Lord Salisbury (1830–1903) is now a subject of intense historical attention. This important new study moves away from conventional biography and presents an original portrait of the mental world inhabited by late-Victorian Conservatives at the time when their world-view was coming under severe strain.

At the centre of the picture is the third Marquis of Salisbury, but *Lord Salisbury's World* does not simply tell the story of his life and politics. Instead, it asks sensitive questions about how the political, intellectual and religious environments of the late-Victorian period seemed to one of its sharpest intellects, and it situates Salisbury and his immediate entourage in a wide landscape of relationships, perceptions and problems.

Its starting points are two: that politics is a situational activity, and that situations reside in the minds of the beholders. For that reason Professor Bentley draws the reader into Conservative assumptions about time and space, property and society, religion and the state, the past and the future – the very language in which they expressed themselves. His book will therefore be required reading for all those interested in British political ideas.

MICHAEL BENTLEY is Professor of Modern History at the University of St Andrews. His many publications include *Politics without Democracy, 1815–1914* (second edn, 1996) in the Fontana History of England. He was also editor of *Public and Private Doctrine: Essays in British History presented to Maurice Cowling* (Cambridge, 1993).

LORD SALISBURY'S WORLD

Conservative Environments in Late-Victorian Britain

MICHAEL BENTLEY

CAMBRIDGE
UNIVERSITY PRESS

PUBLISHED BY THE PRESS SYNDICATE OF THE UNIVERSITY OF CAMBRIDGE
The Pitt Building, Trumpington Street, Cambridge, United Kingdom

CAMBRIDGE UNIVERSITY PRESS
The Edinburgh Building, Cambridge CB2 2RU, UK
40 West 20th Street, New York, NY 10011–4211, USA
10 Stamford Road, Oakleigh, VIC 3166, Australia
Ruiz de Alarcón 13, 28014 Madrid, Spain
Dock House, The Waterfront, Cape Town 8001, South Africa

http://www.cambridge.org

First published 2001

Printed in the United Kingdom at the University Press, Cambridge

Typeset in Baskerville 11/12.5pt   System 3b2   [CE]

A catalogue record for this book is available from the British Library

Library of Congress cataloguing in publication data
Bentley, Michael, 1948–
Lord Salisbury's world: Conservative environments in late-
Victorian Britain / Michael Bentley.
p.   cm.
Includes bibliographical references and index.
ISBN 0 521 44506 X
1. Salisbury, Robert Cecil, marquis of, 1830–1903. 2. Conservatism – Great
Britain – History – 19th century. 3. Great Britain – Politics and government – 1837–1901.
4. Conservative Party (Great Britain) – History. I. Title.
DA564.S2 B46 2001   941.081 – dc21   00–068944

ISBN 0 521 44506 X hardback

Contents

Acknowledgements

I wish to thank H.M. The Queen for gracious permission to consult and quote from material in the Royal Archives at Windsor Castle and to express my gratitude to the staff there for their helpfulness. I owe a special debt, likewise, to the libraries of Hatfield House, Christ Church, Oxford, the Manuscripts Department of the British Library, the National Library of Scotland and Scottish Record Office, Edinburgh, Cambridge University Library and St Andrews University Library. In preparing a study of some eclecticism debts have accrued to a far wider collection of archivists, the staff of county record offices and to individuals with manuscripts in their care. The contribution of such people can never have more than a word of acknowledgement but without their support and readiness to co-operate the enterprise could not begin. A list of all collections and repositories that have been visited in carrying out the research for this book is included in the sources and further reading at the end of the volume and I hope that their custodians will accept this very inadequate word of thanks.

To the British Academy more than a word of gratitude is required for their support in making it possible to carry out part of the research on which this book is based and for providing a semester's relief from teaching duties to expedite the writing. In modern conditions of academic life such help is a *sine qua non* for serious historical work.

No writer works alone and the way has been smoothed in this case by four people in particular who have read and commented on the entire text and helped eradicate some of its more glaring *bêtises*, though they are hardly to blame if the author has persisted in his misjudgements and mistakes. Professor Paul Smith and Professor John Vincent vastly improved the original manuscript through their criticisms. Dr Sarah Foot helped improve the skills of the world's worst proof-reader. Dr Andrew Jones long ago gave up hopes of improving the author but supplied reassurance that Conservative environments still exist.

St Andrews
March 2001

NOTE ON THE TEXT

Capital letters have been reduced to the minimum and stripped from political offices (prime minister, foreign secretary) and general references to institutions (parliament, the church); they have been retained for titles (Church of England, Foreign Office). I have ignored this rule when the result looked odd (archbishop of Canterbury, chancellor of the Exchequer). I have also retained 'Marquis' as opposed to the more usual 'Marquess' because it was the usage preferred by the Salisbury family.

M. B.

Abbreviations

Cecil	Lady Gwendolen Cecil, *Life of Robert, Marquis of Salisbury* (4 vols., 1921–32)
Complete Peerage	Hon. Vicary Gibbs *et al.* (eds.), *The Complete Peerage of England, Scotland, Ireland, Great Britain and the United Kingdom* (12 vols., 1910–59)
Derby, *Diaries*	John Vincent (ed.), *Disraeli, Derby and the Conservative Party: Journals and Memoirs of Edward Henry, Lord Stanley 1848–1869* (Hassocks, 1978); *The Diaries of Edward Henry Stanley, 15th Earl of Derby: Between September 1869 and March 1878* (Royal Historical Society: Camden Series, 1994); *The Later Derby Diaries: Home Rule, Liberal Unionism and Aristocratic Life in Late-Victorian England* (Bristol, 1981)
Hansard	*Hansard's Parliamentary Debates* (third series before 1892, fourth series from 9 February 1892)
RA	Royal Archives – papers and journals of Queen Victoria, Windsor Castle
Salisbury–Balfour Correspondence	Robin Harcourt Williams (ed.), *Salisbury–Balfour Correspondence: Letters Exchanged between the Third Marquis of Salisbury and his Nephew Arthur James Balfour 1869–1892* (Ware, 1988)

Situations vacant

How extensive is a statesman's situation? How long is a piece of string? So much depends on the questions one wants to ask and the angle from which the person is viewed. Seen in one way, the only situation of Lord Salisbury worth the name would take the form of a vast comparative study of modern European aristocracies and their relation to the defining conditions of modernity – economic crisis, the revolution in the social status of particular groups, the coming of various forms of 'democracy' – so that the British variant could be accorded due weight and its deviations identified. The story would concern itself with land and its declining ability to control the *ancien régime*.[1] It would talk about the 'power' of people such as the Marquis of Salisbury or the Earl of Derby to determine the course of politics or retard the onset of 'the people' in comparison with the continuing clout of a Polish noble or a Prussian Junker. It would seek a convertible currency, a sort of argumentative euro, in which the achievements and derelictions of the British case might be assessed. We can always discuss an historical phenomenon as though it had little life of its own, apart from reacting to circumstance, outside some assumed 'process' that is held to drive modernity forwards and account for its transformations. No one doubts that in 1860 conservative landed aristocracies looked more secure than they appeared in 1900 – more confident of their future, more dug in. So one way of situating Salisbury and his circle is to make them look like symbols of this transition toward crisis: a rearguard of privilege concerned to lose ground, where it had to lose it at all, only inch by inch. Complications and singularities disappear in an easier

---

[1] The seminal account of the relationship is Arno J. Mayer, *The Persistence of the Old Regime: Europe to the Great War* (1981). Cf. Avner Offer, *The First World War: An Agrarian Interpretation* (Oxford, 1989) and Dominic Lieven, *The Aristocracy in Europe, 1815–1914* (Basingstoke, 1992).

narrative about the triumph of the masses discovered among a shared experience of progress from Brest to Minsk.

Or one could insert a different filter and train a long-distance lens on Britain from the vantage point of Capitol Hill, producing a negative photograph of American enlightenment and promise. Here, with the Civil War and Lincoln's death at one's back, glad amid the prospect of ever-increasing prosperity and social inclusiveness described in Reconstruction rhetoric, Gladstone's liberal utopia (crafted in the wake of the North's victory) becomes Britain's true and authentic future, one perversely arrested for a time by the arrival of Conservative reaction in the figures of Disraeli and Salisbury. They preside over a period of timid reaction, certainly; but it should be seen as one sandwiched between the healthy progressivism of the People's William, as Gladstone had become known and adored, and the inevitable return to sanity in 1906 when the overwhelming voice of the nation returned Britain to her proper track. The curve of this narrative differs sharply from the story of aristocratic decline informed by a European comparator but it has the same grandeur and same appeal to large structures implicit in the transition to twentieth-century mass politics. Its *dénouement* comes as no more of a surprise than did the other's. Late-Victorian Conservatism dies of suffocation, smothered by enveloping forces far greater than itself, a prisoner of structural constraint that no man can see and none escape. There is nothing wrong with such a view, apart from its intrinsic lack of imagination, but we can reasonably feel uncomfortable when an historical formation turns into passive victim. It is hard to shake off the feeling that agency – the doings of identifiable people in specific situations – helped shape the outcome and that situations may be small and definable as well as huge and ineffable.

But which people? One way of situating political leaders is to locate them among their followers on the ground that leaders do not make parties; the heart of a political formation is seen rather in its popular base and its organisational cadre. This thought leads towards historical sociology and psephology as the best way to explain political events. An account emerges in which we are supposed to understand what was happening by moving away from leadership and concentrating on party machines, constituency politics, grass-roots and the success in elections that is supposed to turn on such things. Two aspects of this situational approach seem striking. First, it views political change as a process whose structural features can be identified and explained – a conclusion that this book will resist, partly out of a disbelief in 'processes', partly because it would like to move beyond 'structures', partly because it just begins somewhere else. Salisbury saw himself as the captain of a ship with a rudder but no destination and keeping afloat as the essence of his problem.[2] We shall follow his mental processes rather than give them a coherence that eluded him. Second (and more damaging), the proponents of history-from-below present the elements they identify as somehow more 'real' or 'fundamental' than the actions and perceptions of those at the top of the system, rejecting in Salisbury's case 'the jaundiced anti-democratic musings of Conservative grandees'[3] in favour, presumably, of the jaundiced pro-democratic musings of Conservative nobodies. It has its place. It frequently does not know its place. The result is a persistent prejudice that historians who write about major political personalities and their thought-world suffer from some sort of simple-mindedness or theoretical *naïveté*. This book focusses on people at the top because that is what Salisbury did and the project here lies in constructing his sense of location. It will not follow Salisbury's injunction to his party managers to study 'villa Toryism' because in speaking of demotic politics he quite literally did not know what he was talking about, having spent very little time in villas apart from the holiday chalets, as he preferred to call them, that he happened to own. We shall take an interest instead in what he did know about: the smaller situation that encompassed himself and his chosen circle.

Small situations arrest the attention of biographers. In Salisbury's case the result is a narrative line along which life-changing thresholds appear: birth in 1830, education at Eton and at home, Oxford, his world tour, parliament, his peerage, India Office (twice), then Foreign Office, the premiership (four times from 1885), his retirement and death in 1902–3. The story widens out at a number of points, like a snake swallowing a victim whole, and becomes what Sir Geoffrey Elton used to call a 'thickened narrative' in which the author glances sideways to fill in context and explain what is taking

---

[2] 'The barque looks crazier & crazier – & the chances of her floating diminish day by day': Salisbury to Balfour, 18 Dec. 1886, Balfour MSS SRO GD433/2/29.

[3] Jon Lawrence and Jane Elliott, 'Parliamentary Election Results Reconsidered: An Analysis of Borough Elections, 1885–1910', in E. H. H. Green (ed.), *An Age of Transition: British Politics, 1880–1914* (Edinburgh, 1997), p. 28. I confess a violent aversion to all 'ages of transition'.

place.[4] It is a crucial task and Salisbury's historical profile has recently undergone significant revision in biographical accounts that have fed on the great archive at Hatfield House.[5] But not every life slides into the mode of biography: there are people whose knees and elbows always protrude. Sometimes their lives seem to resemble a battle against continuity, as that of Joseph Chamberlain so often does in retrospect. Some of them, like Gladstone, live for so long and occupy so many spaces that no single narrative will come close to coping with their complexities. In Salisbury's case the problem does not lie in theological sophistication or philosophical depth so much as in a disposition that resisted the categories most familiar to his students. Religion was central but he would never talk about it. His journalism has been made central but he would never discuss it. His thinking was impressive but he chose to make it sound like common sense. His politics followed rather than led. About Lord Randolph Churchill we can write a 'political life'.[6] For Salisbury this procedure does not work because his life was political in a more distanced and nuanced sense that often took its form from quite different environments. In his case we never crawl out from beneath Carlyle's sisyphian predicament: the brilliant insight that narrative is *linear* but action is *solid*.[7]

The Victorians had a way of dealing with this perpetual problem. They liked to compose a lengthy 'Life and Times' of their heroes in which they made some pretence, often not much more than that, at thinking laterally and examining the broader situation within which their subject ought to be located by posterity. Normally their text would assume the pose of a Time seen through the Life in question. And in a way that is what *Lord Salisbury's World* seeks to do: it wants to put the Times back into Salisbury's Life. Perhaps it goes further, though, in implying that the Life can be examined through the Time as much as vice versa. Perhaps man and context enjoy a mutual conditioning which biography (a mode that always boasts about the distinctiveness of its chosen figure) often misses and which analytical

---

[4] Cf. Elton on narrative and analysis in G. R. Elton, *The Practice of History* (1969), pp. 160–76.

[5] David Steele treats centrally the problems of policy in his *Lord Salisbury: A Political Biography* (1999), while the new official life, Andrew Roberts, *Salisbury: Victorian Titan* (1999) provides a more flamboyant though less sure-footed account. Both of these studies appeared after the completion of the draft of the present account in August 1999.

[6] R. F. Foster, *Lord Randolph Churchill: A Political Life* (Oxford, 1981).

[7] Carlyle, 'On History' (1830), quoted in John D. Rosenberg, *Carlyle and the Burden of History* (Oxford, 1985), p. 44.

monographs can also stamp out through their fascination with the structures and forces that they consider. My own way of thinking about this crux will not be to everyone's taste. We are so accustomed to drawing mental time-lines as we read along that biography feels a more fluent enterprise than a collection of loops and circles of the kind awaiting the reader of this book. Rather than begin with the birth of Lord Robert Cecil and end with the death of the third Marquis of Salisbury, we step sideways and look askance at the whole trajectory, now from one direction, now from another, thinking as we go about Salisbury's relationship to a particular environment and blatantly ignoring some other aspects that a biographer might deem *de rigueur.* Combining these perceptions will leave us speaking French (*mentalité*) or German (*Weltanschauung*) or at least American ('mind-set'). It comes with the territory.

Situating anybody demands a location in space and time, so we start from there. Where to go after that depends on my judgements about Lord Salisbury's temperament and preoccupations but also about the broader context of his age: the elements that he manipulated and the ties that bound his hands. It should be said at once that the choice of environments has its arbitrary side. One could reasonably complain that this book is not about Salisbury's foreign and domestic policies and that these best show his environment. But that world has received so much attention from his biographers and the authors of specialist studies that it seemed to offer a tired and possibly rather dated way of arranging the argument. It could be said that Salisbury's central context lies in the economic depression of the 1870s and 1880s that changed everybody's context. There is much in this view and a strong argument exists for placing political economy and the collectivist drive that often followed from it at the core of this work. But this feature of late-Victorian Conservatism has already been impressively assessed by Dr Euan Green and others,[8] and although we shall tumble into the great depression repeatedly here, it will not be elevated to special consideration in its more strictly economic aspects. It will be said, equally, that Salisbury was a Conservative politician and that this book reaches the Conservative party only in chapter 9. That is deliberate. Too much time has been spent in making Salisbury sound like a premature version of Neville

---

[8] E. H. H. Green, *The Crisis of Conservatism: The Politics, Economics and Ideology of the British Conservative Party, 1880–1914* (1995). Cf. Matthew Fforde, *Conservatism and Collectivism, 1886–1914* (Edinburgh, 1990).

Chamberlain or Harold Macmillan, compelled and impelled by party. Instead, I have chosen domains about which something fresh may be said and which fall within my own sphere of competence. My cue comes partly from Salisbury himself. I have responded to areas of discussion that preoccupied him and those which pressed on him whether he were preoccupied by them or not.

Marx came close to the heart of things when he taught that men make their own history but not in circumstances of their own choosing. He would have missed the significance of Salisbury, none the less, in forgetting that some individuals are clever and powerful enough to make some of their own circumstances. We shall hear throughout this book a conversation between context and control, structure and agency, but the weight accorded to Salisbury's opinions and actions within the environments reviewed here argues against treating him as simply another voice among his colleagues and correspondents. In Victorian Britain some people were more equal than others. For much of the time, therefore, Salisbury holds the centre of the stage, but the subject of the book is the stage itself and the distinctive set on which other actors have walk-on roles or supporting parts. I shall fail to suppress my admiration for Salisbury: I find him bitingly intelligent, focussed and funny. If the book has to have a hero, on the other hand, then it must be the man in a thorn-proof suit at the back of the stage, stroking his setters and fluffing every line. The sixth Duke of Richmond lacked almost every skill known to the world of politics and thought. He brought to his life-long service of country, party and church only a bewildered resolve, his amicability, generosity and code of personal honour. He will leave modern Conservatives pained by a sense of contrast and loss. He thought Salisbury too clever by half, thought the country going to the dogs, saw no point in foreigners, saw murderers and crooks where others saw socialists and radicals. Yet he never abandoned his faith that all could be smoothed over among men of goodwill by human kindness or, in serious cases of misunderstanding, by a haunch of venison and a kippered salmon.

Richmond, Cairns, Carnarvon, Churchill, Derby, on the one side, the Queen, the bishops, the maharajas and Gladstone on the other lent Salisbury's situation a richness of personal contact and friction. He himself was a thinker who located his opinions in the world and not in treatises such as those of his nephew, Arthur James Balfour. It will be important to go to his own medium and inspect his own language. It is not compulsory, on the other hand, to take him at his word. We can make our own historical environment from his letters and the diaries and memories of his circle, evoking a world that none of its participants knew except in glimpses but which we, privileged by distance and years, can construct in our very different situation. Fabrications of this kind give us a Salisbury both larger and smaller than may seem familiar. Larger, because his genius in inventing the world that he wished to govern strikes us constantly from the material that he bequeathed for historical study. Smaller, because life's contingencies spare no one and each of us loses a battle against the ungovernable. The tension between the two makes Salisbury at once a master of the late-Victorian moment and yet its ultimate victim – a man of his time.

CHAPTER I

Time

FAMILY TIME

For the Cecils – or 'Sissels', as they pronounced themselves until quite recently – the historical clock ticks evenly but slowly. They have maintained a presence in British history, sometimes national in their importance, sometimes provincial, since their rise to grandeur through the political careers of Elizabeth I's minister, William Cecil, Lord Burghley (1520–98) and his son Robert, first Earl of Salisbury (1563–1612). The twin genealogies descending from William Cecil's two marriages, one of them issuing in earls and marquises of Salisbury, the other in earls and marquises of Exeter, come down to the present and reflect chronologies no less different than the competing clusters that make up the two wings of the family. Rarely have Exeters captured headlines; the tempo of their existence in the great house at Burghley, near Stamford, has a certain regularity of pulse with a quickening in the late seventeeth century when the so-called Little Bedlam Club brought some society and a certain drunken panache to the house. The Salisburys took a different curve: powerful in the later sixteenth and early seventeenth centuries, quiescent during the eighteenth century, rising to major prominence in the subject of this book, Robert, the third Marquis, and then continuing their serious political and social importance until half way through the twentieth century. In our own century, the Exeters of Burghley have become ghosts wandering the corridors of their property on the occasions when they visit from Canada. The Cecils of Hatfield House still live there and maintain a social cachet reflected in London Clubs (anathema to the third Marquis) and Lord Cranborne's Conservative leadership of the House of Lords until the spaniel in him brought it to a spectacular end at the hands of Mr William Hague. This distended sense of time within one of the most prominent families that England has ever produced helps explain some of the attitudes and approaches sometimes found among its members. It says something pertinent about how Cecils understood themselves in the century after the death of Robert Peel and throws shafts of light across the life of one of them – the most significant since the Tudors – who died in the middle of that recasting of family fortunes. It explains, too, why the story cannot begin with his birth.

Important elements in giving our Salisbury a sense of historical location began, paradoxically, with the second Marquis (1791–1868). 'Paradoxically' not only because Salisbury detested his father for much of the latter's life but because James Gascoyne-Cecil, second Marquis of Salisbury, proved one of the less significant Cecils of the nineteenth and twentieth centuries. Short, vigorous and aggressive, he led the life of a soldier *manqué* with a passion for the county militia, which need not detain us, for estate management at Hatfield House, which became significant when part of it burned down in 1835, and for procreation whose results would prove formidable, not least in making two women and many brothers and sisters central to his famous son's development and providing a context stretching from the first born, the ill-fated James, in 1821, to Arthur, one of the sons to his second wife, who did not die until 1913. The twelve children of the second Marquis divided seven and five: the first batch to Frances Gascoyne and the second to Lady Mary Sackville-West. Both of them stimulate resonances at the end of the twentieth century, one accurate, one not. Frances was the daughter of Sir Bamber Gascoyne whose name indeed lives on in a famous television personality; Lady Mary belonged, on the other hand, to those Sackvilles who were once dukes of Dorset into whom the fifth Earl of De La Warr had married, rather than to the gardening and poetry associated with Vita of Knole and Harold Nicolson. Both of them were to exercise a serious influence on the young and not-so-young Salisbury because one became his mother and the other the lover and wife of a fellow cabinet minister, the fifteenth Earl of Derby, with whom Salisbury would fight his great battles over Near Eastern policy in the 1870s. What the second Marquis inadvertently achieved (and he expired before the consequences became clear) was the union of the houses of Hatfield and Knowsley and the drawing into common threads of a narrative surrounding two great landed families. Like a spider dead in its own web, he left little of himself beyond his sticky extrusions which would envelop all the children and those who came after.

The young Robert Arthur Talbot Gascoyne-Cecil, born in 1830, kept out of his father's way. Lady Gwendolen Cecil, Salisbury's daughter and biographer, would later reflect, in a miracle of under-statement, that the second Marquis generated an atmosphere 'not wholly peaceable';[1] so Robert preferred to become a Gascoyne, close to his mother, though he must in very early years also have had to negotiate the family's slightly dotty dowager, formerly Lady Emily Hill, the first Marchioness, until she perished in the flames of the Hatfield fire when he was five – the earliest of a serious of deaths and calamities that stood always at the young man's elbow.[2] His mother could not protect him for long – she fell ill and died in 1839 – and the hateful years at Eton might have proved a little more manageable had she been waiting at home. Yet even when there, her heart had belonged to the Duke of Wellington (or in Gladstone's memory to Lord Melbourne's father[3]) who did not become one of Salisbury's recollected reference points in the way that some other Tory statesmen did; he deafens by silence. But she had left behind a thicket of siblings that would obstruct or protect Salisbury's life at a number of points. There was James, the eldest son whose frailty turned to blindness, incapacity and early death, thus promoting his younger brother to the courtesy title, Lord Cranborne, in 1865. There were the two elder sisters. Mildred later married an eccentric scholar, churchman and parliamentarian Alexander James Beresford Beresford-Hope (he contrived to acquire the second 'Beresford' in 1854) and by so doing brought her brother within the ambit of a major publicist whose part ownership of the *Saturday Review* gave Lord Robert Cecil, as he then was, a much-needed start in journal-ism undertaken for money after his father had all but cut him off. Beresford-Hope will reappear in this story in the shadow of the nineteenth-century cathedrals whose history he wrote and as the

---

[1] Cecil, vol. 1, p. 5.

[2] Professor John Vincent rightly feels compelled by them all. 'Not everyone has an incinerated grandmother, a mother untimely snatched, a brother dying by inches, a clan of Balfour pulmonaires (Arthur nearly one) ending with a spectacular Balfour death on Mont Blanc. It seems to go beyond the common lot.' (Private communication.)

[3] As late as 1890, Gladstone confided to Edward Hamilton that 'although it was not generally known, he believed there was a doubt as to the parentage of Lord Salisbury caused by the undue intimacy of his mother with Lord Melbourne (father of the Prime Minister)': diary, 19 Apr. 1890, in Dudley Bahlman (ed.), *The Diary of Edward Walter Hamilton, 1885–1906* (Hull, 1993).

commentator on ecclesiastical ritualism which would give Salisbury so difficult a passage in the 1870s.[4] Blanche, who was five years older than Robert, also acquired significance in a longer perspective by marrying a Balfour of Whittingehame and becoming in due course the mother of Arthur James Balfour, who would, like his uncle, become prime minister and a significant force in twentieth-century Conservatism. Salisbury survived both sisters by a considerable margin: Mildred died in 1881 and Blanche still earlier in 1872 after she 'had long been in weak health . . . Her life for many years past had been that of an invalid, and signs of mental eccentricity had appeared at times.' But they vicariously sustained their brother's success and the vitality of the family in the next generation.

With the three sons and two daughters of his father's second marriage, Salisbury had far less to do – reasonably enough – but he could not ignore the dominating presence of their mother who, between her marriage to the second Marquis in 1847 and the death of his heir, James, in 1865, supervised the domestic regime at Hatfield and brought her prejudice and temper to bear on all around her. The children remained 'Cecils' but their upbringing and financial support came predominantly from the future fifteenth Earl of Derby who had probably been the lover of Mary, Countess of Salisbury for some years and who became her husband in 1870. The children of this union were not in any case the stuff of empire or even the stuff of Mary. Sackville Cecil was deemed from the start 'a queer half-mad creature' and remained a focus of disapproval despite his perfectly respectable career in railway management and engineering; perhaps too close to 'trade'. The 'two lads', Arthur and Lionel, failed to run a Scottish farm together and became pensioners of Mary Derby's new husband. Lady Margaret seems to have had a rampant moment with a footman and gone into decline. She refused an offer of marriage from Sanderson, Salisbury's respected under-secretary in the Foreign Office,[5] turned to religion and then lived alone at Burwash. The elder sister, Mary, likewise ended as a *femme seule*, having married 'that awful fellow [the tenth Earl of] Galloway' who 'drank like a

---

[4] See A. J. B. Beresford-Hope, *The English Cathedral of the Nineteenth Century* (1861) and *Worship in the Church of England* (1874).

[5] Thomas Henry Sanderson (1841–1923), who became permanent under-secretary at the Foreign Office in 1894. Yorkshire yeoman family from Armthorpe, near Doncaster. Father Tory MP for Colchester and mother a daughter of the Manners-Sutton, speaker of the House of Commons, who had almost become famous when some Tories tried to make him prime minister in May 1832.

fish' and was deemed disgusting.[6] Mary Derby continued to draw a considerable amount of money from her stepson after her departure from Hatfield – something like £100,000 in his rather bitter estimation[7] – and she lost no opportunity to stir in London society, not least through her close relationship to Shuvalov, the Russian ambassador to London, who seems to have learned much about cabinet conversations from his *confidante*.[8] Happily for Salisbury, Mary Derby became depressed during the 1870s. Increasingly she gave her new husband a burdensome time by complaining about coming to London, and her availability for mischief therefore diminished.[9] By the time she pulled out of her 'melancholy', Derby had been squashed by Salisbury as a Conservative and had become an odd sort of Whig, reasserting the Derby Dilly, led by that generation's Stanley and Sir James Graham, straddling party lines back in the 1830s; so neither he nor she mattered much any more from a Tory point of view. But no one should look at Salisbury in the middle years of his life without seeing behind the curtain an outline of Mary Derby. There is a sour irony in observing how the only mother he ever really knew turned into his covert detractor and enemy.

Probably Salisbury's father would have taken a black view of his son's engagement to Georgina Alderson whether Mary were there or not; but one suspects that she contributed to his resolve to leave Robert Cecil with just £100 a year if he persisted in his determination to contract an unsuitable marriage. He did so, regardless. That she was two years older than him seemed no urgent reason for discontinuing the relationship, though his father found it compelling, presumably worried about her potential for whelping; and he recognized that her relative lack of money – Miss Alderson's father was a judge in the Court of Exchequer – would present some

---

[6] The characterizations are those of 'Eddy' Stanley, seventeenth Earl of Derby: see Derby, *Diaries*, pp. 15–19. Galloway's problems went beyond the bottle and involved a sexual scandal that brought embarrassment to the family. His later letters show a rather pathetic wish to be acknowledged as a force in Scottish politics.

[7] Salisbury explained to his stepsister in 1888 that 'Lady Derby ha[d] been drawing £5,000 a year from [his] estates ever since [he] came into them': Salisbury to Lady Galloway, 1 Jun. 1888 (draft), Christ Church MSS, file E.

[8] Was she in love with him? When he left the country she lapsed back into depression: the only piece of 'evidence' that occurs to me. Her papers have disappeared. Perhaps a post-Soviet scholar will one day find enlightenment in a Russian archive.

[9] By 1877 Derby himself had come to feel the weight of his wife's depression. 'It comes without reason, and seems impossible to cure. I seriously consider whether this being so I can go on with office business': Derby, *Diaries*, p. 386. Her *confidant*, Petr Andreevich Shuvalov, was ambassador from 1874 to 1879.

financial difficulty in the short term. Yet at virtually every level she proved a triumphant success and provided a key rhythm in the Hatfield family for forty years until her death at the end of 1899. Her husband overcame financial stringency, meanwhile, by writing on an heroic scale for the *Saturday Review* and the *Quarterly Review*: he wrote perhaps a million and a half words of polemical journalism between his marriage in 1857 and the offer of ministerial office from Lord Derby in 1866.[10] She herself, meanwhile, confounded any reservations about her fertility, for although her seven children fell short of the rapacious second Marquis's achievement, she outdid him in sons and therefore laid firmer claims on the future of the Salisbury title. They turned out, moreover, sound of mind and limb, though the youngest, Hugh, gave cause for concern on both counts for much of his life. By the time of Hugh's birth in 1869, Salisbury had a future all around him at Hatfield and the succession to the title was to work out beautifully. James ('Jem') would become fourth Marquis on the death of his father in 1903 and, together with his younger brothers Robert ('Bob') Cecil and Hugh ('Linky') Cecil, play a very considerable role in the revival of Tory politics in the 1920s and the extirpation of Lloyd George and his works.[11] The fourth Marquis's eldest son, another Robert, became fifth Marquis in 1947 and offered a consistent version of Conservative reaction through to his death in 1972, teaching the post-war world what was wrong with it and famously finding new Tories 'too clever by half'.[12] Only two of Salisbury's children – Gwendolen and Hugh – remained unmarried. The rest married well and dovetailed the family further into a settled world of landed ascendancy. James followed his father, it is true, in failing to find money, but his marriage to the daughter of an indigent Irish peer, the fifth Earl of Arran, became quite the permanent success that his father's marriage had been. William ('Fish') Cecil, the future bishop of Exeter, married into the Cheshire

---

[10] For an analysis of this output, see J. F. A. Mason, 'Lord Salisbury: A Librarian's View' in Lord Blake and Hugh Cecil (eds.), *Lord Salisbury: The Man and his Policies* (1987), pp. 10–29 at p. 18 and the more detailed information in the same author's article, 'The third Marquis of Salisbury and the *Saturday Review*', *Bulletin of the Institute of Historical Research*, 34 (1961), pp. 36–64.

[11] See Kenneth Rose, *The Later Cecils* (New York, 1975), ch. 4; Maurice Cowling, *The Impact of Labour 1920–1924* (Cambridge, 1971), pp. 60–90; Michael Bentley, 'Liberal Politics and the Grey Conspiracy of 1921', *Historical Journal*, 20 (1977), pp. 461–78.

[12] The remark was aimed at Iain Macleod: see Robert Shepherd, *Iain Macleod: A Biography* (1995), pp. 224ff.

and Lancashire Wilbrahams,[13] Robert into the Durham Lambtons and Edward ('Nigs') into the Surrey wing of the (Dunley Hill) Maxses, though his wanting the daughter of an admiral struck his mother as whimsical. The new daughter kept her courage up with reassurance such as that provided by Lord Pembroke; 'a delicious family (I think) to marry into', he crooned to her. 'Such a large, wholesome life about it . . . You'll find it rather like going to a nice public school . . .'[14]

But the most significant union for the family's past and future in some ways became that of the eldest child, Maud, who confirmed and extended a lengthy narrative in accepting the future second Earl of Selborne whose father had known Maud's from Oxford days. After the horrors of Eton, from where even the second Marquis had ultmately felt compelled to withdraw him in 1845 because of the bullying he had suffered, Robert Cecil had proceeded by way of private tuition at Hatfield to Christ Church, Oxford. There he came across Horsley Palmer, brother of Roundell Palmer (who later became first Earl of Selborne) and a lifelong friendship began, which virtually amounted to a family membership even before Maud's marriage. When Cecil left Oxford with his Honorary Fourth class after two years – his health had not stood the strain of his spiritual and intellectual efforts there – it had been Roundell Palmer who wrote testimonials for him when he went off round the world in 1851 to recover his vitality. To J. R. Godley in New Zealand, he introduced the new friend, 'who is making a tour of the world under medical advice . . . He is not a common person; but unites, with a very high character and principles, good and well cultivated abilities, and a desire to do something for mankind in his time. This, and the circumstance of his being a friend of my brother Horsley, make me feel a more than usual interest in him . . .'[15] Half a century later, Godley's son, Arthur, wrote to Selborne's son, now Maud's husband, recollecting those early years and in particular an occasion when 'Lord Salisbury stayed some days with my Father and Mother at

---

[13] Florence Mary Bootle-Wilbraham (d. 1944), daughter of the first Earl of Lathom. The family was better known in the nineteenth century for supplying earls of Skelmersdale.

[14] Quoted in Violet Milner, *My Picture Gallery 1886–1901* (1951), p. 58. She went on, nothing daunted, to marry Lord Milner after Edward's death and later edited the *National Review* from 1932 to 1948.

[15] Palmer to Godley (copy), 17 May 1851, 1st Earl of Selborne MSS 92 f.40d. John Robert Godley (1814–61) played a central role in the foundation of Canterbury, New Zealand, where he spent three years before returning to a career in the War Office.

Lyttelton. My mother remembers him as a tall, thin young man who, when he walked up a hill with her, had to lie down flat on the ground, midway, to rest.'[16] The tall, thin and ill young man retained his enthusiasm for the Palmers, which led to their living near one another in London, where the children of both played together, and then in Hampshire when the Cranbornes took a house near Blackmoor, the Palmer's home a few miles from Selborne.[17] Quite what the attraction amounted to seems hard to identify now. It can hardly have been political sympathy since Selborne remained a Gladstonian Liberal until the Home Rule crisis turned him into a Liberal Unionist in 1886. Personal magnetism sounds no more probable since Salisbury liked people to be amusing and Selborne's capacity for scintillation was not great: one of his own party described him prettily as 'a cross between a mummy and an icicle'.[18] The most likely explanation would refer to religion; they met during Salisbury's high church phase, which bordered on tractarian commitment, and it may be that Palmer presented a *sympathique* audience and companion.

All these strands from the edge of and beyond the family margin – Derby, Selborne, Balfour – wove themselves into the experience of the Salisburys early in their time together at Hatfield. Derby had made his first visit there nineteen years before Georgina Salisbury became the monarch of Hatfield, as he recalled in 1872. 'My 46th birthday. Just half my life has passed since I was for the first time the guest of Ld & Ly Salisbury at Hatfield, July 21 1849.'[19] By then, of course, the Lady in question had become his wife, the Lord in question was dead and his son was estranged from both his stepmother and Derby himself. But the Selbornes and Balfours helped give the pace of Hatfield its steady, repetitive tempo. They would all be away during the week, apart from Salisbury himself who liked to work at home when possible; but at the weekend everybody vacated

---

[16] Godley to Selborne, 6 February 1902, 2nd Earl of Selborne MSS 92 f.40c. This Godley, later first Baron Kilbracken, was a cousin of the famous classicist and reactionary wit, A. D. Godley.

[17] See Earl of Selborne, *Memorials* (4 vols., 1896–8), vol. II, p. 9; *Cecil*, vol. I, p. 172.

[18] Quoted in David Nicholls, *The Lost Prime Minister: A Life of Sir Charles Dilke* (1995), p. 128. Even Gladstone, a friend until Home Rule for Ireland made Selborne an enemy, came to deem him 'something between ice & ink': Gladstone diary, 4 July 1889, in M. R. D. Foot and Colin Matthew (eds.), *The Gladstone Diaries*, (14 vols., Oxford, 1968–94), vol. XII, p. 215.

[19] Derby diary, 21 July 1872, Derby, *Diaries*, p.112. Plainly any intimacy did not begin at this early stage and, when it did, it is not clear what it involved; but a repeated anniversary-date in the diary refers to the summer of 1855. I am grateful to John Vincent for help with this.

town-houses in London to roost at Hatfield and dinner would normally bring thirteen or fourteen to table: the Salisburys, the Selbornes, Arthur Balfour, Gwendolen and Hugh and the four married Cecils. Arthur Balfour's brother, Gerald, could bring fire and brimstone in Lady Elizabeth Lytton, whom he married in 1887. Frances Campbell, who married Arthur's other living brother, Eustace, visited regularly and brought to the proceedings, by contrast, the rationalist, Scottish Whiggery that a daughter of the Duke of Argyll had little chance of escaping. Her wonderful memoirs, *Ne Obliviscaris*, carry a modern eye into the Great Marble Hall where the six or seven courses, followed naturally by dessert and accompanied throughout by wines of the quality that Salisbury deemed drinkable, were served to the family wearing evening dress and, on the more special occasions, sporting buttonholes that the awesome Newbery, 'ubiquitous groom of the chambers', had doubtless placed on their dressing tables.[20] Daytime rhythms had a certain fixity, too. Chapel came first – the eucharist stood at the centre of Salisbury's life from Oxford to his death – and could begin only when the ghostly clanking of Lady Salisbury's dangling park keys came to rest. (Sunday was different, when all the family went to the eleven o'clock service in Hatfield parish church, of which William for a time was rector.) Then breakfast, which was long, with newspapers. Work, correspondence, perhaps golf in the case of Arthur Balfour, would lead to lunch, after which a succession of carriages would pull up before the door to take anyone driving who wished to go; those not wanted were simply taken away again. The long afternoon might well go in estate matters, for the house and park demanded daily attention, as did the surprisingly large number of people tending them. An account book of 1891–2 suggests an *average* of sixty-five people present at Hatfield every day, counting family, servants and visitors – not abnormal by country-house standards, though impressive.[21] The family did not remain there all year, on the other hand. Increasingly the autumn and winter saw them in France, first at Puys, in their small villa near Dieppe, and later at Beaulieu on the coast outside Nice, until, as Salisbury always ultimately decided about everything, that too became disagreeable. One went to all the

---

[20] Frances Balfour, *Ne Obliviscaris: Dinna Forget* (2 vols., 1930) vol. I, pp. 335, 338; Milner, *My Picture Gallery*, p. 80.

[21] F. M. L. Thompson, 'Private Property and Public Policy' in Blake and Cecil (eds.), *Lord Salisbury*, pp. 252–89 at p. 285 n. 14.

trouble of acquiring land and building villas and tolerating seasickness in order to avoid the rain and fogs and clubs of England, only to find the place infested with mosquitoes all summer, he complained, and with the royal families of Europe all winter.[22]

PARTY TIME

Among those who ran the Conservative party, by contrast, a week seemed a long time. Perhaps it felt so particularly for the generation after Peel as it scampered up and down, thrashed this way and that, looking for any kind of purchase on politics through the years of wilderness in the two decades after 1846. Their narrative threatened to turn into *une histoire événementielle* without the *événements* – except for striking deaths, which merely emphasized disjunction and discomposure. They found Lord George Bentinck collapsed against a wall on the walk from Wellbeck to Thoresby Hall that he never completed in 1848. Had he lived, he might have prevented Benjamin Disraeli from ditching the protection of the farmers, for which Bentinck had given his last years, and brought a thread of continuity with him into the 1850s and 1860s. As it was, he left his life in Disraeli's hands.[23] Or, again, simply imagine those years with Peel in them. It was all so ludicrously *contingent*. If Peel's horse had been young, not old, its owner would not have sought to buy another. Even if he had, he might not have taken the advice of a fellow MP about which one to buy. Having bought it, he got destiny by the tail; and on the morning of 1 July 1850 the beast turned, catapulting Peel on to a hard place on Constitution Hill, near the House of Commons. Disraeli was not exactly on hand, but destiny had a way of speaking to him, or at least to the memoirs that he later drafted, through his guardian angel:

I did not rise, that fatal day, so early as Sir Robert Peel. And in the afternoon, my guardian angel persuaded me, instead of going to Clubs and Houses of Commons, to take a drive in our agreeable environs. We were returning through Regent's Park & two gentlemen on horseback, strangers, stopped our carriage.

'Mr Disraeli,' they said. 'You will be interested to hear, that Sir Robt Peel has been thrown from his horse, & has been carried home in a dangerous state.'

---

[22] Mary Lutyens (ed.), *Lady Lytton's Court Diary 1895–1899* (1961), pp. 94–5.
[23] Benjamin Disraeli, *Lord George Bentinck* (1852).

'Dangerous?', I enquired. 'I hope not. His loss wd. be a great misfortune for this country.' They seemed a little surprised but I spoke [from my heart – *deleted*] what I felt.[24]

Even Disraeli's trowel bent under the weight of 'from my heart' but there was enough in the story to conceal the degree to which tragedy had brought him opportunity. He then employed Gladstone, who loathed him quite as much as Disraeli had loathed Peel, to reinforce the point. 'A day or two after Peel's death', the narrative says, 'Gladstone was at the Carlton [Club], & said "Peel died at peace with all mankind; even with Disraeli. The last thing he did was to cheer Disraeli. It was not a very loud cheer, but it *was* a cheer. . ." '[25]

This baptism, then burial, of Peel by his former detractors gave the Tory party a new start and Disraeli a new role. It drew a line under the experience of Wellingtonian Toryism and the Peelite experiment that had followed it and implied that anti-Liberal forces could rally in some novel posture with the repeal of the corn laws forgiven and some new devices invented to join together town and country as effectively as the previous generation of Tories had separated them. The problem lay in defining the posture; and Disraeli spent hours, days and weeks on it at the beginnning of the new decade, sending out hypothetical thoughts to those whom he trusted or wished to entice, such as the young Stanley[26] who must surely have proved more malleable than his father, the fourteenth Earl of Derby, who was now Disraeli's leader and no Disraelian. His picture emphasized the uselessness of past models and the sense of a new world to be won if all were not to be lost:

As for domestic politics, they are worse than bad: they are hopeless. Neither of the two aristocratic parties being able to govern the country, the community are now curiously investigating the depositories of power so that they may be arranged in some manner wh: will at least secure a parliamentary majority. These analyses do not exactly benefit the cause of the territorial constitution. Prescription justified a landed preponderance as long as the land cd. govern: but the nation will not stand political power mainly deposited in one class, & that class incapable of wielding it. The Movement is irresistible in my mind; and unless an avowedly conservative govt be formed this session, of wh: I see not the slightest prospect, & if formed, successfully maintained, the great towns of the north will govern

---

[24] Draft memoirs dating from the mid-1860s, in J. A. W. Gunn *et. al.* (eds.), *Benjamin Disraeli Letters*, (5 vols., Toronto, 1982–93), vol. v, appendix 5, p. 533.
[25] *Ibid.*, p. 532.
[26] Edward Henry Stanley (1826–93). He succeeded as fifteenth Earl of Derby in 1869.

England in five years time. The aristocratic class are frightened, but protection is a barrier against coalition and reconstruction wh: stops everyone, & Cobden triumphs in the stumbling block. I never saw things tumble down so fast as the landed interest. The new census [of 1851 suggesting a movement to the towns] was a body blow, & the depopulation of Ireland [because of the famine] is another.[27]

His pessimism might have taken a further twist when he visited its true home – Hatfield – three days later. But no; it was a ball for 500 people in the Great Gallery and he was struck rather by 'a multitude of dancing men' and his hostess, 'a very pleasing woman – great simplicity – quite a Sackville with four most beautiful young children'.[28]

Lord Robert was not beautiful and not there: he had begun his grand tour of South Africa, Australia and New Zealand. But when he returned in 1853 he probably already held some notions that would cut across the short-termism that everybody diagnosed in Disraeli. To begin with, he had no time for the cant about Peel: Peel had done harm. During 1845 and 1846, while Peel was making his about-turn over the corn issue (re-ratting after a supposed former betrayal over Catholic emancipation in 1829), Cecil had been enjoying botany in the lanes around Hatfield and absorbing, no doubt, the atmospheric permanence that Hatfield engendered with occasional tirades from his father about iniquity in government. Disraeli had been right to expose it. He had been wrong to trifle with the same tendencies himself. An article of 1865 can be read as a contemporary warning as much as a piece of history, the more so as its title, 'Parliamentary Reform', referred to a growing mood across all parties and one that had to be scotched. 'Of the motives of the late Sir Robert Peel', he conceded, 'there can be no question. In fact his policy at these two junctures [1829 and 1846] was so suicidal, that it is almost a contradiction in terms to impute to him any motives of personal ambition.' But that did not excuse the behaviour of one who 'never seems rightly to have understood the obligations which the exertions of a party impose upon a party chief'.[29] It was not that

---

[27] Disraeli to Stanley, 7 Dec. 1851, Derby MSS 1749/51.
[28] Disraeli to Sarah Disraeli, 10 Dec. 1851, in Gunn *et al.*, *Letters*, vol. v, p. 499.
[29] Lord Robert Cecil, 'Parliamentary Reform', *Quarterly Review*, 117 (1865), pp. 540–74 at p. 554. Sir Stafford Northcote returned to the same theme many years later. 'What the Conservative party must guard against', he warned a backbencher in 1881, 'is, the making [of] promises or holding out expectation which if we were in office we could not fulfil. Anything would be better than that. Sir Robert Peel laid the foundation of evil when he

Cecil thought Disraeli necessarily a danger. Moments in the 1850s gave cause for concern as Disraeli busied himself in looking for opportunities to stir up trouble for the Whigs and Liberals, at whatever cost to policy or consistency, losing sight of the over-whelming Hatfield truth that '[h]ostility to Radicalism, incessant, implacable hostility, is the essential definition of Conservatism'.[30] But during the hopeless days of the great Palmerston government of 1859–65, Cecil felt frequently reassured by Disraeli's willingness to forgo the daily tergiversations and get on with doing his job of opposing. In 1861, for example, Cecil found the parliamentary session 'prosperous but . . . very stupid . . . hitherto'.

Dizzy, converted from evil ways, has behaved like an angel – so that I am beginning to incline to the belief that he really has been baptised. My idea of angelic behaviour consists of supporting Palmerston & opposing Bright on all possible occasions . . . Yet I am afraid the Govt is getting weaker – & I doubt if there are the materials for a Conservative Govt independent of Liberal support. If a Govt is to depend on Liberal support I think it is much better for the reputation of public men that it should be one calling itself Liberal & not one calling itself Conservative – though the names are great trash.[31]

There was the rub. Even when Disraeli became angelic, Cecil raised the spectre of 'the reputation of public men', just as Bentinck had done against Peel. And Disraeli did not think party names were trash: he spent each day trying to find ways to make them more real and develop a formula for Conservatives that would work in the real world.

Oddly enough, their understanding of what a Conservative party needed to be came quite close to an implicit agreement. Disraeli, in his new-party-building enthusiasm of the 1850s, saw that Tories could no longer rely on the countryside and that they would have to move where Peel had directed them, towards the towns. If they did not they would lose all their 'democratic' elements and find them-selves with no constituency beyond the farmers. 'We must', he told Lord Malmesbury in 1853, 'have our eyes opened at last to the futility of attempting to govern the country merely by the landed interest, and not even by its complete power . . . Hitherto the Whigs, by

took up Protection in the years preceding 1842, and then had to depart from the principles on which his party had been brought together. Conservatism has never recovered from the effect of that work': Northcote to Maxwell, 28 Aug. 1881, Maxwell MSS 7043 HEM1.

[30] Quoted by Robert Stewart in Blake and Cecil, *Lord Salisbury*, p. 98.
[31] Cecil to Carnarvon, 'Easter Day' (May 1861), Carnarvon MSS 60758 ff. 20–1.

pretending to lead the towns, have never given us an opportunity of conciliating them. In their eagerness for place they have thrown over the urban interest, which is panting for revenge.'[32] Cecil saw this problem quite as clearly, from an aristocratic perspective, as did Disraeli from an electioneering one. He knew perfectly well that '[p]ure "squire" Conservatism [was] played out'[33] and that only an appeal to a wider base, along the lines recommended by the despised Peel, promised to better the position. But the difference between the two positions remained fundamental because of the divergent conclusions that each drew. Disraeli wanted to acknowledge the problem and then press forward to changing the party. Cecil wanted to acknowledge it in patient resignation and leave the benefit to the Liberals; he could not countenance shifting his position to accommodate electoral turbulence. 'My opinions', he said to Carnarvon, 'are not such as would enable me to work heartily with the moderate Liberals – & it is only under their lead that a Conservative party in the future could be formed.' He chose to walk away rather than become sullied by compromise and shifts of stance of the kind he had been taught to recollect from 1829 and that he had observed in 1846. Deploying a phrase from Victorian theatre, he attacked as un-Conservative 'a policy which produces a transformation scene every two or three years'.[34] The future held at best a sense of mystery and at worst ultimate defeat and withdrawal; but one could not appease it by concession or offering one's tummy for tickling.

Still deeper in these positions lay a core of propositions about party for which Disraeli was not responsible and which would have informed Salisbury's behaviour no matter who led. That 'the old Jew', as Bismarck came to call him, threatened to disrupt the Tory leadership after 1848, assumed the titular role after 1868, and remained there until his death in 1881, remains an obvious reference point for understanding Salisbury's responses. Had anybody else been in charge in the 1860s, then Cranborne would not have resigned and refused to speak to certain colleagues for a number of years. Had Disraeli not 'educated' his party, then Salisbury would have avoided a marked form of political education, which stained the

---

[32] Disraeli to Malmesbury, 26 Jan. 1853 (copy in Stanley's hand), Derby MSS 1749/51. 'All democratic elements have receded from our party. The Reform Bill [1832] took away the Freemen: the Repeal of the Navigation Laws [1849] the great ports.'
[33] Salisbury to Carnarvon, 24 Jul. 1868, Carnarvon MSS 60758 f. 59.
[34] Salisbury in the House of Lords, 8 Jun. 1869, quoted in Cecil, vol. II, p. 30.

way he dealt with the leadership himself after Disraeli's death. But the two men differed in essence because they spent their time differently and saw the importance of the long term within very different frames. Few of the incidents so central to the party's sense of time made much impression on Salisbury, except for parliamentary rituals: a coming debate, a bill needing drafting, finding the right words for a discussion of foreign affairs. Clubs – the focal point of political conversation by the last quarter of the century – he hated; he could rarely be made to visit the Carlton, for all its standing a few yards beyond his front door in Arlington Street, and would go to the Athenæum only sparingly. Grillions, a parliamentary dining club of some repute, often bored him unless some of his intellectual, especially scientific, acquaintances were there; he shared Disraeli's contempt for the bad wine and desultory conversation. He would come to London from Hatfield for a political purpose, see whom he needed to see, normally at Arlington Street or in the House of Lords after 1868, and then go home. At home he read his papers – there exists overwhelming evidence that he read seriously and with concentration, often annotating documents and scribbling notes to their authors – and interacted, as we have seen, with his family. The long round of country house visiting in the summer and autumn, which Disraeli adored,[35] would have left him demented within a fortnight. Moreover, in taking himself off to Normandy or the riviera he dislocated himself from one of the most pressing party rhythms: the annual call to moor and river.

Among senior party managers this call emanated most readily and urgently from the sixth Duke of Richmond, who tried very hard to lead the party in the House of Lords between 1870 and Disraeli's arrival as Earl of Beaconsfield in 1876. He was defeated, but unbowed, by his own lack of attention-span. Indeed there is something glorious about Richmond's struggle to concentrate out of sheer *noblesse oblige*. Letters that were supposed to be about education or the church would elide after a few lines into his subliminal urge to send the correspondent a Kippered Salmon – he was very fond of capital letters – or a haunch of venison or the couple of setters he had promised some time ago. He was, in a word, adorable, and his sheer density of brain still sends screams of laughter around the Record Offices of Britain as one leafs through his long and chatty

---

[35] See chapter 2, pp. 34–5, below.

letters from Gordon Castle or Glenfiddich. ('We have no water in the Spey and consequently the fishing is not very good just now.'[36]) Richmond's party calendar had one date at its centre: the twelfth of August. If parliament were still in session by late summer, he became nervous and restive. As the early days of August came round, he began to accelerate the business as though he were master of it. Getting the 1871 Ballot Bill through 'on 10th or 11th' owed little to his love for democracy and something more to its allowing 'all our sporting friends myself among the number [he disbelieved in commas] to get away on Saturday or Monday'.[37] He plainly pulled it off because we find him in Elysium by the twentieth at Blackwater Lodge, Dufftown, reporting to his close friend Gathorne Hardy on the wonderful time he is having:

> Our sport here is by far the best I have ever seen. Up to last night we have killed 2,068½ brace of grouse . . . We are in all 8 guns. 4 staying here, Prince Edward, Bingham, Turnour and I – at the Glenfiddich March, Algy, Chaplin (Teddy) and Vivian . . . I am happy to say I find myself in first-rate walking trim and am reminded of you frequently during the day by taking drinks out of the flask you gave me.[38]

This matters not for its content but for its ritual and for the company that the ritual helped assemble and cohere. It was not the only one, of course. Later in the century Salisbury would gaze at Lord Hartington's devotion to the turf with the same amused disbelief he had once visited on Richmond's passion for killing grouse and deer. His often-remarked snort that 'Hartington is at Newmarket & all political arrangements have to be hung up till some quadruped has run faster than some other quadruped'[39] spoke again for his estrangement from the uses to which politicians preferred to put their time.

Disraeli did not ride or shoot; he, too, tried to represent himself as a landed proprietor with roots in a distant Conservative past. When he thought of Hughenden, his country home near High Wycombe, and its 'decomposing bowers'[40] he persuaded himself that it put him

[36] Richmond to Cranbrook, 21 Sep. 1879, Cranbrook MSS T501/257.
[37] Richmond to Cairns, 3 Aug. 1871, Cairns MSS 30/51/2/f.42.
[38] Richmond to Hardy, 20 Aug. 1871, Cranbrook MSS T501/257.
[39] Salisbury to Balfour, 15 Oct. 1891, in *The Salisbury–Balfour Correspondence*, p. 362. The arrangement in question concerned Balfour's appointment as Leader of the House of Commons after the death of W. H. Smith.
[40] Disraeli to Derby, 13 Nov. 1875, Derby MSS 16/2/1.

in contact with the great dead and gave him the timeless stature of a Salisbury or Derby or Buckingham. Writing to Stanley as heir to that weight of past, he becomes whimsical and tender through all the cares of the Exchequer.

> The Chilterns are looking very beautiful & I see that yr hearth is now disturbed. What say you to a visit here: a house of work, accustomed to the daily arrival of despatches. We might assist each other, & talk over many things: & sometimes visit the classic haunts of defunct statesmen, for the ghosts of the Grenvilles, & the phantom of Mr. Burke still haunt our hills and woods.[41]

Yet it was all fantasy. He hardly owned the house at all: it had been bought by the younger Bentincks to help him simulate landed respectability;[42] his true time-threshold in politics lay somewhere around the mid 1830s and his days of radical pretensions. When Salisbury dwelled on 1829 and its evils, he pointed at a world before he was born but one he 'knew' more immediately than those around him in the 1870s and 1880s. In that generation memory ran back to the Reform Bill but scarcely beyond, whether one were speaking (or rather shouting) to the frail Earl Russell at the beginning of the 1870s when 'the period to which his mind seemed oftenest to revert was that of the first reform bill' or perhaps, on the Tory side, to Lord Malmesbury who gave up the ghost in 1876 and allowed his mind to go back to the beginning of that Tory time which he had shared with Richmond:

> This ends 30 years of *active* connexion with our Party but you will still feel my knees in yr. back when wanted. Thirty years ago your father and Derby elected me chief Whip in very different times than these, & when we were fighting for very existence as Conservatives & it is a great satisfaction to me that at the end of that period I find myself still acting with & enjoying the friendship of their Sons. As to Dizzy he is immortal . . .[43]

He wasn't. When he died in 1881, Lord Beaconsfield, as he had become, struck the author of a *Times* leader as beginning his important narrative in 1865 – twenty years of the career already forgotten – and worthy of situation beside Palmerston, Derby and Russell. *They* had left, however, a better future to their successors

---

[41] Disraeli to Stanley, 31 Aug. 1852, Derby MSS 1749/51.
[42] Details in Robert Blake, *Disraeli* (1966), pp. 251–3; cf. Paul Smith, *Disraeli: A Brief Life* (Cambridge, 1996), pp. 84–5.
[43] Derby diary, 2 Sep. 1872, Derby, *Diaries*, p. 116; Malmesbury to Richmond, 5 Aug. 1876, Goodwood MSS 868 b 27.

who proved 'their equals in ability and influence'. 'But Lord Beaconsfield has been removed at a time when he was still the foremost statesman of the Conservative party, and while he attracted the attention of the country only in a less degree than MR. GLADSTONE himself.'[44] It did not sound a good augury for Beaconsfield's successors.

Salisbury, who was one of them, nevertheless dominated the last two decades of the nineteenth century without losing his own conception of his place in a longer story. It did not demand the sort of Toryism that refuses all change out of an emotional sense of the past's presence; indeed, Salisbury liked to ridicule people caught 'sticking to the carcasses of dead policies'.[45] Nor did his style of commitment require an identification with the Conservative party as an ancient institution, to be supported whatever its objectives or leadership. He made numerous remarks that have entered the canon of 'Salisbury' quotations that underlined his sense of distance from party association: that party government should be at the bottom of the sea; that 'politics are not all one's life'; that if the Conservative party were ever to change its principles he would would walk out of the Carlton Club for the last time with never a backward glance.[46] But Salisbury's vision of party in the nineteenth century bore a close relationship to his understanding of the dead and the special responsibility that leaders of the present bore in relation to people of previous generations who could no longer speak for themselves or defend what they had once asserted through pain and sacrifice. If he had a *point d'appui* for such thinking, it probably lay in the eighteenth century with an image of party that took its tone from his reading of Augustan politics through to the age of the Younger Pitt. Yet he held a view of the English mind as a slow-moving thing in many matters; and when his own mind moved beyond party, his thoughts ran back deep into the history of England since the Saxons as he sought evidence to help defend the past's legacies against depredation and loot.

---

[44] *The Times*, 20 Apr. 1881, p. 9a.
[45] Salisbury to Lytton, 25 May 1877, in Cecil, vol. II, p. 145. 'When a mast falls overboard', he went on, 'you do not try to save a rope here and a spar there, in memory of their former utility; you cut away the hamper altogether.'
[46] Salisbury to Carnarvon, 10 Feb. 1874, Carnarvon MSS 60758 ff.122–3; Cecil, vol. II, p. 192.

HISTORICAL TIME

Salisbury was not an historian but he had an historian's temperament and enjoyed past environments for their own sake or in their
own terms. He respected intellectuals who wrote about history far
more – as always – than narrow 'experts' who practised the emerging
discipline professionally. Politicians apart, for most of the reflective
ones were Liberals anyway, he would feel more at home in conversation with James Anthony Froude or Sir Henry Maine than with a
Maitland or Gardiner. He read considerable amounts of modern
history, most particularly when he was reviewing on a gigantic scale
during the days of penury before 1865, and acquired an historical
vocabulary which ran from the seventeenth century to the present,
together with some looser images strongly emphasized in the general
literature of mid-Victorian Britain, about the Saxons and the place
of the Norman Conquest. Classical culture he seems to have known
less about, despite the vogue for it among the intelligentsia: he was
far less likely than Gladstone to write a postcard teeming with Greek,
though occasional bits of Latin, especially legal Latin, spatter the
correspondence. The very reverse of a 'Whig', for he suspected
triumphalism for its vulgarity, he kept his Protestantism out of sight
unless the Church of England were under direct attack, distrusted
'liberty' unless negatively defined and abhorred all forms of 'progress'. He shared, none the less, one of the tenets of that school of
historical thinking. He saw the past as a place that held the head-
waters of the present and he saw history as a way of explaining how
the present came about and why it had a particular nature. He also
saw the value of the past as a silent accretion of experience to which
an appeal could be made when validating present behaviour or
institutions. There was little romance in all of this and even less
aesthetic pleasure to which he remained immune in most areas of
artistic expression. Of course he recognized the skill of Lord
Stanhope, say, who tried in his biography of Pitt to 'leave pleasant
illusions on the mind, just as a Richmond head is pleasanter to look
at than a photograph . . . '[47] But he loathed illusion on principle and
taught his children photography, not painting.

---

[47] Cecil, 'Lord Stanhope's *Life of Pitt*', *Quarterly Review*, 109 (Apr. 1861), pp. 531–65 at p. 532.
The thought had an extra edge for him in 1861: he had just sat, or was about to sit, for
George Richmond, who produced one of the best studies of his head ever done. The sitter
doubtless deemed it illusory.

History helped combat illusions held about power: a failure he deplored throughout his conduct of foreign and imperial policy. An example of how he would treat European affairs in the light of history came to the attention of the western world in 1863 when Russia became aggressive against Polish notions of a re-emerging national identity and liberals from Italy to Scandinavia grieved over a crime against humanity. Cecil, while reviewing the great Prussian historian, Heinrich von Sybel, in the *Quarterly*, accused them of inventing a crime in order to feel scandalized by it. The eighteenth-century partition of Poland had been a predictable and unavoidable consequence of developing influence – he saw no real difference between influence and power – among her neighbours; and the attempt to resuscitate Polish independence in the face of that influence could go nowhere. 'An independent Poland is a mere chimera . . . The best that can be hoped for Poland is an improved condition under Russian rule', which might happen if St Petersburg would pay a little more attention to the way it packaged its repressions.[48] It would prove the same with Austria one day. No matter how much noise Vienna made through her blustering ambassadors, the historical record showed 'her destiny to be a cat's paw'.[49] One could rejoice or lament, but killing the cat would remain the only way to divert that destiny. And naturally at the centre of all these dynamics lay the French Revolution and what it had done to the internal and external stabilities of Europe. Salisbury saw them intertwined in a common disaster evident wherever one saw 'those wild democratic theories which the Revolution had left as its legacy to Europe . . . Wherever [democracy] has had free play, in the ancient world or the modern, in the old hemisphere or the new, a thirst for empire, and a readiness for aggressive war, has always marked it.'[50] Only open a history book, his subtext seems to remark; the warnings are all there.

This seemed no less true at home, where values and visible features of English life demanded preservation and respect. Parliament presented one obvious case and Salisbury spent much energy on fashioning a mnemonic language about the House of Commons and the House of Lords within which an appeal to history would often recur. It lurks within the folds of his arguments about a second

[48] 'Poland', *Quarterly Review*, 113 (Apr. 1863), pp. 450–81.
[49] Salisbury to Derby, 7 Jan. 1876, Derby MSS 16/2/7.
[50] 'The Danish Duchies', *Quarterly Review*, 115 (Jan. 1864), pp. 236–87 at p. 239.

chamber. When Disraeli finally went there in 1876 he received the now famous letter from Salisbury trying to dissuade him from any ambition to join 'the dullest assembly in the world'. But his grounds, less remarked, were *historical*. Warnings from the past – Walpole, Pulteney, the Elder Pitt, Castlereagh, Brougham – were made to say with varying plausibility that the House of Lords would prove the kiss of death to a political leader.[51] It appears in his explanation for the centrality of Ireland as a touchstone of party after 1886. Strong feelings about Home Rule abounded on both sides, as all agreed; but one had to place the issue in historical perspective to see what its function had become and appreciate the force of analogy with other great moments:

> You cannot expect to divide the political world into two halves [Liberal and Conservative], and that each half on all possible subjects shall think the same. It would be an ideal and impossible state of things. But if you look into the history of this country since Parliamentary Government began you will find that Parties range themselves . . . on one great issue by which men's minds were turned. First, it was a dynastic issue; later on you had the American War; then you had the French Revolution; then you had the great question of Reform; next the great question of Protection; now we have the great question of Ireland.[52]

Gladstone was so taken by one of these retrospectives that he harped on it when he ran into Lord Acton on the continent. He had in mind an especially unfair *reductio* that Salisbury had imposed on his, presumably bemused, audience of Liverpudlians at the beginning of 1888, which amounted to a history of England as seen from Hatfield:

> You may take from me the history of Europe thus. As a rule I think that wherever communities are in close geographical proximity, and are related to each other by an identity or a close similarity of language, one of two things must happen to them. Either they must combine absolutely or they must separate absolutely. (Hear, hear.) . . . We have seen this kingdom gradually made up, first by the Heptarchy, then Wales, then Scotland, then Ireland . . . The force of circumstances has dictated to those communities the decree that they shall be one (cheers), and if you glance over the history of Ireland you at once see why they must be one. You see a succession of the enemies of England always using her as their opportunity (hear, hear) first from the Yorkists and Perkin Warbeck, then from the times of the Reformation and Philip II, then to the rebellion because of the Puritan movement in England, then to Louis XIV, and later on to the Jacobites at

---

[51] Salisbury to Disraeli (transcript), 27 Jul. 1876, Christ Church MSS, file E, f.143.
[52] In debate on the Queen's Speech, House of Lords, *Hansard*, 27 Jan. 1887, CCCX, col. 32.

the end of the seventeenth century [*sic*] and the Jacobites [*sc.* Jacobins] at the end of the eighteenth century. . . .[T]hey always selected Ireland as the basis of their operations.[53]

If parliament possessed in contemporary perception a past running back to Simon de Montfort or the witenagemot, how much greater depth of temporal weight rested on the rock of the church. Here Salisbury thought in two periods: he dwelled on the 200 years since the Act of Uniformity (1662); and/or he swept an arm over the millennium during which he alleged the English church to have flourished. His parliamentary speeches, in which he normally meant to prevent something happening to the church, frequently shackled the argument to one of these two frames. The first arose whenever Liberals in either House sought to relax subscription to the Thirty-nine Articles of the church of England or to tamper with the Prayer Book. When they did so in 1863, he had the bicentenary of 1662 ready to hand and trounced the malefactors for abusing the wisdom that so long a period must assuredly include. He told them so, probably fortified by wine, four times:

For two hundred years these tests had been constantly and cheerfully subscribed by some six generations of clergymen. All these men, all the great lights of the church since 1662, were by the sweeping denunication of his hon. Friend [Buxton] accused without exception of having been compelled to tamper with their consciences . . . That long experience was the best answer to the statements that had been made. They might depend upon it that an experience of two hundred years was a better guide than the experience of his hon. Friends the Members for Canterbury or Plymouth. Oxford life was but three years in duration, and it was the experience of three years against that of two hundred. Two hundred years furnished a better average of the ordinary tendencies of humanity.[54]

Indeed that last sentence says a good deal about Salisbury's cast of mind: history, in its broadest sense, legitimizes the present but not because it is quaint or glorious so much as because it allows accretion

---

[53] Salisbury at Liverpool, 11 Jan. 1888, *The Times* 12 Jan. 1888, p. 7d. Gladstone's diary refers to a conversation with Acton 'on Salisbury's "History" ': cf. entry under 6 Feb. 1888 in Foot and Matthew (eds.), *The Gladstone Diaries*, vol. XII, p. 98.

[54] Cecil in Commons, *Hansard*, 9 Jun. 1863, CLXXI, cols. 641–2. Charles Buxton was the third son of Sir Thomas Fowell Buxton and an unlikely (Liberal) partner in Truman, Hanbury and Co., brewers. Canterbury was meant to evoke H. A. M. Butler-Johnstone, grandson of Lord Dunboyne, who compounded his wrong views about the church by being an opinionated Tory who later wrote on the Irish, the Turks and *A Trip up the Volga*, which ran to two editions. 'Plymouth' suggests Sir Robert Collier, Liberal son of the reformer John Collier and MP for Plymouth from 1852 to 1871.

of experience to make itself felt as a kind of collective memory. 'Ordinary' experience mattered because Salisbury mistrusted many kinds of exceptional people and had little expectation of the virtues of the mass. The past showed what worked *despite* the worst efforts of those inspired to help and those too malevolent to try. He felt the same about the persistence of manorial rights, about which some people complained. Such legacies may have been wrong or silly: that was not the point. They 'ha[d] existed for a thousand years, and no blame c[ould] attach to those who ma[de] use of them'.[55] When he turned to issues such as church rates or tithes, moreover, he could turn the force of another tranche of time on his persecutors. They were offering 'not a Bill of liberty and enfranchisement', though he doubtless would have opposed that as well, 'but of disfranchisement and forfeiture of privileges which had been held for a thousand years'.[56] They were pressing reform when 'the practice now followed was that which had prevailed for 1,000 years'.[57]

In the years after 1886, when Salisbury settled into the premiership and ran the Foreign Office concurrently, he evolved observations of this kind into a governing style, resting present possibility on past demonstration and dotting the speeches with stories that their lordships could follow. Sometimes he would translate into party time, shortening all the horizons and bringing the subject into a living memory that needed no historical awareness, merely those elements of reminiscence that so easily rested on the red benches. '[T]ake the larger view', he would intone. 'What would you say is the great change which has passed over Europe since the older of us were young men? [Pause for effect while minds turn.] It is this tremendous increase in the burdens which the necessity of self-defence has cast upon every nation of the world.'[58] But he also used his formidable Cecil memory to recalibrate the party mind when it lost sight of the past. Criticized for the form of the Queen's Speech in 1897 – it had been called 'unprecedented' – he effortlessly produced in a private letter the precedent of 1841 – the 'only precedent which is at all analogous'.[59] These reversions amounted to an acquired technique.

---

[55] Salisbury at Manchester, 16 Apr. 1884, *The Times*, 17 Apr. 1884, p. 6a.
[56] Cecil in Commons, *Hansard*, 19 Jun. 1861, CLXIII, col. 1294.
[57] Salisbury in Lords, *Hansard*, 7 Jun. 1887, CCCXVII, col. 7. The issues of church rates and tithe reappear in chapter 8 of this study.
[58] *Hansard*, 19 Jan. 1897, XLV, col. 34.
[59] Salisbury to Beach, 5 Aug. 1897, St Aldwyn MSS PCC/69/146–7.

But he also peppered speeches, and had done so since his earliest days in the Commons, with references to themes beyond memory – to Gibbon, perhaps, who was obviously detestable but, from his own point of view, quite right in his anti-clericalism; to Charles V, possibly, whose thoughts threw light on the English judicial system.[60] Or he might extend his speculations to ancient Greece in order to explain the modern Græco-Turkish problem (the battles of Thermopylae and Salamis had the advantage of having been 'fought 2,000 years ago'); or to the days of Saladin and the crusades to make sense of Turkish ambition, which 'has recalled to them their past of a thousand years ago, when they were victors in every part of the world'.[61] On every front, the point lay in making the membrane between past and present pervasive and porous.

Not so the future. Salisbury derided those who thought that they could see ahead beyond the trifling predictability of a parliamentary schedule. When they did so, trouble resulted in the form, normally, of 'progress', which he took to represent an odious capitulation to forces that should be controlled on the part of people who wanted to travel somewhere quickly without quite knowing where. This was the trouble with innocents such as Joseph Chamberlain in his radical phase. The latter's famous article on 'The Liberal Party and its Leaders' made Salisbury sufficiently unhappy to prompt a reply – not because Chamberlain should be dissuaded from maligning his own leaders of whose perverse tendencies Salisbury already felt acutely aware, but because he should learn to decide on a destination before setting off on his destructive journey. 'It may seem a truism', Salisbury wrote in the *Quarterly*, 'to assert that progress means going somewhere. Yet no one has been able to extract from the "party of progress" where in their case that somewhere is . . . Progress in the abstract, with no itinerary and no goal, is as unreasonable an idea as a pilgrimage to nowhere in particular.'[62] He himself made no pilgrimages toward the future beyond those undertaken out of fear and walking backwards, as in his long-held determination to go if the

---

[60] Third reading of Church Rates Abolition Bill, Commons, *Hansard*, 19 Jun. 1861, CLXIII, col. 1294; Lords, *Hansard*, 21 Mar. 1892, II, col. 1308.

[61] Salisbury in Lords, *Hansard*, 19 Mar. 1897, XLVII, col. 1013; *Hansard*, 8 Feb. 1898, LIII, cols. 42–3.

[62] 'The Progress of the Radicals' (Oct. 1873) in Paul Smith (ed.), *Lord Salisbury on Politics: A Selection from his Articles in the 'Quarterly Review'* (Cambridge, 1972), pp. 312–13.

Queen were to die.[63] This did not make him inactive but it rendered his behaviour the reverse of proactive, a trait that a *Times* obituary took to run in the family. 'BURLEIGH could never had led a Reformation', it said in reviewing Salisbury's long career, 'any more than that his great descendant could have initiated a Reform Bill . . . He was a link, and the only one then existing, between the past and the present.'[64] Even when he could see where he had been, there was sometimes a sense of surprise, chances missed, paths not taken. He hardly saw himself qualified to advise others on their own futures:

When I was younger than you are, by a good deal, I was asked to leave Stamford & stand for Middlesex. My life would have been very different if I had accepted. If I had failed in Middlesex I should probably have abandoned politics. If I had succeeded I should probably have been taken into the Ministry of 1858, & perhaps should have acquired influence enough to prevent the Tories from taking later on more than one step which I deplored. But whether, generally, I should have been wise or foolish, even now, I cannot judge. How should I judge for you?[65]

To the end he remained insecure in his own sense of temporal location. He had, none the less, helped those around him keep some sense of theirs and given politics a retrospect which placed formidable obstacles in the way of those who wanted to remember the wrong parts of the past or who sought after their future with untutored enthusiasm and misconceived zest.

---

[63] Gwendolen Cecil to Cross, 15 Jul. 1902, '. . . the event he had for long fixed upon in his mind as the period of his public life': Cross MSS 51264 f.148.

[64] *The Times*, 24 Aug. 1903, p. 7b–c.

[65] Salisbury to Balfour, 16 Dec. 1883, in *Salisbury–Balfour Correspondence*, p. 102. Balfour was wondering whether to move from his constituency, doomed by impending reform, to Manchester. He decided to do so.

CHAPTER 2

Space

'ENGLAND'

Senior Conservatives enjoyed enviable personal space, for their houses were many and large; but their space brought confinements of body and mind. It was neither random nor dispersed. Its occupants broadcast, without knowing it, a particular sense of place and oneness that echoed Englishness even when they lived regularly in Scotland or Ireland. A century and a half had passed since the Act of Union with Scotland in 1707, while the lives of all participants in the system of late-Victorian Conservatism stood in the shadow of the Act of Union with Ireland at the turn of their century. Yet within the world of perception it often appeared as though these portents need never have troubled parliament with their implications. 'Britain' had no existence apart from the imperative identity found useful in posters or broadsides – 'Britons!' – and England remained the mental ground to conquer, the cause demanding defence. Of course, it was not really a *place* at all so much as a device, a construct, a trope. The notion helped focus time and place within a single image, just as Eliot would later fuse them in a continuity of experience:

> Time present and time past
> Are both perhaps present in time future,
> And time future contained in time past.
> If all time is eternally present
> All time is unredeemable.
> . . . . . . the communication
> Of the dead is tongued with fire beyond the language of the
>   living.
> Here, the intersection of the timeless moment
> Is England and nowhere. Never and always.
> . . . . . . A people without history
> Is not redeemed from time, for history is a pattern

Of timeless moments. So, while the light fails
On a winter's afternoon, in a secluded chapel
History is now and England.[1]

Salisbury lacked this tortured sensibility. But he meant something of the kind when he explained to his contemporaries the consequences of England's having been 'an old country', a place where time passed slowly and sustained in its slowness the place of its passing. 'England' presented thoughts to celebrate or weep over more than a place to live in or a territory to master. Indeed it flew beyond its own borders in this age of imperialism, giving way to Sir Charles Dilke's search for the English overseas in his *Greater Britain* (1868), or Professor Seeley's Cambridge lectures on *The Expansion of England* (1883) or in the fevered projections of fictional expatriots in the colonial Africa depicted by John Buchan or the honorary Englishman, Joseph Conrad.[2]

If 'England' were unreal, its fictive features varied from one depictor to the next. For while a currency existed, ready-minted, in novels and poems and songs for the political classes to acquire, Conservatives, who tend not to rely on imagination (even when they possess it) if personal knowledge can be gained, made their own images and formed their own sense of what 'England' meant. Rambling around the country could inspire that process, of course, and it becomes almost visual as one listens to Disraeli's recollection of the summer he had just spent in 1850. 'We were vagabonds for a month,' he wrote to Edward Stanley, the future Earl of Derby, at Knowsley.

We went to Knebworth, Herts, & stayed with Bulwer [Lytton] a most charming fortnight. He has restored the seat of his maternal ancestry in a manner wh: a 'large-acred' poet cd. alone imagine & accomplish: a Tudor castellated hall, in the richest style: towers & cupolas & twisted columns & embayed windows & glittering vanes: in the midst of an ancient deer park. Then to the William Powletts at Downham in the heart of the Norfolk deserts . . .[3]

---

[1] T. S. Eliot, *Four Quartets* (1944).

[2] I have commented on this style of speculation more generally in 'Liberalism and Nationalism in Britain' in S. Groenveld and M. J. Wintle (eds.), *Under the Sign of Liberalism: Varieties of Liberalism in Past and Present* (Zutphen, Netherlands, 1997), pp. 78–92.

[3] Disraeli to Stanley, 3 Oct. 1850, Derby MSS 1759/51. This Lytton, the novelist, was father of Salisbury's Lord Lytton, who influenced (and provoked) much thought about India, Afghanistan and Russia in the 1870s. The maternal ancestry was Byzantine. Bulwer Lytton added his mother's name – Lytton – to his surname on succeeding to the estate on his mother's death in 1844. She would have been called Warburton but *her* father, Richard, had

The deserts of Norfolk, plumbed with the occasional watering-hole and the single great oasis of Sandringham after Albert Edward, Prince of Wales, acquired it in 1863, still formed something of a border-province in the world of one who found High Wycombe disturbingly provincial. Salisbury, on the other hand, relied on simple intuitions about parts of 'England' that had eluded his experience and talked cheerfully about, say, the men of the north as though they wore woad and ate their women. Normally very cautious about allowing state interference in the lives of individuals, he made an exception of northern fishermen and their 'copers' – boats that sailed not to fish but to supply fishermen with provisions, of which drink putatively formed a significant fraction. His language about such people had the same timbre that he frequently used in discussing the 'lower' races. 'No doubt', he intoned to the House of Lords, 'the sailors in the North Sea Fisheries, coming as they do from various coasts and ports and being composed of a population not all in the highest state of civilisation, must in this matter, to a certain extent, be treated more as children than we should venture to treat other people.' In fact '[t]he position which many of these men still occup[ied] in the scales of civilization' so worried him that he supported a Liberal attempt to save them from themselves – a project that typically would have stimulated his disdain.[4] Northern fishermen failed the 'England' test.

Salisbury's own sense of space had four facets. Hatfield plainly formed one, by far the most dear to him; and it was here that he wrote his letters, read his official papers, entertained friends and dignitaries and took seriously his rights and obligations as a *grand seigneur*. He spent much of his time in a small section of the house: the study, whose battered desk and chair survive as relics; the library to which he added considerably during his time at Hatfield; and the chapel, whose architecture he encouraged towards a version of high gothic. The larger spaces were screamed over by children, prowled

---

taken the name Lytton on inheriting Knebworth on the death of *his* maternal uncle in 1762. And none of these people bore any relation to the *original* Lyttons, who often styled themselves Lytton Lytton, who owned Knebworth in the first place and kept it till 1710. Powlett was an assumed name, too. Lord William Powlett of Downham Hall (1792–1864) had originally been a Vane, since he was born second son to the first Duke of Cleveland. He later assumed his mother's name and changed it back again when he succeeded his brother as third Duke. He sat in the House of Commons for St Ives and Ludlow between 1846 and 1857.

[4] *Hansard*, 8 Jun. 1893, XIII, col. 468.

over by cats and deployed by Georgina Salisbury as public space for
her political receptions, which her husband visited as though
attending the dentist. Only one imposing room – the Great Hall –
remained in constant family use for dinner. Occasionally the outside
world might impinge. (It stuck in the mind of one dining visitor that
the butler brought in a box with the news of Portugal's invasion of
Delagoa Bay as Salisbury was spooning his soup. He sent in the navy,
barely losing his tempo with the spoon.) Yet the world usually came
in a box whose contents he would work through behind double-
doors in his inner sanctum – more a temple of war, perhaps, than
Gladstone's temple of peace at Hawarden, but a sanctum all the
same. The vistas that might propel a man towards *Weltpolitik* did not
exist at Hatfield: it held nothing like the future Cliveden or Blickling,
let alone Berchtesgaden. Like its owner, the space encouraged and
reflected practical tasks at hand. He treated it with a functionalism
that never stopped short of the philistine when it suited him.
Inserting his chemical laboratory in a seventeeth-century mansion
and filling the rooms with smells not known there since the invention
of the water-closet supplied a case in point. The famous and dire
electrical wiring, which he was among the first major proprietors to
install, would have given cause for alarm to residents even if he had
made the right decision over whether to place the circuits in parallel
or in series. As it was, family and guests hurled their cushions at the
ceilings to put out the fires as a sort of surreal parlour game. It hardly
seemed the way to treat a beautiful and near-priceless building.
Salisbury's flexibilities reached their apogee, perhaps, when he
decided to turn the house round and make it face the other way. It
was the need to reach the railway station which drove him on; and
that had been built behind the house. So he called the front the back
and laid a new driveway for his carriage with a lodge and some park
gates.[5]

Carriage and train turned him into a commuter and enabled
Salisbury to avoid living in London for much of the year, except
during congested parts of the parliamentary session or when particular crises demanded consultation with colleagues. These would
normally fall between, say, February and early August when he

---

[5] This programme of work followed the rebuilding of Salisbury's town-house in Arlington
Street and lasted some three years between 1876 and 1879: see F. M. L. Thompson's remarks
in Lord Blake and Hugh Cecil, *Lord Salisbury: The Man and his Policies* (Basingstoke, 1987),
p. 265.

would stay over at Arlington Street because it gave him the space to hold large meetings of cabinet size conveniently and in confidence. He had seen one of his first domestic tasks, after having succeeded to the peerage in 1868, to lie in making this Georgian house more habitable than it had been in the days of his father; and he spent, according to Derby, around £60,000 even before the decorators had finished the final touches. The result was a 'new house . . . very spacious and fine it is, comfortable too'.[6] Even so, Salisbury used it as office space more than a residence and it became prominent as a venue for great matters only once, in 1884, when the so-called 'Arlington Street conversations' between Tory leaders and opposition spokesmen became the foundation for agreement over the redistribution attached to the reform bill of that year.[7] It never became a focus for Mayfair and St James's society because Salisbury did not believe in Mayfair or St James's society. Nor did he use it as a stopping-off place on the way to West End Clubs because he did not believe in those either, and went to the Carlton, the Athenæum or to Grillions out of a sort of hopeless duty. Indeed the sole cachet that he could claim for Arlington Street was that it lay on the right side of Oxford Street, amending for those years of penury in Fitzroy Square after his father cut him off and society ceased to call. Doubtless some of the loathing he felt for the superficiality of London 'society' had its roots in that time when the chimney-piece remained empty of cards. London he saw as the home of parliament and the Queen: a place of intellectual labour and constitutional dignity. He could well do without the *nouveaux riches* of Belgravia with their slick stories, dubious jokes and bad wine.

Left with a little leisure, he might choose to go down to Cranborne Manor in Dorset for the air and the peace; or perhaps to Liverpool to see how his estates in the hinterland had fared. Both contexts ran back into childhood, as chapter 1 suggested. Cecil had spent most of his formative years at Hatfield but the smaller house at Cranborne had played a role in family geography. When he became Lord Cranborne in 1865 he did not reside there but, as we have seen, in a rented cottage at Headley in Hampshire. There were later visits, however, especially when the other houses underwent their

---

[6] Diary, 19 Jun. 1872, in Derby, *Diaries*, p. 109. 'I should have preferred', he added rather typically, 'having kept the £60,000.' The house no longer exists.

[7] For the secluded dramas of redistribution, see Andrew Jones, *1884: The Politics of Reform* (Cambridge, 1972), pp. 205–13.

respective face-lifts. 'I have been down in Dorsetshire', he apologized to a correspondent whose reply had been delayed in 1871; it is clear that the link endured.[8] The Lancashire estates had a younger vintage. Gascoyne lands came into the Cecil inheritance via Robert Cecil's mother. He continued to take an interest in them, if only because they offered a way of repairing relations with the Earl of Derby after his marriage to Cecil's stepmother. 'S. came for one night', Derby noted in his diary at Knowsley in 1873. 'He talked of the Liverpool estates, which appear to be managed in a singular way, by a local architect and a solicitor, without any regular agent: they yield, I believe, £15,000–£16,000 yearly.'[9] This contact with Lancashire land and town came to matter a good deal to Salisbury and should play some part in evaluating his implicit understanding of England. Apart from London, whose seedier parts he knew about through Blue Books and in connexion with his enquiry into the standard of London's housing in the 1880s, Liverpool and its environs represented the one place familiar to him on which to hone his instincts about urban conditions and requirements. Other members of the family cemented this understanding through their own parliamentary careers. Arthur Balfour eventually overcame his anxieties about Manchester in 1885 and held East Manchester against all-comers until the national Conservative catastrophe of 1906. Salisbury's eldest son similarly sat for a Lancashire seat – Darwen – during the decade after 1885. Granted that electoral fortunes among Conservatives seemed increasingly to turn on the experience of London and Lancashire, Salisbury became tempted to use these places as a form of political weather-vane. Frances Balfour would later recall, for example, the interest that Salisbury had taken in the Lancashire contests in 1886 and recorded how 'he had a great belief in Lancashire, and how things went there'. It had become 'again and again the thermometer of his hopes and fears', a place which, he believed, would 'have a decisive effect on other parts of the country'.[10]

Salisbury's 'England' went beyond Hatfield, Cranborne and

[8] Salisbury to Lord de Grey, 22 Jul. 1871, Ripon MSS 43519 f.41.

[9] Derby, *Diaries*, p. 147.

[10] For Frances Balfour, see *Ne Obliviscaris: Dinna Forget* (2 vols., 1930), vol. II, pp. 58–9; Salisbury to Beach, 9 Aug. 1883, St Aldwyn MSS PCC/69/f.20. Northcote, Salisbury's partner in leadership after 1881, pressed Hicks Beach to stand there for different but related reasons. 'We must expect to see in the coming Parlt', he told him in 1883, 'a severe struggle between the supporters and the assailants of Order, Property, and the Unity of the Empire. It is of

Lancashire to involve a fourth kind of distinctiveness. It included France. Perhaps Salisbury was the last of the Angevins, seeing the Channel as a river separating one of his natural domains from the other. France gave him seclusion and a culture given to privacy and *laissez-faire*, qualities he admired. We have Bismarck's word that he could not speak the language very well. But he read its literature with fascinated disgust and his rejection of the new realism did not prevent his buying instances of it by the hundredweight. He absorbed French ease of spirit so completely that Francophilia became part of his personality in a degree unusual among Conservatives until the generation of Baldwin and Austen Chamberlain. Salisbury built two houses there. The first stood on the cliffs at Puys, three miles from Dieppe, and took shape while Arlington Street underwent reconstruction; it was completed in the same year – 1872. Visitors were a pest at first out of sheer curiosity about the 'Chalet Cecil'. They would send home accounts of fun in the sea and an over-relaxed magnate in 'good form'. Sir Stafford Northcote found the children's pranks as anxiety-making as he found everything else:

> I don't think I can tell you much in the way of gossip, unless you like to have an account of Salisbury's villa at Dieppe, and of the wonderful little *perissoirs* [pedal-boats] in which the children venture out to sea. They are small twin canoes about 12ft or 13ft long and about as many inches wide, united in the middle like Siamese twins by a seat on which the paddler sits. They look most dangerous, but seem to stand the roughest sea . . . Salisbury was in great force.[11]

The second house at Beaulieu we have already encountered: it was the one that suffered royal infestations. But that was a grander affair in a more exclusive place on the riviera; and when Salisbury bought the land on which to build it in 1888 he was prime minister and in no position to close his door on overmighty subjects or to swat European princes as vigorously as he might have wished.

Family fun and personal withdrawal concealed a more serious side. Salisbury decided to commit himself to France at the very moment when others, especially Conservatives, feared for the stability and friendliness of the new republic – a word with unconservative associations. One of the Earl of Derby's characteristics was an eagerness to pick up gossip about the end of the world for the landed

---

great consequence that we should obtain the aid of as many as possible of the great centres of Commerce and Manufactures': *ibid.*, PCC/77/unfol.
[11] Northcote to Cairns, 14 Oct. 1874, Cairns MSS 30/51/5/f.13.

classes and he found a good deal of it by the end of 1869 as people applied French experience to the British situation. There was the worry that Paris would disseminate its challenging doctrines, 'because a violent republican outbreak c[ould] not fail, if it occur[-red] to create a corresponding feeling here'.[12] There was a less hysterical anxiety that 'Republicans are not agreeable neighbours' and that greater demands would be placed on the British taxpayer to resist aggression if it came.[13] Salisbury remained cool and measured. He had felt for some years, possibly since the failure of the British government to interest itself in the fate of Denmark when Prussia bullied it in 1864, that the English had become an isolationist people, 'glad to seclude themselves' behind their Channel moat:

> I wish that there was any chance of awakening England to the necessity or the duty of sustaining upon the Continent the position which she acquired and held in former times. Such a revival of feeling on her part would not only draw classes together in this country and purify our internal conflicts from the material element which is coming to be dominant in them; but it would prove an important guarantee for the maintenance of the present structure of Europe.[14]

Certainly this argued the need for a strong army and, in particular, for a powerful reserve in case an emergency should erupt. Yet the tone of Salisbury's letter to Carnarvon as he wound himself up for the parliamentary session of 1871 avoided all intemperate commitments to either France or Prussia and warned, as he so often would in later years, of the danger of substituting emotion for perspective. 'I doubt the expediency', he wrote, 'of dwelling much upon the conduct of either of the belligerents . . . It is not our function to compose history. Criticisms of the conduct of foreign powers are only in place where they serve as an argument addressed either to the feeling of [*sc.* or] the reason of their own Govt. or people to determine them to some particular course.'[15] No such course seemed obvious in 1871 and no agitation would make it so.

Many of the characteristics of Salisbury's spatial experience found some reflection among other landed Conservatives of his generation. He belonged, after all, to an English class with common character-

---

[12] Derby diary, 7 Oct. 1869, in Derby, *Diaries*, p. 37.
[13] Hardy to Cairns, 2 Sep. 1870, Cairns MSS 30/51/7/f.30.
[14] Salisbury to Bille, 18 Apr. 1871, quoted in Marvin Swartz, *The Politics of British Foreign Policy in the Era of Disraeli and Gladstone* (1985), pp. 25–6.
[15] Salisbury to Carnarvon, 30 Jan. 1871, Carnarvon MSS 60758 ff.85–6.

istics, one that shared many of its attitudes with Scottish aristocrats and the Anglo-Irish ascendency. He had no monopoly of stately homes, as Knowsley or Highclere or Goodwood at once make palpable. He was not the only senior Conservative to have a French hideaway: his Irish chancellor, Edward Gibson, Lord Ashbourne, kept a place at Boulogne and left it as little as possible.[16] Salisbury hated county balls and suffered at the sessional courts at which his presence was demanded; but others, too, knew those pressures and differed from him only in finding them less appalling. The often-recalled arrival at Hatfield of Lord Randolph Churchill's resignation as Chancellor of the Exchequer in December 1886 occurred in the middle of a great ball and inserted a minor occasion into the history books. But the Duke of Richmond held at least as many and inclined to finding a ball helpful in a grim sort of way, 'not a cheerful thing in itself', he would say, 'but [he was] able to meet a good many people of the County and so keep up one's influence which [was] a necessary thing in these days'.[17] The county would press quite as hard on Carnarvon as it did on a Salisbury or a Richmond, no doubt feeding his wish to be at Highclere rather than in Portman Square ('If out of office he would probably be out of London', Derby had said of him[18]), but also providing a *raison d'état* that other colleagues in the system would be bound at once to recognize and allow. 'I am unfortunately bound to be in Hampshire on some really important county business . . .'[19] It was as good as a sick note.

All the same, Salisbury presents a sharp study in contrast despite these structural similarities. His rootedness in the country had little to do with the farming around which so many Tory lives revolved. Though he tried to learn a little about it when he succeeded to the estates, he continued to understand land as a problem and responsibility constrained and secured in history, economics and law; he was unsure what to do with it beyond letting it out to tenants or covering it with cottages and charging rent. He could not expand his thought-world far enough, therefore, to find the wavelength of the Duke of Richmond, by whom he was deeply distrusted out of native density

---

[16] He leased the Château de la Cocherie and made increasing use of it from the mid-1870s: see A. P. Cooke and A. P. W. Malcolmson (eds.), *The Ashbourne Papers, 1869–1913* (Belfast, 1974), p. xvii.

[17] Richmond to Cairns, 4 Jan. 1874, Cairns MSS 30/51/3/f.1.

[18] Derby to Cross (copy), 12 Sep. 1875, Derby MSS 16/2/5.

[19] Carnarvon to Richmond, 17 May 1871, Goodwood MSS 863 x 4.

and the clever teaching of Lord Cairns. Now Disraeli, who had no more idea than Salisbury about how to farm, picked up Richmond's low frequencies very quickly once he had received a couple of uncomprehending letters. He soon learned how to begin a letter to his rural friend – like this one in the middle of the Russo-Turkish war, which might unduly have preoccupied Salisbury. 'The Grouse is the King of Birds!' he began, in order to thank Richmond for a parcel of game that had arrived from Scotland, '& tho' I hear guns firing about me in all directions, I know the Partridge tribute that I shall receive, cannot for a moment shake him on his throne. The Turks go on fighting . . .'[20] This was *correct*, like invading England via Thanet. Salisbury could no more have attempted such lubrication than pretended to be a sportsman. It was part of his marginality. His nephew, who swung a golf club with some success, spent every September at North Berwick where he would play thirty-six holes most days and write philosophy in the evening, when he was not taken away by visits to dine and sleep.[21] Uncle Robert did not accompany him, though he occasionally visited Whittingehame, Balfour's house in East Lothian. It all took effort and he did not like it. He was delighted that Hatfield did not lie astride the road to Scotland or indeed anywhere that might bring to his door every Tory worthy who happened to be passing – a privation supposedly enjoyed by the Duke of Northumberland at Alnwick – which would have struck him as a form of social perversity.[22] Not that his privacy could always be counted to his advantage. When he retired to Hatfield to ponder the serious issues surrounding the question whether to take minority office in 1885, the opposition gloated without contradiction that he had 'thrown up the sponge' and gone home in a sulk.[23] Confidential spaces make the best soil for rumour.

London presented Tory strategists with a cluster of confidential spaces. These had their own geography in the later nineteenth century, one not always distinguishable from Liberal patterns of

---

[20] Beaconsfield to Richmond, 4 Sep. 1877, Goodwood MSS 865 w 63.

[21] 'My plans are of the usual kind. I go to Balmoral for a day or two on the 29th: North Berwick on the 2nd of September . . . Then perhaps Glen [Glenconners]: and *then* Wynyards [Londonderrys].' Balfour MSS SRO GD433/2/67.

[22] 'Found there a large party, none known to us before: it is the custom of the Duke and Duchess, as I am told, not to invite parties made up beforehand, but to ask all their friends to stay with them in passing . . . which is apt to make a dull house . . . They remain at home from August to January, receiving in this way . . . We sat down to dinner some 25 persons': diary, 30 Sep. 1873, Derby, *Diaries*, p. 145.

[23] Edward Hamilton to Gladstone, 21 Jun. 1885, Gladstone MSS 44191 f.13.

residence but one also that did not follow the shape of previous exclusive castes. The days of High Whiggery still had their ghosts in Devonshire House or Lansdowne House, though Holland House was now a walk from civilization rather than a carriage expedition.[24] Tory barons had come to copy them, as the Londonderrys did in their ghastly mansion where receptions flooded onto the street and threatened to kill the guests by asphyxiation.[25] But the Conservative managers of Salisbury's generation visited one another at home in Mayfair or St James's in order to resolve matters best dealt with privately – 'a single conversation is worth a dozen letters'[26] – which meant most Conservative matters; and the spatial layout and proximity of their houses, encouraged by often literal forms of peer pressure, made this feasible. While many discovered that they could only afford (or perhaps even find available) a house in Belgravia – a quaint thought a hundred years later – Tory grandees hung onto their town-houses further east to remain closer to Westminster and closer, after 1880, to Salisbury. Standing at his front windows in Arlington Street, he must have felt the eyes if not bullets of colleagues all around him. His fellow leader, Northcote, who led the Commons after Disraeli went to the Lords as Earl of Beaconsfield, lived a snowball's throw away in St James's Place when not at Pynes in Devon, where, thankfully, he frequently contrived to be. Next door on Salisbury's left, at number nineteen, was the Marquis of Zetland, Irish Viceroy by the end of the decade, who at least looked likely to give no trouble.[27] From the upper windows, Salisbury might have caught the backside of the Carlton Club to remind him of human ambition and party squabbles. Further to his left and his rear, in life as much as in political art, roamed Lord Randolph Churchill in Berkeley Square. Cranbrook in Grosvenor Crescent at least helped keep Mayfair among friends, and a coming middle-class man, W. H. Smith with his bookstalls, could afford Grosvenor Place and had his uses when resolving organizational strife. To Salisbury's right,

---

[24] Its historian dates the embrace of London from 1840. The former turnpike was celebrated for its bandits as well as its discomfort. See Leslie Mitchell, *Holland House* (1980), p. 10.

[25] Carol Kennedy, *Mayfair: A Social History* (1986), pp. 137–9, 146.

[26] Disraeli to the Duke of Marlborough, 30 Jan. 1868, Marlborough MSS 9271/3/12.

[27] His gloomy house still stands, though number twenty disappeared long ago. His heart in any case lay in Yorkshire. Briefly MP for Richmond before his creation as first Marquis in 1892; later mayor. Seat nearby at Aske Hall, where he died in 1929. Nearly 12,000 acres in the North Riding. Prominent Mason. Master of the Zetland Hunt 1876 to 1911. His unhappy tenure of the lord lieutenancy between 1889 and 1892 was his only intervention in national politics.

beyond St James's Palace, stood the impressive uniformities of
Carlton House Terrace, with the young Curzon eventually imperial
in number one, Sir Matthew White Ridley, Salisbury's home secretary after 1895, in number ten (now home to the British Academy),
the Prince of Darkness in number eleven, when the electors of
Midlothian or the quiet of Hawarden did not detain him, and Lord
Granville in number eighteen. Carlton Gardens had a more encouraging clientele with nephew Arthur at number four and Henry
Chaplin, Lincolnshire squire and agricultural spokesman, at number
two after he had waited years for it to come on the market.[28] Perhaps
there was one casualty in this translation of ambition into brick. As
the new Arlington Street house came into use after 1872, the old and
very desirable address 1 Grosvenor Gate went out of service. Disraeli
had only been able to keep it so long as his wife lived. With her death
he began to rattle around Whitehall Gardens and Curzon Street,
with little more than the royalties from *Endymion* keeping a suitable
roof over his head and making Hughenden ever more attractive, if
only the gout would leave him alone.

Passing one another's door gave political life an expansion slot to
accommodate discussion of a problem when corridors and lobbies at
Westminster might prove over-public or when being seen talking to a
particular person might portend a hundred conspiracies and lead to
oblique embarrassments in tomorrow morning's *Times*. 'I will call in
Arlington St tomorrow at 3pm', said Carnarvon, 'on my way to the
House', a normal way of proceeding, just as a letter could become a
tainted thing when one 'meant to have *said*, not written this to you
. . .'[29] For the party leaders, meanwhile, a potentially divisive
discussion could be staged in a manageable, controllable *milieu*.
There was much to be said for holding shadow- or, as they said, ex-
cabinet discussions or smaller colloquies of central people in one's
own house because it conferred the advantage of making dissent or
outrage a form of social solecism. Thus Lord Ashbourne was told to
come to Lord Beaconsfield's house for his induction into cabinet-
level talk. He found himself 'ushered upstairs to the drawing rooms,
which appeared to be slightly perfumed'.[30] It is hard to become

---

[28] The foregoing walkabout is intended to supply atmosphere more than chronology. These
addresses were not occupied simultaneously.
[29] Carnarvon to Salisbury, 25 Jun. 1884, Salisbury MSS (Carnarvon, f.471); Spofforth to
Churchill, 23 Jan. 1884, Churchill MSS 9248/2.
[30] Diary, 6 Jan. 1881, in Cooke and Malcolmson (eds.), *Ashbourne Papers*, p. 5.

noxious in a perfumed room. Upstairs had another virtue, for all of Tory London lived their domestic life there on the first floor. Seldom had high politics been so high. When Cranbrook reflected that 'London is really the base of Tory principles',[31] he commented on its electoral potential but could equally have pointed to the centrality of parts of London to his colleagues' clandestine operations and the place of drawing-rooms more than basements. By placing most of its participants in a domestic cocoon that hovered above the real world – each in his urban *Berghof* – leaders confirmed their position as patrons to those outside, reassured themselves of their stature within the cocoon and emphasized what all of them knew as a gardener knows his plants – that a Conservative political style wilts in open spaces. It needs glass, a brandy glass, for its germination and propagates through the warmth of an open fire.

SCOTLAND

A well-known team of English satirical writers published many years ago a Tory map of the world. It integrated all of India and bits of Africa into the Conservative understanding of 'abroad' and reduced European peoples to a series of racist slurs: 'Frogs', 'Wops', 'Krauts' and so on. And it redesigned Britain to fit the Tory vision. There was a globule of territory around London and the Home Counties – this was England – which connected through a long capillary, perhaps a motorway or railway, to another ill-defined globule in the north that spread over the Western Highlands and east towards the River Spey (whisky) and Balmoral (the Queen). It was a land close to the centre of Tory sentiment because one went there on ritualized occasions to shoot grouse and stags and to fish with a fly for salmon. Like the rest of the caricature, this image depended on its inaccuracy for its humour. But like all caricature it had to reflect an acknowledged truth in order to bite. Several parts of the message certainly had held good in the later decades of the nineteenth century. 'Scotland', the image, made little fit with Scotland the place: only a few sectors of the geography came within its definition. The 'Scotch' likewise behaved as an English invention.[32] They had a supposedly deviant

---

[31] Quoted back at him by Salisbury in Salisbury to Cranbrook, 10 July 1886, in Cecil, vol. III, p. 309.

[32] This point is more sensitive now than it felt in 1880 when the adjective and noun, 'Scotch', were universally used by the *English* when describing Scottish people and culture. The

history, a strange sociology taken from Sir Walter Scott and subsequent tartanophile publicists; and they presented to the English imagination an alleged cultural homogeneity which would have surprised any three people drawn at random from Motherwell or Arbroath. Edinburgh meant Morningside, the university, the lawyers and the New Club – home from home, as it were. Glasgow had industrial money and an imperial political economy; it therefore contained, or so one would have assumed, proto-Tories on the make. Nowhere else mattered much, though one could conjure reassuring images about the Lowlands from Balfour or Lord Lothian and feel pleasantly confident about the Tory values of great estates in the west and north, such as those of the Duke of Buccleuch at Drumlanrig or of the Duke of Richmond at Gordon Castle.[33]

Fictions had their place, but facts were stubborn things. One snap of the fingers from the Grand Old Man of Midlothian and vast crowds of Scots would gather to worship. When Tories decided to have a meeting, they had to hire small rooms or pull in people from outside to avoid embarrassing gaps.[34] Salisbury's first major sortie took place in the autumn of 1882 as a way of trying to neutralize some of the Gladstonian success in the Midlothian campaign and the subsequent general election. He went up for the week, staying over at Whittingehame with Balfour and committing himself to a series of engagements for Edinburgh Tories, culminating in an enormous banquet to 'make up in spirit for what they lack in strength', as the poisonous *Times* report remarked. Indeed the reporter looked forward to the next couple of days with the sour glee that his newspaper usually brought to Salisbury's difficulties. He ought not to be denied his audience.

For this event, preparations are being made on the most elaborate scale. The interior of the vast and bare chamber is being completely transformed, so as to make it a fit banqueting-hall for the reception of the hundreds of

---

demise of 'Scotch', except as a vulgar term for whisky, came with the rise of cultural nationalism north of the border where 'Scottish' is currently *de rigueur*. The text here will use 'Scottish', therefore, except within quotations.

[33] For a more serious treatment of these ideological and perceptual problems, see the academic debate on 'Where was Nineteenth-century Scotland?', *Scottish Historical Review*, 73 (1994), pp. 89–102.

[34] e.g. Balfour to Churchill, 2 Nov. 1883, arguing that the organizer of a forthcoming meeting in Edinburgh will have to pull in '*county voters*' because [h]is own adherents will hardly fill his room!': Churchill MSS 9248/2. Cf. Balfour to Churchill, 3 Nov. 1880: 'Conservatives in Scotland do not grow like blackberries. We can hardly produce enough in the same town, I should fear, to form *two* imposing meetings', *ibid.*, 9248/1.

lords and ladies and the thousands of commoners who are expected to be present. Extensive kitchen accommodation, with furnaces, hot plates, boilers and hot presses, is being extemporized in and around the building, so as to secure, in the words of the local organ of Conservatism, 'that the cuisine shall be of the most complete and satisfying description'. It further appears that provision has been made for keeping 7,000 plates hot at opposite sides of the hall, and that, in order to give a national character to the feast, a 66-gallon boiler has been erected 'for the cooking of the haggisses'. The decorations of the hall – floral and textile, civil and military, armorial and baronial, pictorial and legendary – have received special attention, and that the soothing charms of music may not be wanting, a pavillion for the accommodation of the band has been erected opposite the entrance to the hall.[35]

By all accounts it went well and Lord John Manners reported later that Salisbury had been 'much gratified' by how kind everyone had been.[36] But of course the leader-writer was right: all it would achieve was the suppression for a single evening of 'the irremovable pre-dominance of Liberalism'.

Scotland was *Liberal*: by tradition, by culture, by religion, by education. The Conservative party won at best about a third of the seventy parliamentary seats, which it did in 1874 or 1900; it could drop to eight or ten, as in 1885–6 and again, crushingly, in 1906.[37] Its tenantry worked with land-law and customs quite different from England's (or Ireland's); its emerging working class had a strong tinge of independent socialism on the Clyde and romantic, wistful Speyside socialism, judging from the early years of James Ramsay MacDonald; its people committed themselves to a vision of education, by which they meant religious education, which suggested a seriousness about learning that English Tories never quite understood, let alone shared. What was taking place 'on the ground' in later-Victorian Scotland bore little relation to Conservative images of the bold Highlander or pipe-smoking Lowland farmer. But images feed perceptions and hopes; and there was always the dream that one day the Scots would conform to the role assigned to them and turn Caledonia into a haven of stable loyalties.

The first task for the English was to get there and it became more urgent once the Queen had done so. Indeed it seems likely that

[35] *The Times*, 22 Nov. 1882, p. 4a.
[36] Manners to Northcote, n.d. [3 Dec. 1882], Iddesleigh MSS 50041 f.126.
[37] For the electoral details, see the very helpful survey by I. G. C. Hutchison, *A Political History of Scotland 1832–1924: Parties, Elections and Issues* (Edinburgh, 1986).

Scotland would have remained vastly less visited by English Conservatives – and the Isle of Wight still less – had Queen Victoria not
chosen to spend much of her time at Balmoral and Osborne. The
original decision to have a romantic seat in the Highlands had owed
something to Prince Albert; and the famous family portraits with
children and dogs and the scion of Saxe-Coburg-Gotha in a kilt
became their own form of legitimation once the royal purdah began
with Albert's death in 1861. And there was more than just the house.
When Derby made his duty visit as minister-in-attendance at
Balmoral in 1874, his landlord's eye scanned the horizon and beyond
to the subsidiary parts of the now considerable estate:

Abergeldie is leased by the Queen from the Gordon family, for a term of 40
years: Birkhall is owned by the P. of Wales: and Balmoral itself, about
10,000 acres, by the Queen. The three together give the family command of
about 40,000 acres, besides which they have leased the shooting on the
opposite side of the Dee from Farquharson of Invercauld.[38]

This serious holding gave visiting ministers the opportunity to meet
people on their walks (for the boredom of Balmoral stretched
endurance) and perhaps even to challenge preconception. Derby's
Bold Highlander took a dent on this visit, for example, when a walk
with Cairns revealed that the Lord Chancellor had lived with the
species for four or six weeks every year and 'denie[d] that they were
a hardy race' at all.[39] Once called, all the same, the obligation to
attend Her Majesty became a sort of jury service that a minister
could rarely dodge; and one by one they made their way to northern
Scotland to suffer a week, perhaps even a month, of stultifying
privation, never let out until tea-time (in case the Queen required
them), shivering behind the newspapers 'with all the windows open
and a scanty allowance of fires'.[40] At least it became easier to reach
after 1889 because the Tay Bridge reopened after the disaster of ten
years before when, famously, it had plunged into the water with a
train on its back, killing many people on the last Sunday of 1879.
Once the Marchioness of Tweeddale, wife of one who was not a
pillar of Scottish Toryism,[41] opened the West Highland Railway in

---

[38] 26 Aug. 1874, in Derby, *Diaries*, p. 177. The Farquharsons held the mansion of Invercauld in
south-west Aberdeenshire where they owned almost 90,000 acres.

[39] *Ibid.*, 22 Sep. 1874, p. 179.

[40] Richmond to Hardy, 2 Sep. 1877, Cranbrook MSS T501/257.

[41] The tenth Marquis of Tweeddale (1826–1911) sat as a Liberal for a few years in middle-life
but most of his working experience, following training at Haileybury, was spent in the

1894, the sleeper-express had begun Auden's poetic journey, 'past cotton grass and moorland boulder / shovelling white steam over her shoulder...'.

Toryism in Scotland, devoid as it was of numbers, turned on notables – great names with baronial castles and wide acres – who acted as spindles around which the thin thread of Conservative politics might be woven. The most important of them was the loved and hopeless sixth Duke of Richmond, to whose seat at Gordon Castle colleagues were brought with their guns and rods and from where haunches and braces sped off on the railway to the kitchens of the Home Counties. His letters from the Highlands tell of his legs (gammy or no), his dogs, his horses, his farms, his tenants; and the rain, endless rain. Politically he did his best. He tried to organize some Conservative support in his locality, though rarely saw beyond 'difficulties' that beset 'the whole situation'[42] and reported on his efforts to the man he admired above all others in politics, Hugh, later Earl Cairns. Thus we find him in the dog-days of Gladstone's first ministry, when it is clear that an election cannot be held off for long, seeking to ward off the threat from the house of Fife, whose earls had a disturbing Liberal involvement. He hoped that he might thwart Viscount Macduff (heir to the Fife earldom) in 'Morayshire' (i.e. Elgin and Nairnshire) and keep one of the Grants in place there as they had been on and off, with the Bruces, since 1832. But 'he is not a very good candidate. He has disgusted some of his Conservative supporters by some Radical votes, upon the Burial Bill, Ballot &c., and now of course his Radical friends whom he pleased will all vote for Macduff.' Richmond could not be gainsaid: they did, and Grant lost the seat. As for Banffshire, he went on, there was not much to be done, 'but we are organizing a society to see if it is not possible to turn out Duff of Fife'. Not only did they not turn him out but they failed to find anybody who would even oppose him.[43] Aberdeenshire again promised nothing beyond humiliation until the party persuaded a Gordon to stand at a by-election in 1875. Further to the

---

Bengal civil service. He chaired the Board of Directors of the North British Railway Co. until 1899.

[42] Richmond to Hardy, 2 Sep. 1877, Cranbrook MSS T501/257.

[43] Richmond to Cairns, 16 Nov. 1873, Cairns MSS 30/51/2. 'Ballot &c.' referred to the introduction of the secret ballot in the previous year. Burial Bills remained a thicket of controversy in Scotland through what were read by Tories as Dissenter-inspired plots to infiltrate episcopalian property by using the issue of burial in churchyards as the thin end of an unthinkable wedge.

west and south, very much the same stories emanated from the
direction of Buccleuch's domains. If the party intended doing
anything serious after the cataclysm of 1880, one correspondent
argued, it would have to persuade Buccleuch's son to stand, for
although the Earl of Dalkeith had built a considerable reputation for
incompetence, '[t]he Conservative Party are loyal & true to the
Buccleuch family & . . . if he cannot win our battle for us, *no one else
can*'.[44]

Part of the problem for Conservatives lay in the obstacles facing
any project of mimicking English models for sustaining deference;
and space played its role as a major obstacle. Edinburgh did not
function as London did in providing an intimate cell within which
strategies might be hatched. Indeed there was something plaintive
about Richmond's calling to his London house in Belgrave Square a
gathering of 'Peers, Members of Parliament & Landowners Connected with Scotland',[45] as though they could not muster in the
country whose future they wanted to discuss. Sheer localism
impeded conversation across distance, especially away from the
Edinburgh/Glasgow hinterland where Toryism had to rely on
isolated activists such as Sir Herbert Maxwell – the novelist and
Creevey's future editor – at Monreith in Wigtownshire, out on the
western peninsula where no writs ran. His plans to get up a county
ball and play the local Richmond or Salisbury foundered on there
being nowhere to hold one. And even if there had been, no one
would have gone because the distances would have proved too
tiresome. Now in the Borders the situation was different. Here the
gentry lived more compactly and traditions of county society had
taken firmer root. Yet even in this denser environment, a distance of
just twenty miles could worry the party-goers. Here is a very young
Charles, later Sir Charles Dalrymple, a friend of Maxwell and a
future Tory wirepuller from his home just outside Edinburgh. It is
ball season in the autumn of 1865:

We had good fun in Berwickshire, and two topping balls at Floors [Castle,
the Roxburgh seat]. The Kelso Mace ball was also very good, much better

---

[44] Illeg. to Maxwell, 27 Oct. 1882, Maxwell MSS 7043 HEM1 (emphasis in original). Cf.
Richmond's urgency before the 1874 election – 'It is absolutely necessary that Buccleuch
shd go with us': Cranbrook MSS T501/257. This Dalkeith, for all his frailties, lacked the
cosmic inadequacy of one of his forebears whose enemies had a volume printed detailing
'The Political Accomplishments of the Earl of Dalkeith', which they filled with entirely
blank pages.
[45] Colville to Maxwell, 19 Jun. 1883, Maxwell MSS 7043 HEM1.

than usual. The only drawback (almost) was the distance wh: we had to go – 13 or 14 miles – and that certainly goes far to shorten one's life . . . I wish you had been there. The Pss of Wales is quite too lovely & the other Royalties made themselves vastly agreeable, & spoke to all who came in their way very pleasantly. After the Milne Homes we went to Wolflee near Hawick, where Sundry Elliots live . . .[46]

Had every county town thrown together a ball with the promise of royal or noble glitter, possibly more could have been done with local sentiment. As it was, activists had to bring in their 'swells' from outside, and not uncommonly from England.

Viewed from Westminster, this image of Scottish space as a lush deer-farm policed by isolated notables lent an undue prominence to the 'Scotch peers' question. For they were unlike English peers in having a so-called 'representative' aspect. They did not sit in the House of Lords as a matter of right. Instead, the eighty-five Scottish peers (in 1886) were allowed to elect among themselves just sixteen 'representative peers' at the beginning of each parliament. Not only were those who failed to secure support excluded from the House of Lords, but they could not stand for election to the House of Commons either – something Irish peers were permitted to do. Another grievance did not remain repressed for long. While the Irish peers, once elected, held their representative function for life, the Scottish ones had to face re-election with every new parliament.[47] Now in fact, the pressure on the Scottish system enjoyed some release from the dual-holding of titles in the English and Scottish peerage: over half of the catchment held titles outside Scotland and therefore acquired seats in the conventional English way. But the disparity of treatment scratched an inflammable skin and Richmond spent miserable hours trying to soothe his peers when, for example, Lord Inchiquin floated in 1874 a clever Irish device to flood the House with yet more Irishmen – a ruse seen through by Derby and squashed by Salisbury.[48] By the summer one of Scotland's scratchiest peers, Lord Elphinstone, was warning his leader that he had 'been

---

[46] Dalrymple to Maxwell, 25 Oct. 1865, Maxwell MSS 7043 HEM1. Dalrymple is probably referring to his contemporary, David Milne-Hume of Paxton House, Berwick, MP for Berwick-upon-Tweed 1874–80 and 1880–5. The Elliots of Wolflee married into the Elphinstones (see n. 49).

[47] I am indebted here to Andrew Adonis's unravelling of these complications in his *Making Aristocracy Work: The Peerage and the Political System in Britain, 1884–1914* (Oxford, 1993), pp. 40–1.

[48] See the correspondence from Inchiquin and Malmesbury to Richmond, 17 and 28 April 1974, Goodwood MSS 866 ff.289–90, 867 f.294.

told by more than one, that if elected as a representative they would seriously consider the question as to sitting upon the Cross benches instead of upon the Conservative side of the House', hitting back where it hurt most.[49]

The stress placed on the peers north of the border came out especially in 1885 when Salisbury had to appoint the first secretary of state for Scotland – not his idea, but one taken over from Gladstone's second Liberal government of 1880–5. His mental checklist of candidates ran, inevitably, through the peerage and landed gentry: Lothian – too ill, though he turned out to be irritated ('not I fear an uncommon thing')[50] for not having been asked; neither Dalrymple nor Sir James Ferguson had the right weight; Balfour of Burleigh was possible but he had little authority and seemed unpopular with the party managers in Scotland.[51] That left the inevitable and wonderful Richmond if only he could be persuaded to do it. Salisbury plainly took advice and got it *right* for once, in a letter that the Scottish Office ought to exhibit on its walls. He dismissed other candidates as 'too insignificant':

The Scotch people would declare that we were despising Scotland & treating her as if she were a West Indian Colony. It really is a matter where the effulgence of two Dukedoms [Richmond and Gordon] & the best salmon river in Scotland will go a long way.[52]

Sadly it went nowhere at all. By 1885 Salisbury probably knew himself that any appointment of this kind could hardly penetrate to the heart of Tory weakness in Scotland. Notables and their potential support formed only a part of the problem and arguably the lesser. The main difficulty lay in what they were supposed to talk about.

---

[49] Elphinstone to Richmond, 22 Jun. 1874, Goodwood MSS 867 f 210. The thirteenth Lord Elphinstone (1807–60) was a baron in the peerage of the United Kingdom. When he died without issue, however, that title became extinct, though the *Scottish* title, with all its restrictions and irritations, devolved on his first cousin. It was brought back into the fold as a barony in the United Kingdom peerage in 1885.

[50] Cranbrook to Salisbury, 6 Aug. 1885, Salisbury MSS (Cranbrook 1868–85, f.212). Lothian considered himself 'a prime author' of the bill to establish a Scottish secretary.

[51] Salisbury to Cranbrook, 9 Aug. 1885, Cranbrook MSS T501/267. The ninth Marquis of Lothian did indeed become secretary of state but not until 1887. Sir James Ferguson, Bt (1832–1907) had an Edinburgh brahmin background and married into the Dalhousies. Salisbury made him parliamentary under-secretary at the Foreign Office, instead. The sixth Lord Balfour of Burleigh (only distantly related to the Whittingehame Balfours) eventually had a period in the Scottish Office from 1895.

[52] Salisbury to Richmond, 7 Aug. 1885, Goodwood MSS 871 d 45. Richmond agreed to serve, but not without reminding the prime minister that he regarded the Scottish Office as 'quite unnecessary': Richmond to Salisbury, 9 Aug. 1885, Salisbury MSS (Richmond, f.175).

Scottish issues did not rerun English ones, except at certain moments of legislative activity, as during the education preoccupation of 1870–2. The cries that Tories could use with some power in England – the empire and its expansion, keeping the Russians out of Constantinople, repressing Irish lawlessness, dallying with economic protection, resisting further dilution of the franchise – these did little to endear Scots to them and in some cases would be likely to alienate a nation struck, increasingly, by its otherness, sickened by class oppressions in the countryside and suffused by a diffuse but real egalitarianism of mind and spirit. Burning in popular politics were the twin brands of school and church; and both gained their fire from the way in which Scottish people saw them as emblems of a national and cultural identity. Westminster Toryism felt the heat of these issues in England from time to time, a thought that will return in chapter 7, but as political problems to be 'solved' or avoided rather than as crusades for a higher cause or test of true citizenship.

The Conservatives tried hard between 1882 and 1885. Northcote, leader of the Commons, made a post-Midlothian trip. Salisbury had his banquet. In the following year he went again to do a tour of western Scottish towns and to take in Inveraray now that his nephew had involved Conservatives with the house of Campbell. The visit became something of a morality tale: in the great house he was received with spacious civility while in Dumfries people threw stones at his carriage. (Typically, he kept one that came though the window as a paperweight for his desk.)[53] Northcote, Waterford and Chaplin tried their hand at Edinburgh in 1884 and claimed to find considerable sympathy for the House of Lords in the midst of the reform agitation at Westminster.[54] Salisbury made a further lunge at Glasgow. This became desirable not least because that city's Conservatives had turned out to contain a cell of 'Fourth Party' supporters – those who wanted to see Lord Randolph Churchill and his henchmen Sir Henry Drummond Woolf and John Gorst come to the fore and who had been encouraged in this view by the coming man, Charles Dalrymple.[55] So there was fanfare and parade: a special train

[53] Frances Balfour, *Ne Obliviscaris*, vol. I, pp. 387–8.
[54] Lord John Manners to Salisbury, 17 Sep. 1884, Salisbury MSS (Manners, unfol.): 'there has never been such a Conservative gathering in Edinburgh before'.
[55] See Churchill to Gibson, 5 Nov. 1880, in Cooke and Malcolmson (eds.), *Ashbourne Papers*, p. 102. The proposed demonstration in favour of Churchill in Glasgow never took place, though Woolf remained 'very glad of Dalrymple & look[ed] to Scotland for a good deal': Sir Henry Drummond Woolf to Churchill, 25 Oct. 1883, Churchill MSS 9248/2.

from Blythswood on 1 October for a meeting with great notables in attendance – the Marquis of Lothian, the Earl of Galloway, Sir Michael Shaw-Stewart. Then on to the St Andrews Hall, after a private Conservative dinner, for a few slashes at Gladstone for having become the master of the platform in its railway sense; and then home again.[56] It seemed more magnificent than warlike and the results at the election in 1885 hardly suggested mass conversion.

There were further eruptions after 1886 when at least the dominating issue of Home Rule for Ireland helped Scottish Tories by producing a new Liberal Unionist wing with whom they could work. The subject gave local Tories a rare moment of aggression when they could express convictions with genuine passion. Sir Herbert Maxwell was a backbencher in 1889 and he turned on one of his Home Rulers with some violence:

> You are very welcome to a brief expression of my opinion . . . on the question (which I observed you dignify by the name of a 'movement') of Home Rule for Scotland. I look upon the action of those who have, as it seems to me, inconsiderately flung down this apple of discord before people who must necessarily, for the most part, be imperfectly acquainted with the history of their country, the perils it has passed through and the developement [*sic*] of its institutions, as entirely deplorable . . .
> . . . The motives [of both the sincere and cynical] differ in dignity but the effect is equally mischievous, and you may rely upon any influence I may have and any action I may take being uniformly employed and strenuously directed in opposition to the establishment of a legislative Chamber and separate Ministry in Edinburgh.[57]

Scottish Home Rule even made an appearance in the House of Lords when the embittered Lord Camperdown, reflecting on Irish misfortunes, asked whether Gladstone's third ministry intended to give Scotland Home Rule as well. The Duke of Argyll, ancient, deaf, sulphurous and bellicose, got onto his legs to shout resistance. The Earl of Rosebery gently but firmly repressed him on behalf of the government but forgot that Salisbury would follow with a venomous account of how the Irish affliction had been brought on in the first place, not by frontal assault but by lethal injections of evil. What point had the Scottish patient reached in her demise, he asked.[58]

---

[56] Account in *The Times*, 2 Oct. 1884, p. 7a–d. Blythswood, 'a neat, large, modern edifice, surrounded by a finely-wooded park', was the seat of Sir Archibald Campbell in Renfrewshire. The Prince and Princess of Wales had visited in 1876.

[57] Maxwell to Andrew Reid, 14 Dec. 1889, Maxwell MSS 7043 HEM3.

[58] *Hansard* (Lords), 30 Jun. 1893, XIV, cols. 529–35.

It all made admirable parliamentary material. Any good done by resistance to Home Rule, on the other hand, suffered from the embarrassment of the crofters of the Western Isles and the government's deafness to their plight despite the Scottish Secretary's persistent screams for help and some glimmer of understanding for his proposals to expedite emigration for the stricken families. He wound up with the usual solution: three ships sent to Stornoway with 100 marines and 40 men of the Second Battalion Royal Scots to keep down disturbances.[59] Any strengthening of the party in Scotland would in any case be confused by an arousal of unionist feeling, which was by no means committed to the Conservative position. Indeed by 1889 Salisbury had all but given up. When the Scottish local government bill entered the parliamentary agenda – the corollary of the English reorganization of 1888 – he thought merely of the effects any discussion might have on *English* landowners and 'our right wing'. About the Scottish dimension he was, as usual, brutally clear. 'We have so little to lose (or to gain) in Scotland at present that if the effects were limited to that country, I should not, in a purely Parliamentary sense, regard the matter as important.'[60] He allowed his mind to return to its 'English' horizons, molested less by Scottish fantasies than Irish realities.

IRELAND

In the case of Scotland or of Wales, space and time united to suggest that they could be regarded as minor versions of England, umbilically joined. They seemed strange places because they possessed pressing and un-Conservative characteristics. Wales, with its developing working class engaged in primary industry and its overwhelming Nonconformity in religion, offered little hope of party advance but equally little fear of disruption, except in the matter of church tithes which gave Salisbury serious headaches, as we shall see in reviewing his ecclesiastical context. By the mid-1880s all that party managers could reasonably expect was that a couple of boroughs would hold on (Denbigh and Montgomery) and a couple of county seats likewise (South Monmouthshire, Radnor) until the attachment of the Liberal Unionists helped leaven the lump after

---

[59] Lothian to the Queen (copy), 31 Jan. 1888; Lothian to Knutsford (copy), 22 Mar. 1888, Lothian MSS GD40/16/58/ff.140–3, 156.
[60] Salisbury to Balfour, 6 Feb. 1889, in *Salisbury–Balfour Correspondence*, p. 284.

1886.[61] But the subjugation of the principality in the early fourteenth century plus the implausibility of any mass revolt in the absence of an homogeneous peasantry gave rise to little alarm, unless someone were to suggest changes to governance or law that might have repercussions in England. So Salisbury might hear alarm bells if the land laws in Welsh were threatened with liberalization, as in the 1890s. Otherwise, one could assume that the organic link would continue amid occasional noise. Scotland stood largely in the same case, since Conservatives remained incredulous of its nationalist potential, as their treatment of the crofters made all too clear, and disbelieved the claims of Scots even to a separate culture. Balfour would have been more impressed by Scottish identity, given the racial preoccupations of his generation, if its progenitors were still, properly speaking, Celts; but he doubted that they ever had been, as he explained to his sister-in-law in 1912:

As regards Scotland, I believe that the most recent investigations shew that at the time (say) of the Battle of Bannockburn there was one dialect of the Anglo-Saxon language from the Humber to Aberdeen, and there is, as you well know, a great Norse element round the coast and islands in the north and in the west. I suspect that of all the races now inhabiting our island there are fewer Celts than any other; but there is, of course, an immense amount of pre-Celtic blood, and probably this pre-Celtic element is strongest where forms of Celtic, Welsh, Gaelic and Erse are still spoken.[62]

It was all rather reassuring.

Ireland could give no such (imaginary) solace and it did not function in the same way within English Tory conceptions of the world. For Ireland, unlike England, could only come into focus as foreign or extra-terrestrial. It was China; it was Mars.[63] It presented to the mind mythologies about the sapping effect of Roman Catholicism, the limitations of Celtic blood and brain, how not to arrange

---

[61] Three of the four representatives – respectively Hon. G. T. Kenyon, P. Price-Jones, Hon. F. C. Morgan, Hon. A. H. J. Walsh – plainly relied on apprentice-noble status and the cachet of land. A recent study of Carmarthenshire by Matthew Cragoe confirms the power of the aristocracy there and points out that, for all their poor electoral performance, the Conservative party won a significant share of the vote in the mid-Victorian period: Matthew Cragoe, *An Anglican Aristocracy: The Moral Economy of the Landed Estate in Carmarthenshire, 1832–1895* (Oxford, 1996), pp. 116–17.

[62] Balfour to Frances Balfour (dictated and not sent), 4 Dec. 1912, Balfour MSS 49830 ff.223–4.

[63] '. . . it is amazing how in England its atrocities are read as if they happened in China or another planet': Cranbrook to Salisbury, 14 Jun. 1882, Salisbury MSS (Cranbrook).

inheritance and land law, about the overwhelming incapacity of these distinctive *Untermenschen* to run their own lives in a responsible way. Unless a property-owner there oneself, or invited by a member of an Irish or Anglo-Irish family, or unless one were *sent* (the usual reason), there seemed no great point in going, which meant that ignorance grew by what it fed on. Knowing next to nothing about Ireland hardly figured among Tory monoplies: Liberals, even Gladstone himself, knew very little and, what little they gathered, they got from books or chance conversation.[64] Lord John Russell had acquired a reputation for eccentricity in his young Whig days by insisting on making a visit. Lord Randolph Churchill in his brash, Tory moments aroused similar unease through his liking for Dublin society, which he doubtless found closer to that of Paris than of London.[65] Mostly politicians assured one another that 'Ireland cannot be governed entirely from London'[66] while trying simultaneously to do precisely that. They lamented that the party's writ did not run there when chaotic local arrangements helped inspire electoral defeat.[67] But Tory Ireland did have some spatial peculiarities. Its Protestantism and Unionism combined, from the mid-1880s, to make it a defender of Ulster practice and identity, suggesting that parts of Ireland could not and should not suffer severance from 'England'. Landlordism and Unionism became Tory tunes so repetitively sung that even Salisbury and his fellow peers tired of them.

Years before this continuo had became urgent, banishment to Ireland hung about the heads of Tory magnates and politicians as a persistent threat. The administration of the country required two leading functionaries: a lord lieutenant who was largely honorific and a chief secretary who worked at the sharp end of government.

---

[64] There is a suggestive example in the account of Bobby Spencer (brother of Lord Spencer, Gladstone's lord lieutenant of Ireland) lunching with the prime minister in 1882: 'it was very interesting indeed, but at the same time I was much struck by the evident way he thought Ireland was as quiet really as here with only a row or outrage every now and then . . . It startled me a little I must own . . .' C. R. Spencer to Lord Spencer, 4 Jun. 1882, in Peter Gordon (ed.), *The Red Earl: The Papers of the Fifth Earl Spencer* (2 vols., Northampton, 1981–6), vol. I, p. 204.

[65] See Roy Foster, *Lord Randolph Churchill: A Political Life* (Oxford, 1981), pp. 33–57.

[66] Beach to Salisbury (transcript), 28 Jul. 1886, St Aldwyn MSS PCC/31/unfol.

[67] E.g. when Cork went wrong in 1891. 'I have often told you that we ought to have some sort of organization in Ireland where at present my writs do not run': Akers-Douglas to Balfour, 27 Oct. 1891, Balfour MSS 19772 f.3. The by-election produced by Parnell's death in Cork City brought in an anti-Parnellite Nationalist and left the Unionist candidate a poor third.

The former functioned as a viceroy – he was formally lieutenant-general and governor-general of Ireland – and the post was filled by peers, thirty-four of them between the Act of Union and the division of Ireland in the treaty of 1921. The chief secretary was often a marginalized or aspiring politician and rarely lasted, Balfour apart, more than a couple of years of backbreaking work in the later years of the nineteenth century, carrying, as the historian of Irish administration contends, 'almost the whole range of Irish business'.[68] Filling these posts caused Tories significant pain. Disraeli did well with Lord Naas's return to the chief secretaryship in 1866: he came from a prestigious Irish family, had considerable ability and drive and would have turned into a major player had not an assassin decided otherwise while he was Viceroy of India in 1872.[69] Salisbury achieved a similar *coup* in sending Balfour in 1887. Here the success followed from Balfour's clear-headedness about his objectives, from the accident of his family connexion with the Cecils and through his holding a seat in the cabinet: he did not feel so cut off from the game as many others had come to feel in Dublin. With his lord lieutenants, on the other hand, Salisbury had a grim time. The appointee always needed a private income because the outlay on receptions and hospitality was traditionally prodigious and the salary did not suffice for meeting it. Carnarvon had always been a close friend and at one level looked a sensible choice; but he had already shown himself pink over Russia during the Russo-Turkish war of 1877 and once in Ireland he began to turn green.[70] In the age of Home Rule after 1885, he could not be reappointed. Others kept their orange colour but lacked the closeness to Salisbury that Carnarvon had once had; so they soon fell into the Dublin Castle mood of having travelled a great distance to an uncongenial place only to find that nobody consulted or listened to them. For both Lord Londonderry and Lord Cadogan the episode ended in regret and bitterness. 'They must do as they like', spat Londonderry when his term of office moved towards its blessed end. 'I can do no more, and am thankful to think that my time is drawing to a close, and the most unenviable and

---

[68] R. B. McDowell, *The Irish Administration 1801–1914* (1964), pp. 52, 33.

[69] Richard Southwell Bourke, Lord Naas from 1849 until he succeeded as 6th Earl of Mayo in 1867. Chief secretary for Ireland 1852, 1858–9, 1866–8. Viceroy and governor-general of India 1868–72. Murdered by an Afghan convict in the Andaman Islands, February 1872.

[70] As Salisbury observed in a family conversation, 'I am not easy about Carnarvon, – he is getting so very "green".' Quoted in Cecil, vol. III, p. 155.

thankless part of the whole government can be handed on to someone else.'[71] A later 'someone else', the Earl of Cadogan, who had once enjoyed the Privy Seal which allowed him a cabinet seat and the civilities of Chelsea House, left in precisely the same mood. His complaint in 1898 that nobody had asked his opinion about founding a Catholic university, before Balfour's letter arrived announcing one, stood as one fulmination among several.[72] Abolishing the lord lieutenancy, which is what the Liberal Unionists were said to favour, perhaps seemed to him a less radical plan than it had appeared in 1895.[73]

To the extent that communication took place regularly between Conservative governments and the Irish, it tended to pass through the Irish Chancellor, Edward Gibson, Lord Ashbourne. His appearance in works of political history often comes under the index-entry 'Ashbourne Act', because it is the one intervention in Anglo-Irish relations for which he is known. Nor should it be downplayed: his land act played some role in making the purchase of land by tenants more thinkable than either of Gladstone's land acts had achieved.[74] But his political importance lay elsewhere – in his carefully constructed longevity. Gibson went to much trouble to make sure he got the job he wanted when the Conservatives came back to office in 1885. Having spent some time as attorney-general for Ireland he felt in a position to insist on the real plum when Salisbury formed his first government. The Irish chancellorship carried an income *for life* – no small consideration, particularly for a man with a château in France; and once there, an individual with the appropriate expertise would prove difficult to dislodge. Ashbourne remained lord chancellor of Ireland until the Conservatives left office just before their catastrophe at the polls in 1906 and his papers show him to have

---

[71] Londonderry to Ashbourne, 20 May 1889, in Cooke and Malcolmson (eds.), *Ashbourne Papers*, p. 149.

[72] Cadogan to Gerald Balfour, 18 Nov. 1898: 'I was startled this morning by Arthur's "bolt from the blue" . . .' Balfour MSS 49831 f.5.

[73] Devonshire to Cadogan, 31 Aug. 1895, Cadogan MSS CAD/723. Salisbury seems not to have taken these threats too seriously.

[74] Ashbourne's objectives were three: to advance money to tenants from the state at 4 per cent, repayable over the more generous period of forty-nine years; to loan the whole of the sum required, up to £5 million, with one-fifth retained by the Land Commission, 'at moderate interest', until the tenant had matched that sum in repayments; and to open what was left of the Irish Church surplus, available since disestablishment, 'to save the State from any ultimate possibility of loss'. Ashbourne in Lords (maiden speech as lord chancellor of Ireland), *Hansard*, 17 Jul. 1885, ccxcix, cols. 1045–6.

acted as something of an interface between Westminster and bruised
sectors of Irish landed society.[75] For some, Ashbourne's associations
with the tenantry laws made him a target more than a confidant.
Neither man spoke to the other for a long time after this outburst
against Ashbourne from the Marquis of Waterford when the Conservative government's land bill of 1887 came on:

I hear the plan of campaign [i.e. an organized scheme of resistance to
paying rent] has been adopted on my property, and no rents are paid,
which would never have been the case if the bulk of the tenants did not
know that under the new *Conservative* measure they can stay on for 7 months
after a decree [for eviction] is granted. I never expected to be ruined by the
party that my family had spent hundreds of thousands to support. I only
wish I now had back the money I myself and my ancestors have spent to
support them. I should have plenty to retire from Ireland upon then. As it
is, it has all been wasted, or used for my own destruction and that of my
friends, in addition to the destruction of the country I used to be so fond of.
The act of 81 [Gladstone's land act], which you fought so well, was a joke to
the act of 87, many of the clauses of which are put down to you.[76]

Nevertheless, Tory relations with Ireland would have remained even
more distant without Ashbourne's presence and the more so when
the Queen eventually vetoed in 1897 the long-germinating plan of
establishing a royal residence there as a way of making loyalist
Ireland feel less beleaguered.

Dual administration from an overseas state; an affronted peasantry
deemed to be racially suspect; social polarization around issues of
religion and caste; a constant preoccupation with policing and
insurrection: Ireland resembled nothing so much as India. Salisbury
felt this very early and made the connexion long before he himself
gained experience of the India Office, though his two periods at that
desk assuredly did little to soften his appreciation of how perilous it
had become to govern India without a sword. One of the long
reviews he submitted to the *Quarterly* in the 1860s focussed on
Castlereagh and amounted to a defence of the Irish peer who, for all
his reputation of repression and heartlessness, had at least 'effected

---

[75] For the details of Ashbourne's career and a good range of letters to him during this period,
see Cooke and Malcolmson (eds.), *Ashbourne Papers*.

[76] Waterford to Ashbourne, 16 Nov. 1887, *ibid.*, p. 188. Apart from penury, Waterford also
suffered from an excruciating back-complaint, which meant that he had to give his speeches
in the House of Lords sitting down. It is said that he purchased Flogger Keate's whipping-
block, which, if it gratified more than nostalgia, can hardly have helped. The combination
of his collapsing domestic economy and continual pain in his back unbalanced his mind and
he shot himself on 23 October 1895. See *Complete Peerage*, vol. xii/2, p. 424, n.

the Irish Union' and laid a foundation in policy for 'the growing prosperity of Ireland'. He did not spell out the contrasting case he had in mind but five years after the Indian Mutiny everyone knew what Salisbury meant when he wrote about 'the calamities into which other empires have been plunged by co-ordinate and independent legislatures under one crown'.[77] It stayed with him as a theme, alternating now and again with the African comparison that he made notorious in his 'Hottentots' speech of 1886, which represented the Irish as being no more capable of running their own affairs than an African tribe. Of course, the eruption of Home Rule for Ireland as an issue 'brought on' by the Liberal party gave Salisbury many opportunities for rehearsing this view of Irish incapacity. Moving the Queen's Speech in the House of Lords in January 1887 he thought the Home Rulers 'idle to talk of leaving the Irish people to govern themselves. You know very well that they will not govern themselves, but that the majority will govern the minority in a way utterly inconsistent with its rights, and in a manner utterly fatal to all its industrial and commercial hopes.'[78] It is the last phrase that turns the Irish from green to black: they will turn Ireland into a banana republic because their racial (and religious) characteristic is to be lazy and servile. They lacked the Protestant ethic and capitalist energy of the White Man. They did not, to be fair, tell quite as many lies as other inferior races and Salisbury rose almost to a defence of the Irish as 'a rather truthful people' compared (as usual) with the Indians.[79] The racial tone in all this is important and we shall return to the preoccupation. But the point here lies in seeing the way in which Irish space became as distant as Indian, as foreign, as colonial, as *unpleasant*.

Distance emerges in almost every category of discussion, not merely at the explicit level that the Irish are, for example, 'emotional' and that they 'cannot take care of themselves', as Carnarvon (a sympathizer) apparently told the cabinet,[80] or that 'the existing race

---

[77] 'Lord Castlereagh', *Quarterly Review*, 111 (Jan. 1862), pp. 201–38 at p. 204.

[78] Salisbury in Lords, *Hansard*, 27 Jan. 1887, cccx, col. 35.

[79] Salisbury in Lords, *Hansard*, 22 Apr. 1887, cccxiii, col. 1610. Again there was code. Lying was more predominant 'in certain races lately ruled over by the noble Marquess opposite . . .', with a glare, possibly, at the Marquis of Ripon who had been Indian viceroy during Gladstone's second government.

[80] Related in Cranbrook's diary, 18 Jul. 1885, in A. E. Gathorne-Hardy, *Gathorne Hardy, First Earl of Cranbook: A Memoir* (2 vols., 1910), vol. II, p. 223. Cf. Nancy E. Johnson (ed.), *The Diary of Gathorne Hardy, Later Lord Cranbrook, 1866–1892* (Oxford, 1981), pp. 569–70 for context.

of tenants' will acquire the soil and kill the country, as Lord John Manners (a critic) had come to believe.[81] It informed less obvious areas such as the disestablishment of the Church of Ireland by Gladstone's first government in 1869. Salisbury voted *for* it – an inconceivable proposition if the Church of England's status were called into question – contenting himself with the observation that capitulation in this case was inevitable and that its delay would only bring still more trouble.[82] But Ireland was different all the same. It affected how politicians who dreaded Roman politics approached the question of the secret ballot in 1872. 'What a show up of priestly intimidation in this Galway election', Richmond railed in May of that year. 'It rather shakes my opinion about the Ballot for I suppose the priests would coerce and never be found out.'[83] It inspired Churchill's fervent 'hope to goodness the outrages w[ould] not slack off', once the Tory party had lost the 1880 election, on the good Tory ground that they were the only thing holding the party together.[84] It informed the less messianic views of Stafford Northcote, who argued simultaneously that he did not understand Ireland and that its better representation within the British polity had become 'a terrible *crux*':

> Salisbury (not being a member of our body) accepts it as the best way out of difficulty. Beach is strongly opposed to it, and says, with some reason, that if you begin adding members you may go on adding them. He will vote against the proposal anyhow. So will those of our Irish friends who kick against the large proportion of Home Rulers. I am afraid they will not be satisfied with the argument that first loss must fall upon Ulster.[85]

Similar prisms operated in Salisbury's vision of having a land bill for the Scottish crofters. It would be a bad thing because it would be 'a pity to reduce the Highlanders quite to the condition of Ireland'.[86]

81 Manners to Smith, 24 Jul. ?1887. Manners would have preferred the landlords to buy out the tenants rather than the other way round; 'but the bowl has been set trundling in one direction, and must, I suppose trundle till it stops – and drops': Hambledon MSS PS14/62.

82 Salisbury in Lords, 17 Jun. 1869: 'It is no courage, it is no dignity to withstand the real opinion of the nation. All that you are doing thereby is to delay an inevitable issue – for all history teaches us that no nation was ever thus induced to revoke its decision – and to invite besides a period of disturbance, discontent, and possibly worse than discontent': *Hansard*, CXCVII, cols. 81–2. Carnarvon followed the same path, though only one bishop did (Thirlwall): see R. Davidson and W. Benham, *Life of Archibald Campbell Tait* (2 vols., 1891), vol. II, p. 31.

83 Richmond to Hardy, 30 May 1872, Cranbrook MSS T501/257.

84 Churchill to Gibson, 5 Nov. 1880, in Cooke and Malcolmson (eds.), *Ashbourne Papers*, p. 102.

85 Northcote to Dilke, 23 Feb. 1885, Dilke MSS 43893 f.20.

86 Salisbury to Richmond, 23 Dec. 1885, Goodwood MSS 871 d 80.

Examples pulled almost randomly from the period's archives leave a sense that Ireland came to life in politicians' imagination as the armed madman loose in the grounds. In one respect, however, it impinged directly and overwhelmingly and in ways that registered across all parties. Once Gladstone's sympathy for an Irish parliament had been revealed and publicly debated over Christmas and New Year of 1885–6, Salisbury and his Conservative colleagues found themselves with a rhetorical gift as well as a new potential ally from the summer of 1886 in the Liberal Unionist party. The preservation of the northern Protestant minority and the retention of cohesive empire as a theme had been pressed by Salisbury before Gladstone's *crise de conscience*. In his Mansion House speech as prime minister in November 1885, he could hardly have been plainer:

With respect to larger organic questions I have nothing to add . . . The traditions of our party are well known. The integrity of the Empire is more precious to us than any other possession. (Cheers.) If I may add another consideration, we are bound by motives not only of expediency, not only of legal principle, but by motives of honour, to protect the minority, if such exist, who have fallen into unpopularity and danger because they have maintained either as champions or as instruments the policy which England has deliberately elected to pursue.[87]

It would be easier to believe that Gladstone did not understand Salisbury's view had Gladstone not copied out this extract in his own hand, making nonsense of his supposed expectation that Salisbury would introduce Home Rule himself.[88] Once in place, 'Irish' politics became a Tory language of resistance, neither more nor less. With the two attempts by Gladstone to pass a Home Rule bill having failed in 1886 and 1893, Salisbury saw no need to kill Home Rule by kindness, making 'concessions' he did not need, as he told St John Brodrick in a crushing minute of 1894:

I understand that the object of the proposed movement is to exchange certain advantages & securities we now possess for advantages & securities which it is believed will be greater. Our present security against further legislation for stripping the Irish landlords consists, first, in the power which the state of business, & the recent habits of the House of Commons, give of obstructing such a measure in its passage through the House. Secondly, the resistance of the House of Lords. Thirdly, is the presumed refusal of a

---

[87] *The Times*, 10 Nov. 1885, p. 6f.
[88] Memo by Gladstone, n.d., Gladstone MSS 44769 f.256. He underlined 'larger organic questions' in his version.

Unionist Government to entertain such a proposal, if the resistance can be prolonged until a change in the majority takes place.[89]

And so, of course, it did. Not that the Conservative party lost interest in Irish legislation or failed to propose ameliorative legislation. Salisbury had left office when George Wyndham's bill travelled through parliament; but it would prove one of the more signal moments of Irish legislation for this generation. From 1886, all the same, 'Ireland' offered opportunities that had nothing to do with the Irish and everything to do with re-establishing the hegemony of Conservative politics at Westminister. Had anyone, Liberal or Conservative, had the precocious vision to see Ireland as an island undergoing industrialization against a background of agrarian distress and religious conflict, rather than as an icon for the strengthening of 'mission' or as a collection of ghosts and devils, a test case for imperial coherence or an avatar of landed property, then those living there might have fared better at the hands of the British state. But its images confined its realities and eliminated a variety of ways of treating them. Meanwhile, Salisbury and his fellow leaders were left needing not to talk about Ireland the place at all, except in the language of outrage and regret. They could and did grant Gladstone the privilege of ploughing the sands by himself.

---

[89] Salisbury to Brodrick (minute), 20 Oct. 1894, Christ Church MSS, E21. William St John Brodrick was under-secretary at the War Office and went on eventually to become secretary of state for war and India secretary in the Salisbury/Balfour governments of 1900–5 before succeeding to the family peerage as ninth Viscount Midleton (d. 1942). Easily confused with his uncle, G. C. Brodrick, former *Times* leader-writer, who was Warden of Merton College, Oxford from 1881 to 1903, and had been a Liberal in his younger days (he was the defeated candidate against Churchill at Woodstock in 1874). Closest, this one, to Goschen – they got their Firsts together at Oxford – and he followed his friend towards a sort of Liberal Unionism in later life. Impressive mind. Both Brodricks were buried at the family seat, Peper Harow, near Godalming.

CHAPTER 3

Society

THEM AND US

The Conservative understanding of society has always suffered from a compound fracture. On the one hand, a tradition of hostility to the idea of society as a singular entity lies embedded in the literature: society does not exist at all, as Lady Thatcher liked to emphasize, only individuals do. Each of those individuals has around him or her an immediate family, who legitimately accept responsibility for their members' welfare, and a circle of friends and perhaps benefactors. Beyond such assistance everybody has to make his or her own way; no one should rely on 'the state' to provide a living. 'Society' simply provides a label for millions of individuals engaged in this task. It is not in itself a thing or super-person: it cannot think, make moral decisions or carry out any action that is not the product of an individual or a finite and identifiable collection of individuals. Yet, side by side with this account, one finds another to which many Conservatives feel drawn. It implies the possibility of a coherent 'society' characterized by organic values, a sense of shared historic experience, a celebration of community and common reference. It has a place, after all, even in Salisbury's denial of society in one of his most remembered passages. Otherwise there would have been no point in lamenting the *absence* of such a 'society' in the course of a letter to W. H. Smith during a depressed moment of the parliamentary session in 1889:

We are in a state of bloodless civil war. No common principles, no respect for common institutions or traditions unite the various groups of politicians, who are struggling for power. To loot somebody or something is the common object under a thick varnish of pious phrases.[1]

---

[1] Salisbury to Smith, 5 Feb. 1889, Hambledon MSS PS 14/11. Probably this remark will not

It remains moot whether Salisbury or anybody else believed that a
time had ever dawned during which 'common principles' and
respect for institutions and traditions had marked British society. But
the idea runs through Tory sentiment at all points from Burke
forwards. It informs the judgements that Conservatives made about
the stability of their social fabric, about race, 'otherness', class,
women and the notion of a British identity. Much of this appeared
(as it does in this book) outside formal comment on social issues; but
we should pause a while to consider Conservative comment on
contemporary society as a screen on which to project other kinds of
image about property and the nature of the state. The ambiguity
with which we have begun will rarely seem far away.

Society for late-Victorian Tories was, like God, English. Other
places had their own societies of a kind, of course, but there was
always something wrong with them and they were in any case not
our business. In a world dominated by 'our' past, 'our' government,
'our' people, 'we' could not be expected to solve the globe's social
problems, beyond those places that 'we' had conquered or annexed,
but should instead concentrate on the real society at home – the one
encountered every day and about which everyone possessed some
lived experience. This was why Salisbury could not accept that the
American Civil War was about slavery so far as English people were
concerned. When white people (like us) were dying and when cotton
exports (to us) had all but ceased, the problems of black Americans
had to be kept in proportion. '[W]hen we read the weekly narrative
of American carnage', Cecil wrote in the *Quarterly Review* in 1862, 'or
the daily tale of Lancashire starvation . . . we cannot stop to inquire
into wrongs under which [the Negro] apparently thrives and is
happy, when the blood of our own race is being poured out like
water, and our fellow-citizens are perishing by inches.'[2] It was a
matter of priorities and Southerners showed their gratitude. When
the radical W. E. Forster later visited the United States and
introduced himself to a Southern lady, she told him precisely what
she thought of him but sent a kiss 'to the dear old gentleman', Lord

stand the weight often put on it: the context of parliamentary pressure, Irish nightmares and
the particular urgency of socialist language in the second half of the 1880s are relevant to its
meaning. Little in Salisbury's language is said *sub specie æternitatis* and it may be best not to
place it there.

[2] 'The Confederate Struggle and Recognition', *Quarterly Review*, 112 (1862), pp. 535–70 at
p. 570.

Salisbury, who alone deserved her affection.[3] As for foreigners and Negroes in 'society' at home, they could not hope for inclusion in Conservative categories of social acceptability. Some Jews made it through long-standing integration, especially among the highly exclusive London families of Anglo-Jewry who were often *plus royaliste que le roi*, though even here barriers could appear.[4] But blacks suffered the double problem of rarity – their number may actually have been decreasing through the Victorian period[5] – and visual prominence. Like the less detectable Irish they also suffered from contemporary styles of humour: jokes about them would always go down well with an audience that had no sense of squeamishness about racial typologies. Here is Salisbury on a public platform, congratulating Colonel Duncan on having held Holborn in a by-election in 1888, albeit with a smaller majority than he had achieved in the general election:

But then [in 1886], Colonel Duncan was opposed by a black man (laughter), and, however great the progress of mankind has been and however far we have advanced in overcoming prejudices, I doubt if we have yet got to that point where a British constituency will elect a black man to represent them. (Laughter.) Of course, you will understand that I am speaking roughly and using language in its ordinary sense, because I imagine the colour is not exactly black; but at all events he was a man of another race who was very unlikely to represent an English constituency.[6]

It had been Salisbury, too, who only the previous year had observed to Lady Manners, in a moment of unusual vividness, that the Queen of Hawaii looked for all the world 'like Lady Rosebery stained

---

[3] W. E. Forster to Mrs Forster, 2 Nov. 1874, in T. Wemyss Reid, *Life of the Rt. Hon. W. E. Forster* (2 vols., 1888), vol. II, p. 79.

[4] Closest to this subject is perhaps Todd M. Endelman, *Radical Assimilation in English Jewish History, 1656–1945* (Bloomington, IN, 1990), but this subtle and elusive subject awaits its historian. Historians of the Jewish community are understandably preoccupied with issues of mass immigration and its effect on popular politics and working-class life, as in David Feldman's excellent *Englishmen and Jews: Social Relations and Political Culture* (New Haven, CT, 1994). But the phenomenon of concealing one's Jewishness among the social elite, or suffering when others reveal it, is very hard to penetrate.

[5] See Peter Fryer, *Staying Power: The History of Black People in Britain* (1984), p. 236. Some cities, Liverpool and Cardiff most prominently, retained a black community.

[6] Salisbury at Edinburgh, 30 Nov. 1888, *The Times*, 1 Dec., p. 8b. The loser in question, one Naoroji, went on to further failure at Finsbury Central as a Liberal in 1895 and Lambeth North as an Independent Liberal in 1906. How depressed Salisbury must have been when, closer to home, a Parsee merchant from Bombay won Bethnal Green for his, Salisbury's, own party three years later. Among Mancherjee Merwanjee Bhownaggree's other achievements was his translation of the Queen's *Our Life in the Highlands* into Gujarati.

walnut'.[7] It becomes easier to see why the former King of Oude remarked after an invitation to Hatfield in 1879 that he would rather have spent the weekend in the jungle.[8]

'Otherness' could relate to race or, indeed, simple nationality – 'who can trust a Russian?'[9] – and those encountering it surmounted the difficulty by pretending that the 'other' was alien, if flexibility allowed, or by treating it, when there seemed no alternative, as though it were really one of 'us'. So Salisbury and Cranbrook would put up with Ambassador Shuvalov's interminable opinions 'on the subject of dry champagne, Bismarck's beer, the Greek representative &c' when once he had been included in the local hunt whose hounds had mustered on the front lawn of Hatfield House.[10] But internal othernesses also operated. They extended to various social strata within British society. They often extended also to women, whose role reflected a vertical division of society that many Conservatives took seriously. Laughs about women could be got quite as readily as those about the Irish and Negroes: the distinctiveness of their world seemed no less overt. And within an elite whose rural outlook still outshone their urban, it felt 'natural' to ensure that women did what suited their sexual characteristics – tenderness, frivolity, woolliness of mind, patience, submissiveness, emotionalism. Even so sympathetic a human being as the Duke of Richmond became immediately huffy 'agst women being Elected as Mayors and Alderman', as the Liberals seemed bent on proposing in 1894. 'They had much better confine themselves to the duties which naturally belong to them.'[11] Counter-argument would have left him quite as baffled and injured as if one had suggested that the weather could be improved by act of Parliament or a sow persuaded to service a stallion. Oddly enough, some of his colleagues did indeed attempt a different point of view, among them Salisbury himself. He may have shown himself as *outré*

[7] Salisbury to Lady Manners, 3 Jul. 1887, quoted in J. A. S. Grenville, *Lord Salisbury and Foreign Policy: The Close of the Nineteenth Century* (1964), p.8.
[8] Duke of Somerset to Lady Katherine Parker, 18 May 1879. 'He said, apropos Lady Salisbury's party of the night before, that he would rather go into a jungle than to such people.' See W. H. Mallock and Lady Gwendolen Ramsden (eds.), *Letters and Memoirs of the 12th Duke of Somerset* (1893), p. 412.
[9] Derby diary, reflecting on Shuvalov, 15 Jul. 1875, in Derby, *Diaries*, p. 230.
[10] Hardy diary, 8 Feb. 1879, on a three-day party at Hatfield, in A. E. Gathorne-Hardy, *Gathorne Hardy, First Earl of Cranbrook: A Memoir* (2 vols., 1910), vol. II, p. 109; the extract is omitted from Nancy E. Johnson (ed.), *The Diary of Gathorne Hardy, Later Lord Cranbrook, 1866–1892* (Oxford, 1981).
[11] Richmond to Cranbrook, 22 Jun. 1894, Cranbrook MSS T501/257.

as the next Tory on issues of class or blood, but Salisbury saw woman as potentially one of 'us'. The reasons run deep and probably have much to do with the nature of an imperial society suffering from a series of insecurities and requiring shoring up from within. Salisbury venerated women in the same way, and for some of the same reasons, that Southern society in *ante-bellum* America honoured its women. He saw them as a breath of purity capable of bringing sweetness to the defilements of modern living. They must not be sullied. On the other hand he rejected the view, so often held by imperial Tories, that politics would sully them. It might be, *au contraire*, that they would lift politics out of the mire if treated properly.

He never pressed his personal opinion that women ought to have the vote in the manner, say, of the 'progressive and independent Conservative' Sir Albert Rollit who built a reputation by doing so, but it mattered that he held it and his commitment often came to attention – public and private – from the discussions surrounding the 1884 extension of the franchise[12] and in particular from the late-1880s. In the same speech that he courted posthumous outrage by his dismissal of black men, he won contemporary enthusiasm by praising the Primrose League – Britain's first major political organ-ization to draw on the support of women[13] – for seeing the need for a female role in politics. The old form of constituency organization still had its importance, he said. But the League was 'freer . . . more elastic; it brings classes more together, and I think its greatest achievement is that it has brought the influence of women to bear upon politics in a way which it never bore before. (Cheers.) . . . Well, I am now speaking, mind you, for myself only . . . But . . . I earnestly hope that the day is not far distant when women will also bear their share in voting for members in the political world (loud cheers) . . .'[14] Reminded of this outburst in the House of Lords during the next session he scurried away into his personal dis-claimer;[15] but his views continued to show an awareness of the

[12] Carnarvon announced in 1884 that he would support a female suffrage bill provided somebody else introduced it. Salisbury thought any such move would have to come from the Commons. Carnarvon to Salisbury, 15 Dec. 1884, Salisbury MSS (Carnarvon, f.494).

[13] For the Primrose League, see Martin Pugh, *The Tories and the People 1880–1935* (Oxford, 1985) and his essay on 'The Limits of Liberalism: Liberals and Women's Suffrage, 1867–1914', in Eugenio Biagini (ed.), *Citizenship and Community: Liberals, Radicals and Collective Identities in the British Isles, 1865–1931* (Cambridge, 1996), pp. 45–65.

[14] *The Times*, 1 Dec. 1888, p. 8c.

[15] *Hansard*, 18 Mar. 1889, cccxxxiv, col. 5.

potential of female contributions in politics, sometimes even a sense of female existence that could carry across the normal boundaries of class. In 1900, after his crippling last illness and when close to retirement, he came to the Lords to contest a doomed early closing bill which would have curtailed shopping hours. Doubtless part of his resistance stemmed from an inherent dislike of meddling in commercial matters; but his language proved interesting for its passion about those who had to do the shopping:

[T]here are few Members of this House who will want . . . to shop after seven o'clock; but there are hundreds of thousands of women in our large towns who spend their days in work and who have not the time for making the requisite provision for their necessities and their household goods until after six o'clock . . . [Y]ou shut her out [in this bill] from that commerce at the only time of day when she has leisure to pursue it.[16]

Perhaps he placed the wives of the respectable poor above the fate of the sweat-shop girl, but at least he placed them somewhere and took an interest in their difficulties.

Whenever the subject of discussion took the form of a universal category (Negroes, Russians, women), it often concealed a cluster of particulars relating to a named person or a specific and delimited group. The rules, frequently held with passion, often became honoured in the breach, simply because Tories rest uncomfortable with any system of conduct or attitude that claims a global legislative force. Judging the case 'on its merits' (always a way of preferencing arbitrariness) seemed fairer and more sensible than assuming postures and constructing lattices within which everybody was supposed to act. They believed, largely, in patronage as a social device, not only because they shared Disraeli's regard for 'an outward and visible sign of an inward and spiritual grace', but because it conformed most naturally to Conservative assumptions about how a society ought to work.[17] These assumptions took much of their colour from a view of human nature as fallible and weak and a view of personal knowledge and experience that lent especial weight to a sense of craft and apprenticeship. That sons should benefit from their fathers' efforts, or fathers from the solicitude of their sons,

---

[16] Salisbury in Lords, *Hansard*, 22 May 1900, LXXXIII, cols. 869–70. The bill went down on second reading by 77 to 16.

[17] For Disraeli, see Robert Blake, *Disraeli* (1966), pp. 682–9. The phenomenon of patronage as a social instrument is well discussed in J. M. Bourne, *Patronage and Society in Nineteenth-century England* (1986) which is good on the first half of the century but thinner on the later years.

appeared too obvious to state until someone like William Godwin had questioned the self-serving nature of the transaction. 'I *ought* to prefer no human being to another because that being is my father, my wife, or my son, but because . . . that being is *entitled* to preference.' Salisbury quoted this sentence from Godwin's *Political Justice* in order to show his readers that Godwin was ridiculous, ludicrous beyond all need for further argument, since his doctrines were 'manifestly repugnant to the commonest and not the worst feelings of our nature'.[18] The feelings of our nature argued for beginning with the particular altruism found in the family and then easing it outwards in a series of concentric circles until 'society' became the expression of a universal altruism of the kind that Hegel had seen in the rise of the state. Accorded a special pedigree in this account were, therefore, relatives by blood and marriage, school-friends, university contemporaries, neighbours, acquaintances; and these partialities could be made in certain cases to overcome taboos about class or religion. Patronage often began with a thought about contiguity. 'We know Dr. Church here as a good neighbour', Salisbury might begin, '. . . but I am not closely acquainted with his professional merits.' His being a neighbour might make Salisbury interested enough to find out.[19] His correspondent, W. H. Smith, was theoretically despicable: all middle-class money and commercial vulgarity. Yet once the cabinet circle had come to know him as a person, their boundaries collapsed and Tories from Salisbury and Derby to Richmond greeted his premature death with perfectly genuine lamentation.

Of course, cosiness of this kind could not survive perceived threats, so perhaps Smith died just in time. The last decades of the nineteenth century saw a steep intensification of class feeling and aristocratic insecurity, be it from socialist awareness, death duties, doctrines of degeneration among Europe's noble stock or the drawing of the Queen's life peacefully to its close. For the Cecils, who see trouble even when it is not there, the rot set in at the 1880 election and began a quarter century of concern about the class war. Salisbury sounded the clarion himself after Gladstone's popular election triumph of 1880 and half-persuaded himself that something serious was afoot:

---

[18] 'Competitive Examinations', *Quarterly Review*, 108, (Oct. 1860), p. 569.
[19] Salisbury to Smith, 16 Nov. 1889, Hambledon MSS PS 14/124. This was not the more famous R. W. Church, Dean of St Paul's.

The hurricane that has swept us away is so strange & new a phenomenon that we shall not for some time understand its real meaning. I doubt if so much enthusiasm & such a general unity of action proceeds from any sentimental opinions – or from a new academic judgement. It seems to me to be inspired by some definite desire for change: and means business. It may disappear as rapidly as it came: or it may be the beginning of a serious war of classes. Gladstone is doing all he can to give it the latter meaning.[20]

Salisbury's nephew, to whom the letter had been addressed, took it seriously enough to recall and print it in his *Chapters of Autobiography* half a century later. And when he, Arthur James Balfour, met his own Waterloo at the election of 1906 he wrote an equally famous letter containing equally epochal predictions which reflected the precise timbre of what he had seen so many years before.[21] In fact Salisbury came to change his mind (sometimes) and to take the more cheerful lesson away from 1880: that it had been a passing whim. But whether one took the class war to represent a rhetorical challenge to be used or an all-too-real threat to be faced, the point remained inescapable. Rather than bleat about the class war, one had rather to *win* it.

INEQUALITIES

Salisbury belonged to a collection of self-conscious aristocrats who remembered enough Greek to know that the word had its roots in a conception of government by the best. This sense of *arete* impinged on Tory minds: 'best' in the sense of most virtuous and cultivated rather than moneyed or forceful. The Greek statuary that obstructed their hallways, the Ciceronian postures assumed by their ancestors for their portraits, the very plans, proportions and locations of many of their houses, made remarks about the present by placing modern representatives of Britain's great families in the tradition of Pitt and Burke, emblems of a ruling class that sought to be effective in its administration but also special in its recruitment and deportment.[22]

---

[20] Salisbury to Balfour, 10 Apr. 1880, *Salisbury–Balfour Correspondence*, p. 40.

[21] Balfour to Lady Salisbury, 17 Jan. 1906, quoted in Sydney H. Zebel, *Balfour: A Political Biography* (Cambridge, 1973), p. 143.

[22] For some background to the Hellenism of this generation, see Richard Jenkyns's well-known study of *The Victorians and Ancient Greece* (Oxford, 1980). Cf. Mark Girouard's point that clever layout of a house might produce a form of male insulation for those not up to the pentathlon. 'If the billiard room was placed next to the owner's study or business room with a w.c. and wash basin adjacent, one had the makings of a comfortable little male territory': *The Victorian Country House* (New Haven, CT, 1979 (1st edn 1971)), p. 35.

Naturally, life and art frequently diverged. It was sometimes hard to spot regality in a chinless defective who had squandered the family money on women and drink or simply succumbed to those ordinary characteristics of the titled English that Salisbury had come to loathe by the time he came of age – 'the dwarfed, languid, nerveless, emasculate dilettantism of the "higher classes"'.[23] Yet art had its own power as an image of what society ought to be and how aristocracy, properly understood, would feature within it. Many portraits of the ideal come readily to mind from a generation obsessed by democratic degeneration, but few surpass Salisbury's own:

> Every community has natural leaders, to whom, if they are not misled by the insane passion for equality, they will instinctively defer. Always wealth, in some countries birth, in all intellectual power and culture, mark out the men to whom, in a healthy state of feeling, a community looks to undertake its government. They have the leisure for the task, and can give to it the close attention and the preparatory study which it needs. Fortune enables them to do it for the most part gratuitously, so that the struggles of ambition are not defiled by the taint of sordid greed. They occupy a position of sufficient prominence among their neighbours to feel that their course is closely watched, and they belong to a class among whom a failure in honour is mercilessly dealt with.[24]

That virtually every sentence of this pæan would draw a smile or a cringe from Salisbury's colleagues and friends does not diminish its force as a 'public doctrine', a cluster of intimations in which an educated public ought to be made to believe in order to ensure the continuity of British (and normally English) civilization.[25]

The court of Queen Victoria supposedly capped this palladian structure, providing example for all and a daily guide to conduct. Until 1861 this seemed plausible when Prince Albert still lived and Prince Albert Edward had not yet made his mark. Thereafter it became something of a sad parody. Grief that ought to have been immeasurable became a thing of inches: a black edge an inch and a half wide was applied to all the royal stationary in every royal

---

[23] Journal, 7 Nov. 1851, in Cecil, vol. I, p. 28. He was drawing a contrast with the 'manliness and heartiness and freedom from all cant' that he had found in South Africa, though he loathed the Boers as well.

[24] 'The Confederate Struggle and Recognition', p. 547. For other portraits of aristocratic superiority, see in particular the writings of W. H. Mallock, and Anthony M. Ludovici, *A Defence of Aristocracy* (1915).

[25] See Maurice Cowling, *Religion and Public Doctrine* (2 vols. and continuing, Cambridge, 1980–), vol. I, pp. xi–xiv.

residence; only after decades had passed did it shrink to three-quarters of an inch. The black dresses became candidates for caricature. Self-pity, relieved by John Brown's devotion or her Indian favourite's antics, made a troubled marriage with self-assertion. 'She has said to me more than once "*I want someone to sympathise with me*" '; and of course Richmond always did during those interminable visits to Balmoral.[26] Others found it harder. Lord Randolph Churchill's lifestyle more closely resembled Albert Edward's than that of the Queen and wild reindeer would not have pulled him to Balmoral. Indeed it was all Salisbury could do to get him as far as Windsor when the new government took office in the summer of 1885. Churchill's account, written to his mother, manages no more than his customary level of gravitas. 'Windsor was deadly,' he wrote on the following day.

> After dinner the Queen talked for $\frac{1}{4}$ an hour to [Hicks] Beach, 10 mts to [Lord] G[eorge] Hamilton and 7 mts to me; then 3 mts more to Beach and, oh joy! took herself off to bed, then 20 mts more deadly work with the household, then a cigarette in the Smoking Room which was exactly $6\frac{3}{4}$ miles from my bedroom. I was in ecstasies at taking myself off this morning at eight o'clock and only pray it may be a long time before I go again.[27]

The Prince of Wales did nothing to heal such wounds but spent his time running from country park to grouse moor with his gun – 'the P of W shot 6 stags on Friday'[28] – looking for hot luncheon, liqueurs and cigars even when halfway up a hill. (Richmond used to send a portable marquee after the guns and servants would stagger up the slope with soup, entrée and pudding.) In the evening following a day of such athletics he wanted cards and dancing with local girls whose curiosity outshone their reticence. Few hosts were left with an overwhelming sense of *arete*.

And yet . . .; to say that court life had become a mere embarrassment comes too easily and misses the point about its social function. For a Churchill who would not go, one could substitute a Carnarvon who was not asked – he wanted to give away Ireland – and who minded dreadfully.[29] Rather than dwelling on the Queen glowering

---

[26] Richmond to Cairns, 30 Oct. 1876, Cairns MSS 30/51/3/f.123.

[27] Churchill to Duchess of Marlborough (copy), 5 Jul. 1885, Churchill MSS 9248/6.

[28] Cairns to Richmond, 7 Oct. 1879, Goodwood MSS 869 c 25.

[29] 'Hardy told me that Twitters [Carnarvon] was much disturbed at not being summoned to Balmoral . . .': Richmond to Cairns, 10 Sep. 1877, Cairns MSS 30/51/4/ff.28–9.

in supine misery at Balmoral, one could report instead Beaconsfield's amazement that she was taking the night train in order to conduct an audience with him at Windsor. 'What energy! What nerve! What muscle! Her minister is, I fear, deficient in all three.'[30] What seems to have happened is a slide, paradoxically, away from the dignified role in the constitution that Walter Bagehot had seen in 1867 as the royal role and back towards a place in the state rather than in society.[31] Such social events as she hosted in these later years were always likely to court scandal with the Prince's indiscretions on the one hand and the now sclerotic *amours* of her relatives on the other. The Queen of Holland seems to have kept her passion for the Whig Lord Clarendon out of the public eye.[32] The Queen of Denmark had coped less secretively when in her youth she had received the ardent attentions of a duke. Only Disraeli could have done justice, with a pen sharpened on characterization, to their reunion at a state dinner when they were in their dotage. 'It was a family dinner [at Windsor] yesterday', he wrote to Derby in 1875, 'but State: I mean gold plate & diamonds, in honor [*sic*] of the Queen of Denmark. Her ancient lover the D of C sate next to the mother of the ruler, & returning to his first loves, bellowed out the most tender reminiscences into almost insensible ears.'[33] Scenes of this kind kindled affection of a kind but they lacked a certain dignity.

Where the court made an entry into day-to-day political life was through the numerous offices that it made available to members of the aristocracy and in particular their wives through the Bedchamber – a fact that Sir Robert Peel would have done better to ponder.[34] It continued indirectly through the bishops or other significant churchmen such as the Dean of Windsor who obtained much of the Queen's ear for a time; and, of course, the army, especially when the Duke of Cambridge played a role in its direction as commander-in-chief between 1856 and 1895, and politicians grew used to notes from the Duke pressing them for an urgent talk, usually in their London

---

[30] Beaconsfield to Duke of Marlborough, 26 Nov. 1879, Marlborough MSS 9271/4/68.
[31] I defend this line of argument in an essay on 'Power and Authority in the Victorian Court' (forthcoming).
[32] Diary, 3 Jun. 1877, in Derby, *Diaries*, p. 406.
[33] Disraeli to Derby, 30 Nov. 1875, Derby MSS 16/2/1.
[34] In the so-called 'Bedchamber crisis' of May 1839 Peel's insensitivity to the Queen's wish to control household appointments and the monarch's umbrage over this trivial issue cost him the chance of forming an administration.

homes. Nor was the Prince of Wales politically negligible. Through his clubs and his circle of 'fast' playmates, he made his views known and sometimes took it on himself to lecture cabinet ministers about their failures of strategy or resolution, as when he and other members of the royal family deemed Beaconsfield's team pusillanimous in the face of Russian bullying. Albert Edward's determination to make Salisbury a member of the Marlborough Club 'as it is free from political bores, and the food particularly good' landed on the stony ground then guarded by the secretary, Sir Schomberg McDonnell, who told his royal patron that the Prime Minister found the Athenæum and both Carlton Clubs more than enough.[35] Others would doubtless have shown themselves more lubricated and have slid thereby into privileged conversation and knowledge with the frictionless dynamics that marked the mechanisms of high politics. Behind all of this lurked the formidable danger to those at the very top that the Queen herself might come to visit – and that would not be at all lubricated. The near ruination visited on Burghley by the changes made to the house to accommodate her visit of 1844 was avoided by Beaconsfield and Salisbury; but the reminder of whom policy was supposed to protect would not have been lost on either of them. It is clear, and rather moving, that Salisbury lost interest in politics when the Queen died in January 1901. She exasperated and ranted at him from time to time; but he felt something approaching love for her and took very seriously the concept of 'the Queen's Government'.

Readers of the 'Court' pages in *The Times* he did not take seriously; he earnestly despised them. The mood came on early when he lived north of Oxford Street: it had been people like that who had weighed with his father who failed to raise his allowance when he, Cecil, married beneath him. He did not change his mind when he moved to the right side of the tracks: he continued to find so-called 'Society' repellent and avoided it when he could avoid giving offence. Disraeli could hardly have behaved more differently with his adoration of gilded halls, tiaras, titles and fluffy conversation that judged success by its flippancy. Salisbury could be made to go occasionally to the parliamentary dining club, Grillions, on a Wednesday evening during the session (Monday after 1876) – the club so disliked by Disraeli. In

---

[35] Memo by McDonnell for Salisbury, 22 Feb. 1899. Salisbury minuted 'Very happy'. Christ Church MSS, no file.

1868, after he had avoided it for three years, the latter found that he had not missed its 'dozen prigs and bores (generally) whispering to their next door neighbours over a bad dinner in a dingy room'.[36] Disraeli found no more attraction in 'The Club', a similar grouping with a more intellectual flavour, while Salisbury, typically, much preferred that kind of company, particularly if scientists might be there as on the evening in 1869 when the journalist Henry Reeve reported a 'Good party'. The participants sitting around Salisbury included Spencer Walpole, Tyndall, Hooker, Lecky and Lyall.[37] Exclusion from such society would have caused Salisbury pain and he would have sympathized with anybody else suffering exclusion from interesting people. What he genuinely could not understand was anyone wanting to indulge in social climbing – Cecils have so little left to climb – in order to meet and endure people who were patently unsound. Never one given to writing homilies, he became almost a Polonius in 1891 when counselling the red-necked Charles Beresford against pursuing his allegation that the Prince of Wales had 'cut' his wife and thus closed doors to society. 'The acquaintance of no illustrious person', he wrote (with acid in the adjective), 'is necessary to one's true happiness: & if any illustrious person whom you know withdraws from intimacy you have no reason to trouble yourself further in the matter than for his sake to regret the opportunities of enjoyment he has lost. Your position in society & in your profession are not affected by the friendship of any one however highly placed . . . I strongly advise you to sit still & do nothing.' Beresford ignored the lapidary advice, but its quality said much for

[36] Disraeli to Cairns, 9 Dec. 1868, Cairns MSS 30/51/1. Grillions's schedule is explained by Nancy Johnson in her introduction to the diaries of Gathorne Hardy, p. xxvii.
[37] J. K. Laughton (ed.), *Memories of the Life and Correspondence of Henry Reeve* (2 vols., 1898), vol. II, p. 369. Walpole (1806–98) was home secretary in all three of Derby's governments in the 1850s and 1860s. Grillions commissioned a bust of him for the club from George Richmond. John Tyndall (1820–93) was a friend of Huxley and succeeded Faraday as superintendant of the Royal Institution in 1867. The distinguished botanist Joseph (later Sir Joseph) Hooker (1817–1911) was close to Darwin and a friend of Kelvin. W. E. H. Lecky (1838–1903) owed his fame as an historian at this time to his *History of the Rise and Influence of the Spirit of Rationalism* (2 vols., 1865). He was about to begin work on his magnum opus, *The History of England in the Eighteenth Century* (8 vols., 1878–90). Sir Alfred Lyall (1835–1911) sailed closer to the forbidden winds of politics as a former minister of the Indian government and lieutenant-governor of the North West Frontier, though he became a great clubman after his retirement in 1887 and joined Balfour and Rayleigh in the Synthetic Society. Archbishop Benson's diary in 1886 records a more stridently political gathering with Ashbourne, Harrowby, Cranbrook and Derby as well as the perennial Walpole. Salisbury would doubtless have avoided it for that reason: Benson diary, 5 Apr. 1886.

Salisbury's social sanity, just as the neglect of it spoke strongly for Beresford's often-remarked stupidity.[38]

Much Conservative social contact took the form of male association – often through the London clubs but also via certain key institutions among which, for Tories, the church and the army had become important locations. The late nineteenth century saw a flowering of St James's clubs, perhaps because some of the older and more fashionable ones such as White's and Brooks's had long waiting lists but also because the City had attracted much new money looking for outward expression. Toryism, with the dandified image of a Churchill or Henry Matthews, supplied (unusually) a form of chic. It looked unsavoury from the other side, as Edward Hamilton would later reflect in a dark diary entry in 1895. 'The Upper Classes have become much more Conservative', he sighed, 'and the fashion which they set filters down from one class to another.'[39] Some of the newer clubs announced a political leaning of some kind – the Beaconsfield, the Devonshire, the Junior Carlton; others, including some long-established institutions, had a well-worn label of another sort such as the Thatched House Club (civil service), Boodles ('chiefly for country gentleman'), the Garrick ('literary men and actors'), the Athenæum (intellectuals), the Travellers' (a journey 500 miles from London was the minimum qualification in 1881), the United University, the Turf.[40] Most politicians aspired to become members of the two senior political clubs, the Reform Club for Whigs and Liberals and the Carlton for Tories. The latter's membership (950) figured among the smallest in St James's and many hopefuls had to wait out their time in the Junior Carlton before ascending. Not so the military. A rank of major or above in the army or commander in the navy would open the United Service Club in Pall Mall; or there was the Army and Navy on the north side of Pall Mall with a membership of 2,200. Many Conservatives who lacked Salisbury's aversions chose to become members of several of these

[38] Salisbury to Lord Charles Beresford, 10 Aug. 1891. Christ Church MSS, E29. When Beresford resolved to press ahead with his plan to write a letter of complaint to the Prince of Wales, Polonius instantly became Henry V: 'This looks like war . . . [C]all legal advice in to determine how matters can be shaped so as to bring in the Prince least – & hurt the Beresfords the most' (to McDonnell, 21 Dec., Christ Church MSS, E47–8). It is one of Salisbury's charms that he found philosophical detachment a wearisome doctrine.

[39] Diary, 30 Jul. 1895, in Dudley W. R. Bahlman (ed.), *The Diary of Sir Edward Walter Hamilton, 1885–1906* (Hull, 1993), p. 309.

[40] Quotations from the 1881 edition of Baedecker: see Carl Baedecker, *Great Britain: Handbook for Travellers* (Leipzig, many editions).

clubs where the politics of privacy could proceed agreeably over drinks, luncheon and dinner.

Churchmen had their own modes of association. Their styles of patronage differed from secular forms because of the complicating presence of religious doctrine. Except, of course, in Gloucester where such views really had to be kept in proportion:

> Has Claughton got any money? If he has, he might like to be Dean of Gloucester. I should not think of offering it to any one without money – for under agricultural distress the income has fallen from £1500 to £300 a year. But it may revive to some extent . . . It is vacated by Dr. [Montagu] Butler who takes the Mastership of Trinity.[41]

Deanery, Varsity, Salisbury: three nodes of social power interfacing over a single transaction among thousands in this world of male arrangement and accommodation. By the 1870s that world had come under pressure from inside the state, as we shall see: the crippling combination of the Crimean war and the coming of Gladstone had disturbed peculation in the civil service and the possibility of buying commissions in the army. But it also engaged with a broader difficulty. Men could do most things on their own; but one thing they could not. And doing it became the subject of strategy as well as instinct as the depression bit and income shrivelled.

Marriage could do a lot for Tory Man. A single, well-aimed contract (perhaps in return for conceding a double-barrelled name) could relieve pressure on an estate by bringing in wealth – maybe from the eldest daughter of a peer or great landowner, possibly from a rich American family or from an industrialist seeking to move daughters up the social ladder. It could confer status if one had money of the wrong sort. It removed suspicion, often levelled at the unmarried, that a man's tastes were, well, unnatural. On the other hand, marriage had a trailing edge and could lacerate a person in social trouble if the acquisition turned out to be unpresentable, lustful, mad or divorced. The latter, of course, always proved the most consequential of these afflictions and would remain so up to and beyond the days of Mrs Wallis Simpson. Imagine the feelings of Lord Egmont when told, in a formal interview with Lord Leconfield on behalf of the 'County', that his new wife could not be received in society 'for the dangerous precedent it would create, & the fact of

---

[41] Salisbury to Richmond, 31 Oct. 1886, Goodwood MSS 871 d 102. Claughton, who was a personal friend of Richmond, in fact went to Worcester and Salisbury found 'another and richer man' for Gloucester.

having daughters', even though everyone agreed that she had behaved quite unexceptionably since her marriage. The most that Leconfield could do was to send a report of the conversation to the county leader (Richmond). Egmont left virtually in tears.[42] Presumably some similar misfortune befell the son of Disraeli's Lord Chancellor since we find Salisbury gossiping in a mood of serene malice about the choice. 'Cairns is very happy at having got rid of his daughter-in-law,' he confided to Carnarvon, 'though at a considerable expense.'[43] Getting rid of one's own daughters had its darker moments, of course, and London was the place to do it, which often meant hanging about the city when a free spirit might wish to be finding some country air. It left Herbert Maxwell perplexed that his English friends seemed so obsessed; and his publisher, Blackwood, agreed with him that it was a mystery. '[A]ll you say,' he wrote in sending Maxwell some proofs, 'I have been preaching to my country house friends for [the] last ten years & how they can waste their time in London even after the middle of May beats my comprehension. [B]ut alas so many are wedded to fashion & must get their daughters out & married & so on it goes.'[44]

But if the plans went well, if one's wife were *all right*, then a woman could become not merely helpful to her husband in his career but a significant force in political society, especially among aristocrats whose women enjoyed a quite different status from that accorded other wives.[45] The astuteness of Georgina Salisbury in organizing political gatherings at Hatfield – writing to Aretas Akers-Douglas to find out whether people were proper Conservatives and what their spouses were called[46] – could find some echo in county

---

[42] Leconfield to Richmond, 26 Aug. 1886, Goodwood MSS 871 d 99–100. Charles George Perceval, from the same family as Spencer Perceval, the assassinated prime minister of 1812, seventh Earl of Egmont (1845–97). Married in 1869 Lucy King of Horndean, Hants. She remarried after his death – a son of Sir Robert Brisco, Bart. The Egmont seat was Cowdray Park, near Midhurst, where the family owned 14,000 acres, the core of which comprised the estate bought in 1909 by Sir Weetman Pearson, later Lord Cowdray, the Asquithian financier during Liberalism's dark days after 1914. The Egmont line had itself become eccentric before then in the eighth Earl, our man's cousin, who became serially a seaman, a fireman, keeper of Chelsea Town Hall and the victim of a failed cement business. 'He was a Conservative.'

[43] Salisbury to Carnarvon, 14 Feb. 1884, Carnarvon MSS 60759 f.121. Cairns's son had embroiled himself in a breach-of-promise suit with a disappointed actress.

[44] Blackwood to Maxwell, 9 Jun. 1890, Maxwell MSS 7043 HEM3.

[45] This aspect of female society is well argued in K. D. Reynolds, *Aristocratic Women and Political Society in Victorian Britain* (Oxford, 1998), pp. 1–25.

[46] Lady Salisbury to Akers-Douglas, 24 Apr. (no year), Chilston MSS C/19.

politics throughout the country. It needed a Lady Bradford, perhaps, to 'know everything down to the most minute details of everything that passe[d]',[47] and a Disraeli (or an Asquith) to tell her. Yet Salisbury's mother's relationship with the Duke of Wellington and his stepmother's with Derby and Shuvalov call the exceptionalism of female power into question, just as social effluvia from Lady Londonderry's parties made all too manifest to contemporaries the scale of possibility.

First sight suggests, all the same, that on a literal reading of the manual on social climbing many Conservatives married ingloriously. This impression is probably a distortion produced by a more realistic sense of what was desirable in a world which turned increasingly on money and the need to construct a career. Naturally, there were still aristocratic marriages aiming to draw together 'appropriate' families with much to lose. It feels inevitable that a Whig Grenfell, having turned Tory, would have a Fane for a wife.[48] Or that Lord Elcho, son of the Adullamite and later extreme individualist Earl of Wemyss, should have married a daughter of the Earl of Lichfield.[49] Or that Lord Hylton's son and heir should have married into the family of the Marquis of Bristol. There were also promotions for some, ascending from commonalty to the peerage through the marriage market. Everybody wanted to marry a Churchill or a Cecil or a Balfour – itself a political compliment as much as a social. There were quieter ways to advancement for those who failed. Henry Chaplin, the party's agricultural spokesman, showed himself ob-sessed by the soil and completed the process by marrying it, even at the expense of compromising party ties.[50] The same result could be achieved in other ways, of course. Albert Brassey was no agricul-turist, for example, but where there was Brassey there was money,

---

[47] Richmond to Cairns, 27 Jul. 1876, Cairns MSS 30/51/3/f.102.

[48] William Henry Grenfell, later Baron Desborough. Harrow Eleven; swam across Niagara (twice); Harcourt's private secretary for a while. He resigned his seat over the second Home Rule bill in 1893 and became a Conservative in 1898. This and much of the following detail comes from John Bateman, *The Great Landowners of Great Britain and Ireland* (1878) and M. Stenton and S. Lees, *Who's Who of British Members of Parliament* (4 vols., Hassocks and Brighton, 1976–81).

[49] Hugo Charteris, later eleventh Earl of Wemyss. He partnered Charles Dalrymple in the Ipswich seat between 1886 and 1895 after a period in his father's former pocket borough of Haddingtonshire. Sixty-two thousand acres helped him along.

[50] He married Florence Leveson-Gower (pronounced Looson-Gore), daughter of the Whig third Duke of Sutherland whose Scottish acres were vast, if covered in more rock and heather than Chaplin would have liked.

which brought him an address in Berkeley Square and the Hon. Matilda, daughter of Lord Clanmorris. In the case of Henry Blundell-Hollinshead, a portentous name perhaps helped him enter the society of Admiral Byng and his wife, Maud, who was maid of honour to the Queen. He duly won their daughter, the Hon. Beatrice.

More commonly, however, the marriage patterns among parliamentarians reflected the importance of a changing social fabric as commercial Tories increased their number and new occupations entered the parliamentary record.[51] Riffling through the backgrounds of Tory MPs during Salisbury's high period, one comes across the inevitable farmers (with a nod towards tenantry as well as owners), lawyers (solicitors, now, and not only barristers), brewers and distillers; but there are also surveyors, engineers, shipowners, plus numerous representatives of the City-based world of banking and insurance. There is a maker of fertilizer (Fison), a chemist, a wholesale grocer, a bleacher, the director of a telegraph company, a trader in silk, a wire-rope maker and a boomerang-thrower.[52] Perhaps for this newer clientele parliamentarians seemed their own aristocracy: a political class into which it made sense to marry and more relevant to social position than a crumbling pile of stone in the counties with an estate sinking under encumbrance and unpaid rent. Certainly these Tory MPs took to marrying daughters of other MPs or functionaries within the political system. The egregious Lord Charles Beresford may have had his wife 'cut', for example, because he married, as a son of the Marquis of Waterford should not, the daughter of an MP from Leicester. Similarly, the son and heir of Lord Newton married Evelyn Bromley-Davenport whose father represented Warwickshire. Edward King-Harman, who was a notable power in the politics of land on both sides of the Irish Sea and a straight-up-and-down Eton and army man, married a Hovingham Worsley whose father held the Isle of Thanet for a time. More evocative of the new mood, however, were less exalted men

---

[51] For a study of this development, see G. R. Searle, *Entrepreneurial Politics in Mid-Victorian England* (New York, 1983) and John Turner, *Businessmen and Politics: Studies of Business Activity in British Politics 1900–1945* (1984).

[52] The last was the eccentric third son of an earl from the ever-eccentric line of Winchilsea. The Hon. H. S. Finch-Hatton, MP for Newark between 1895 and 1898 and younger brother of the future eleventh Earl, was author of *Advance Australia!* (1885) and, apparently, an expert with the boomerang. His elder brother, Lord Maidstone, enlisted as a common soldier and died from drink. Yet they had a very respectable seat at Eastwell Park, Kent.

such as Charles Wing Gray, a tenant farmer and son of a barrister, who sat for Maldon in the Salisbury long parliament of 1886–92 and who married Alice Bentall, daughter of the former Liberal MP for the same seat and a force in the manufacture of agricultural machines.

To parliament and trade one must add empire and America, not least because a single biography might encompass all four environments. America became especially compelling for Conservatives in the last quarter of the century. Doubtless Lord Randolph Churchill's wedding to the beguiling Jenny Jerome helped articulate a fashionable development. For a stateless wanderer such as the well-known editor of Thomas Croker's published correspondence, Louis Jennings, periods of residence in India and then the United States established the conditions in which his bride would come from New York. But among parliamentary bankers, in particular, business connexion would also have the same effect, whether because, as in the case of John Saunders Gilliat, the family firm was based in America or, as happened to a Tory Baring, the ordinary course of international banking brought New York to the doorstep.[53] And of course there could be sheer serendipity. So grim a line as the Barons Grimthorpe, whose first embodiment had married a Feversham and defended the Church of England's traditions as though Satan himself had stuck his tail through them, produced a nephew who followed him into parliament but preferred Lucy Tracy Lee of New York to the desiccated frumps of much Anglican county society.

In marrying a judge's daughter, if not an American, Salisbury reflected a mild loosening of social identities, as did Brownlow Cecil, Lord Burghley, who contented himself with a daughter of a mere baronet, Isabella Whichcote. But it has to be asked whether Salisbury's circle felt many of these new breezes and it seems unlikely that it did. The Cecils and Balfours married 'well' for the most part. Arthur Balfour confused the account by not marrying at all but it would probably have been a Lyttelton had he ever raised the energy. Gerald, his brother, married Lord Lytton's daughter; another brother, Eustace, married the firebrand daughter of the Duke of Argyll. As a family nexus the Cecil/Balfour clan scattered itself across

[53] Gilliat married into the Leicestershire Babingtons at whose seat, Rothley Temple, Thomas Babington Macaulay had been born in 1800. Thomas Charles Baring was a nephew of the (Whig) Lord Northbrook and married Susan Carter Minturne of New York.

the pages of Burke's Peerage like dandelion seed, as did the families of many of their senior colleagues unless they 'married' one another by joining sons and daughters to their rivals' spawn. Even when one reaches the more minor functionaries of the party such as Acland-Hood or Hart-Dyke, the stability of marital expectation remains clear, with only Akers-Douglas reflecting minor gentry in his choice.[54] This habit pushed a contemporary social mechanism below the common horizon of those directing Conservative fortunes and increased the social isolation that high politics managed to enforce in so many ways, with important implications for the ability of this political class to understand a good deal of what was happening in their immediate social vicinity, to say nothing of much that was not.

BEYOND THE PALE

Removed from Westminster's sight, and banished from mind by park gates, lime groves and estate walls, the great British public led its own life. What Conservative politicians thought about its members often defies easy reconstruction, though it seems clear enough that most members of the Tory political classes could pass the greater part of their existence without coming into close contact with anybody beyond their own world, except for encounters with a land agent, solicitor or local party organizer when the time came to give a speech. There were classes of people: they knew this much. Lower classes had their own customs and habits, like tribal peoples in Africa. Something approaching magic seemed to dominate the relationship between great figures and these unknown creatures of the abyss. There would arrive an invitation to go down to speak to (say) the Lancashire and Cheshire Conservative Association, 'most tiresome but worthy';[55] a crowd of enthusiasts would be whipped up to excitement by a chairman who bridged the gap between audience and exalted guest; and then the speaker would drone for an hour – sometimes far longer – about policies of the moment with interjections, 'laughter' and 'cheers'. But what any of it *meant* to anybody

---

[54] Sir Alexander Acland-Hood, later fourth Baron St Audries, married a daughter of Lord Ventnor; Sir William Hart-Dyke married the eldest daughter of the seventh Earl of Sandwich. Akers-Douglas chose Adeline Austin Smith of Hayes Court, Kent.

[55] Balfour to Ashbourne, 12 Feb. 1896, in A. B. Cooke and A. P. W. Malcolmson (eds.), *The Ashbourne Papers 1869–1913* (Belfast, 1974), p. 67.

in the audience proved as baffling to contemporaries as it does to historians. The Earl of Derby supplies a case in point. As King of Lancashire he could not avoid some contact with the towns around him, not least the smoke and smells of St Helens that drifted across his park at Knowsley and made him think of moving his residence. On Whit Monday 1870 he went into Liverpool to be received by the mayor and to lay the first stone of a new hospital. Then he made a speech. At the end of the day he wrote analytical reflections in his diary just as an anthropologist might have done in his note-book after a few hours' field work among the Algonquin or Matabele.

The scene of today has raised in my mind some curious thoughts. What is – what can be – the inducement to some thousands of persons receiving wages, and not too high wages, to pass several hours of one of their holidays, in a crowd, hot, dusty, and generally uncomfortable, merely to see a few notabilities pass? What makes them cheer such people? There is no motive for affecting enthusiasm, if it does not exist: yet what they have to be enthusiastic about is perplexing to me . . . One practical moral may be drawn – that in some inexplicable way, these public appearances of local magnates do give pleasure to, and create popularity among, the masses; and that therefore they ought not to be wholly neglected.[56]

That Derby was right in his conclusion ought not to drown his observation that he did not understand why he was right. Indeed the rhetorical distance between notable and audience seems to have been important to the relationship's functioning in the way that Derby described. When once politicians became capable of understanding those for whom they spoke, they lost whatever popular interest they had stimulated in the first place, unless they could use a populist language like that of Lloyd George in the next generation, which Victorian Tories could hardly do. 'The people' apparently wanted their governors, when they wanted Conservatives at all, who were beyond them in economic power and social mystique.

Conservatives of Salisbury's circle shared Derby's ignorance of what the public was like and sought to lead and manipulate it by using suitable and resonant public language.[57] They felt more *au fait* with those they deemed the 'middle class', perhaps because they heard more about the undesirability of such people from parents and educators, but also because the nastier characteristics of this

---

[56] Diary, 6 Jun. 1870, in Derby, *Diaries*, p. 62.
[57] This theme is taken further in chapter 10.

supposed class had become lampooned in Victorian novels, and because members of that group impinged increasingly on their own lives as politics became more professional. Not that anybody received a salary as an MP in Victorian Britain: that innovation dates from 1911. But men of the stamp of Richard Cross and W. H. Smith on the Tory benches, or Joseph Chamberlain on the Unionist side, brought the enemy closer and even into the cabinet room. In one way this encroachment overcame prejudice and made Smith a popular figure with, say, Richmond or Derby as well as Salisbury.[58] On the other hand, Smith had acquired in 1877 a 5,000 acre estate in Suffolk which turned him into a 'big squire' and confused the categories. Disraeli had allowed himself to be persuaded of the merits of Smith and Cross[59] – Marshall and Snelgrove, as Churchill preferred to call them – but resistance to middle-class men did not end with his death in 1881: a tradition of dislike and mistrust persisted in Tory circles until well into the twentieth century. Quite what it meant to be middle class was specified by very few observers, with some wonderful results in social depiction. There is delicious blurredness, for example, in Balfour's compliment to W. L. Jackson that he suffered from 'middle class tact and judgement . . . but good of their kind'.[60] He doubtless took some of his attitudes from his uncle. In his Tractarian days, Cecil had shown himself hostile – 'turbulence as well as every other evil temper of this evil age belongs not to the lower but to the middle class'[61] – but he had become sunnier by 1866, at least when defending a middle-class man from the deprecations of the second Marquis. 'It is not the poor man's fault that he enjoys the honour of Mr. Spofforth's protection or Lord Ranelagh's friendship. I believe he has very fair ability – and so far as I know there is nothing against his moral character – except that he sits for Stafford. He takes good care of himself, & will lose nothing for want

---

[58] For example, Richmond to Cairns, 5 Aug. 1877: 'I have formed a very high opinion of W.H.S. since we have been in office': Cairns MSS 30/81/4/f.23. It was to Richmond that Salisbury sent his plainly genuine letter of disappointment at Smith's death. 'What a terrible blow this is – the death of Smith. He was such a good, loyal, self-sacrificing man! It is wretched to think of': Salisbury to Richmond, 10 Oct. 1891, Goodwood MSS 873 t 39.

[59] Neither had been first choice for their respective posts. Cross had been pressed by Derby and Sandon had initially been preferred to Smith. I am grateful to John Vincent for this caution.

[60] Quoted in James Cornford, 'Parliamentary Foundations of the Hotel Cecil', in Robert Robson (ed.), *Ideas and Institutions of Victorian Britain: Essays in Honour of George Kitson Clark* (1967), pp. 268–311 at p. 296.

[61] Journal, 28 Mar. 1852, Cecil, vol. I, p. 32.

of asking; but that I imagine to be the characteristic of "our enlightened middle class".[62]

The patronage remained, but its tone became less bitter and defensive in the later decades of the century. For good or ill, Conservative politics had come to rely on middle-class favour, and prudence would dictate that a crucial ally in the contest against loot and depredation should not be snubbed. An older middle class in the countryside – the social catchment evoked by a term such as 'country gentleman' – could no longer function as the mainstay of a modern political party: it lacked numbers by the 1880s and Gladstone seemed bent on destroying what little influence it still possessed.[63] If Tories claimed an interest in winning the towns and cities, which they did consistently after their defeat in 1868, then they needed to swallow prejudices against the inhabitants of suburban villas whose help as local notables they would undoubtedly need. Salisbury lacked the genius of Baldwin in sensing instinctively what such people wanted; but he knew that they mattered and that he must listen to those who had a finger on the pulse.

He claimed, interestingly, that one person who had this skill was the least plausible candidate in the kingdom. One does not think of Victoria as a middle-class queen. But her *attitudes*, as opposed to her background and riches, frequently had the ring of *bourgeois* commitments: a constrained and pursed humour, a belief in the elevating character of misery, an ethics which went no further than dilated convention, a collection of opinions whose ordinariness would have raised no ruffles in any chamber of commerce or wives' knitting circle. After her death, Salisbury reverted to this aspect of her help to him during his period as prime minister. 'I have said for years', he told the House of Lords, 'that I always felt that when I knew what the Queen thought, I knew pretty certainly what view her subjects would take, and especially the middle class of her subjects.'[64] In his earlier experiences of government this doubtless took the form of telling ministers without ambiguity what the public wanted to do with Russia. By the later years, Salisbury had insulated foreign policy

[62] Cecil to Marquis of Salisbury, 29 Oct. 1866, Christ Church MSS E61. Markham Spofforth was approaching the end of his reign as 'the last of the old breed of electioneering attorneys': Richard Shannon, *The Age of Salisbury, 1881–1902* (1996), p. 123. The seventh and last Viscount Ranelagh (1812–85) had an army career. Died unmarried.

[63] Salisbury to Richmond, 17 Apr. 1880, Goodwood MSS 869 c 46.

[64] Quoted in Cecil, vol. III, pp. 186–7.

from the attention of the public and, indeed, just about everybody.
His attention turned rather to internal politics in this epoch of state
expansion, which he always mistrusted, and middle-class man
became something more than a repository of attitudes; he became a
victim, a ratepayer. So when Lord Hardwicke's aliens bill came on in
1898, Salisbury threw his weight behind it, not out of his often-
rehearsed problems with black men but rather out of a concern that
the camel's back of impositions on (Tory) ratepayers now audibly
creaked and might give way:

> I know no more helpless, no more pathetic figure in our present community
> than the English ratepayer . . . Boards have been called into existence,
> whose chief duty appears to be to pile new burdens on his shoulders, and
> his inability to combine is so great that he is at the mercy of every spoiler.
> The rates are rising, rising, rising . . . I wish, at all events, to save [the
> ratepayer] from a burden [in supporting foreign paupers] which he ought
> not to bear.[65]

Like almost all senior Conservatives and Sir Robert Walpole a
century and a half before, Salisbury had come to see that the politics
of taxation had a particular purchase on middle-class voters and that
the future of Toryism had something to do with negotiating it
sensibly.

Two contexts lent this predicament a particular piquancy: the loss
of buoyancy in a free-trade capitalist economy after 1873 and the
acceleration of socialist doctrine among the forces of labour in the
second half of the 1880s. Both of these long-term processes have an
importance outside the evolution of party politics. They impinged,
nevertheless, on politics through this painful thought: both of them
began and took on their character during periods of Conservative
government. Much could be done historically (and not enough has
been) with the realization that Gladstonian Liberalism only worked
when the economy did. The thought's opposite facet is no less
notable and some contemporaries noted it. Conservative governments had the joy of coming into power as trouble got into its stride.
Only Salisbury's last government, from 1895 to his retirement in
1902, could claim to have seen some upturn after the crisis in jobs
and rents; and it lifted its face just in time to feel the slap of the Boers

---

[65] In the Lords, *Hansard*, 23 May 1898, LVIII, col. 287. His remark recalls a letter to the Queen
some years before in which he described one item in the day's cabinet as concerned with
'the mode of protecting the ratepayers from excessive taxation': RA VIC/A67/56.

in 1899 with its implications for defence spending and further taxation. All of this gave social thought a certain flexibility when Tories ruminated on middle-class politics. It gave it a special harshness of texture in approaching the working class.

Apart from his statements about the evils of democracy, which almost everyone knows, Salisbury's remarks about the working class have entered a treasury of quotations intended to show how horrible was his personality and how mean his spirit. Most are authenticated, all are striking and no one should disbelieve that he meant what he said in loathing the dirty hands and greasy chops that he had always associated with the hustings. Much of this commentary fixes inadvertently, however, on the early years – not simply because that period saw his fight against the 1867 extension of the franchise but because it was then that he wrote the polemical journalism that modern historians like to quote, even though he forbade any mention of it in his own house since he regarded it as a form of literary prostitution. The perspective needs balancing by views he developed later when charged with the responsibility for governing and when the working-class threat took on its particular shape in the last quarter of the century.

1880 supplied a threshold, since Gladstone's rhetorical violence at Midlothian led Salisbury to believe that a frontal assault on the possessing classes lay in the forefront of Liberal strategy. Before then, the pressures of rural depression had stimulated some thinking about the housing of the rural poor, not least on his own estate where he conceded that 'the cottages . . . were only on the road to perfection & had not yet attained it'.[66] The concern with rural housing stayed with him all the same and acted as one test of depravity in the urban housing that became a preoccupation in 1883. Already Northcote had gone some way to effect reform of the artisan's lot by adjusting taxation schemes governing urban housing. He boasted to Derby after the release of his budget in 1874 that 'Rathbone of Liverpool said to me in the Park this morning that we had been very cruel in cutting into the heart of the Liberal strength in the boroughs by untaxing the tradesmen's horses; but that they deserved it for having been such fools as not to have thought of it before!'[67] Derby himself

---

[66] Salisbury to Carnarvon, 2 Jun. 1873, Carnarvon MSS 60758 ff.115–16. Recent work suggests that Salisbury's modesty about the state of his cottages was fully justified.

[67] Northcote to Derby, 17 Apr. 1874, Derby MSS 16/2/6. Northcote's financial statement, made the previous day, had announced a penny on income tax, more subventions towards

continued to be exercised by the growing strength of labour – a subject about which he would become virtually unbalanced during the 1880s – while Salisbury's energies were distracted by India, Russia, Turkey, the Afghans and the Zulus. The Artisans' Dwellings Act of 1875 went some way to give the government credibility in his area but its permissive tendencies made it less than revolutionary.[68] It was in the period out of office, especially at a time when his political leadership had come under severe challenge in the House of Lords, that Salisbury turned to the housing problem, fired, as were so many sensitive observers, by Andrew Mearns's pamphlet on *The Bitter Cry of Outcast London* which appeared in the autumn of 1883. And, like the Congregationalist Mearns himself, Salisbury approached the issues as a churchman distressed and repelled by the moral consequences of bad housing. Cholera was a bad word, but incest a worse; and the disclosure that sexual temptation had increased in conditions of severe overcrowding prompted Salisbury into print – unusually by this date. His well-known piece on 'Disintegration' deserves its centrality in the Salisbury corpus of journalism and it dates from this year. But perhaps 'Labourers' and Artisans' Dwellings', which appeared in the *National Review* a month later in November 1883, should be seen as the more momentous if less spectacular.

He focussed on urban housing – by which he meant London housing – and distinguished the problems found in the town from those he knew about as a landlord. In the latter sphere he sounded at once authoritative with figures at his fingertips and gave the impression of a clearly grounded sense of experience coming into play. Building cottages for the poor, he argued:

depends on the existence of a class of labourers sufficiently at ease to disregard exact considerations of profit and loss. The cost of a healthy cottage at present prices may be put at an average of £150 . . . To pay four per cent. interest on this sum, and to lay by two per cent. for repairs and replacement of capital, the rent must be not less than £9 a year or three and sixpence [17p] a week – a sum which is beyond the ordinary means of an agricultural labourer, if it be true, as is generally assumed, that a man

local taxation, and the abolition of the Sugar Duty and the horse tax: *Hansard*, 16 Apr. 1874, ccxviii, col. 676. Rathbone (1819–1902) represented his city of Liverpool, where he was himself a merchant, from 1868 to 1880 as a 'decided Liberal'. He then sat for seats in Carnarvonshire until his retirement in 1895. Father of the better-known and more significant Eleanor, the social reformer, feminist protagonist and, like her father, Liverpool patriot.

68 See Paul Smith, *Disraelian Conservatism and Social Reform* (1967), pp. 218–23.

cannot pay, without embarrassment, more than a sixth of his income for his lodging. There is no practicable remedy for this state of things until wages rise to a higher point; for the cost of building is not likely to fall.

He distinguished, however, between the private role of the land-owner building cottages on his estate and the urban context where the state might be expected to play some role, at least in supplying loans. Otherwise the analysis seemed equally bleak: he judged a wage of £1 3s per week the minimum to make loan-financed building feasible in London and he doubted, from ignorance, whether this sum were realistic.

We know little – far too little – of the material conditions of the vast masses who are congregated into modern towns. But we may assume with confidence that there are multitudes whose nominal wages fall short of this sum . . . The number of labourers and artisans in London who earn this sum are probably far from being a moiety of the whole labouring population.[69]

Nothing in this analysis suggested a solution other, perhaps, than the need for enquiry and research. But the Royal Commission on the Housing of the Working Classes, suggested by Cranbrook in *The Times* before the end of the year, proved an important fruit of Salisbury's ideas and it served a helpful purpose if only in revealing how great the problem had become.[70] Similarly, his hopes that the setting up of a Poor Law Commission a decade later would mitigate the severity of provision for the old and infirm betrayed a streak of genuine sympathy in Salisbury's conception of the (deserving) poor and their problems.[71]

Sympathy had its limits. If Salisbury never took the view that all state intervention in the life of the working classes had to be seen as wrong in principle, in the way that, for example, the Earl of Wemyss tended to do, he avoided in practice forms of intervention that

---

[69] 'Labourers' and Artisans' Dwellings', printed in Anthony Wohl (ed.), *The Bitter Cry of Outcast London* (Leicester, 1970), pp. 111–34 at pp. 114–15, 123–4.

[70] The Commission did give rise to the housing act of 1885 through which the Metropolitan Board of Works received powers to build and let houses for working people. At the end of his career Salisbury expressed his sadness, none the less, that conditions had actually deteriorated rather than improved in London as a result, he thought, of people moving in from the countryside in order to live near their workplace: *Hansard*, 26 Jun. 1899, LXIII, cols. 546–51.

[71] Salisbury in Lords, *Hansard*, 31 Jan. 1893, VIII, col. 26. He was arguing in private by 1899 that 'some relaxation of the Poor Law in favour of Old People would be (within the limits of financial possibility) both just & wise'. But he did not rate the issue an urgent one against the background of war. Salisbury to Beach, 18 Oct. 1899, St Aldwyn MSS PCC/69/f.177.

implied compulsion and opposed legislation that offended his fastidious sense of precision. So he greatly disliked the Liberal bill that tried to build on recommendations of the Royal Commission because it seemingly opened unwelcome doors by 'put[ting] it in the power of any Board of Guardians to build out of the rates as many cottages, with half acres attached, as they like[d], taking for the purpose any land that they please[d]' – implications he would always want to see written out of sloppy bills.[72] He liked to see what he called 'Conservative Labour candidates' standing for the party in constituencies that they had some chance of winning;[73] but he had no strategy for finding the money that such people would need in order to contest a seat. He set his face against meddling bishops who wanted to use legislation to curb drunkenness.[74] Yet the most he could offer the working class (who, he thought, were undeniably drunk) was the model of the upper and middle classes (who were growing less drunk) by trusting to an undefined 'education and enlightenment' that would seep down through society. He sincerely regretted what commentators on the 1890s came to call 'the labour wars' – the eruption of trade union militancy against an employers' offensive that manipulated the law as its instrument; but he saw no possible conclusion other than that 'the labourers w[ould] get the worst of it' and only after they had succeeded in persuading employers to organize against them 'into Federations and Trusts & such like things', when his sympathies would be with the consumer rather than the labourer.[75]

Above all, Salisbury's fragile sense of common-cause with the lower classes rested, like that of all Conservatives, on a view of social cohesion and loyalty. His world coped with 'Hodge'; it excluded Eleanor Marx or Tom Mann. Because this was a fundamental principle about the health, as he would have put it, of British society, it did not evolve or soften. Here Lord Robert Cecil, Viscount Cranborne and the Marquis of Salisbury truly fused into the same man and the passions of the 1860s came through quite as sharply thirty years later. All the arguments and prejudices about countenancing revolutionary forces that he had derided in the reform crisis in

---

[72] Salisbury to Dilke, 4 Jun. 1885, Dilke MSS 43876 ff.91–2.
[73] Salisbury to Akers-Douglas, 3 Apr. 1885, Chilston MSS C18.
[74] Salisbury in Lords, 12 May 1893, speaking against the Bishop of London's attempt to introduce a Licensing Boards Bill: *Hansard*, XII, cols. 750–1.
[75] Salisbury to Cranbrook, 18 Dec. 1896, Cranbrook MSS T501/263.

1867, when he resigned from Derby's government rather than remain associated with its flexibility, reappeared in the quieter times of 1884, even though the argument from fear had even less plausibility then than it had in the days of the Hyde Park riots.

> [T]he arguments which are addressed to us having reference to existing agitations, or to impending processions and demonstrations, seem to me the idlest of all. We know perfectly well that demonstrations and expressions of anger can be produced to order by our adversaries so long as the balance at their bankers remains unexhausted. We know that there are plenty of Radicals in this country; and if it pleases them to walk up and down the roads, and spend their Sundays in the Parks, and to do other things from which they derive wholesome exercise, and exhibit themselves in the open air, we know that that gives no indication whatever of the real opinion of the majority of the constituencies, which is the only opinion for which we care, and by which we are bound.[76]

This struck him as a crucial ethical insight as well a constitutional or social one. To permit behaviour outside the law would undermine the existence of any society at all and reduce civilization to the snake-pit. Not least, it would place at risk those social institutions which acted as bastions of private and public personality and allowed the individual some legitimate self-expression. A constitutional monarchy with its parliament and judiciary supplied the framework for such an existence in 'England'. And the point of that constitution lay in upholding law and securing property.

---

[76] Salisbury in Lords, *Hansard*, 8 Jul. 1884, ccxc, col. 468.

CHAPTER 4

Property

CONTRACT

Lord Robert Cecil read for the Bar. It seems a small fact, one made smaller by his never having practised and by the legal luminosity of others, most especially his least favourite Conservative colleague, Hugh McCalmont Cairns, later Earl Cairns, the formidable Lord Chancellor. Small facts can have great weight, none the less – especially when they refer to formative stages of a life and present pointers to how a public figure might develop. Cecil disliked the aridities of the law, to be sure, and even the most sympathetic historical imagination struggles to turn him into a decent lawyer: too much passion, too much temper, not enough human understanding or interest, insufficient flexibility when faced with supposed evil. Yet some of the training and vocabulary stayed with him for the rest of his life and marked the way in which he would respond to particular issues. If we lose this facet, then we lose a crucial part of his mind and situation.

Nowhere does this background impose itself more clearly than in Salisbury's language about property. Doubtless this indebtedness owes something to the existence of well-established sectors of legal studies devoted to the law of land ownership and transfer (with all its Scottish and Irish niceties) and to the complexities of inheritance over which the most unlegal of landlords forever fretted. In Salisbury's case, though, these became subordinated to a wider concern which would expand his conception of society and inform his view of the significance of history. He dwelled repeatedly, insistently and consistently on the inviolability of contractual agreement between consenting parties. And the starting point for any understanding of his despair about the status of property throughout his public career lies in the realization that, for Salisbury, the entire second half of the nineteenth century stood in breach of contract with what had gone before.

It did not begin with Sir Henry Maine, for all the importance of Maine's *Ancient Law* of 1860 and for all Salisbury's respect for Maine as an intellectual figure. It may have originated – certainly he commented on them in retrospect – with the Encumbered Estates Acts of 1848 and 1849, a Whig attempt to intervene in the mechanism of land sale in Ireland to the disadvantage, Cecil argued, of the landowners. It continued through what he conceived to be attacks on the colleges of the ancient universities, when government expressed a wish to amend historic contracts with their founders and benefactors; through a pogrom against hares and rabbits by an ignorant state, an interference with the relationship between tenant and landlord at almost every level, and, most urgently and piteously for the starving aristocracy, through the continual and disastrous meddling with the framework of law in Ireland. All of these matters of high policy require comment and example. But best to begin in a lowlier way, with a letter from Salisbury to a humble person, not his lord chancellor or a cabinet colleague, but to his gardener at Hatfield:

Mr. Bowman,
You have put me to great inconvenience as I have refused other gardeners besides purchasing the furniture you asked for. I have a right to ask for some explanation why having engaged yourself on Tuesday you now refuse to come . . . You are legally bound after having engaged yourself to give me a week's notice before you go: you must give me some reason for breaking your contract.[1]

Nothing could more vividly illustrate the depth of this commitment to contract. It became a life-principle for him, a fundamental approach to thinking about issues that usually involved property but in which the recourse to contract as the essence of the matter would require his intervention. Rarely at ease elsewhere in the role of mentor, Salisbury *taught* his colleagues and his peers about the importance of law.

Ultimately this teaching became a familiar public doctrine which fused with Salisbury's 1890s language about loot, theft and pillage. A speech at Nottingham in 1889 will suffice as exemplar. The audience learns that investment is crucial to everyone's prosperity and that the essential condition for providing security, which is the stimulant for

---

[1] Salisbury to Bowman (draft), n.d. (Jun. 1875), Christ Church MSS, no file.

investors, is a 'scrupulous respect for existing contracts'. Off he then
goes into his robbery motif: 'All kinds of depredation are pleasant at
the moment; you get all you want and nobody is much hurt except
the man who is robbed – and he, of course, doesn't matter. But
depredation becomes unpleasant when you come to want the
assistance of the person robbed and find that you are unable to
obtain it, and that you have lost ten times more by losing your
character for legislative honour than you could possibly secure out of
your ill-gotten gains.'[2] Yet the theme had begun thirty years before
out of a concern about the University of Oxford (a lifelong commitment) and the perennial anxiety that someone, somewhere, had a
plan to do down the church.

The Oxford case turned on two things: first, medieval contracts
undertaken by philanthropists for particular purposes that could not
now (he contended) be overridden and, secondly, on the new
contract enforced by the state after the Commission enquiring into
the University of Oxford reported in an act of Parliament in 1854.
This made the extraction of oaths and declarations no longer
necessary for matriculation or a precondition for obtaining a
bachelor's degree and authorized colleges to amend their statutes
accordingly. When, in 1860, the right of veto on the part of colleges
permitted by that 1854 legislation against ordinances issued by the
University seemed to be under threat from a new measure, Cecil
pounced on it since the bill 'was nothing less than a breach of
contract which was entered into between Parliament on the one
hand, and Oxford University on the other in the year 1854'.[3] The
church had its turn three years later when the burial issue – dead, as
it were, in the twentieth century but very live in the nineteenth –
gave him the opportunity to look behind current claims from
Nonconformists to be buried on church land and draw gasps of
horror by the offensiveness of his resort to contract:

Persons attached to the Church had, of their own free will, given plots of
land in which the services of the Church were to be performed. They had
not given them in order that the services of Dissenters, whether Baptists or

---

[2] Quoted in Cecil, vol. IV, p.164. The contract/investment/stability motif recurred frequently
in Salisbury's post-railway director's experience. So a *point d'appui* for his resistance to
Gladstone's second Irish land act was that 'they have invented a doctrine of free contract
which, if it ever comes to be applied to the industries of this country, will produce the utmost
confusion and the most bitter contention': in Lords, *Hansard*, 1 Aug. 1881, CCLXIV, col. 262.

[3] Cecil in Commons, *Hansard*, 30 Jan. 1860, CLVI, col. 322. Perhaps the anniversary of Charles
I's execution gave his language about parliament and corporations a certain urgency.

Quakers, or Ranters, or Jumpers, should be performed . . . Parliament had of late years played strange tricks with private property, but nothing of the kind had been proposed before . . . [This] was as plain and simple an act of spoliation as if they were to take the Churchyards and convert them into theatres or dancing rooms. [*Cries of* Oh!][4]

Some 'oh's doubtless came from Conservative colleagues, for many of them did not understand the sheer violence of Cecil's manipulation of historical contract as a basis for present argument. They would become more accustomed to its tone when Salisbury modulated it as prime minister to make it sound more responsible.

Meanwhile 'the duty of the state to enforce contracts'[5] and the duty of everybody else to leave them alone appears in the speeches and letters like a mantra. It 1863 it was, burials apart, the case of Joseph George Churchward. The latter has not been much celebrated in the history of nineteenth-century injustice but Cecil became enthusiastic about him. He held a contract, signed in 1859, to convey the mails between Dover and Calais and Dover and Ostend until the contract expired in 1870. The Report of the Committee of Supply announced to the Commons in 1863 that, his contract notwithstanding, no payments would be made to Churchward after 20 June of that year. Cecil contrived to make out that the failure to pay Churchward everything due to him represented an 'attempt to crush an innocent man in order to gratify [Liberal] political passions'. This apparently became clear if '[he] asked the House to consider the question merely as one of contract'. There had been an agreement in 1859 that Mr Churchward 'should have certain services to perform until 1870'; Mr Churchward had consequently invested money in a business; and now the government wished to escape their commitment because they contended he had broken the law. Imagine the cosmic consequences if ministers should succeed in destroying Mr Churchward. 'From this time forwards there would never be any certainty that any contract into which any Government might enter might not be quashed, because some political partisan might afterwards discover that the contractor had been guilty of resorting to corrupt expedients.'[6] Fifteen years later, long after

---

[4] Cecil in Commons, *Hansard*, 15 Apr. 1863, CLXX, col. 146.
[5] Salisbury in Lords, *Hansard*, 26 Jun. 1891, CCCLIV, col. 1577.
[6] Cecil in Commons, *Hansard*, 28 May 1863, CLXX, cols. 2053–6. Cf. Cecil on the Bishops of London and Durham Retirement Bill seven years earlier on the breaking 'of a compact to which the House was asked to set its seal . . . It was not easy to comprehend in what sense the word "contract" should be understood if that was not a contract': *Hansard*, 23 Jul. 1856,

Churchward's memory had faded, it was hares and rabbits that struck Salisbury as embodiments of contract – a conclusion in which he received support from an unlikely quarter, since the Duke of Richmond usually repeated everything that Cairns said when he could understand it and Cairns never said anything that helped Salisbury. Of course, hares and rabbits lived in the world close to the essence of Richmond's existence and he received letters and pleas from landlords of all kinds:

I have had a letter from [Lord] Stradbroke about the Hares and Rabbits Bill. His views I am afraid can not be carried out, to leave matters as they are and to be an arrangement between landlord and tenant – I have told him I agree with him but I am afraid it is too late. I have also a letter from Lord Onslow objecting very much to the use of the gun . . . I have told him that my objection to the Bill was its interference between me and my tenant[.] [A]s to details I do not think they are so important as interfering with freedom of contract.[7]

Salisbury could hardly have said it better, though the worm turned when it suited him.[8] In 1889 the theme returned, quite apart from the Dock Strike and the publication of *Fabian Essays*, with another attack on the constitution by clause 4 of Hart-Dyke's Technical Instruction Bill, which its author may reasonably have taken to be innocuous. Not so the prime minister. He had spotted the phrase 'local authorities' (which always brought out the blue pencil) but also, and worse, 'school boards', set up after 1870 and which Salisbury had already demonized as 'the most recklessly extravagant bodies in England'. He explained his outrage to a presumably bewildered Cranbrook:

I do not know what end [clause 4] is required to serve – but it is a most insidious and dangerous clause – and one to which I should have a very strong objection . . . The Education Act gives power to managers of school boards to violate their trust deed [another Salisbury idiom] so far as is necessary to enable them 'to fulfil the conditions required in pursuance of

---

CXLIII, col. 1281. He lost, as usual: see Cecil to Carnarvon, 15 Aug. 1856, Carnarvon MSS 60758 f.11.

[7] Richmond to Cranbrook, 15 Aug. 1880, Cranbrook MSS T501/257. Salisbury owed nothing to Richmond in his lifelong campaign to resist 'the claim that Parliament has a right to interfere . . . in the contracts between landlord and tenant'. See Salisbury in Lords, *Hansard*, 16 Feb. 1893, VIII, col. 1555.

[8] After receiving an admonition from Hatfield for his supporting compulsory provisions in the Agricultural Holdings Bill in 1882, Richmond swept away at once the familiar mantra: 'I know there is a great deal to be said about interfering with freedom of contract.' Richmond to Salisbury, 20 Jan. 1882, Salisbury MSS (Richmond, f.67).

the Act to be fulfilled in order to obtain a parliamentary grant'. But the clause 4 in the bill goes a great deal further. It gives power to managers of schools to violate their trust deed so far as is necessary to fulfil any conditions of grant laid down *by the school board or local authority*. When we passed the 99th clause of the Education Act we knew what we were doing – we were setting aside trust deeds so far as they were inconsistent with the Act we were passing. But here we are to set aside trust deeds so far as they may be inconsistent with the wholly unknown requirements which any school board or local authority may require in any part of England.[9]

Trust deeds, violation, setting aside, possible escalation all over the country: this passage could form a set text in the understanding of Salisbury's style of resistance-politics at the point where property met law. It so easily became a complicated compound of precision and polemic which mixed the undeniable with the implausible and presented it as a kind of graven wisdom designed to divert 'England' from its wilfully chosen path to ruin.

Contract implied a structure of rights and duties which best defined Salisbury's view of the function of property. It had relevance to any form of ownership but took its special character from land; and when Salisbury remarked about property in general, he usually betrayed a conception of the relationship between a landlord and a tenant with an idealized 'agreement' between them in a written contract relating to period of occupation, rent, powers of eviction and so on. If he spoke of 'the ordinary rights of property,'[10] this was the spatial location for his understanding of what these comprised, just as 1,000 years (or in this case the 600 since the Statute of Merton) frequently supplied its temporal justification. If he became aggressive about assaults on property, he did so predictably during periods of Liberal government and especially in the context of Liberal interference with Irish landlords. This latter context played a role of particular importance, as we shall see, in exposing Conservative conceptions of property and their limits during the last third of the nineteenth century – not so much because of Gladstone's obsession with altering the constitutional status of Ireland after 1885, but through his no less urgent fixation on altering the basis of landlordship in two major land acts of 1870 and 1881. From the Radical point of view this legislation attempted to confine the

---

[9] Salisbury to Cranbrook, 4 Mar. 1888, Cranbrook MSS T501/263. The italics were probably supplied by Salisbury, though it is possible that Cranbrook was highlighting the text for his own purposes. The Bill was withdrawn in July.

[10] In Lords, *Hansard*, 27 Jul. 1893, xv, col. 605.

exploitation of the tenant by absent and unscrupulous landlords during a period of agrarian distress. From Salisbury's, it took the world of parchment in which he believed and set fire to it. 'The Irish Land Act', he wrote in a polemical analysis of 1873, 'has sanctioned the principle that when two parties have made a contract as to land, the State may lawfully step in and wrest it aside in favour of one of them; presenting him with a contingent right to money payments [i.e. reduction of rent] of which, when he made the contract, he never dreamed. The only claim to this act of violence, committed on its behalf, that could be pleaded by the favoured class was that it was organized, unscrupulous, and politically strong.'[11]

By the time of Gladstone and Lord Rosebery's unhappy administrations of 1892–5, much of the battle for Irish land had been lost and the landlords, for whom personally Salisbury had often little respect, had become a class marked by wailing and gnashing of teeth. But the argument over contract he never failed to press, narrowing or widening it as the situation demanded, warning always about the black future which must follow depredation as surely as the night the day:

[The Liberal Government] will follow the last landlord, or landlord's right, to the grave with a dry eye. But I want them to consider that – by that mysterious inter-connection which brings together all human actions and all human procedure, and forces the human mind that has once given way to a particular set of motives to give way to them again on any analogous occasion – other contracts besides those of land will be subjected to the same idea. The feeling will very soon spread that anybody who has a right to anything, and who uses any process of the law to recover it, is liable to the thunders that are pronounced against the evictor and the land-grabber. 'Base is the slave that pays!' That is the philosophy of the future.[12]

The difficulty of the position he adopted was twofold. First, it left little room for change of any kind, even change in order to conserve, because every amendment of former practice involved an implied rupture of 'contract' between parties who might, had they been alive in the present, have approved the change but who could no longer do so. Secondly, it rested on an image of Conservative property that bore increasingly little resemblance to the complicated patterns of wealth-holding and generation that characterized Salisbury's own

---

[11] 'The Progress of the Radicals', (Oct. 1873), in Paul Smith, *Lord Salisbury on Politics: A Selection from his Articles in the* Quarterly Review, *1860–1880* (Cambridge, 1972), p. 322.

[12] In Lords, *Hansard*, 14 Aug. 1894, XXVIII, cols. 961–2.

period of experience. He spoke not only on behalf of a class whose economic power had waned but in favour of a conception of property more suited to Palmerston's era than his own.

REALTY VERSUS REALITY

Land was alpha and omega, beginning and end. It supplied to the Conservative understanding something far beyond economic interest through its vocabulary of aspiration, duty, virtue, stability, influence, deference, propriety. It provided natural space in the imagination for the good and memorable characters encountered in Jane Austen, Sir Walter Scott and Anthony Trollope. Its woods and fields coloured the mental landscape as much as the visual. It supported the villages that Tories treated as though they had sprouted from the soil; it caught the shadow of spires deemed by Anglicans the tallest of its trees. But the images and resonances seemed harder to sustain once the impact of rural depression made selfish interest a more urgent subject than poetry and rendered the security of an income from ownership a bitter fiction. From the end of the 1870s, the *problem* of land became a theme and the realities of trying to defend it – or agreeing to sell it – acquired their own persistence. Information derived from the so-called 'new Domesday Book', based on data from 1873, helped blur the picture in some ways by confirming the Conservative instinct that most land was held by a very small number of people. John Bateman, who popularised the material in his *Great Landowners of Great Britain and Ireland*, reckoned that a mere 1 per cent of proprietors owned around 60 per cent of landed wealth. His figures are certainly open to question: the original data had excluded London from the reckoning (a major omission in the late nineteenth century) and counted acres rather than their capital values when many of the largest acreages earned next to nothing. A recent analysis suggests instead, in the wake of such doubts, that perhaps only 30 per cent of land in Bateman's day remained in upper-class or wealthy hands.[13] Nor does it always seem the case for historians, as it did to contemporaries, that rent plummeted during the great depression after 1873. If one takes into account urban rents, often mushrooming in this period, and the opportunities provided

---

[13] See the important observations of Avner Offer, *Property and Politics 1870–1914: Landownership, Law, Ideology and Urban Development in England* (Cambridge, 1981), pp. 106–7.

for landowners by railway development, mining and so on, rents seem to have stabilized at around 12–14 per cent of national income which is not very different from the proportion observed in previous periods.[14] Nor was it the case that moor and heather raised no money: renting them out to the guns of an aspirant *bourgeoisie*, as on the Galloway estate, brought considerable reward for little effort. Perception, however, moved in a different groove and it is perception that informs behaviour and shapes that world of judgement that is our subject.

The more mundane forms of this perception looked to land as a form of investment, at least until 1880. In the case of the Duke of Richmond, it dominated his entire outlook. At seven in the morning we find him in the saddle, trotting around his farms, speaking knowledgeably to tenants and labourers about every aspect of agriculture and horticulture. His anxiety is that government will interfere in what it knows nothing about – setting up Boards of Agriculture to confuse the farmers or threatening his return from salmon (one of the many happy consequences of owning a stretch of the Spey).[15] In Derby's case the motive was security rather than profit in 1875. His solicitor ran through the possibilities: mortgages (not very safe and difficult to find the right property for the amount one had to invest); railway debentures (hard to find an outlet for a large sum); Indian securities ('too high'); and then the buying of land, which would pay little back but which would be safer than anything else.[16] This view did not endure far into the depression with the Land Wars in Ireland, the crofting agitation in Scotland and the perceived crisis of rent in England. Even in 1875 the time was not far away when Salisbury would describe 'the supposed security of an income from real estates, which was its great charm' as 'now a matter of past history'.[17] Yet for all its ownership having become grounds for condolence rather than envy, land and its farming remained a Tory preoccupation long after economics recommended

---

[14] *Ibid.*, p. 105.

[15] As early as 1868 Richmond reported an income 'to me *clear* [of] about seven or eight thousand a year' from ten miles of water at the mouth of the Spey: an astonishing profit and a considerable investment. Richmond to Hardy, 2 Apr. 1868, Cranbrook MSS T501/257.

[16] Diary, 9 Nov. 1875, in Derby, *Diaries*, p.250. The depth of this rejection across generations is emphasized when one notes that Derby's father had already decided to get rid of these estates and that his brother decided to take cash rather than Irish land as his inheritance. Information from John Vincent.

[17] Salisbury to Cairns, 30 Dec. 1881, Cairns MSS 30/51/6/f.64.

that it should. Conservatives ranted about the insanity of governments (including their own) who tried to make tenants better off at the expense of the landlord. 'Where is the law', Lord Stradbroke wanted to know, 'to make tenants liable for reducing the value of a farm by bad cultivation so that no respectable tenant would hire it[?] I have nine farms thrown up in this sad state, and have lost two whole years' rent in restoring them.'[18] They pined for their hares and rabbits, which Gladstone seemed determined to take away with the vindictive swipe of someone who could not tell a turnip from a cucumber, leaving even Salisbury with the 'dim apprehension that we shall none of us have any rents, rabbits or religion when the session is over'.[19] And they became still further consumed with worry about the Tory disease.

There is a certain irony in the wake of the 1990s, surrounded by the greatest disaster to affect beef cattle in the twentieth century, to recall how *normal* was cattle disease as a Victorian fact of life. Cattle plague (or the German form *Rinderpest* from about 1865) could with little exaggeration be characterized as the continuo of agricultural politics in the second half of the century with a fluctuating insistence. Richmond, not Cairns, became on these occasions the man who could save England. Consulted by Disraeli himself, sent down to agricultural meetings to put the government case, rubbishing the ignorance of those looking for quick solutions, patronizing urban politicians for knowing nothing about agricultural markets or the history of the problem, the Duke discovered political status and revelled in it.[20] Farming MPs had this issue on their minds as they listened to speeches on parliamentary reform or foreign policy, for it cut closest to home by threatening their livelihood. It cut Salisbury by threatening his credibility as co-leader of a party that supposedly championed farmers' interests; so when the issue of cattle disease again pressed in 1883–4, he put considerable pressure on Richmond to do something beyond stating that he had the situation under control. 'Pray think over the possibility of proposing *something*,' he

---

[18] Stradbroke to Richmond, 9 Aug. 1880, Goodwood MSS 869 c 50.

[19] Onslow to Richmond, 10 Aug. 1880, Goodwood MSS 869 c 51–2; Salisbury to Lady Manners, 8 Jul. 1880, Cecil, vol. III, p. 36.

[20] 'I hope I have got the better of the Cattle plague': Richmond to Cranbrook, 30 May 1877, Cranbrook MSS T501/257. For the most concerning outbreak, see Arvel B. Erickson, 'The Cattle Plague in England, 1865–67', *Agricultural History*, 35 (1961), pp. 94–103. Cf. John R. Fisher, 'Cattle Plagues Past and Present: The Mystery of Mad Cow Disease', *Journal of Contemporary History*, 33 (1998), pp. 215–28.

urged in the spring of 1883. 'It is a question on which we shall carry
with us *all* our friends, both Landlords & tenants: & in that respect it
has the advantage over the compensation question in dealing with
wh. we should certainly tread heavily on the toes of some of our
landlord friends.'[21] Richmond remained immovable, both now and
when Salisbury returned to the charge during the following year, out
of a congenital hostility to countenancing interference with property
and relations between landlord and tenant, as well as his usual
suspicion of Salisbury as a man of extreme and sometimes impenetrable views.

What he did concede was that those who owned considerable
acreages needed tenants to farm them; and how to secure and hang
on to good tenants in sufficient numbers to make the system operate
smoothly became the critical dimension of landed property in the
last two decades of the century. Salisbury was used to thinking in
large numbers when he discussed acreages and capital value. He did
not lose sight, however, of the political strength of a smallholder
society. When Richmond's long-awaited report came close to its
appearance in 1882, Salisbury pressed the point on its author as a
key ingredient in a Conservative view of landed property. His earnestness lost itself, as usual, in wit:

The great difficulty seems to me to be to make any legislation on this matter
elastic enough – so as to suit not only rich soils & enterprising cultivation –
but also the more modest aspirations of those who have got poor soils & do
not care to risk much upon them. Moreover I hope we shan't sweep away
the *gradation* of tenantry – & leave nothing but big capitalist farms, who go
in for radical politics because their wives are not admitted to county society.
Be merciful to primitive Hodge.[22]

It had not escaped the Conservative leader in the House of Lords
that primitive Hodge was about to get the vote. Like villa Toryism in
the towns, there was a good deal of farmhouse Toryism in the
countryside to be cultivated. Salisbury's rural vision after 1880 found
a balance betweeen owner and tenant and a sense of Conservative
mutual dependence. It was not a soft-centred image: very few of
those projected themselves from Hatfield. The balance required firm
control and representation from all sides, particularly in any political

---

[21] Salisbury to Richmond, 31 Mar. 1883, Goodwood MSS 871 d 13–14; by the following
January the backbench expert on the rural community, Chaplin, discovered '[t]he
agricultural mind . . . red hot upon the question': *ibid.*, d 22.
[22] Salisbury to Richmond, 15 Apr. 1882, Goodwood MSS 871 d 4.

organizations, such as the proposed County Boards of the early 1880s, where 'the two classes [ought to be] sharing the votes in equal proportions'. This was the only way, he told Northcote, 'in which any reliable security for Conservative interests [was] to be looked for'.[23]

His colleagues were not averse to small tenants. They simply could not find any. During the 1880s the problem seemed patchy, with farms standing empty in some places and finding takers easily enough elsewhere. So the agricultural districts generally reflected the particular experience of Lord John Manners and W. H. Smith (the latter now a country landowner). 'The farming affairs are a little less unprosperous,' Manners reassured Smith in 1883; 'but, like you, my brother has still several farms in hand. In Derbyshire on the contrary every farm is occupied, and every rent paid.'[24] Compared with disasters taking place in the Irish countryside, this seemed tolerable and there was always the hope that the cycle would reverse and land become a desirable investment again. But it did not happen. By the mid-1890s, before the upturn around 1896, the situation had become desperate for landowners in many parts of the country with no one to work the farms, so unattractive had the investment become. Salisbury's solicitude for tenants had turned into a pugnacity for property generally and a determination to squash any attempt by (Liberal) government to make owners do what they did not want to do.[25] Richmond had an especially black time and would have been happy to have the soil swallow him up by 1898, replying to Cranborne's complaints with still louder moans. 'I am like you a fellow sufferer,' he wrote, after the summer months of 1895 had left parts of his Sussex estate an unvisited desert:

I have seven farms on hand all on the north side of the downs in that valley that connects the Midhurst Road and the Petworth Road . . . They are mostly sheep farms and as sheep are very high in Price now they ought to be made to pay. I hope not to lose money by them. The Strange thing is no one will come to *look* at them: It is not a question of *rent*. No one *asks* about them. I can not imagine what is to be done. I have suspended any outlay upon Buildings. I have told the tenants they must put up with what they

[23] Salisbury to Northcote, 20 Jan. n.d. [1883], Iddesleigh MSS 50020 f.54.
[24] Manners to Smith, 27 Jan. 1883, Hambledon MSS P58/61.
[25] See his reply to Herschell's attempt to abolish settlements in estates in order to diffuse land among more owners, Lords, *Hansard*, 25 Apr. 1887, cccxiii, col. 1771; and his anti-compulsionist mood about small-holdings and the crofters: Salisbury to Balfour, 28 Jan. 1892, *Salisbury–Balfour Correspondence*, pp. 390–1.

have got. The necessary outlay of Capital is very serious in as much as I have to borrow it.

I have of course to keep my labour Bill as low as possible. I do not see what more can be done at present. I should put down in grass any land not necessarily kept in arable. I mean for the sake of growing roots &c for the keep of Stock.[26]

The situation left Salisbury himself depressed and impotent. He had 3,000 acres that were not producing a penny of profit and there seemed nothing to be done but to wait for better times, *pace* 'our agricultural friends' who thought he ought to be able to do something about it.[27]

Against this portrait of property in crisis, place a rather different one. These individuals who felt so racked by their lack of rents and so oppressed by their inferiors in the rural social scale often drew most of their income, and thus the basis of their property, from activities far removed from farming. Many of them owned land on which stood, not barns and dairies, but hotels and railway stations. Bury in Lancashire and Eastbourne in Sussex grew up on land owned largely by the Tory Earl of Derby and the Whig Duke of Devonshire respectively.[28] Millions of pounds would, for similar reasons, eventually pour into the coffers of Hugh Lupus, newly created first Duke of Westminster, not from rural rents but those escalating city rents due to him as owner of so many acres on which the West End of London rose.[29] For the Tory Londonderrys, a vast mansion in the fashionable West End became possible not through the ownership of land in itself but rather through the possession of coalfields. Others, like Salisbury himself for a time, experimented with commercial directorships – in a railway company, perhaps, or, in the case of the seriously rich W. H. Smith, with exploiting their

---

[26] Richmond to Cranbrook, 11 Oct. 1895, Cranbrook MSS T501/257. Three years later he still had five farms on hand with no interest shown in any of them and the prospect of lambing 3,000 ewes without help. To Cranbrook, 18 Feb. 1898, T501/257. In Scotland, a neighbour of Balfour's had a farm that formerly he had let for £900. As early as 1885 the most he could get was £150. Sidgwick's diary, 30 Sep. 1885, in A. and E. M. Sidgwick, *Henry Sidgwick: A Memoir* (1906), p. 425.

[27] Salisbury to Cranbrook, 19 Dec. 1895, Cranbrook MSS T501/263.

[28] For Bury, see H. J. Hanham, *Elections and Party Management: Politics in the Time of Disraeli and Gladstone* (Hassocks, 1978), pp. 79–80, 284–322; for Eastbourne, David Cannadine, *Lords and Landlords* (Leicester, 1980), pp. 229–417.

[29] This Whig duke (1825–1899) married a daughter of the Duke of Sutherland and extended thus his connexion with vast territories. As in the case of the Bedfords, however, but to a still greater degree, London remained the nub. The Westminsters' London wealth has remained unrivalled.

platforms and foyers. Further down the social scale, marriage-worthy beer and whisky had their attractions as a business as well as a pastime and 'Merchant' became, as seen in the last chapter, a familiar descriptor in the parliamentary manuals of backbench Toryism. So, although rural preoccupation bit hard during the dragging depression, *money* had not dried up: it flowed and coursed through Tory politics by finding new ways to follow. Rarely had large-scale money so readily grown among those in the position to seek it and possessing the courage to try. When the Registrar of Births, Marriages and Deaths reported in 1858, his figures suggested that only sixty-eight estates at death ran to £100,000 or more. In 1900/1901 the number of millionaires had not changed much – nine as opposed to seven in 1858 – but there were now 298 estates valued at over £100,000.[30] And while more than half of the 1858 cohort could attract a label derived from landed society – 'gentleman' or 'esquire' – very different categories were needed by the turn of century to depict the *nouveaux riches*.

From the carriages of the very rich there fell very little muck or brass. Indeed the period from about 1880 imposed a pattern of wealth that has largely persisted in Britain – a movement away from land as the sole repository of capital and enterprise and a trajectory towards commerce and the vastly important (and fragile) structures of banking. Thus the historian of the phenomenon stresses that 'the wealthy in Britain have disproportionately earned their fortunes in commerce and finance – that is as merchants, bankers, shipowners, merchant bankers and stock and insurance agents and brokers, rather than in manufacturing or industry'.[31] When W. H. Smith shortened his life by trying to save Barings in 1890[32] – poignantly, granted what a single employee would do to the house a century later – he presented to posterity a cameo of the new politics of property: a man from the middle classes responding, as perhaps he best could, to the challenge of wealth from a German-Danish banking family, watched over, of course, by George Joachim Goschen, who ran the Exchequer with the aplomb expected from a

---

[30] W. D. Rubinstein, *Men of Property: The Very Wealthy in Britain since the Industrial Revolution* (1981), p. 30.

[31] *Ibid.*, p. 61.

[32] Barings had extended themselves to a dangerous, indeed all but catastrophic, degree, through speculations in the fast-growing but unstable South American market and by 1890 they were nearly £20 million adrift. Smith helped Goschen and the Bank of England put together a life-raft.

German Jewish family. That Jewishness, moreover, had become as important as it was new in Tory politics. Long gone were the days in which Lord Robert Cecil had deprecated the admission of Jews to parliament, as he had with such dedicated offensiveness in 1858. From 1880 Jews had to be seen as part of the parliamentary classes because they had become part of the Tory classes: a new and highly significant twist in the account of Conservative wealth. Possibly given some impetus by the racial flavour of Gladstonian pronouncement on the Turkish question in 1876, possibly enhanced by Beaconsfield's magisterial and now thoroughly-accepted figure through the same period, possibly spurred by the Rothschilds' crossing to the Tory side in the 1880s, Anglo-Jewry brought its paramount financial weight over to Conservative politics at exactly the time when its domination of certain social strata, particularly that of the super-rich merchant class, approached its zenith.[33]

Juxtaposing these two images of rural traditionalism and urban novelty helps sharpen a particular problem. Why did Conservative strategy so frequently dwell on the difficulties faced by land when land had ceased to be the central pillar of economic interest? An easy answer speaks about a general cultural mind-set in Britain – one that could no more free itself from an atavistic longing and a revulsion against 'trade' than could seventeenth-century hidalgos inspire commercialism in Spain.[34] Undoubtedly some Conservatives lived mentally in the 1850s when they should have been assessing the developments of the 1880s. If any political thinkers suffer from time-lag, after all, Tories stand high among them. But there seems more than this to the preoccupation. Beyond the land and its agricultural management, much revolution was clearly taking place. It was happening also, however, within landed society and politics. The collapse of land as a foundation of civilized society appeared unprecedented in this generation's experience. Most of the parliamentary Conservative party of the 1880s and 1890s had grown up through a time of peaceful development on the land and considerable growth in the landed economy, apart from the beginning of rural unrest among the labourers after 1870. Grandfathers' stories of

---

[33] Cf. Geoffrey Alderman, *Modern British Jewry* (Oxford, 1992), pp. 100–1. Rubinstein calculates that, of thirty-one merchant millionaires at the end of the nineteenth century, twenty-four were Jewish.

[34] The thesis of cultural blocking was advanced in Martin Wiener, *English Culture and the Decline of the Industrial Spirit* (Cambridge, 1982).

bread or blood, of Captain Swing, of tithe riots: these things belonged to a time before Peel had made the world safe. Of course they expected competition; and with the manifest opening of the wheatfields of Canada and the United States and then the coming of refrigerated ships with their threat to flood Britain with imports of cheap foreign meat, the future could only hold difficulty. There were further exasperations in the American Henry George's perambulations around Britain and his insistence that rent lay at the heart of all evil, together with repeated moves towards a graduated death duty that found its eventual outlet in Harcourt's famous budget of 1894.[35] ('We are all Socialists now.') Yet there was a further situation over which historians of Liberalism spill their life's blood and which historians of Conservatism sometimes occlude or neglect. Once Gladstone took it into his head to pacify Ireland, no one could read a newspaper without watching the unravelling of a culture at the very core of which lay the landlord and his tenants' contested concept of property. Every burned rick, each hamstrung bullock, the tortured narratives of eviction, boycotting and despair: all of them had an eastern aspect or an English resonance. Between 1870 and 1903 there was neither a moment's respite for Conservative property in Ireland nor any confidence, whatever the result of a particular engagement, that the siege of proprietors could be lifted.

ALIENATING IRELAND

Historians of British politics often think instinctively of nineteenth-century Ireland as a Whig property. Those immense acreages and rent-rolls come to mind at once when thinking of the Irish aristocracy: the Marquis of Lansdowne's 130,000 acres, for example, nearly 100,000 of them in Kerry, Earl Fitzwilliam and his 90,000 acres in Wicklow, the Duke of Devonshire and the quarter of that vast estate that lay in Cork and Waterford, the Earl of Bessborough's substantial holdings in Kilkenny and Carlow, or Dufferin's in Down. Nor is the association illusory, before 1886 at least. It proclaims itself repeatedly throughout the list of Irish landowners even though the names were

---

[35] Churchill was playing with the idea in the days before his spectacular resignation in 1886. And it is pertinent that Salisbury objected to the death-duty notion less for its intrinsic un-Toryness than because it would affect realty disproportionately and become 'more of a grievance to the landowner than the fundholder': Salisbury to Balfour, 18 Dec. 1886, Balfour MSS SRO GD433/2/29.

better known to Irish society than to English unless they played a part in politics as representative peers or as MPs. Palmerston, their most famous alumnus, had hardly needed to fear social exclusion in London society. Viscount Powerscourt frequently came up in Westminster conversations during the period – close to forty years – that he served as a representative peer in the House of Lords; so his 53,000 acres in Wicklow and Wexford had their own voice. Similarly, the Marquis of Clanricarde's 60,000 acres in Galway had helped him to a seat there in 1867 (as Viscount Bourke). Or one might take the traditional route to glory by marrying a Big Whig, as did the Duke of Leinster who potentially attached tracts of Scotland to his 70,000 acres in Kildare by marrying a daughter of the Duke of Sutherland. How very different was the Irishness of these grandees from that of the Tory party's leadership. Men like Hartington (later Duke of Devonshire) and Lansdowne with their Irish experience were set for the highest office within Whig/Liberal politics until the crisis of 1886 blew it all apart. But Salisbury, Derby, Richmond, Northcote, Beach, Smith – all of them owners of landed property – possessed scarcely a foot of land in Ireland. Peel, for his part, went so far as to insist in his will that no portion of his bequest was to be invested there.[36] Derby had admittedly once had some Irish property. He got rid of it when Gladstone's Irish land act first began to have an effect in 1871 and he cited, interestingly, four reasons for his sense of relief at having cut his losses:

First, the annoyance of the land act, and the attitude of the tenantry, making it practically impossible even to change the boundaries of a farm without the consent of the occupier: next the effect of the church disestablishment [of 1869], which would have thrown on me, as nearly the largest proprietor in Tipperary, the burden of supporting half the Protestant clergy in that country [*sic*]: thirdly, the general feeling of disaffection which prevails throughout the south of Ireland, making it impossible to look forward to a safe future: and lastly, the wish to diminish encumbrances by the sale of an estate which gave me neither pleasure nor influence.[37]

This was not the way to contest Whig supremacy but it did display a moment of signal prescience on Derby's part, for the time was soon

---

[36] Malmesbury's diary, 15 Jan. 1854, in James Harris, *Memoirs of an Ex-Minister: An Autobiography* (2 vols., 1884), p. 323.

[37] Diary, 1 Jan. 1872, in Derby, *Diaries*, p. 95. The increase in his net income of £2,000 a year through the sale perhaps also made a difference.

to come when acquiring land in Ireland would become an affliction meriting messages of sympathy rather than congratulation.

An image of Whig stewardship in Ireland nevertheless requires considerable refocussing. The close relationship between the Irish peerage and Whig/Liberal politics can be overstated (none of the five great families who cleaved to Gladstone in 1886 owned Irish land[38]) and, once Gladstone's Irish obsessions became clear in the mid-1880s, the landed Irish moved solidly towards the Conservative party as their only hope of salvation from land acts, arrears acts and a politics of 'selling out'. The massive holdings of the Marquis of Sligo (115,000 acres in Mayo) turned from Liberal to Unionist in colour after 1886, for example, a process that often produced a contentious generational divide when sons saw the direction of the wind from Westminster and took cover, as did Donegal's brother when he succeeded to the Marquisate in 1885, Fitzwilliam's son as MP for Wakefield after 1895, and the Earl of Normanton's son when he succeeded to that Irish peerage in the following year. The young Viscount Clifden had no son or wife but dragged his piece of Kilkenny toward the Conservative camp on his own account before pneumonia took him off at the age of thirty-one.[39] Gladstone frequently declared himself happy to be rid of his Whigs, and with some justification: they promised a future full of recalcitrance and negativity. Tories are more used to these things and accommodate their implications more freely. But the acquisition of Irish land via Whig landlords did nothing to suggest stability and it would imply that a Conservative leadership should have listened to people whom they had not previously taken too seriously; and their failure to do so would bring all too audible frictions in the later 1880 and 1890s. Few men are so resentful as those plucked from the waves and then dropped again.

A second point about Irish property complements this unease over Whig supremacy. Much of it had never been Whig in the first place. It is not simply that the Whigs dazzle through the glamour of their estates and palaces; one comes across Tories like the Earl of Lucan

---

[38] Granville, Harcourt, Kimberley, Rosebery, Spencer. Granville did not own land on any scale in England or Scotland either: his fortune (and future lack of one) depended on failing industrial concerns from which only Derby's generosity saved him.

[39] He had 35,000 acres in Kilkenny. It seems to have been a doomed family: Clifden's father had scarcely made his fortieth birthday before he succumbed to 'softening of the brain' (*Complete Peerage*, vol. III, p. 289).

who, with his seat in England and his 60,000 acres in Mayo, could look any Whig potentate in the eye.[40] The Earls of Longford and Rosse, similarly, could at least look them in the waistcoat buttons.[41] But the pattern of Tory landowning in Ireland was generally different, with more spread of property into smaller lots and consequently a lower social profile which masks the extent of Tory presence. Some followed Lucan's example in holding land on both sides of the Irish Sea. The Stanhopes made a particular mark both politically and intellectually. Their 14,000 acres were located for the most part in the region of their seat at Chevening but their 2,000 acres in Queen's County kept interest alive in the future of Irish landlords.[42] Or take the case of Lord Templemore, who reversed this emphasis. His seat near Basingstoke brought with it 2,500 acres but these seem derisory when compared with the 23,000 stretched across Wexford, Donegal and Londonderry. Lord Rathdonnell managed to get his name on the deeds of land from eight counties, Lord Portarlington from four, Lord Ormathwaite on two neat parcels of 11,000 acres in Kerry and Cork, while simultaneously speaking for Tory interests in the less revolutionary district of Leominster in Herefordshire. The coupling of land with a parliamentary seat proved as common, of course, in Ireland as anywhere else. Edward King-Harman lacked a peerage but did not lack land – over 70,000 acres bunched in Longford, Roscommon and Sligo – and though the latter constituted his smallest holding, it sufficed to support his Tory seat. Sir Roger Palmer's 80,000 acres likewise did him no harm in Mayo, Sir James Stronge got by on 13,000 in Armagh, and Lords Templetown and Trevor managed famously in, respectively, Antrim and County Down.[43] These are points of light on a dark landscape,

[40] Although the seventh Earl (1851–1928) never acquired the fame of the sixth, he was a representative peer after 1890 and married into the Bessboroughs.

[41] Longford owned 15,000 acres in Westmeath and the County of Dublin; Rosse 24,000 acres in King's County and Tipperary.

[42] The most political was the second son of the fifth Earl, Edward Stanhope, who sat for Lincolnshire seats from 1874, was under-secretary at the India Office in the 'Derby' reshuffle of 1878, and held first the Colonial Office and then the War Office in the Salisbury government of 1886. Died 1893. His father was the noted historian and scholar (*History of England from the Peace of Utrecht* (7 vols., 1836–54), *Life of the Rt. Hon. William Pitt* (4 vols., 1861)); and his elder brother, the sixth Earl (1838–1905), likewise distinguished himself intellectually as antiquary to the Royal Academy for half a century from 1855.

[43] Sir Roger Palmer (b. 1832) sat for Mayo, 1857–65. Sir James Stronge held Armagh for a decade after 1864. Lord Templetown crowned military glory at the Alma and Inkerman with the Antrim seat from 1859–63. Lord Trevor embodied County Down at Westminster for thirty-five years.

possibly, but a picture begins to evolve of quiet solidity rather than glamour, with a Tory section of the ascendancy resting on pieces of land around the 10,000–30,000 acre mark, often broken into a series of sub-plots and with an owner who frequently had a career in the army and whose clubs were Dublin clubs as frequently as St James's ones.

Dispersed ownership of this kind provided Westminster with a pressure group hovering around the lower levels of Tory political society with some strength on the Commons' backbenches and among representative peers when they could be enticed from their estates. Yet Ireland mattered more than the dimensions of this direct influence might imply. So long as Ireland remained across the sea, granted, its undoubted difficulties could sink to the depth of Scotland's without arousing English preoccupation. On the other hand, when the Fenians attacked the mainland, as contemporaries would have phrased it, in the 1860s and when Ulster doctrines of tenant-right upset the English farmers' representatives during the same decade,[44] Ireland crept closer to the centre of politics, and worried those who controlled it . But then, in the 1870s and 1880s, the sea all but dried up as the custodians of an 'English' structure of property and law found themselves staring at the dissolution of law in Ireland, the stark alternatives of concession or coercion, the spectre of Irish landlords losing the soil to their tenants with the apparent consent, even blessing, of the Mother of Parliaments. Perhaps that is why so many accounts of these years talk about the land acts of 1870 and 1881 and their various amendments and extensions as though they amounted to essays in Gladstonian politics rather than developments in Tory psychology. Certainly the narrative unfurled around Irish grievance, Irish intractability and the Liberal search for answers. Its subtext could be read, all the same, as a story about the future of 'English' property. For it was not only Salisbury who put an edge on his language about Ireland and the tearing up of contract. Many of those who had never been there, had no relatives there, knew nobody from there, who despised all that they had heard about that miserable Celtic fastness, brought to their discussion of Irish landed property a bloodiness of mind that could only reflect a fear over matter. Refracted in the colours of Ireland

[44] For the Fenians, see John O'Leary, *Recollections of Fenians and Fenianism* (1896) and John Newsinger, *Fenianism in Mid-Victorian Britain* (1994).

they saw light from England returning to them and striped in darker bands. Ireland became the prism of English Conservative anxiety.

Naturally the bands became displaced toward the red end of the spectrum. Both parties had worried or enthused about the 1870 Land Act; but for Tories the Agricultural Holdings Bill of 1875 seemed an English and dismal corollary. For Liberals the land act of 1881 held the centre of their attention when speaking of Irish property. For Conservatives the Arrears Act of 1882 formed the greater concern. For Liberals the Home Rule issue dominated all in 1885–6. For Tories, the land act of 1887, because it was a *Conservative* action, provoked party crisis. For Liberals the period after 1886 lost itself in the single and doomed obsession of giving Ireland Home Rule. Among Conservatives the same period reflected alternative emphases of coercing the Irish into submission and the partially successful strategy of finding ways in which tenants could be helped to purchase their own land. And it would be Tory trimming, caught in the veering winds of Unionism, rather than Radical utopianism that would make the greater mark in giving Ireland back to the Irish.

The land act of 1870 became a bench-mark in Conservative memory within which it would become the initiator of a process that no one could stop. By making the landlord pay tenants compensation for 'improvements' that they may have made to the property, or for 'disturbance' suffered by tenants when landlords carried out their own projects, it implied a structure of rights in the land that landlords vigorously rejected. At the time, it was the scale of the compensation that seemed disturbing – as much as the equivalent of seven years' rent which, granted that rent normally would be assessed as one-twentieth of the value, made the tenant a part-owner of one-third of the property. 'It is not easy', Derby wrote when the details of the bill emerged, 'to see by what arguments a transfer of property of this nature is to be justified.'[45] Justification depended, as so often in the next thirty years, on the plea of exceptional circumstances, but those who knew Irish circumstances better than Gladstone remained firmly unpersuaded that any piece of legislation would achieve much on behalf of law and justice in a country run increasingly by the gun, knife and rope. Lord Doneraile claimed to know a great deal about Ireland's problems and confessed to Richmond, who always understood when land felt threatened, that

---

[45] Diary, 16 Feb. 1870, in Derby, *Diaries*, p. 50.

he could not see where changing the land law in this way would help anybody, because even if the tenants gained something from the Act there was nothing to prevent them returning to their ancient methods of getting more through 'an appeal to the blunderbuss!'[46] After a few years the effects had become plain enough. The act had not worked as a remedy for unrest but it had alienated landlords to the point that they wanted nothing to do with any Conservative adventures in the direction of greater 'tenant right':

> Mr. Gladstone's land bill has hit us very hard; I can no longer let my land for fair value; and some of the decisions [over] questions of indemnity for removing tenants have been most painfully oppressive on Landlords . . . By the Land bill, if I wish to take up the land let to a pauper tenant for £10 a year, I must give him seven years rent, 70£!!! being fully $\frac{1}{3}$ of the value of the land.[47]

It was all beginning to sink in.

Conservatives would naturally have preferred not to interfere in English land law in the ways in which Gladstone had so disturbingly compromised the Irish. But England had its own troubles. The so-called 'revolt of the field' on the part of Joseph Arch's agricultural labourers, combined with news of a better deal for Irish tenants, meant that the issue of rural relations could not be kept out of practical politics. Richmond's greatest fear, perhaps, was that some form of Ulster practice would find its way across the ocean and swamp English tradition by making the so-called 'Lincolnshire custom' the rule rather than an exception, a consummation to lament not only because of its theoretical implications for political economy but because of the fear – so dear to Richmond – of 'practical difficulties' and because it would turn, like most Tory things, into 'the thin end of the wedge'.[48] The Agricultural Holdings

---

[46] Doneraile to Richmond, 17 Mar. 1870, Goodwood MSS 862 v 70. The eighth Viscount, Doneraile clocked up thirty-two years as a representative peer (1855–87) on the basis of his landed strength with nearly 30,000 acres in Cork and Waterford. Died in 1887 after a bite from a rabid fox.

[47] Stradbroke to Richmond, 17 Jan. 1875, Goodwood MSS 867 a 18. The second Earl (1794–1886), Stradbroke was an Irish Wellingtonian relic: he had been born early enough (just) to have served in the Iberian and Dutch campaigns at the close of the Napoleonic Wars. Bateman gives him no Irish land in his survey of *The Great Landowners of Britain and Ireland*, based on data from 1876: the Stradbroke estate lay then entirely in Suffolk, of which he was lord lieutenant for over forty years. Presumably the Irish holding had been sold in 1875/6. It seems plausible that such land had existed through Stradbroke's maternal family. Also likely that he was a Mason, like his son and grandson.

[48] Richmond to Cairns, 12 Dec. 1873, Cairns MSS 30/50/2/ff.144–5.

Act, introduced by Disraeli's government in 1875, avoided some of Gladstone's calamities and did its best to avoid Ireland's. It was given, in the first place, to the Duke of Richmond as the spokesman most likely to keep agricultural opinion with him. It fostered, secondly, its particular rhetoric which depended on there being a crisis of food production in the country and a corresponding need to bring the maximum improvement to the land. The argument gave Richmond an opportunity to say that the main obstacle to food production could be traced to the insecurity of any capital that tenants might wish to invest in their holdings; so the Irish cure could be provided with an English disease. In a tentative and uncomfortable presentation, Richmond persuaded the peers that a bill of this kind had to happen *despite* its undeniable interference with contract. He sweetened the pill by making compensation for improvement payable only where the letting value of the farm reflected a clear increment as a result of the tenant's investment.[49] Even Salisbury swallowed it. Indeed, he showed himself combative for a while about bad landlords who 'have no more right to rent than a pickpocket who is made to give up his neighbour's pocket handkerchief'.[50] He found the language harder to sustain as the demands for further concessions to tenants increased and the rights of landlords degenerated into a legal fiction.

Between the summer of 1880 and the summer of 1882, Salisbury went badly wrong in his political judgement of Irish property, so much so that the end of the 1882 session left his ability to lead the Conservatives in the House of Lords open to serious question. His own instincts remained unchanged and it might all have worked better had he followed them. His profound pessimism over the 1880 election and his fears of a 'Socialistic anti-rent agitation' organized by Michael Davitt, combined with an impending nervous collapse that would send him off to the south of France for the winter, left him violent about one of the Liberals' first moves – a Compensation for Disturbance Bill that he saw as nothing more than 'a suspension of

---

[49] See Rutland, speaking *vice* Richmond, in Lords on committee stage of the Agricultural Holdings Bill, and Richmond's later glosses on his remarks: *Hansard*, 22 Apr. 1875, CCXXIII, cols. 1422–41. Cf. Derby's encomium on the level-headedness of the Lords on this occasion: 'I never heard a better or more thorough sifting of the clauses of a bill. No long speeches, and very little nonsense.' Diary, 22 Apr. 1875, in Derby, *Diaries*, p. 209. The bill sought to define a category of 'unexhausted improvement' and arranged periods of expiry for compensation under three classes of improvement.

[50] Salisbury to Cross, 3 May 1875, Cross MSS 51263 ff.10–11.

eviction, and, consequently, a suspension of rent'.[51] But what really concerned him, like all Tories, was the impending land bill that would plainly go further than the loathed act of 1870. In Nice over New Year, Salisbury felt as much bewildered as concerned,

utterly puzzled at the proceedings of the Government. I cannot make out what they have in mind – what they are driving at . . . If they mean to govern Ireland by giving the Irish all they want – why did they not say so long ago & spare themselves the humiliation of this successful rebellion[?] If they mean to coerce – why have they patiently allowed their task to become so formidable as to be almost . . . unattainable by any means Liberals are likely to use[?][52]

Once back in the fray, his language returned to its normal, decisive register but he saw that not everyone shared it, especially Cairns with whom relations had turned cool. A long-standing Liberal friend such as Roundell Palmer regretted the difference of tone between the two and found far more to applaud in Cairns's moderation than Salisbury's venom.[53] At the end of the day Salisbury was a constitutionalist before all else and he agreed that the tradition of passing government bills at their second reading should not be broken. It sank deep into his memory all the same and the land act of 1881 would be brought out for a flout or jeer in later years: by 1887 it had become 'one of the most unfortunate measures ever submitted to the British Parliament'; a decade beyond then it had turned iconic as 'this bold defiance of the laws of political economy which Parliament sanctioned 16 years ago'.[54]

Essentially the land act moved toward bestowing the three famous Fs: Fair rents, Free sale of improvements and Fixity of tenure. Three Fiddlesticks, Disraeli had said when they were first mooted.[55] And indeed Gladstone's act pleased nobody. The Land Commission, which it established and which survived until 1923, dealt with

[51] Salisbury in Lords, *Hansard*, 2 Aug. 1880, CCLIV, cols. 1926, 1929–30.
[52] Salisbury to Stanley of Alderley, 4 Jan. 1881, Austin MSS.
[53] Roundell Palmer to Willie Palmer, 14 Aug. 1881, second Earl of Selborne MSS 96 f.104.
[54] Salisbury in Lords, *Hansard*, 22 Apr. 1887, CCXII, col. 1604, and 23 Jul. 1897, LI, col. 864.
[55] Beaconsfield to Salisbury, 29 Dec. 1880. It is the last of his letters held at Hatfield and has the wistfulness of a *nunc dimittis*: 'nothing will induce me to support the 3Fs: three fiddlesticks. During a long parliamentary life, & long before I was in Parliament, I have been profoundly convinced that the greatness & character of this country depended on our landed tenure. All the rest I look upon, & have ever looked upon, as "leather & prunella"': Salisbury MSS (Disraeli, f.554). Looking forward to Bloody Balfour, he felt no less certain that '[t]he harm that Gladstone's land legislation in Ireland and in the Highlands has done is almost beyond calculation': Balfour to Zetland (copy), 15 Feb. 1893, Balfour MSS SRO GD433/2/69.

applications to reduce rent, but the plan to advance tenants money to help them purchase their holdings over a long period was unrealistic in its image of what tenants could afford and few of them had recourse to it. Meanwhile the owners believed that they had ceased to be owners *tout court*: the landowner had become joint-owner with his tenants, 'a sort of mortgagee upon the estate', as Salisbury preferred to put it, 'with an uncertain and precarious hold upon his income'.[56] This seemed bad enough, but news that the government intended to legislate on the widely dispersed arrears of rent that had built up in Ireland alarmed landowners there even more. Leader of the House of Lords since Beaconsfield's death in 1881, Salisbury knew all too well about 'growling' and 'starving' Irish peers: they would make a good deal of noise over any arrears bill.[57] He hoped that the deleterious effects of the 1881 act would be revealed by a House of Lords committee that had been appointed to enquire into them and pressed Cairns to be more aggressive about this aspect of the problem through the spring of 1882.[58] Meanwhile the defenders of Irish property had begun to rail against the idea of subsidising people who had failed to pay rent and had even used criminal means to avoid doing so. '[P]eople whose husbands and fathers have been butchered', raved the still-Liberal Goldwin Smith, 'or whose property has been destroyed for doing what the law enjoined them to do, and to whom the government has failed to afford protection, are left without any compensation, while we pay out of the public purse the private debts of robbers and assassins.'[59] Even on the Tory benches, sympathy for afflicted landlords took often the form of silence and a biting of the lip. From John Gorst's Fourth Party point of view, for example, the holier-than-thou rhetoric of that class took some swallowing:

The Ulster Landowners do not seem to me to be capable of regarding the Land Bill from any but a selfish point of view, and are apparently ready on every occasion to sacrifice both sound policy and common sense to their

---

[56] Salisbury in Lords, *Hansard*, 1 Aug. 1881, cclxiv col. 257. The historians of Irish land law agree that the 3Fs 'amounted to the recognition of dual ownership of land': C. F. Kolbert and T. O'Brien, *Land Reform in Ireland* (Cambridge, 1975), pp. 35–7. For Salisbury's reflection on fixity of tenure and free sale, see Salisbury to Balfour, 31 Jan. 1881, in *Salisbury–Balfour Correspondence*, p. 63.

[57] Salisbury to Carnarvon, 1 Jan. 1882, Carnarvon MSS 60759 f.66.

[58] Salisbury to Cairns, 30 May 1882, Cairns MSS 30/51/6/ff.84–5: 'We have dealt chiefly with the working of the Act – not yet with its *effects*.'

[59] Goldwin Smith to Gibson, 29 Jun. 1882, in A. B Cooke and A. P. W. Malcolmson (eds.), *The Ashbourne Papers 1869–1913* (Belfast, 1974), p. 171.

financial interests . . . I have too much regard for liberty of opinion to wish to prevent the Ulster members going their own way . . . What I protest against is their insisting upon dragging the whole Conservative party in bondage at their heels, and expecting people to subordinate opinions based on actual experience to the crude ideas which they hastily take up as most in accordance with what they imagine to be their own interest.[60]

The *politics* of property had shattered into three shards, each of them with very sharp edges. One piece, to which Salisbury was originally attached, wanted to drive opposition as far as rejection at second reading and precipitate a dissolution in order to drive out the government from office. One piece opposed doing so because expectation had been raised so high among the Irish tenantry that disorder or worse might follow. Another took the view that second reading should be passed but the bill then emasculated in committee. Salisbury dropped the first fragment and gingerly picked up the third; and since the amendments that he wanted to use against the bill offended Cairns and the moderate wing, he now contrived to upset each section of Conservative opinion about Ireland. Whatever he said to the ex-cabinet or to the party meeting that he called to explain his position did little to appease his critics; and among those who were starving and growling his reputation would never recover, for all his having persuaded Waterford and other leaders to refrain from voting against the second reading. More ominously, the argument could be given its English twist and it was not without significance for property that the most extreme, indeed incoherent, expostulation in the Lords came from one who wept for those who held land on both sides of the Irish Sea:

. . . he wished their Lordships would look at the question in an English point of view, for it affected England as well as Ireland . . . Many of their Lordships were landowners, not only in England but in Ireland; and what would they be able to say to their tenants in England, who in consequence of bad seasons and bad times, were in arrears? The legislation on which they have now embarked in Ireland would touch England tomorrow; and

---

[60] Gorst to W. H. Smith, 14 Jul. 1881, Hambledon MSS P57/58. By 1885 Salisbury himself had decided that the Irish landlords were 'troublesome & unreliable allies': Salisbury to Churchill, 16 Nov. 1885, Churchill MSS 9248/9/unfol. In the mind of one ex-Liberal critic this amounted to sheer posturing to cover a more fundamental political point after 1884: 'they know that the landlords are not a popular class, and that the spoliation of them will arouse very feeble indignation in the breast of the average household suffrager': Henry Sidgwick to J. A. Symonds, 4 Jul. 1892, in *Sidgwick: A Memoir*, p. 524. This implies, of course, what Liberals always imply, that Tories live by bread alone.

so far as he was concerned he was sorry the Bill was not to be divided upon. He, however, washed his hands of it, and protested against it altogether.[61]

His leader had missed the mood. It produced a 'cataclysm of convictions' that left him bewildered and resentful.[62] He justified his behaviour as best he could to Cairns and refused to accept that the mess was his fault; but he learned important lessons all the same. The first was that all unacceptable legislation must be squashed at second reading. The second was that he had no feel for Ireland and ought to keep out of it. '[S]ince the affair of the Arrears Act,' he confided to Cairns when they were on better terms in 1885, 'I have avoided meddling in questions of Irish Land as much as I could.'[63] The story brought to a close a long narrative of rivalry, mistrust and active enmity between Salisbury and Cairns and the dénouement had not gone in Salisbury's favour. He may have succeeded in keeping the Cairns/Richmond axis at bay when Disraeli's leadership had come into question after 1871 and resisted Cairns's designs on the church, but the latter now threatened a good deal or would have done if his health had allowed.

Not so Lord Ashbourne, who threatened little. He, like the milder flavours of Irish Tory opinion represented by Carnarvon, worried about the Irish land market and came to accept that the only solution to the purchase issue was to find a way of advancing *all* the purchase-money to tenants on repayment terms that they could manage. He, unlike Carnarvon, showed few signs of flirting with more radical political treatments of the issue and so long as he stuck to purchase as the issue he would not inflame Tory passion. Confiscation was their issue, not purchase. When Ashbourne introduced a scheme for more effective purchase during the minority Salisbury goverment of 1885, it produced, therefore, little party wrangling. Two-thirds of the needed advance had been promised in the 1870 act, three-quarters in

---

[61] Bury in Lords, *Hansard*, 27 Jul. 1882, CCLXXII, cols. 1952–3. William Coutts Keppel, seventh Earl of Albemarle, was styled Viscount Bury until 1891. Originally a Liberal (sat for Norwich, Wick and Berwick-on-Tweed in his early career). But under-secretary at the War Office for short periods under both Disraeli and Salisbury. 2,500 acres in Leitrim but 7,500 in Norfolk where the seat was Quidenham Hall, near Attleborough. Received into the Roman Catholic Church, 1879. His opinions on *The Rinderpest treated by Homeopathy in South Holland* (1865) seem not to have established a national reputation.

[62] Salisbury to Cross, 10 Aug. 1882, Cross MSS 51263 f.68.

[63] Salisbury to Cairns, 12 Mar. 1885, Cairns MSS 30/51/6/f.173. He retained this unease for meddling: cf. his review of recent experience – 'Just look at the history of the legislation of this subject' – in 1891, when he stressed that 'the feelings of the British taxpayer' could not be ignored: Salisbury in Lords, *Hansard*, 26 Jun. 1891, CCCLIV, col. 1576.

1881. Ashbourne went for the full amount with safeguards for the landlords in case of default and piloted much the most successful act of the decade in stimulating take-up from tenants. Something like 16,000 of them availed themselves of the opportunity presented by the legislation, financed on a 4 per cent annuity over forty-nine years. For Home Rule, the Conservatives had rhetorically substituted home possession. They would retain power at the cost of property. It hurt. But it was 'the best hope for us landlords'[64] in the situation of 1886 when Ireland became threatened by someone larger and stronger than either tenants or peasants.

Gladstone's lurch toward giving the Irish a form of Home Rule at the end of 1885 introduced new dangers and imperatives. By splitting his own party he gave Tories the chance of recruiting from what would become known as the 'Unionist' wing of Liberalism provided that they had a policy for Ireland that could be swallowed by ex-Liberals – the more so once Gladstone's Home Rule bill had failed in the House of Commons in June 1886 and the Unionists had formed their own political party. For Salisbury the message seemed too insistent to allow much trimming. He could and would stamp on anybody who had the wrong language about Parnell or Home Rule: this spelled the end of Carnarvon and ensured his exclusion when Salisbury came back to power in 1886. Yet he would need to do more than that. He would have to move in the direction of further curtailment of the rights of landlords for two compelling reasons. The first concerned agitation and its future course, as he gathered from his new chief secretary in the autumn of 1886:

From all parts of the country I hear reports of a better tone among the people. Landlords are giving considerable reductions of rent: and tenants seem less unwilling to pay, when they can. Some of the Parnellites are stumping the country: but their speeches are more moderate in tone than formerly, and in some of the worst parts (eg. King Harman's neighbourhood in Roscommon) their agitation has fallen flat . . . At the same time, there is another side. The secret societies are more active; and though at present we hear of no definite plans, we have information as to schemes for outrages . . . next month. Rents will then be due: if not paid, and pressed for, trouble is very likely to follow.[65]

---

[64] Kavanagh to Ashbourne, 26 Aug. 1886, in Cooke and Malcolmson (eds.), *Ashbourne Papers*, p. 140.

[65] Beach to Salisbury (transcript), 20 Oct. 1886, St Aldwyn MSS PCC/31/unfol. Edward King-Harman owned nearly 30,000 acres in Roscommon, with another 40,000 in Longford, Sligo, Westmeath and Queen's County. He sat for Sligo (1877–80), Dublin County (1883–5) and the Isle of Thanet (1885–8) and functioned as a useful barometer of Irish rural opinion.

The development of the so-called 'Plan of Campaign' made this no idle prediction. Tenants took to withholding their rent and diverting it to a trustee until the landlord met their terms or until the money could to be used to defend other farmers threatened with eviction. It was the landlords' turn to reach for the blunderbuss; or to find a better way through concession. A second point was still more urgent, politically. The Liberal Unionists had to be attracted and held and that might mean baiting the hook with something slimy and wriggling. Contemporary documents speak rhetorically of the Union and the need to save it at whatever cost. Salisbury helped future historians a few years later by calling a spade a spade when he looked back on the land bill of 1887 that he had so hated having to propose. 'That was a bill', he confessed to the Viceroy in 1895, 'containing some very bad provisions – but they were the price of obtaining the votes of the Lib. Uns. & of the left wing of our party, for the Crimes Act.'[66] Neither his exposition nor his situation in 1886 left much scope for ambiguity. Coercion would have to happen; bleeding hearts would bleed; something would have to be done for the tenants of Ireland and the frailer spirits at Westminster.

Together, these constraints explain what otherwise seems inexplicable: the refusal of the Conservative majority government of 1886–92 to reverse Liberal land law in Ireland. Salisbury tried to cover his discomfort with unpersuasive language about Gladstone's recent threat having overmastered all others and about the need for 'continuity'. ('My Lords, we have no other choice . . . If every Government were to make it its business to reverse in most vital matters and in connection with critical measures the policy of its Predecessors, confusion and absolute chaos would result.'[67]) In private he did not bother to do so: it was all 'pain & grief to me'.[68] The problem, of course, was that any interference with contracts already in force, rather than simply future ones, represented another case of 'tearing up' agreements entered into in good faith by owners who now would see their lien on their own property further attenuated.[69] We have already seen the response of the Marquis of Waterford and his wish to have his money back from the party that

---

[66] Salisbury to Cadogan, 22 Nov. 1895, Cadogan MSS CAD/756i.
[67] Salisbury in Lords, *Hansard*, 22 Apr. 1887, cccxii, col. 1605.
[68] Salisbury to Beach, 3 Jul. 1887, St Aldwyn MSS PCC/69/69.
[69] Cf. Salisbury to Balfour, 8 Mar. 1887, *Salisbury–Balfour Correspondence*, p. 178.

now betrayed him.[70] He was not alone in his denunciations in the House of Lords. All the same, it seems remarkable how little trouble was encountered by Salisbury's government in pushing the land bill through. Many of the Irish owners had perhaps already thrown in the towel and come to see tenant-purchase as their only future. They also ran up against the manifest contempt of no small number of Tories – Salisbury included – who saw them as an unimaginative coterie of irresponsible owners who had brought much of the trouble on themselves by their bone-headed selfishness through years of exploitation and then their lack of courage in bringing cases to court against their malefactors.[71] It was Carnarvon, rather than Salisbury, who voiced this prejudice in 1885 but he spoke for an important English persuasion. 'Doubtless they have their difficulties,' Carnarvon conceded, '– & many great ones – though as far as I can perceive they have suffered *very* much less than we have in England – and if they have suffered, the tenants have lost still more'.[72]

It was not the end of the narrative but from the point of view of property its remaining pages lose their urgency. Thoughtful statesmen tried to improve the mechanism for making Irish property over to its smallholders: W. H. Smith tried to encourage a little liberal capitalism in the government's approach to that problem in 1889;[73] Gerald Balfour tried to push a more generous scheme for repayment past the unbudgeable nose of Hicks Beach, who 'w[ould] not be bullied', in 1896.[74] No one wanted to push the other way. Defence of property now became a defence of giving it away in order to defend the structure of society itself. Salisbury presented the new language when recommending purchase to the peers in 1891:

Our object is to multiply proprietors of land in a country which, owing to a great variety of causes, has come into a thoroughly unhealthy condition, and which, without the support of a class in the highest sense Conservative, of a class which has a deep and ineradicable interest in the existing state of things, cannot come back to the hearty condition in which we all desire to

---

[70] Above, chapter 2, p. 60.
[71] Salisbury to Halsbury, 22 Dec. 1886, Halsbury MSS 56371 f.31.
[72] Carnarvon to Beach, 25 Sep. 1885, St Aldwyn MSS PCC/78/unfol.
[73] Smith to Balfour, 8 Oct. 1889: 'What do you say to a general conversion of rent upon this basis, the landlord to receive payment in Irish Consols bearing 3 per cent interest for 25 years like the local loan Stock, secured first by the law, next by the local taxes and backed by an ultimate Imperial Guarantee[?]' Balfour MSS 49696 ff.102–4.
[74] Gerald Balfour to Cadogan, 28 Feb. 1896, Cadogan MSS CAD/894; Cadogan to Ashbourne, 26 Mar. 1896, in Cooke and Malcolmson (eds.), *Ashbourne Papers*, p. 71.

see it . . . I should have thought it was now one of the commonplaces of politics that where [a class of peasant freeholders] exists it is a sheet-anchor of the social stability of the country.[75]

In a sense the anxieties of 1870 could be inverted, too. Ireland had been made to look like England rather than the other way round – a place where property had diversified, albeit by force, in order to accommodate social change and a shifting political order. Perhaps the surgery had indeed brought pain and grief to the patients; but as the operation proceeded in the theatre of politics, Salisbury wore the gown and Gladstone came under the knife.

---

[75] Salisbury in Lords, *Hansard*, 26 Jun. 1891, CCCLIV, cols. 1573–4.

CHAPTER 5

Thought

SALISBURY AND THE CLERISY

Salisbury thought deeply about a wide range of issues and problems. This was unusual. Conservative politicians tended, then as now, to shy away from intellectuals, universities and the life of the mind. They did so with good reason because Conservative politics often turn on the instinctual and inadvertent rather than the cerebral or the purposive. Tone leads strategy; tradition overtakes abstraction. When thinking becomes the sort of dismantling in which the Enlightenment once delighted, it becomes by its very nature an anti-Tory instrument just as it produces a scepticism about religion ready-made from its own tool-box. All these intimations and suspicions were shared by Salisbury: indeed, he lavished some of his choicer disdain on those whom he suspected of *dixhuitième* deviations. But in his way, through his own abilities, he developed one of the most powerful minds of the nineteenth century. He then concealed it, as one might a revolver. It suited him to have others deem him unread, uninterested and unaware. 'Hatfield is Gaza, the capital of Philistia.'[1] Slogans of this kind might not only unsettle a nervous young woman but also confuse the world at large. One has to probe behind them in order to see the degree to which Salisbury requires some intellectual situation; behind them, too, his determination to owe nothing to anyone. Gwendolen Cecil saw this individuality in her father clearer than she saw its limits. 'I doubt', she said, when collecting material for her biography, 'whether he ever became clear about anything which he did not think & work out for himself. That was an undoubted weakness – his extreme independence of thought,

---

[1] The welcome boomed at Violet Maxse when her future husband, Edward Cecil, brought her home: Violet Milner, *My Picture Gallery 1886–1901* (1951), p. 57.

incapacity alike to appropriate other men's ideas, or work out his own ideas through them.'[2] This made him as unlike Lloyd George as, in a different way, it distanced his mind from Balfour's or suggested a flirtation with Gladstone's that he would have thought unsavoury. He believed all the same in the existence and desirability of a sort of Conservative intelligentsia – a clerisy of thinkers, writers, churchmen, dons – whose function lay in presenting in some scientific way the residual Toryism that he identified in most educated people. For 'in the long run the more highly educated portion of society leads and indicates the course which the whole community will undoubtedly pursue'.[3]

Commentators dwell on his journalism as principal evidence for Salisbury's thought. Doing so raises as many difficulties as it removes, however, for several reasons. First, his enormous output of articles for the *Quarterly Review* occupied an early phase of his life which he did not replicate during the years of power, apart from isolated famous instances such as his piece on 'Disintegration' in 1883.[4] They give a picture of Cecil and Cranborne but leave little sense of the mature Salisbury. Second, the articles take the form of rhetorical exercises composed against the clock for money. Read carefully, each paragraph contains one sentence which is written ten times in various ways in order to spin out the content to the length required. They have a virtuoso quality, certainly, but reflect nothing of the terse expressions of later years where the power comes through in sheer, brutal economy. Third, and most compelling, Salisbury himself would tolerate no word said about his periodical contributions in his hearing. Diners ran into a wall of glowering silence if they hinted at his authorship. Their (anonymous) author did not call attention to them in his speeches or letters. Salisbury was not ashamed of once having had to write for his living and seems never to have begrudged the massive labour that these performances demanded; but neither did he see his periodical articles as other than ephemeral remarks for *pièces d'occasion*. Where they offer so much is in their language and individual characterizations – shafts of light and wild stabs in the night. After he died, Salisbury's son, Robert,

---

[2] Lady Gwendolen Cecil to St Aldwyn, n.d. [Dec. 1913/Jan. 1914], St Aldwyn MSS PCC/69/203.

[3] Salisbury at Edinburgh, 3 Nov. 1888, *The Times*, 1 Dec. 1888, p. 9a.

[4] *Quarterly Review*, 156 (Oct. 1883), pp. 559–95.

began to leaf through some of these articles and found the right frame for them in a private letter to his cousin:

I've been going on with my Quarterly readings . . . They are all interesting to me, of course, & many of them would be to the outside world. For instance, there is one written in Jan. 1862 (vol III) on Castlereagh which gives a description of the perfect Foreign Minster. It might have been written as far as opinions go in 1900. Then there is one on W[ar] O[ffice] Reform in 1871 . . . which among other things shows that the problem is unchanged in the last 30 years. Scattered through them are passages of immense interest on Sir Robert Peel, on Gladstone, on the Church & on Political Principles generally . . . I suppose at present the secret of their authorship should be kept.[5]

But interest cannot be made to do service for authenticity and these pieces make a quarry more than a monument to Salisbury's thought. One has to look elsewhere for complement and correction.

This is far from easy. He did not, like Balfour, write books. He did not, like Gladstone, keep a diary. He did not, like Lloyd George, keep a mistress who kept a diary. His 'thoughts' reached paper mostly in his private correspondence – which, though massive, remained laconic – or in office memoranda, which presented often masterly arguments in favour of specific courses of action, but left to the reader or future researcher any pulling out of general intellectual positions or tendencies. The temptation becomes one of dismissing Salisbury's wider intellectual interests once his chemistry set and experiments with Hatfield's electrical wiring have been given their due. And he set about encouraging that result by writing semi-public letters such as the one directed at the enthusiasts of Beverley Road Wesleyan Young People's Association who wanted to know what he thought of Robert Blatchford's *Merrie England*, which had come out the previous year. ('I have never read the book.'[6]) But other remarks suggest a different story: his returning to Cranbrook an unnamed volume on banking in 1894 and offering a crisp and critical account of it, or his thanking Richmond for a work by Jacob Wilson which he had already read and admired.[7] Occasionally, moreover, he reflected overtly on a particular book such as *Lux Mundi*, a collection of theological essays edited by Charles Gore in 1889 and widely

---

[5] Robert Cecil to Balfour, 17 Nov. 1903, Balfour MSS 49737 ff.7–8.

[6] Memo by Salisbury, 7 Nov. 1895, Christ Church MSS, no file.

[7] Salisbury to Cranbrook, 23 Apr. 1894, Cranbook MSS T501/263; Salisbury to Richmond, 15 Apr. 1882, Goodwood MSS 871 d 4. The Wilson volume is unclear; it may have been his *Practical Life and the Study of Man* (Newark, NY, 1882).

regarded as an important attempt to harmonize Christianity with Darwinism. Not only did Salisbury know the book, but he also took on holiday with him some of the continental criticism on which the volume's more radical recommendations had been grounded. He dismissed the lot as 'an inverted pyramid of argument',[8] of course, but he knew whereof he spoke.

One can say that his very dismissiveness betrayed a lack of seriousness and application in reading: it does not surprise posterity that Salisbury leaves no evidence of having read about Schopenhauer on a train, as the earnest Earl of Derby once did, or of having drawn up a checklist of Benjamin Kidd's pros and cons, as the still more earnest Gladstone tried to do.[9] It makes stronger sense to acknowledge nevertheless that Salisbury could bring his formidable mental powers to bear on an economic or theological text and say something of his own about it if the spirit moved.

When life was too short, his repertoire of fictional reading rarely left his memory and his letters and speeches often contain some allusion to English literary classics from Shakespeare to Scott. These latter figures supplied sanity when all around were losing their heads. Twitters Carnarvon lost his so frequently that colleagues tired of his tantrums and threats of resignation; but it catches the eye that when Salisbury calmed him down during one of his storms over the Near Eastern situation in 1877, he did so by sending his tiresome friend back to the beginning of *Henry VIII*.[10] In public, *Waverley* could get an airing (as so often for this generation), especially through the Baron of Bradwardine and his better-known phrases:

---

[8] Cecil, vol. I, p. 107.
[9] Perhaps one should stress irony more than earnestness in Derby's reading a life of Schopenhauer in the middle of the cabinet crisis over the Russo-Turkish war in 1877: see his diary, 27 May 1877, in Derby, *Diaries*, p. 403. Cf. Gladstone's diary entry for 6 Apr. 1894: 'Read Social Evolution (many pros and more *cons*) . . .': M. R. D. Foot and Colin Matthew (eds.), *The Gladstone Diaries* (14 vols., Oxford, 1968–94), vol. XII, p. 407.
[10]
>   Be advis'd;
>   Heat not a furnace for your foe so hot
>   That it do singe yourself: we may outrun
>   By violent swiftness that which we run at,
>   And lose by over-running. Know you not
>   The fire that mounts the liquor till't run o'er
>   In seeming t'augment it wastes it? Be advis'd:
>   I say again, there is no English soul
>   More stronger to direct you than yourself,
>   If with the sap of reason you would quench
>   Or but allay the fire of passion.

Cf. Salisbury to Carnarvon, 24 Mar. 1877, Carnarvon MSS 60759 f.24.

Ae half the speech wi'Phoebus grace did find,
The t'other half he whistled down the wind.[11]

Allusions of this kind helped decorate the published articles and gave them a patina of shared association. Jonathan Swift also had his uses in polemic, especially Laputa which attracted Salisbury more than other parts of Gulliver's travels for its sardonic possibilities. The idea that professors might try to extract sunshine from cucumbers struck him, after all, as only mildly overstated and whether the target were about 'Laputan financiers' for the *Quarterly* or 'the politicians of Laputa' for the benefit of the House of Lords, he lost no opportunity to call satire to his side in argument.[12] Probably most of this reading dated from his early years. In the later ones he read most connectedly when in France and there his tastes would run to French literature that found less expression, if only because it disgusted him in a compelling sort of way, rather like the tendency towards nudity that continentals seemed to indulge. Even there, however, note the moment of aesthetic interest implied at the end of an outburst intended to amuse the peers around him. He wanted to see, he said, 'some canon as to the course artists should pursue in dealing with the question of clothes or no clothes'. Presumably some smiles among the sparse audience urged him forward into an unscripted announcement:

Artists take a different view of the subject from that taken by a majority of mankind, and some of the matters which they represent as wholly innocuous and, indeed, praiseworthy would, if translated into ordinary life, attract the attention of the police. As far as my experience goes – though that be a small one – even in the representation of sacred subjects I have observed on the part of artists that a desire to exhibit their knowledge of the human form and their command of flesh tints, has overcome the inclination to clothe saintly persons with a sufficiency of garments. I would invite my noble Friend [Stanley of Alderley] the next time he goes to the Continent to visit the Magdalen of Guercino at Naples and the Magdalen of Correggio at Paris.[13]

Genuine philistines take a pride in having visited neither.

When he wrote rather than read, Salisbury wrote almost always about politics. Indeed he complained to one supplicant in 1881 that there were now 'more years than I care to remember since I wrote anything which was not in some way or other connected with

---

[11] Quoted in 'The Income Tax and its Rivals', *Quarterly Review*, 109 (Jan. 1861), pp. 212–47, at p. 219.

[12] *Ibid.*, p. 214; Salisbury in Lords, *Hansard*, 13 Jun. 1893, XIII, col. 876.

[13] Salisbury in Lords, *Hansard*, 17 Jul. 1891, CLV, col. 1521.

politics'.[14] And in that sphere he broadcast his anti-intellectualism as a counter-Enlightenment position mixed with a number of cynicisms about the possibility of theory having any relation to political activity. It was as though all political statements, like electoral addresses, had the 'merit . . . [of] . . . hav[ing] no thought to conceal'. As for theory in general, it was better left to the Germans or over-rational Voltaireans in Paris. 'Hard-headed Englishmen', he claimed to believe in the *Quarterly*, 'seem for a time as if they were metamorphosed into German Professors. Even the oldest statesmen seem bitten with the fancy of grinding out Constitutions upon the calculating machine; and the Universities pour upon us troops of rising statesmen, all armed to the teeth with formulae for the logical government of mankind.'[15] Beside remarks of this kind one has to set his respect for a writer such as Sir Henry Maine, for whom Salisbury had an obvious regard and whom he tried to place on commissions over which he had control. When Maine wrote the articles that were to turn into the four essays that made up *Popular Government* (1885) – theoretical to a fault – Salisbury neither sneered nor claimed that he had avoided reading them, at least in private:

Maine has always spoken to me in strong dislike of the acts of Modern Liberals & I believe he was to have stood as a moderate Conservative at Cambridge. I take him to be of the same politics as many of the Liberals of thirty years ago, who are now Conservative. I believe he writes for the St James Gazette & he has written four articles against Democracy in the Quarterly which have attracted a great deal of attention.[16]

A concentration on the public face of Salisbury's politics omits this dimension entirely. It focusses on an area of discussion in which Salisbury deemed thought largely irrelevant and then attributes to him a view about its irrelevance elsewhere.

Once we redirect the lens, this distortion disappears at once. He spent much of his time nurturing the University of Oxford, for example, albeit in a style that Modern Liberals would not always have approved, especially when he insisted on retaining forms of

---

[14] Salisbury to Austin, 30 Dec. 1881, Austin MSS.

[15] 'The Elections', *Quarterly Review*, 118 (Jul. 1865), pp. 280–95 at p. 281; 'Parliamentary Reform', *Quarterly Review*, 117 (Apr. 1865), pp. 540–75 at p. 573.

[16] Salisbury to Cross, 2 Jul. 1885, Cross MSS 51263 ff.94–5. Sir Henry Sumner Maine (1822–88) was one of the century's most prominent legal minds. Christ's Hospital and Pembroke, Cambridge. Junior Tutor at Trinity Hall for a time. Regius Professor of Civil Law, 1847–54. Bar, 1850. Reader in Roman Law and Jurisprudence at the Inns of Court, 1852. Wrote for *Saturday Review* from 1855. Master of Trinity Hall, 1877–88.

Anglican hegemony there. Throughout a very long period as chancellor (from 1869 until his death in 1903) he discharged his functions punctiliously and took a serious interest in the intellectual direction of the university as well as its administration. These two preoccupations came together in 1876 with the appointment of another commission of enquiry into the working of the university. Salisbury did what he could to manage the investigation in such a way that Oxford would not be damaged by secularism; but he showed his usual intelligence by incorporating thinkable liberals to cloak his intention. Replying to Cranbrook's suggestions, he by no means followed the churchman's reflexes and urged a more latitudinarian view, playing in a relaxed letter with some of the more famous intellectual personalities of the day:

I should be delighted to have Dean [R. W.] Church, if we can get him. I know nothing of [W. H.] Fremantle. I am quite content to have Lords Selborne & Blachford if there is room for them. The Abp. of York [Thomson] I think is dangerous. He would alarm both our Ch[urch] & Conserv[ative] friends. I do not know Sir Henry Maine – though I think him very able . . . My impression is that there should be 2 Liberals; and I feel sure the scientific world will not be satisfied with less than two. Can you not reconsider your objection to [H. W.] Acland? He is as harmless a sort of scientific man as you can have – & he is intensely Oxford in all his thoughts & objects. He is nominally Liberal but would not meddle with Clerical Fellowships.[17]

Acland, indeed, showed a touch of inspiration helped by familiarity with an old Christ Church friend. Whatever his Liberal tendencies, he remained in touch with Conservative leaders and shared all

---

[17] Cranbrook MSS T501/267. Dean Church appealed because of his sympathies with the 'Oxford movement', as his seminal history would show (R. W. Church, *The Oxford Movement: Twelve Years 1833–45* (1891)). W. R. Fremantle had more liberal tendencies in his publications. Frederic Rogers, Baron Blachford, had been an Oriel man in the generation of Hurrell Froude and Newman; permanent under-secretary at the Colonies in the 1860s. The despised William Thomson, Archbishop of York from 1863–91, had worse than liberal tendencies of a Jowettian kind until *Essays and Reviews* (1860), after which he separated himself to a degree. At York he had already begun by 1876 his trajectory towards something resembling socialism. He was proud of having been given a canteen of cutlery by the steelworkers of Sheffield. Sir Henry Wentworth Acland (1815–1900), scion of the distinguished Liberal family whose seat was Killerton in Devon, was Regius Professor of Medicine at Oxford from 1857 to 1894 and Radcliffe Librarian. One of his recent papers was *Faith and Knowledge: A Paper Read before the Metaphysical Society* in 1873. For his life, see J. B. Atlay, *Sir Henry Wentworth Acland, Bart.: A Memoir* (1903). Salisbury's political arts and devices ultimately gave way to the possible. Following several refusals he wound up with 'three very stout Tories, three mild Liberals & a neutral judge' (to Cranbrook, 2 Mar. 1876). He tried, but failed, to persuade Selborne to retract his refusal to chair the commission: Salisbury to Selborne, 8 Mar. 1876, first Earl of Selborne MSS 1866 f.201.

Salisbury's worries that the impact of science and 'abstract political ideas' threatened to undermine the basis of society, 'unless the popular leaders [were] disciplined Christian souls'.[18]

Salisbury saw, too, a function for the university within the wider community. The vision was assuredly not that of Canon Barnett or T. H. Green: no missions set out from Hatfield to bring succour to the East London poor. But he saw that the university ought to do something beyond impart further flourishes to the Latin and Greek learned at school; and he had many constructive prejudices. He hated professors almost as much as he loathed bishops. So when someone like Max Müller argued that the study of Eastern languages should be augmented at the Imperial Institute, Salisbury retorted that the money would be far better spent by adding junior tutors to the University of London and then 'giving very *good* prizes for conversational proficiency – not of course literary proficiency which [was] of no use at all'.[19] His very functionalism thus turned him into a radical. Pressed to say what a university ought to do, his Conservatism returned very quickly, of course, but it had the virtue of breadth and did not reflect John Henry Newman's vision of knowledge for its own sake rather than as vocational training.[20] It ought to see itself 'preserving the variety and the elasticity which are so necessary to our English habits of mind'.[21] The advice doubtless would not have impressed the Universities of Edinburgh and Glasgow, but then it was not meant to. Outside the universities, he took part in conversations intended to force Eton into teaching science: hardly the recommendation of a reactionary but one quite natural in a fellow of the Royal Society, which Salisbury became, to his lasting and genuine pleasure, in 1869.[22] He brought a similar sense of duty and width to his dealings with the British Association

---

[18] Acland to Smith, 31 Jul. 1869, Hambledon MSS PS14/68.

[19] Salisbury to Beach, 2 Jan. 1896, St Aldwyn MSS PCC/69/114. Friedrich Max Müller (1823–1900). Educated in Leipzig. Worked under Schelling in Berlin. England from 1846; he settled in Oxford. Taylorian Chair of Modern European Languages 1854–68. Fellow of All Souls. The first Professor of Comparative Philology in Oxford from 1868. His collected works appeared first in German, later in English. Cf. *Ausgewählte Werke* (13 vols., Leipzig, 1897–1901).

[20] See, in particular, Discourse v, 'Knowledge its Own End', of Newman's well-known text: 'I consider, then, that I am chargeable with no paradox, when I speak of a knowledge which is its own end, when I call it liberal knowledge, or a gentleman's knowledge, when I educate for it, and make it the scope of a University': J. H. Newman, *The Idea of a University* (1873), ed. Frank M. Turner (New Haven, CT, 1996), p. 83.

[21] Salisbury to Cranbrook, 9 May 1888, Cranbrook MSS T501/260.

[22] See Salisbury to Carnarvon, n.d. (1874), Carnarvon MSS 60758 f.151.

for the Advancement of Science, whose president he became in 1894 and to whom he gave an address on evolution in 1894 that baptized Darwin and found him not at all consistent with Design in the universe,[23] but whose more menial commissions he would also take on, such as finding out for them whether Northcote would raid the Exchequer to help set up an observatory in India for the study of sun-spots.[24] There were even moments when the peers at Westminster found themselves compelled to suffer a discourse on astronomy, though the subject may have been so uncosmic as the Gladstonian policy towards Egypt:

> The proof of a scientific law is that you can prophesy from previous occurrences what will happen in the future. That is exactly what will take place in the present instance . . . As astronomers, observing the motions of a comet, can discover by observation the future path by which that comet is to travel, so we could prophesy what would happen in the case of General Gordon . . . [for] . . . by that time we had ascertained the laws of motion and the orbits of those eccentric comets who sit on the Treasury Bench.[25]

Despite his postures reflecting dislike of 'experts', secular 'thinkers' and aesthetic snobs, Salisbury's private and public language constantly suggested an engagement with an intellectual world.

The Balfours played no small part in sustaining this contact. Arthur's role in cementing ties with an intelligentsia can be overstressed; his own langour insulated him from much that went on – witness his not bothering to attend Salisbury's evolution lecture at the British Association – and a preference for sleepy remarks echoed his uncle's penchant for keeping his powder dry. Yet even at the public level, Balfour's national prominence as the author of *A Defence of Philosophic Doubt* (1879) and his *Foundations of Belief* (1895) brought him into contact with a range of intellectual figures and a fitful correspondence with them would sometimes ensue. His reading and

---

[23] Details and quotations in Andrew Roberts, *Salisbury: Victorian Titan* (1999), pp. 593–6.

[24] Salisbury to Northcote, 15 and 19 Sep. 1875, Iddesleigh MSS 50019 ff. 28–31. Not much sunshine came back. 'I suppose we ought to study the Sun,' wrote the dismal chancellor, 'though I don't see that we are likely to get any good out of the spots': Northcote to Salisbury, 25 Sep. 1875, Salisbury MSS (Northcote, f.87). On the 1894 lecture Balfour reported, 'I need not tell you that Uncle Robert's Address at Oxford and John's [Rayleigh's] discovery of a new gas, were the two most exciting incidents of the British Association. Nora and Evelyn were both there, and I was not': Balfour MSS 49831 ff.187–8. It might be added that Salisbury also played a role in founding the National Physical Laboratory (1899): see Frank M. Turner, *Contesting Cultural Authority: Essays in Victorian Intellectual Life* (Cambridge, 1993), pp. 217–18.

[25] Salisbury in Lords, *Hansard*, 26 Feb. 1884, CCXCIV, cols. 1317–18.

width would occasionally come out there, almost always in sub-clauses or by implication. So when an acquaintance, now inspector of schools, produced an edition of Swift in 1892, Balfour made a point of referring to it before entering upon the business of Scottish secondary education and threw in, with his congratulations, a secondary thought. 'I hope, in the second volume, you will not miss out "Reasons against abolishing Christianity", in some ways the best thing of its kind that either the Author or anybody else ever did.'[26] This Augustan temperament extended to music and especially to Handel, of whom Balfour displayed great knowledge and for whose works he expressed the closest he came to passion. Privately, his critical sense of much of his contemporary culture could be savage. For George Saintsbury, the guru of literary taste and seemingly immortal Regius Professor of Rhetoric and English Literature at Edinburgh, he showed, for example, little patience because Saintsbury did not investigate the weaknesses of his authors, especially Tennyson, and thus missed how 'it [was] quite possible . . . to hold that nine-tenths of "In Memoriam", nine-tenths of the Idylls, and more than nine-tenths of some of the other volumes might be pitched into the sea with no great loss to anybody'.[27] This had became a theme. His rectorial address at St Andrews in 1887 caught Edmund Gosse's fastidious eye for its courage in sweeping away the 'humbug which the pedantic and the ignorant have been combining to throw over the subject of Reading . . . an unwholesome idolatry for the situation of the past [that] threatens to close round living literature, & positively stifle it'.[28] On the other hand he rejected materialism and positivism which made him attractive to a post-Christian sensibility such as that found in Henry Sidgwick, F. W. H. Myers and the enthusiasts for psychical research. Visiting Cambridge in 1888, Myers felt especially grateful for a recent paper of Balfour's dissenting from the fashion of decrying metaphysics and the spiritual:

There is I am sure – I see it here – a real danger that men will lose energy and enterprise, from the conviction that death ends all – & then this loss of enterprise – of the spirit, so to say, of cosmic adventure – prevents them from giving their minds to those problems whose solution is of all things the most important – & not beyond hope.[29]

[26] Balfour to Craik, 2 May 1892, Craik MSS 7174 f.15.
[27] Balfour to Betty Balfour, 20 Feb. 1895, Balfour MSS 49831 ff.68–9.
[28] Gosse to Balfour, 11 Dec. 1887, Balfour MSS SRO GD433/2/34/1.
[29] Myers to Balfour, 7 Oct. 1888, Balfour MSS SRO GD433/2/31.

Balfour was neither beyond hope nor much possessed by cosmic adventure. He was never, as Sidgwick judged his brother Gerald to be, an Hegelian and held no very coherent philosophical position. His persuasive prose made him, all the same, an intellectual publicist of considerable force among those thinking Tories who believed in God rather than the church and looked back with some nostalgia, in a Leslie Stephen sort of way, to the cool eighteenth-century mind.

The other Balfours brought their own tone and energies and should not be envisaged as reflections of Arthur. His sister-in-law, Frances Balfour, brought into the family all the capacity for disputation that the Duke of Argyll might have desired in a daughter and brought it in particular to Hatfield, whose society she adored. Her wavelength was also Salisbury's and she plainly brought out his intellectual side quite as much as, perhaps more than, the more famous Balfour in the room. Her memoirs[30] take one into Hatfield society more compellingly than any other recollection, though she was later to quarrel bitterly with many of its members. Gerald was a brilliant classicist whose political career became overshadowed by his brother's rise to national prominence but whose mind was not: he has never received the attention he merits. And then there was Frank: equally unsung and prematurely dead. When he fell from the south face of Mont Blanc in July 1882, Frank Maitland Balfour vacated a fellowship of the Royal Society and a chair of animal morphology at Cambridge to which he had just been appointed, an irreparable tragedy to everybody but Salisbury.[31] It is hard to believe that a family circle constituted in this way helped Hatfield remain the capital of Gaza, Tennyson notwithstanding.

Beyond Hatfield, Salisbury saw the intellectual world in particulars more than in structures or categories. He had little time for the press and, unlike Disraeli, he did not spend his energies on tuning it, though he listened when it spoke.[32] But he could be attracted to an enterprise if he thought it might serve a specific purpose in reaching

---

30 *Ne Obliviscaris: Dinna Forget* (2 vols., 1930).

31 *Ibid.*, vol. I, p. 349. Salisbury, hearing the news, revealed the glacial face that came naturally to one who believed tragedy to be part of life's texture and irreparability a matter of degree. 'Science,' Frances reports him saying, 'like any other Truth, never suffers from the loss of any individual' (*ibid.*).

32 Stephen Koss argued, for example, that he did not accept office in 1874 until he felt 'prodded' by *The Times, Daily News, Spectator* and *Pall Mall Gazette*: Koss, *The Rise and Fall of the Political Press in Britain* (2 vols., 1981), vol. I, pp. 204–5 and n.

the Conservative thinking-classes. Perhaps this explains his otherwise inexplicable generosity to Alfred Austin, whom he made poet laureate in 1895. (It could hardly have been the poetry.) In 1882 Austin had conceived, together with the distinguished literary critic W. J. Courthope, a new journal to be known as the *National Review*, written from an avowed Tory perspective in order to present current issues in an acceptable frame. Carnarvon was roped in at a meeting in the Junior Carlton and pressed the notion on Salisbury, who seemed taken by the idea. 'The country will be greatly indebted to it & to its promoters', he assured Austin, 'if it can give something of a scientific shape to the mass of Conservative thought which lies at the bottom of most educated men's minds.'[33] Of course, at one level this merely gave an intellectual twist to his instinct about 'villa Toryism' as a popular disposition except that in this case he knew rather more about it. But 'the mass of Conservative thought' implied an elitist perception quite as much as the villa Tories invited a demotic one: a worry to those like Carnarvon who had rather hoped that the journal would cut down deeper into the masses and 'reach a lower class'.[34] Salisbury wanted a journal like the *Quarterly* of his youth. Indeed, Austin achieved the startling success of persuading Salisbury to write for his new periodical, albeit sporadically. *Blackwood*, the standard-bearer of ultra sentiment for generations, felt itself rather snubbed. 'I see the Press today very full of Lord Salisbury's article in the "National Review"', wrote a plainly miffed proprietor. 'I suppose he has sent it there in order to bolster it up. It was too bad of him throwing over the Quarterly, or Old Maga [*Blackwood's Magazine*] for such a stripling.'[35] Salisbury wrote virtually nothing for publication by the 1890s and this piece flashed in an otherwise empty pan; but it suggested the depth of his concern for an intellectual Conservative journalism aimed at the clubs and common rooms. He never reflected Disraeli's priceless waving-away of this mid-Victorian initiative – 'No, my dear boy; I hate your new magazines'[36] – whose limited audience and civilized tone appealed to Salisbury because Conservative society ought to be limited and civilized.

To the extent that Salisbury ignored the press, he destroyed an

[33] Salisbury to Austin, 29 Oct. 1882, Austin MSS.
[34] Carnarvon to Salisbury, 16 Oct. 1882, Salisbury MSS (Carnarvon, f.400).
[35] Blackwood to Maxwell, Maxwell MSS 7403 HEM4.
[36] Lord George Hamilton, *Parliamentary Reminiscences and Reflections, 1886–1906* (2 vols., 1922), vol. I, p. 60.

important asset amassed by his predecessor. Not that Disraeli had spent all his time with newspaper editors: he had been happy to leave liaison with them to a party manager such as Gorst in the way that Salisbury would later allow colleagues to pursue journalistic contacts on their own initiative. But Disraeli had clearly understood the power of the national press and *a fortiori* of *The Times*, which he always pursued with some ardour. The days had long passed when he could write blithely to his leader, 'I hear the Times is going to support us. So much for public opinion',[37] as he had done during the more spacious days of Palmerstonian England; but he knew that Conservative opinion in London – the sort that interested him – might absorb significant teaching from the editor of *The Times*, so he courted that influence through written contacts and social engagements. He did not want to be told how to make policy: that emerged through political leaders and found its expression in parliament. 'The office of the press', he said, played its part 'afterwards, to enforce, illustrate, develope [*sic*] [policy]: reply to criticisms & vindicate it agst all comers.'[38] This turned editors into led more than leaders, apart, perhaps, from J. T. Delane who, Salisbury was complaining by 1868, may have gone around London 'talking Whig' but whose *Times* nevertheless displayed his 'writ[ing] Dizzyish'.[39] Other readers of Tory print counted the *Standard* and the *Globe* among 'our press'; but when Northcote tried to persuade Disraeli's secretary, Monty Corry, to book an appointment for the *Globe*'s proprietor so that he could inform Disraeli 'of the state of politics in Edinburgh', one suspects that the the champion of the 1867 reform bill had other things on his mind and complained of a prior engagement.[40] In other words, Disraeli interested himself in editors to the extent that they formed a section of the Conservative clerisy rather than because he saw them as a way of turning himself into a Gladstonian tribune.

Salisbury never managed even this much and his neglect told by the 1880s when his negative cast of mind found its fuller expression amid reform at home and Little Englandism abroad. He once allowed himself to be pulled out of the House of Lords by Algernon

---

[37] Quoted in W. D. Jones, *Lord Derby and Victorian Conservatism* (Oxford, 1956), p. 228.
[38] Disraeli to Stanley, 15 Aug. 1852, Derby MSS 1749/51.
[39] Cranborne to Carnarvon, 6 Mar. 1868, Carnarvon MSS 60758 f.57.
[40] Diary, 13 Aug. 1872, in Derby, *Diaries*, p. 113; Northcote to Corry, 18 Feb. 1867, Hughenden MSS B/XX/A/52.

Borthwick of the *Morning Post*[41] and he naturally was aware that the
Standard of W. H. Mudford had some importance. It is less clear that
he had any clear vision of the degree to which Tory journalism for
the masses had become a major power in the land or at least in
London.[42] He was right that neither J. T. Delane nor G. E. Buckle –
the two great Thunderers of the late nineteenth century – liked him
as Conservative leader, though he had some helpful support in
constructing foreign policy from Donald Mackenzie Wallace, the
foreign assistant editor from 1891.[43] Buckle, for example, merely
followed long-held instincts when he pushed for the Duke of
Devonshire to lead the Conservative government of 1895.[44] But
Delane and his successors would have made more effort on behalf of
Salisbury had the latter tried harder to encourage him. The cost
came in attacks such as this one as the 1884 reform bill preoccupied
press and parliament:

> Great organic reforms of this kind are really effected far more by the
> general consensus of the community than by the predilection or caprice of
> individual statesmen, and the academical schemes propounded by LORD
> SALISBURY in the *National Review* do not belong to the domain of practical
> politics. Conservatives and Liberals alike must move with the general
> movement of the national mind if they are to enjoy the national confidence,
> and LORD SALISBURY will not find it easy to secure the confidence of
> those classes in which in his earlier speech of yesterday he professed to
> discern the promise of Conservative strength in the future, if he persists in
> standing in the way of a great scheme of popular enfranchisement.[45]

It was the same with so many intellectuals of the era, though with
less justification. Salisbury attracted distaste for his sharp tongue,
certainly, but mostly for his illiberalism in a generation of great
liberal consistency before 1880. The high-minded writers of the
Fortnightly and *Contemporary* reviews sought something loftier – a good
liberal word – than Salisbury's cynicism: indeed they often missed its
point. Few flew higher than Goldwin Smith and, until he changed

---

[41] Oliver Borthwick to Lady Bathurst, 3 Aug. 1900, in Reginald Lucas, *Lord Glenesk and the Morning Post* (1910), pp. 391–2.

[42] For the growth of the Tory press in these years, see Koss, *Rise and Fall*, vol. I, pp. 199–200, 211, 320. 'Preponderantly Liberal when Disraeli took office, the metropolitan press was preponderantly Tory when he left it': *ibid.*, p. 198.

[43] See *History of the Times* (6 vols., 1935–93), vol. III, p. 135.

[44] Salisbury to Austin, 1 Jun. 1900: 'I think he has always quite frankly & loyally preferred that the Prime Minister should not be a pure Conservative': Christ Church MSS, no file. The background to this relationship will be developed in chapter 9.

[45] *The Times*, 2 Oct. 1884, p. 9b.

his mind, few felt so certain of his own views. '[Lord Salisbury] may gain support for his party by honourable views,' the prophet intoned in 1882, 'but he must not think that patriotism can be perverted to the uses of reaction.'[46] Press and periodical alike reinforced Salisbury's isolation. And that he rejoiced in their contempt did not increase their benevolence.

Two thoughts mitigated that rather bleak situation. First, some others within the Tory hierarchy maintained their own contacts with the intelligentsia, broadly defined, and helped relax the image of Conservative austerity and philistinism. 'Reading Renan's new essay . . . very original and striking.' Had Salisbury kept a diary we may be sure that this remark would have found no place in it. That it appears in Derby's[47] says something for the future foreign secretary's intellectual range and his ability to transcend Schopenhauer. He was one of the few Tories in a position to say that he had just received a letter from Darwin – 'the Darwin'.[48] But then, Derby's first-class degree seemed superficially stronger evidence than Salisbury's honorary fourth that the party deserved a better appellation than that of 'the stupid party'.[49] Or consider Carnarvon. 'Twitters' did not command respect for the weight or decisiveness of his intellect, to be sure, but his first in classics brooked no denial. His problem, from the point of view of the thinking Tory, had nothing to do with intelligence or culture so much as a certain manner, described variously as mincing or (rather worse) liberal.[50] He also had a worrying brother in the libertarian theorist and eccentric, Auberon Herbert, who sat as a Liberal for Nottingham at the beginning of the 1870s. When he made a speech there in 1871, the Duke of Richmond flagged its disturbing content to Gathorne Hardy by wondering what Carnarvon thought it meant; he himself had plainly struggled to

---

[46] Smith to Gibson, 25 May 1882, in A. B. Cooke and A. P. W. Malcolmson (eds.), *Ashbourne Papers 1869–1913* (Belfast, 1974), p. 171. Cf. Sidgwick's dismissal of the *Saturday Review* for its 'dominant tone' of 'conceited orthodoxy and cynical worldliness': diary, 22 Feb. 1885, in A. and E. M. Sidgwick, *Sidgwick: A Memoir* (1906), p. 401.

[47] Diary, 19 Jan. 1872, in Derby, *Diaries*, p. 97. He was referring to *La réforme intellectuelle et morale* (Paris, 1871).

[48] Derby to Cross, 17 Apr. 1878, Cross MSS 51266 f.17.

[49] Illness, of course, lay behind Lord Robert Cecil's result. Nor should it be seen as a contemptible achievement after so short a stay in the university, though it loses some of its majesty when compared with Ruskin's honorary *double* fourth.

[50] 'Very cultivated and refined, he has a manner which is too mincing to inspire confidence . . . he wants both grit and grip': *Society in London* (1885) quoted in *Complete Peerage, sub* Carnarvon (p. 48, n.).

make out its muzzle from its brush.[51] Then there was W. H. Smith, who at least *sold* books. He knew, moreover, the Mallocks of Cockington, near Torquay, who put him up when he visited south Devon, and thus made another contact, albeit a slightly *déclassé* one, with the ubiquitous William Hurrell Mallock who seems to have made little personal impression on Salisbury, though Carnarvon pressed Mallock's claims on him as 'a useful auxiliary' and 'one of the purely literary class whom it is desirable to secure'.[52] Certainly Mallock's country-house presence often enters the contemporary literature to which he also contributed through important critiques of current fashions in liberal thought.

Like the Herberts, the Mallocks give pause to any history of Conservative ideas in Victorian England by articulating the lack of fit between family and persuasion. The Devon family had none of the grandeur of the Carnarvons: Cockington was no Highclere. But they have that same smudging between Tory and Liberal universes of which our Mallock's middle name stands as reminder. William Hurrell Mallock's mother was a Froude, daughter not of the memorable Tractarian Hurrell Froude but of his brother, Robert Hurrell Froude, which made Carlyle's great friend and apologist James Anthony Froude her uncle. In marrying a rural vicar from south Devon she unconsciously joined a heritage of potential intellectual Liberalism to a form of bucolic Toryism ably embodied in her son, born in 1849 among the embers of Tract 90[53] and the ashes of his great-uncle's *Nemesis of Faith* which was burnt in the streets of Oxford when it appeared during that year. Mallock retained his ambiguities for a time, taught privately by a pupil of Thomas Arnold who claimed also to be friend to Tennyson. But by the time he went up to Balliol to cultivate his deep, relentless and mutual hatred of Benjamin Jowett and all he stood for, Mallock's colours had dried. He developed a churchmanship that never quite tumbled over into

---

[51] Richmond to Hardy, 10 Apr. 1871, Cranbrook MSS T501/257.
[52] Carnarvon to Salisbury, 3 Dec. 1881, Salisbury MSS (Carnarvon, f.359). Carnarvon seems to have offered Mallock financial support from party funds: 3 Dec., *ibid.*, f.362.
[53] This was Newman's celebrated contribution to the *Tracts for the Times*, from which the Tractarian Movement takes its name, which was deemed to have unacceptable Roman tendencies in its assertion that the Thirty-nine Articles of the Church of England were compatible with the doctrines of the ancient church. It thus 'led to the end of the Tracts, shattered Newman's self-confidence, and hacked away at those roots in Protestant tradition out of which the [Oxford] Movement had grown': Owen Chadwick, *The Spirit of the Oxford Movement: Tractarian Essays* (Cambridge, 1990), p. 43.

Romanism but bore the marks of his heritage.[54] He formed for himself a way of laughing at modernity as if it were a conspiracy of stupidity got up by the chattering classes; and in 1877 he brought many of its more risible personalities together in a fictional seminar whose members he made say sillier and sillier things, a method of discursive destruction that became his mature style. *The New Republic* (1877) expressed a Disraelian moment but it could better be read as a document seeking its Salisbury. Its appearance made intellectually respectable many of the propositions to which Lord Robert Cecil had so signally failed to lend dignity in the 1860s. From there Mallock went on to construct a mystique about country-house society that resembles that invented by those other Tory social climbers John Buchan and Evelyn Waugh. But he also reversed Ruskin in a series of portraits of capitalism as a thing of beauty that held at its heart not greed but genius.[55] Mallock became obsessed by talent as the only hope for the world and he saw it as the intangible spirit that drove capitalism along through its enterprise and vision. He saw as clearly as Marx that capitalism gave rise both to forces and relations of production; and, like Marx, he thought attempts to wish away the consequences of their mutual relation at best brainless and at worst corrupt. But Marx was hopelessly, comically wrong, he said, about commodities and what gave the products of capitalism their value. Labour was not at the basis of the thing at all: it was brains. And brains were not equally distributed, indeed they turned out remarkably scarce among the population as a whole. Elites reflected that scarcity and were as crucial to civilization as the wealth which they – and only they – ultimately created. A labour theory of value, confusing the instrument with the hand that guided it, made as much sense to Mallock as a horse theory of navigation.

In a professionalizing society, Mallock's amateurism debarred him from making certain kinds of impact. But to him one could add another loss to liberalism, James Fitzjames Stephen, whose elegant swipe at Gladstonian Britain, dressed up as an attack on the French Revolution,[56] carried the weight that a practising judge could carry,

---

[54] John Lucas is helpful about this and other aspects of Mallock's biography in his introduction to *The New Republic* (Leicester, 1975), p. 8.

[55] See, among other books, *Social Equality: A Short Study in a Missing Science* (1882); *Labour and the Popular Welfare* (1893); *Classes and Masses; or, Wealth, Wages and Welfare in the United Kingdom* (1896); *Aristocracy and Evolution: A Study of the Rights, the Origins, and the Social Functions of the Wealthier Classes* (1898); *A Critical Examination of Socialism* (1907).

[56] *Liberty, Equality, Fraternity* (1873) became a key text in clearheadedness for a generation of

just as Maine's contribution a decade later drew some of its force
from the stature of Maine in professional circles. Cumulatively these
points of contact, peripheral in the day-to-day management of Tory
politics, prevented Hatfield from becoming an island and brought to
Salisbury's table styles of reading and conversation he would never
knowingly have sought but which none the less fed his intelligence
and capacity for ironic destruction.

A second point concerns time. Before 1880 the intelligentsia who
had cut their teeth on the higher journalism of the 1860s and whose
world was that of Darwin, Spencer and *Essays and Reviews* maintained a liberal orientation that was often capital-L Liberal as well:
they acted as 'lights' for a progressive generation who declared
themselves impressed by scientific advance, economic success and
the righting of wrongs by Gladstone.[57] But the lure of a sophisticated
imperialism from the late 1870s, the collapse of trading optimism,
the onset of socialistic propaganda and the crippling effects of Irish
nationalism undermined these comfortable thoughts. First of all the
Whigs, then the more radical currents within Liberalism felt
troubled by the new moods. Come the collapse of Gladstone's
second government in June 1885, the ties that joined the intellectuals
to the Liberal party had already frayed. News of Gladstone's
unilateral and unaccountable 'conversion' to Home Rule at the end
of the year snapped those cords immediately and permanently.
Rarely has any single act on the part of a politician lost hard-won
intellectual support virtually overnight: one has to turn to Ramsay
MacDonald's 'betrayal' of socialism in 1931 for a similar provocation
among the thinking classes. But the result was manifest in 1886. The
clerisy screamed its outrage à la Goldwin Smith or shook its mane in
gloomy disbelief in the manner of Selborne, whose attitude to
Gladstone became a mixture, as Sir Charles Dilke said, of ice and
ink. They did not become supporters of Salisbury, at least not at
once. They saw the politics of Unionism, none the less, as a new crux
against which other priorities must henceforth be weighed. Some of
them irritated their potential allies by their past iniquities and their
present reluctance to commit themselves to the Conservative cause.

Tories. It was hated by socialists, for obvious reasons, but most ferociously by feminists
because of Stephen's dismissive attitude towards women. There were responses in print
from Lydia Becker and Millicent Garrett Fawcett.

[57] See Christopher Harvie, *The Lights of Liberalism: University Liberals and the Challenge of Democracy*
(1976).

Firebrands such as Alfred Milner, himself originally a Balliol Liberal closer to Morley and W. T. Stead than to Salisbury but a convert to Unionism *à l'outrance* after 1886, saw nothing to celebrate in an acquisition like Edward Dicey of the *Observer*. 'He may or may not call himself a Liberal Unionist,' Milner spat, 'but if there is one man in England who has failed to appreciate the difficulties or comprehend the motives of the Unionists, it is precisely Dicey.'[58] Union was plainly going to be hard to effect at home, whatever happened in Ireland. Still, a threshold had been crossed by Salisbury's style of Conservatism; and for the next fifteen years he proved able to rally a considerable section of Britain's intellectual classes in passive support if not active acclamation.

DEMOCRACY, SOCIALISM, REVOLUTION

By no means did the thoughts of those classes turn exclusively on political subjects. For many members of the intelligentsia the function and future of religion furnished, for example, a preoccupation during years of challenge from and accommodation with scientific method and attitude. For others, the ability to restate familiar problems in the language of science in itself acted inspirationally and became a surrogate for religious certainty. The emerging 'science' of economics, fertilized by an older tradition of 'political economy' and rendered urgent by the collapse of prosperity in Britain in the 1870s, altered both the discourse of the subject itself and the mental horizons of those who addressed it. Intellectuals concerned themselves with race and its biology, German philosophical idealism and its relevance to British thought, the nature of the British past, a search for the moral and the manly. Conservative thinkers were not intrinsically above such interests; but they often felt happier below them all the same. Religion often meant, as we shall see, the Church – not even the churches. 'Society', lacking all intellectual substance, became for them the state, which seemed a tangible and real thing.

---

[58] Milner to Austin, 3 Aug. 1887, Austin MSS. Edward Dicey was Albert Venn Dicey's elder brother and helps to cement a connexion already developed here, since his mother was a sister of the first Sir James Stephen which made James Fitzjames Stephen his uncle. He lacked his brother's intellectuality (as a third from Trinity College, Cambridge, confirmed) and he took, first, to business, then to freelance authorship and eventually to full-time journalism. He spent some years on the *Daily Telegraph* in the 1860s but is better known for having edited the *Observer* for nearly twenty years between 1870 and 1889. Keen clubman: Athenæum and Garrick.

Politics meant party, for no formation in Britain has ever enjoyed so powerful a sense of association and so rigid an intolerance of he-who-is-not-with-me. When Tories chose to think of higher purposes, however, they shared a common and natural concern with the health and future of their order and discussed, or rather declaimed from an intuitive platform, the perils of what must come if Britons were to relax their vigilance. Conservatives always know that their country is going to the dogs. What is interesting about them across time is the particular route by which they judge the national catastrophe will be reached. Salisbury's generation plotted a path to disaster marked by the milestones of democratic advance. Their thought frequently began with a vision of this partially trodden path and a determination at all costs to find a diversion that would take them around the ultimate nihilism of revolution and terror.

The path to ruin had originated in France and America. 1789 lay in no one's memory for the Salisbury generation: he had been born in the year of renewed revolution, 1830. But the horrors of the revolution they learned from witnesses such as Edmund Burke and Mme de Staël; they had Thomas Carlyle's narrative of the events, written in a prose that trembled and despaired as though the text itself were waiting for the guillotine; and they found themselves surrounded by memoirs and histories of the revolution and the terror as the century advanced and Napoleonic France became the end of history. And what a century the French had suffered since the joy of revolution: eruptions again in 1830, 1848 and 1870; constant instability of regime to the point of comedy; a seeming inability to become a dictatorship, a republic or an empire. French experience offered itself to the dread of democracy as a ready resource and illustration: democracy would make the British like the French – QED. On the other hand, at least Paris held pockets of *ancien régime* sensibility, just as libraries contained a Benjamin Constant or a de Maistre to sound the alarm. Salisbury was clearly comfortable on the edge of Dieppe or Nice with his novels and his children. America provided a very different story. It was not a democracy, but *the* democracy. From their very inspiration, the United States of America proclaimed themselves custodians of a new sense of justice drawn from self-evident first principles. America claimed success in that role, relished her self-awareness that a great work was being done there, boosted by the writing of a Frenchman, Alexis de Tocqueville, whose *Democracy in America* (1835–40) said much that the

British did not want to hear. And when the republic fell into crisis, Lord Robert Cecil had just come of age, ready to chronicle the fall and write a treatise on original sin.

He had been sardonic enough about America before the Civil War tore to tatters some of Washington and Jefferson's more dubious claims. Corruption within the American political system offended many British Conservatives, not least because it seemed so *public*, though Cecil himself preferred a soft irony about that because he thought corruption, sensibly and quietly applied, had its uses in an historic polity.[59] Once North and South had raised their flags, however, nothing was to be gained from understatement for, in the very act of self-dissolution, the United States had exposed the contradiction and incoherence of *unum in pluribus* and rendered vacuous the democratic promise of the New World:

> They never ceased to assure us that democracy was a cure for war, for revolution, for extravagance, for corruption, for nepotism, for class legislation, and, in short, for all the evils with which the states of Europe are familiar. It is too late for them, not that America is a prey to all these old-world maladies at once, to turn round and tell us that the model Republic is not worse than an average despotism, or no worse than England was four hundred years ago . . . A twelvemonth of stern experience has covered with confusion the foolish boasting of twenty years. A man would be laughed at now who should claim for democracy any special thrift, or purity, or love of peace.[60]

How wonderful that it had all gone wrong: it was 'the most ignominious failure that the world ha[d] ever seen'[61] and Conservatives ought to enjoy it while it lasted. Nor had democracy run into the sands just because of slavery or other taints from the Old World. It had collapsed from the nature of democracy itself, 'the great political fallacy of their institutions'. 'They are reaping a harvest', Cecil wrote in 1862, 'that was sown as far back as the time of Jefferson. They are without any leaders worthy of the name [!], because, in deference to a dreamer's theory, their natural leaders have been deposed.'[62] And why this usurpation? Because democrats

---

[59] '[A] healthy diet will kill a sick man outright. Sir Robert Walpole's bribery saved his country; Necker's purity ruined his': Cecil, 'Competitive Examinations', *Quarterly Review*, 216 (Oct. 1860), pp. 569–605 at pp. 571–3.

[60] 'The Confederate Struggle and Recognition', *Quarterly Review*, 112 (Oct. 1862), pp. 535–70 at pp. 538–9.

[61] *Ibid.*, p. 545.

[62] *Ibid.*, p. 547.

persuade themselves that anything done by the few, however wholesome, lacks value, while anything done by the many, whatever its
results, reflects virtue. When one of the bloodiest, most bitter
conflicts of recent times came to an end, Cecil reflected on 'The
United States as an Example' and saw the moral in nothing so
elevated as Lincoln's vision or even in inexplicable tragedy. It had
been all too explicable, its moral all too patent. The United States
had shown what happens when majorities tyrannize minorities; and
it was a lesson to bring home. If with this knowledge the governing
classes allow themselves to be duped into an 'advance' towards
democracy, 'their recompense will not be slow to reach them, and
will be richly merited when it comes'.[63]

America's impact on Conservative thinkers remained powerful for
the rest of the century.[64] But between 1864, when Gladstone
famously proclaimed the moral right of men to come within the pale
of the constitution, and 1867, when a sizeable fraction of working
men actually did so, the lesson of America pressed especially hard as
the franchise issue again came to centre-stage. Neither Gladstone
nor Salisbury put it there; but it would affect the political posture of
both of them and transform the potential of Disraeli over these few
years. All three had known about the problem virtually since they
came into politics. Whig claims that the extension of 1832, though
small, must be seen as 'final' had failed to carry conviction in the
1850s as the number of enfranchised men increased through natural
expansion as prosperity returned and property flourished. In particular it lost its credibility in face of the Irish Franchise Act of 1850,
which greatly extended the vote in ways that could hardly long be
held off in Britain. Even Salisbury's father, not exactly one to whom
the pundits turned, could see what was bound to come. 'It is
obvious', he railed at Disraeli, 'that from the day on which we passed
the extension of the franchise in Ireland Ld. John Russell's finality
was at an end . . . It is difficult to give a reason why an £8 occupier
in Ireland should be entrusted with a franchise which you would only
allow to a £10 occupier in England. It is difficult to argue that a £6

---

[63] 'The United States as an Example', *Quarterly Review*, 117 (Jan. 1865), pp. 249–86 at
pp. 285–6.
[64] Cf. H. A. Tulloch, 'Changing British Attitudes towards the United States in the 1880s',
Historical Journal, 20 (1977), pp. 825–40. It is significant that virtually all the authors
considered in this article were Liberals. Cf. Tulloch, *James Bryce's American Commonwealth: The
Anglo-American Background* (Woodbridge, 1988).

occupier is not as fit to be intrusted [*sic*] with it as one who is rated at £8.'[65] Quite so: the door had been opened as Peel had always warned and pressure from without would push it wider. The son of the second Marquis shared his father's sense of the mechanics at work and improved on his level of despair. He began with the idea of corruption – not the helpful sort but petty venality that came into play simply because 'the franchise had been extended to people who were so poor that they were liable to be bribed'.[66] He had sat on election committees investigating bribery in 1859, particularly one relating to Gloucester, where such depravities at any time before the First World War would have brought dejection to the heartiest democrat. Perhaps it stimulated a mood. It certainly found its way into his writing again a few months later when he sneered that '[w]hen so many men purchase[d] their seats for hard cash, it [was] not to be looked for that they should disdain to purchase them by the less costly, and less substantial sacrifice of their opinions'.[67]

This became one wing of the argument: that democracy means giving the vote to poor people who will sell it and encourage adventurers to bid for that commodity with their wallets or pliable convictions. A second took flight from his understanding of property and the right of property-owners to enjoy protection from parliament against forms of spoliation. In the wake of Gladstone's 'pale of the constitution' speech, Cecil wrote one of his sharpest polemics about what the House of Commons was *for*: it was to reflect the character of 'the English social system which supplies it with members, . . . the political climate in which it has been put together' and 'the inbred instincts of those who drive it'. These people respond to 'the political opinion of an educated class, among whom they live'. Democracy, on the other hand, excludes such people out of class jealousy and produces a form of political behaviour in which no sensitive person would wish to participate. '[E]ducated men do not like going round, hat in hand, begging for the votes of a mob . . . [who] are their inferiors in the ordinary concerns of life, are rough and crass in their manners, and delight in humiliating a "gentleman", and require him to swallow the most claptrap pledges as the condition of their

---

[65] Second Marquis of Salisbury to Disraeli, 17 Jan. 1852, Hughenden MSS B/XXI/C/129. For the Irish context in 1850, see Theodore Hoppen, *Elections, Politics and Society in Ireland 1832–1885* (Oxford, 1984), esp. pp. 1–33.

[66] Lord Robert Cecil in Commons, *Hansard*, 26 Jan. 1860, CLVI, col. 187.

[67] 'The Conservative Reaction', *Quarterly Review*, 108 (Jul. 1860), pp. 265–302 at p. 270.

support'. What property supplied to the argument was, for Cecil, its crucial weapon in the battle against those who sought a wider franchise:

[T]hey persist in forgetting that 'the suffrage' means something very much more than a share. It means an equal share. To give the suffrage to a poor man is to give him as large a part in determining that legislation which is mainly concerned with property as the banker whose name in known on every Exchange in Europe, as the merchant whose ships are in every sea, as the landowner who owns the soil of a whole manufacturing town. An extension of the suffrage to the working classes means that upon a question of taxation, or expenditure, or upon a measure vitally affecting commerce, two day-labourers shall outvote Rothschild.[68]

In other words Cecil cleaved to a theory of 'virtual' representation that had been familiar to Burke and Blackstone. Parliament should contain representatives of property of all kinds; those who could not participate directly in the House of Commons and House of Lords had their interests protected by those who indirectly represented their concerns by reflecting their status and occupations. 'The question [was]', quite simply, 'whether England sh[ould] be governed by property and intelligence, or by numbers.'[69]

Within a decade, numbers seemed to govern Britain – at least to Salisbury and his circle. Many elements contributed to that suspicion but two of them preoccupied Conservatives more morbidly than others: the reform act of 1867, instigated by their own party, which effected a more radical extension of the vote than anybody, least of all Disraeli, had anticipated; and the coming of the secret ballot in 1872, which placed the hordes beyond control by allowing them to do their worst in a private act of subversion. The first of these events belongs to the history of party and we shall have cause to reconsider it.[70] But in prompting their decision to resign from Derby's minority government of 1866–7, Disraeli's reform bill not only brought about a significant party rift but confirmed Cranborne and Carnarvon in their fear of numbers. Perhaps other issues had intruded or even dominated. Perhaps 1867 had as much to do with a question of who was to lead the Conservative party as with the end of the Conservative party. It remains clear that the sheer scale of the enfranchisement (and this before radical amendments greatly enhanced it) made the

---

[68] 'The House of Commons', *Quarterly Review*, 116 (Jul. 1864), pp. 245–81 at pp. 247, 273, 266.
[69] 'The Elections', p. 295.
[70] See chapter 9 below, pp. 252–64.

blood run cold at Hatfield and Highclere. Cranborne's refusal to countenance so great a shift in the political structure (or his political failure in pretending to refuse) removed him from all co-operation with his party and left him morose about the country's future. He and Carnarvon wrote sad letters to one another. 'You know I heartily concur in all your gloomy views,' Carnarvon was reassured in 1871. 'As a nation we have reached the valetudinarian stage. We are perpetually consulting doctors, & trembling at the possible risk of remedies. Decay is not far off.'[71] Undoubtedly the events of 1867 with their burden of concession to popular demand and pandering to the worst instincts in society greatly contributed to his instinct – one that he never abandoned. At just the moment when his anti-democratic theories had most venom in them, moreover, he rather pulled away from journalism, apart from one memorable attack on Disraeli whose fault it all was. The mass of prose written between 1859 and 1865 he left behind him, turning to his railway chairman-ship, to the Hatfield improvements and the obligations following from his succession to the marquisate. To Disraeli he left the task of 'secur[ing] the New Constituency' through a programme of registra-tion[72] whose beneficiaries he avowedly despised; nor was he de-pressed when Disraeli failed to secure it and crashed in the general election of 1868. Even so, the depredations of Gladstone, now leader of the Liberal party and prime minister for the first time, could only confirm the drift of British institutions in the direction of popular control and participation. When Lord Clarina thundered from the depths of Limerick that right-thinking men must 'oppose the Demo-cratic spirit that seems to pervade every measure of the present Government',[73] everyone in the late cabinet knew exactly what he meant.

The damage ranged from attacks on the army and the universities to an obsession with populist rhetoric about class and interest, for this was the new Gladstone, the People's William. While other Conservatives suffered seizures over army reform, however, it was the ballot issue that most incensed Salisbury and brought him back into political engagement, aided by Disraeli's not being in the House of Lords. As with reform itself, Disraeli's line on the ballot never went beyond the pragmatic: he disliked it in principle but would

---

[71] Salisbury to Carnarvon, 30 Jan. 1871, Carnarvon MSS 60758 f.92.
[72] Disraeli to Cairns, 'Whit Sunday' 1868, Cairns MSS 30/51/1/f.31.
[73] Clarina to Richmond, 8 Mar. 1870, Goodwood MSS 862 v 64.

swallow his dislike if, as seemed to be the case, the party showed signs of splitting in the Commons.[74] Salisbury remained convinced to the end that the ballot was simply 'a very bad thing'. 'It will produce great abstention from the polls of the respectable classes,' he forecast to Carnarvon, '& proportionably [*sic*] increase the power of busybodies, enthusiasts, & party wire-pullers.'[75] Carnarvon needed no priming, but his anxiety focussed not on who would attain power, but rather *where*:

In itself I own I like the measure less & less the more that I look at it – and my dislike is strengthened by recent events and agitation among the agricultural labourers [i.e. Joseph Arch's campaign in Warwickshire]. I have very little faith in our gaining any *real or permanent* advantage from it as some people believe & if things sd. turn out badly our hold on the Counties, which after all is the real source & centre of our strength, might be affected.[76]

By the time Tory peers met at the Carlton to consider their line on the ballot bill, most of them had bitten Disraeli's bullet. Salisbury had not.[77] And he never moved away from his position, despite accumulating evidence that the ballot made very little difference to stability or actively encouraged democratic advance. '[U]nder the Ballot all is uncertain.' 'The Ballot is the regime of surprises.'[78] Like John Stuart Mill, who had also preferred it,[79] Salisbury saw in open voting a check on 'random impulses' and perhaps also a moral quality that raised the citizen above furtiveness by charging him with responsibility to defend the judgement on which he had staked his name and reputation.

Good strategists occasionally win wars while losing battles and Salisbury, once he emerged from the despair of 1867–72, saw the best chance of success in accepting *faits accomplis* and turning the argument elsewhere. In this sphere, as in foreign policy, he found Carnarvon's jitteriness poorly-grounded and Derby's sense of doom

---

[74] Disraeli to Richmond, 16 Sep. 1871, Goodwood MSS 863 x 43.

[75] Salisbury to Carnarvon, 20 Feb. 1872, Carnarvon MSS 60758 f.100.

[76] Carnarvon to Richmond,12 May 1872, Goodwood MSS 863 y 31.

[77] Derby diary, 13 May 1872: '. . . the second reading of which we decided not to oppose, Salisbury only having doubts': Derby, *Diaries*, p. 107.

[78] Salisbury to Balfour, 19 Jul. 1873, *Salisbury–Balfour Correspondence*, p. 15; For his later views, see, 'Disintegration', *Quarterly Review*, 156 (Oct. 1883), pp. 559–95.

[79] '. . . the duty of voting, like any other public duty, should be performed under the eye and criticism of the public; every one of whom has not only an interest in the performance but a good title to consider himself wronged if it is performed other than honestly and carefully': *Considerations on Representative Government* (1905 (1st edn 1861)), pp. 192ff.

over-excited. The point lay in maintaining and servicing the ramparts that already existed to prevent democratic waves from overwhelming the constitution and the classes for whom its mysterious character had been evolved. Certainly one had to play the sub-democratic game to the extent of amending political practice so as to reach new voters. This meant giving Akers-Douglas, or those who shared his world-view, his head in organizing the constituencies; it implied that the Primrose League, designed to advance the popular reach of Toryism, should be supported at least in public.[80] His central thrust, however, lay in stressing forms of resistance or diversion. For resistance he looked to the House of Lords – not out of some revival of constitutional doctrine but as the best hope of stopping the radical-dominated House of Commons from doing anything dangerous. This position produced no friction with a Conservative understanding of how the constitution ought to work, and resistance could be given a theoretical cloak which made it appear disinterested and prompted only by a wish to protect the electorate's higher wishes. Writing to a supporter in the Cirencester Constitutional Club in 1894, he stressed – inevitably – the constitution. 'If the House of Commons were elected every six months or even every year,' the argument went, 'there might be some ground for contending that their decisions were necessarily in conformity with the views then held by the electors . . . But to assume that a house that is elected for several years must necessarily be at all times voting in accordance with the views of the electors upon bills which have not been referred to them, appears to me a rash inference, unsupported by any arguments of a practical kind.'[81] This view underpinned the justification of using the power of the House of Lords consistently after 1880 to try to arrest democratic tendencies visible in the Commons or at least to emasculate that which could not be prevented. Secondly, Salisbury shifted the argument towards redistribution. If the battle over franchise had gone wrong, he could still argue that the question of how the new electorate was to be redistributed now became a subject of central political importance – taking Carnarvon's anxiety about *where?* and substituting it for *how many?* Pulling off the change of stance without falling over demanded

---

[80] Privately he thought that the initiative would collapse because its authoritarian nature would not suit the English character: Salisbury to Northcote, 23 Dec. 1883, Iddesleigh MSS 50020 f.69.

[81] Salisbury to Harmer, 15 Dec. 1894, Christ Church MSS, no file.

some careful amnesia, so that the speeches in 1884 would not look at all like the ones of 1867. He remained within the memory of many of his audience all the same when he spoke to the House of Lords on the potential democracy envisaged in 1884:

I am in a condition to know what are the opinions of Conservatives, not only within these walls, but in various parts of the country; and there has never been any adverse feeling to the extension of the suffrage on the ground of the presumed incapacity or unfitness of those to whom it has to be extended. But the issue turns on a totally different question. The question is – How is political power to be so distributed that all classes may receive their due position in the State, that all interests may be respected, that a true mirror for the actual numerical condition of opinions in this country may be produced within the walls of the other House of Parliament, in order that minorities may be able to receive that just power of expressing their opinions, which is essential to the just protection of their interests . . .[82]

This portended not a new liberalism in face of *demos* but an artful performance over the redistribution clauses when the Tory leadership would rally to the cause of the countryside and limit the impact of radical towns.

Other cards remained up the sleeve. Provided that the power of the state were controlled, Salisbury did not believe that a serious democratic attack could succeed. He saw democracy as a form of political organization that had gained its credibility in countries such as America which protected its citizens from legislative attack with a framework of fundamental constitutional laws that no radical administration could subvert.[83] Britain would never trust democrats in the absence of such protection: 'the feebleness of our government is our security'. Secondly, he looked to the nature of society itself and the characteristics that would not only retard democracy but also act as a dyke against socialism and revolution. Partly he had in mind the possibility of enfranchising women – a move he recognized would not come about in the short term but which he often saw in his later years as a helpful injection of stability, morality and detached wisdom into British political life. Yet there was more than this. In what he thought of as 'English' society there inhered serious obstacles to any form of revolutionary upheaval. Perhaps that was

---

[82] Salisbury in Lords, *Hansard*, 8 Jul. 1884, CCXC, col. 456.
[83] Salisbury to Balfour, 29 Mar. 1886, Cecil, vol. III, p. 297.

why he felt so much less fear of socialism and revolution than many around him announced in their correspondence and public remarks.

Of course, creeping socialism and the potential for revolutionary disturbance formed an important context for all Conservatives after 1867 and its significance should not be downplayed in understanding their responses to the political conditions of the 1870s but especially the late 1880s when the exposure to socialist thought seemed at its most intense. The responses show interesting and no less significant modulations, however, both between individuals and across time. For a Carnarvon or Derby, the threat became an enervating certainty, its only question whether one could contrive to die before it came about. For Disraeli it was merely part of a materialist decadence from which religion offered some escape and death would supply a release. For an ideological capitalist like W. H. Smith, the country was 'drifting into radical socialism very fast indeed' by the early 1880s and the constitutional system heading for inevitable destruction.[84] Richmond tried to think about it but it only made him miserable, so he sent everybody a kippered salmon and hoped that Cairns would pull the country through. The intellectuals poured out their ink – James Fitzjames Stephen, Sir Henry Maine and Mallock especially with his jeremiads about socialist idiocy, the indivisibility of wealth, the sacredness of brains and enterprise. Some sections of the intelligentsia took heart from the accommodations practised by the missionary moods of Oxford and Cambridge; some of them saw spirituality where others saw abdication and betrayal of one's class. Meanwhile the bishops often had their own secret heartaches hidden behind sermons in which they could hardly confess to the new public that they thought the 'democracy-strata' behaved like 'tyrants'[85] or who saw England becoming uninhabitable if these trends persisted:

Surely of all government that by *hysterics* is the worst, and England is being more and more governed by the hysteria of half-educated men and women.

The aristocratic oligarchy of the last century was selfish and short-sighted as regards domestic policy; but it was cool, far-seeing, and prompt, as regards foreign politics.

The boorish voter who sustained that aristocracy and squirarchy was dull and impassive, and open to bribery and beer; but he was stolid and bovine, and never got into a fury except against the Pope. But your modern, half-taught, newspaper-reading, platform-haunting, discussion-club frequenter,

---

[84] Smith to Cranbrook, 23 Jan. 1882, Cranbrook MSS T501/260.
[85] Benson diary, 17 Jan. 1885.

conceited, excitable, nervous product of modern town artisan life, is a most dangerous animal. He loves rant and cant and fustian, and loves too the power for the masses that all this rant and cant is aiming at, and he seems to be rapidly becoming the great ruling power in England . . . The England of thirty years hence . . . will surely be the nastiest residence conceivable for anyone save infidel prigs and unsexed women.[86]

It was a desperate thought. And in these years of fenianism, the Paris Commune, the spread of Marxist ideas in the 1880s, the first march of the unemployed in 1886 and the onset of mass strikes by unskilled labourers at the end of the decade, only the deaf and the blind could avoid a sense of transformation.

Yet if Salisbury shared and absorbed these images as complement to a native pessimism, he shared also the perceptions of the dead who had called revolution's bluff. He would take his note as much from the Duke of Wellington as the Duke of Omnium and incline to meet adversity with force when argument failed. Like Wellington, he did not fear the mob nearly so much as he mistrusted the courage of his own class; and, like Wellington, he saw dissolution coming not from revolutionary assault but rather from internal collapse at the hands of the tremulous and stupid. Here at least England was not France. 'One night's neglect may place a mob in the possession of the Tuileries and terminate a dynasty,' he wrote in a crafted passage. 'But this sort of revolution can never take place in England[:] . . . the example of the capital assuredly would not shake the allegiance of a single English county . . . [I]t is quite clear that the British Constitution has nothing to fear from revolution, unless the owners of property are beguiled into helping to undermine the institutions which protect them.'[87] But of course that is precisely what he saw happening in 1867 when owners of property, beguiled by Disraeli, allowed themselves to crumble into concessions that could never be revoked. Riots in Hyde Park doubtless played their part in inflaming public opinion; he conceded that they turned rather ugly at one point. They could have been suppressed by a less neurotic home secretary than Spencer Walpole. They certainly provided no excuse for what followed. His initial position did not alter, however. Revolutions could only be produced in England by the dithering of a nerveless elite. He could greet the formation of the Communist

---

[86] Magee [Bishop of Peterborough] to MacDonnell, 4 Mar. 1878 in J. C. MacDonnell, *The Life and Correspondence of William Connor Magee* (2 vols.,1896), vol. II, pp. 91–2.

[87] 'Parliamentary Reform', *Quarterly Review*, 117 (Apr. 1865), pp. 540–75 at pp. 562–3.

International with equanimity while Carnarvon bleated on his walks with Derby that a new order in history had come into existence.[88] The solution of some – that 'one nation' ideals must prevail and the divide between rich and poor close – he rejected as contrary to sound Conservative strategy. Better to reinforce that divide and make sure that the rich part was Conservative. Rather than throw up one's hands about the class war, better to win it. As he turned Conservative thought to a defence of property, he knew full well that sharper divisions in society would result between the Haves and the Have-Nots. But he saw the likely result as less revolutionary rather than more, because people would learn that they could win a stake in the nation and acquire something to protect – an insight developed by Margaret Thatcher a hundred years later. He would not have been surprised at Lord Onslow's unsteadiness after the London County Council elections of 1898:

. . . I am afraid for landowners, share holders et hoc genus omne . . . [especially] . . . if one looks at the map. Except Chelsea (which was a fluke) the whole of the 'Haves' of the West End form a serried rank in opposition to the 'Havenots' of the East End & though the number of votes on both sides was practically equal, the 'Havenots', save for the fortunate protection of a Parliament containing at present a Conservative majority, have the larger rate-payers & property owners at their mercy.[89]

The prime minister would perhaps have reversed the logic. It was precisely the promulgation of counter-revolutionary doctrines by the Conservative party that had put the majority there in the first place and the best way to keep it there lay in sharpening that image rather than blurring it. As Baldwin would discover in the 1920s, revolution was the Tories' friend, for nothing so rallies one's supporters as a sense of impending extermination.

Socialism proved more of a difficulty and Salisbury had none of Baldwin's finesse in pretending to half-believe in it.[90] Neither, however, did he seek to trample socialists in the mud, at least in public. Instead he used arguments similar to those of Mallock: socialists and radicals of various kinds deluded themselves about the nature of political economy and in particular they failed to see that the purpose of good government lay in encouraging enterprise to

---

[88] Diary, 26 Jun. 1871, in Derby, *Diaries*, p. 83.
[89] Onslow to Cadogan, 11 Mar. 1898, Cadogan MSS CAD/1321.
[90] See Philip Williamson, *Stanley Baldwin: Conservative Leadership and National Values* (Cambridge, 1999), where the links of the Baldwin family with Christian socialism receive some stress.

increase the size of the national cake rather than slicing it into ever-smaller pieces. So '[t]he Conservative points the working man forward to obtain wealth which is as yet uncreated', rather than 'say[ing] that the wealth which has already been obtained is badly divided, that some have got something, that others have got nothing at all, and that the real remedy is to look back and fight among yourselves for the wealth that has already been obtained'.[91] During the second half of the 1880s the urgency of parliamentary argument quickened, not least through the shrill predictions of doom in which the Earl of Wemyss had come to specialize. On three occasions during these years, Wemyss placed the spectre of socialism before the House of Lords to terrify the peers into greater awareness. The first two proved less than arresting: in 1887, for example, he attracted a total of seven peers to the debate. On the third occasion, in 1890, he did better and presented the House with his familiar warnings about where the ever-increasing body of legislation was tending. 'Now, my Lords, what is the character of all this legislation? It is to substitute State-help for self-help, to regulate and control men in their dealings with one another with regard to land or anything else . . . The whole tendency is to substitute the State or the Municipality for the free actions of the individual.' Not for the first time, Salisbury (though pressed as prime minister with more immediate concerns) chose to reply to him and his speech is worth recalling for its patient picking-apart of Wemyss's contentions and his fundamentally relaxed description of what 'socialism' meant:

I take Socialism in its strict meaning to be for the State to do that which is usually done by private people for the sake of gain. I believe that this is sometimes a very unwise thing; on the other hand, it is sometimes a very wise thing. There is nothing so Socialistic as the Mint or the Post Office. No doubt my noble Friend is right in saying that at the present day there is a strong leaning towards bringing in the interference of the State on every possible occasion, and I think that is a tendency against which it is right that we should be upon our guard. *It is not that we sin against any principle*, but that we expect from the State what it cannot possibly do if we impose upon it tasks which it cannot fitly perform or burdens beyond its power; and all we shall do will be to create an indefinite source of expense, and ultimately an unlimited cause of corruption and inefficiency. My Lords, it seems to me that Socialism is a great mistake, but I do not think it is an irremediable evil. What it really means is spending money on a useless object . . . No

---

[91] Salisbury at Victoria Hall, Lambeth, 4 Nov. 1885, in *Cecil*, vol. III, p. 263.

irremediable evil will be the result, only a certain amount of legislative goose-step will have been performed.[92]

This position camouflaged occasional outbursts in private. His genuine anxiety about the outcome of the 1880 election we have already noted; and the same concern would erupt from time to time at elections when he considered that socialism had turned into the litmus test of opinion. Consider the year of the great dock strike, 1889, an apotheosis of socialist advance in the trade unions and within the clerisy through the publication of *Fabian Essays*. At a by-election during the spring (Lambeth, Kennington), the Conservative candidate had done badly. One of the Beresford-Hopes had watched a government majority of 430 degenerate into a Liberal win by over 600 votes. Salisbury thought that it had been lost on the socialist question and brought his anxiety to the Brighton election in the autumn where he expected the changecoat Sir Robert Peel to take the seat for the Liberals because the socialists and artisans would vote against the government to a man.[93] He may well have been wrong about the first and certainly was about the second, for Peel went down by 2,500 votes; but the anxiety could flare up from time to time. More significant, perhaps, is Salisbury's awareness of the flaring and his insistence, when more at his ease, that other issues would prove more testing in the long run. His preoccupation was property and that the Conservative location of property pointed to Ireland. In 1885 he shared the Queen's unease about 'a "Socialist" current' but thought it probable that the interest in it would show itself a 'transient' one.[94] By the end of the year he was reassuring the jumpy Austin that whereas the socialist question had 'the habit of making a burst for a year or two, and then disappearing', the Irish problem had 'shewn its vitality by centuries of undiminished vigour'.[95]

Salisbury's definitions help explain the neglect. If by 'socialism' one intends to convey the connotation familiar to a modern ear – a doctrine denying the ability of capitalism to construct or maintain a fair society and recommending the deployment of state power in

---

[92] Wemyss and Salisbury in Lords, *Hansard*, 19 May 1890, CCCXLIV, cols. 1218, 1240–2 (emphasis added).

[93] Salisbury to Manners, 20 Mar. 1889 and 22 Oct. 1889, in Charles Whibley, *Lord John Manners and his Friends* (2 vols., 1925), vol. II, pp. 251–2.

[94] Salisbury to the Queen, 18 Oct. 1889, RA VIC/A67/93.

[95] Salisbury to Austin, 2 Dec. 1889, *Cecil*, vol. IV, p. 206.

order to secure social and economic equality – then Salisbury was its implacable opponent and so were 99 per cent of his colleagues in all parties. But if socialism had the gentler resonance that Salisbury ascribed to it – a series of questions about what the state could reasonably be asked to achieve – then it touched the sensitivities of every sector of political opinion during a period when Liberals, quite as much as Conservatives, found their ideas about state interference undergoing a major transformation and when thinkers, quite as much as politicians, had become preoccupied by the relation between the state and social policy.[96] Behind all such questions lay older ones. *Qu'est-ce que l'état?* Had the Victorian state changed its character from the primordial one known to the Enlightenment? What relation should be seen to subsist between people and government in this new, sub-democratic environment? Most important for Conservative thinkers and parliamentarians, what would a *Conservative* state look like and with whom could it legitimately permit itself to interfere? Few Tories had framed any answer before 1870. Not a few resented the degree to which all the 'answers' had been invented by Liberals.

[96] For a useful perspective, see José Harris, 'The Transition to High Politics in English Social Policy' in Michael Bentley and John Stevenson (eds.), *High and Low Politics in Modern England* (Oxford, 1983), pp. 58–79.

CHAPTER 6

The state

THE CONSERVATIVE CONSTITUTION

At the moment when Cranborne's scepticism about democracy darkened into night during 1867, a liberal vision of *The English Constitution* appeared in print and made its author famous. There is not much to suggest that Walter Bagehot would have become famous otherwise, except as a prolific writer of occasional pieces across the spectrum of mid-Victorian subjects. His brief account of English governance nevertheless found its audience in the aftermath of 1867's reform bill (which made the book at once out of date) and, more puzzlingly, retained its power as an insight into British constitutional practice for subsequent generations. This is odd, not least because *The English Constitution* seems as occasional as most of Bagehot's other books and as liberal as all of them. On the other hand, the English intelligentsia has nurtured its Victorian liberalism in the twentieth century, so perhaps like still speaks to like. A process of revision is underway, all the same, and modern students of the constitution – to the extent that Britain can be said to have one – see much in Bagehot that requires correction.[1] More pressing for our theme here is an understanding that Conservatives saw a different constitution from the one sketched by Bagehot and one of which one needs some awareness if Tory assumptions about how to govern are to make more sense. A conception of power residing in an 'efficient' House of Commons which acted in tandem with 'dignified' elements such as the monarchy and House of Lords found little fit with Conservative expectation of these institutions as operative and

---

[1] See, for example, H. J. Hanham, *The Nineteenth Century Constitution, 1815–1914: Documents and Commmentary* (Cambridge, 1969); G. H. L. Le May, *The Victorian Constitution: Conventions and Contingencies* (1979); James Vernon (ed.), *Re-reading the Constitution: New Narratives in the Political History of England's Long Nineteenth Century* (Cambridge, 1996).

important locations of authority. Perhaps particularly during the last thirty years of the century, as Conservative leadership looked to the 'establishment', the monarchy and House of Lords for its inspiration and resistance to popular pressures, the liberal understanding of how the state ought to function cut across Tory sentiments so manifestly that distinct languages about the state's nature and responsibilities emerged in parliament, the higher journals and the day-to-day apprehensions of Conservative leaders. To see this Conservative language as an articulation of new constitutional theory is to pulp the politics of Toryism, which loathed theories about the constitution as much as it mistrusted theories of any kind. Intimations of difference there certainly were, none the less, and they made their mark from Balmoral to Goodwood, from Knowsley to Hatfield.

Balmoral mattered socially in the lives of Tory politicians. It would blur contemporary perceptions, however, if we followed Bagehot in leaving the power of the monarchy there. Of course it is the lesson of all textbooks that 'the power of the crown' diminished in the nineteenth century; and so it plainly did if one is speaking about the ability of a monarch to dismiss ministers, which was done for the last time in 1834, or the command of patronage that (say) George III had enjoyed and which Victoria unquestionably did not. But the Queen remained head of state in a way that Tories found resonant: they may have disliked her personally, for few found her post-Albert incarnation other than spoiled, selfish, emotional and poorly-advised, but they saw her as the apex of Britain's pyramid of political forces and as a formidable *problem* when they crossed her. She also gained some status in Conservative eyes from her patent detestation of Gladstone. This meant that Gladstone's emergence after 1868 as Liberal leader and the Queen's emergence from extreme purdah at around the same time wove together a useful thread of Conservative influence at court. Every time she exploded that she was 'very much annoyed at Mr. Gladstone's course of action',[2] no constitutional doctrine came under threat; but the spin generated by her firmly held opinions was still on the ball by the time it reached Arlington Street or the cabinet room. Salisbury read that spin well: he treated Balmoral and Osborne as a sort of department of state and usually contrived to go with the Queen's mood of the moment rather than

---

[2] Cross to Derby, 20 Sep. 1876, Derby MSS 16/2/5. This instance commented on Gladstone's agitation over Turkish atrocities in Bulgaria.

resist. His context explains this complaisance to some extent, for the revival of Victoria's political prominence predated his arrival in power and took its toll of Disraeli long before he felt the weight of royal displeasure. The Disraeli/Beaconsfield ministry of 1874–80 supplied the locus for royal resurgence because it interfered with the church, about which Victoria minded,[3] and was itself interfered with by the Russians, whom Victoria had learned to hate for what they had done in the Crimea twenty years earlier. It also turned out by accident to supply the period of Albert Edward's coming of age politically – an event to upset any ministry.

Through her favourite channels of communication – Richard Cross, Lord John Manners and the Duke of Richmond in the 1870s, W. H. Smith in the 1880s – the Queen energized, cajoled and browbeat: she rarely argued, let alone persuaded. She saw herself as having an especially prominent role in the formation of foreign policy, about which constant demands for information and counsel emanated from her secretaries and captive politicians. 'I am desired by the Queen to say', wrote Cross rather wearily and without conviction to the foreign secretary in 1875, 'she wishes to hear any thing you may have to say about China. [I]t will be quite enough if you write to me & I dare say you have not much to say.'[4] This amounted to no more than conventional management of a difficult personality and neither required much footwork nor revealed much influence. The shift of sensibility seems to have come with Disraeli's decision to elevate the Queen to the title of Empress of India (a move which Salisbury, incidentally, opposed[5]), for it gave wing to royal ambitions to govern more than the Indian subcontinent. By the autumn of 1876 she had turned to glare at the Bear, warn the ministers of his ambitions and announce 'that when the Spring comes a veritable Russian army may invade Turkey from Servia.' Lord John Manners was told to tell Derby; she herself would alert the prime minister.[6] This initiative became more of a bore through its relentlessness. The court wanted war if Russia went anywhere near Turkey; and that inescapable fact sapped the will and dogged

---

[3] This subject will recur in the next chapter.
[4] Cross to Derby, 7 Oct. 1875, Derby MSS 16/2/5.
[5] See Richard Shannon, *The Age of Disraeli, 1868–1881: The Rise of Tory Democracy* (1992), p. 273.
[6] Manners to Derby, 12 Oct. 1876, Derby MSS 16/2/5. Cf. Richmond to Cairns, 7 Nov. 1878: 'She charged me to write in the strongest possible terms to the Prime Minister and state what she felt': Cairns MSS 30/51/4/f.37.

the travels of ministers. If they went to court they found her rejuvenated and 'very warlike' with her son and heir 'talk[ing] loudly and foolishly in all companies'. If they crept away for a Sunday in the country, as Beaconsfield did in the summer of 1877, no less than three messengers might follow, not to mention the telegrams that littered the table like leaves.[7] By the end of that month Salisbury came back from Osborne 'unpleasantly impressed with the state of the Queen',[8] who had clearly begun to take more time and patience than ministers had formerly allowed her. Richmond seems to have been at least as exasperated by Albert Edward: the encounter destabilized his punctuation even more than usual.

I have had conversations with P[rince] of W[ales] and D[uke] of C[ambridge] about affairs in the East both are very keen that we shd have done more than we have done. I pointed out our very awkward position. The former energetic in his view. said we ought to have occupied Gallipoli with fifteen thousand men that it was no use having a majority if we did not use it: and the usual arguments that we have heard so often. Most of which I have seen in the Pall Mall Gazette.[9]

This particular eruption climaxed in the weeks before and after Christmas 1877 when the Queen lunched at Hughenden on 15 December, dragged Beaconsfield to dine and sleep on the 18/19th, paid further visits on the 22nd and 27th and left Derby not a little apprehensive in the New Year that she was losing her sanity[10] – a not uncommon fear in Conservative circles, especially given the family history.

Salisbury felt comparatively little of this pressure before 1878 and the resolution of the Eastern crisis in the Congress of Berlin in that year siphoned off much of it. But it educated him towards a politics of partial compliance when the royal crisis of his own premiership broke in the attempt to keep Prince Alexander of Bulgaria out of the hands of the Russians in the autumn of 1885 when Salisbury was nursing his caretaker government until elections could be held on that year's register. He had already been warned by Hicks Beach that

[7] Diary, 22 Jun. 1877 and 16 Jul. 1877, in Derby, *Diaries*, pp. 412, 420.

[8] Diary, 26 Jul. 1877, in *ibid.*, p. 423.

[9] Richmond to Cairns, 1 Aug. 1877, Cairns MSS 30/51/4/f.20. Edward VII's accession in 1901 showed at once that he had not forgotten these moments of intervention, for Balfour's government had to tolerate incursions into their business. In the case of the King's Speech in 1903, for example, Edward demanded textual changes in reporting the Alaska Treaty to Parliament: Knollys to Halsbury, 14 Feb. 1903, Halsbury MSS 56371 ff.221–2.

[10] Diary, 15 Dec. 1877 and 7 Jan. 1878, in Derby, *Diaries*, pp. 475, 481.

the Queen ought to stop sending personal communications to the Viceroy of India through the India Office, because 'the recipient can hardly help supposing that they not only represent H.M.'s private views, but are more or less confirmed by the Government'.[11] In the case of her many European relatives he had to tread still more warily. It was all very well for the prime minister to tell W. H. Smith that the Queen could be reassured that she and the government did not differ on any essentials in their view, 'but [Smith was] nevertheless directed to express to [Salisbury] the anxiety with which Her Majesty regards the present situation of affairs in South Eastern Europe and her hope that no time and no opportunity will be lost in effecting a settlement which shall maintain Prince Alexander in Bulgaria and Eastern Roumelia; as Her Majesty is convinced that any change will place those countries under the direct control of Russia'.[12] Salisbury could and did point out the degree to which foreign affairs did not lie uniquely in the hands of the British government and he knew that, when push came to shove, the Queen would have to be content with what he decided.

Her presence preyed on his mind, all the same, and he went to unnatural lengths to win her round, just as he had only taken minority office in the first place to express his sympathy for her constitutional position. Both he and she recognized that she could no longer dictate the composition of his government – though the thought rarely deterred her from trying – but she referred her prime minister continually to a royal 'constitution' which only she understood. 'She expects I fear impossibilities,' Cranbrook reported in 1886, 'and does not make enough allowance for our Parliamentary system.'[13] She did not allow for it because she started from somewhere else. Salisbury could not follow, but he never took the view reflected in Gladstone's dealings with the Queen that she could ultimately be ignored. Perhaps that is why his advice was not ignored as Gladstone's so notoriously was in 1894 when Rosebery found himself made premier by the Queen and nobody else. That famous occasion is taken as a blip on a Whig monitor of royal decline but there are grounds, universally recognized among late-Victorian Conservatives, for seeing the process in a different light as a blatant exercise of power that remained far from fictional or 'dignified' to

[11] Beach to Salisbury (transcript), 17 Aug. 1885, St Aldwyn MSS PCC/30/unfol.
[12] Smith to Salisbury (copy), 3 Oct. 1885, Hambledon MSS PS/10/2.
[13] Cranbrook to Salisbury, 30 Aug. 1886, Salisbury MSS (Cranbrook, ff.304–5).

the end of Victoria's reign and which came into play whenever the royal finances, the peerage or especially the church came under discussion. With Balfour as much as with Salisbury, one finds genuine sympathy with the Queen's plight during the early days of the South African War in 1899. He discovered the Queen 'most anxious that [he should] stay' at Balmoral. 'She is, naturally enough, depressed and worried, and she seems to find some comfort in having a minister to hand to whom she can put questions.'[14] This is not the world of gold carriage and cheering crowds but a more private one to which Tories felt themselves drawn by both prudence and heartstrings. It also supplied a significant social function by providing 'one of the few bonds of cohesion remaining in the community'[15] and for a persuasion committed to social cohesion those bonds could not be swept aside by a Whig understanding of constitutional 'progress' or 'advance'.

The House of Lords had a place in that world, too; and its story, like the Queen's, accelerated in the 1870s and came into its own with Salisbury's domination of it after Beaconsfield's death in 1881. Disraeli's interest in the peers was social: he collected tufts and loved dukes. The business side he expected to be managed by a competent leader whom he could trust and he thought he had found one in Earl Cairns. But Cairns went wrong. As a lawyer who needed to earn his living and with an eye on the Woolsack, Cairns never settled as leader in the Lords: he could not make the time to sit through appeals; he felt that old blood would work better than new in the post; and (the salient point) if the Conservatives came back to power, after Gladstone had done his worst, he would want to be Lord Chancellor and would not be able to lead then in any case.[16] Besides, his health had deteriorated and his Bournemouth villa beckoned. If not Cairns, however, then who? Salisbury would be unacceptable because of the row over reform in 1867, which had led Cranborne, as he then was, to resign, though being a non-starter did not prevent Cairns from trying to start him. Disraeli wrote one of his sniffier letters in reply:

The Leader in the Lords must be one who shares my entire confidence & must act in complete concert with myself. I do not know, whether Lord Salisbury & myself are even on speaking terms.

[14] Balfour to Alice, 4 Nov. 1899, Balfour MSS 49831 f.189.
[15] Memo by Salisbury, 'secret' (copy), 15 May 1886, RA VIC/A65/1.
[16] Diary, 18 Nov. 1869, in Derby, *Diaries*, p. 41.

You contemplate making a man Leader of a party, of wh: he is not even a member.

If we show strength in Parliament and the country, it is probable, in due time of course, he will join us. If we try to force the result we shall only subject ourselves to humiliation.[17]

He was quite right. On the other hand, his certainty about Salisbury did not make the problem go away, which is one reason why Disraeli was furious with Cairns for leaving his post in 1869 and causing all this trouble. What ensued is well known to political historians and we need not exhume the details of a familiar narrative; but once Salisbury had been tried and had refused,[18] the choice fell on Derby, who thought about it for twenty-four hours before replying crushingly in the negative. Lord Colville took it rather badly. 'I received a letter from Derby this afternoon – <u>declining</u>!!! I never was so astonished . . . What is to become of us?'[19] In writing thus to the Duke of Richmond he perhaps knew that he could arouse a sense of honour in one for whom honour led intellect, intuition and personal comfort. Pressures mounted on Richmond to stand in the breach and he felt he could not let his friends down. 'I do not think I am up to it', he confessed to the person he could always confide in, 'but I must do my best.'[20] Besides, there were compensations in not being brainy, as the Earl of Selkirk sought to reassure Colville while plainly holding Salisbury in mind as the alternative model. 'I think we shall get on much better with the Duke of Richmond than with the more brilliant speakers with whom we have scarce had time yet to get acquainted, and there is less room for personal jealousy under his guidance than there might have been under the other proposed arrangements.'[21]

---

[17] Disraeli to Cairns, 14 Dec. 1868, Cairns MSS 30/51/1.

[18] Salisbury was quite as clear as Disraeli that the two could not work together and 'the worst leader, who could act with the leader in the H of C would be better than one who could not': Salisbury to Carnarvon, Carnarvon MSS 60758 ff.74–9.

[19] Colville to Richmond, ?16 Feb. 1870, Goodwood MSS 862 v 3–4. Charles John Colville, first UK (as opposed to Scottish) Baron 1885. Representative peer 1852–85. Master of the Buckhounds 1866–8. Chamberlain to Princess of Wales 1873–1901. Chairman Great Northern Railway 1880–95. Viscount 1902. Small landed estate but died in Eaton Place, Pimlico.

[20] March to Mother, 25 Feb. 1870, Goodwood MSS 862 v 12. Although the Earl of March had succeeded to the Richmond dukedom in 1860 he seems to have retained for his mother the name by which she knew him as a child. The eldest son took the courtesy title of Earl of March from 1860 until Richmond's death in 1903.

[21] Selkirk to Colville, 1 Mar. 1870, Goodwood MSS 862 v 29. Selkirk had been a Scottish representative peer since 1831 and continued for a further thirty-three years until his death. 20,000 acres in Kircudbright. Seat: St Mary's Isle.

And so, in some ways, it proved. From the completion of the succession in 1870 until Disraeli went to the Lords and assumed the leadership there in 1876, Richmond ruled with a rod of tallow. He did not want to change very much: indeed he opposed changing anything at all. Derby's sense that members of the House of Lords lived 'out of the world, politically'[22] would have struck Richmond as part of their strength. He knew that Tories had their moments of bias, of course, but it had to be a good thing for the constitution that this bias resided permanently in the second chamber to stop bad things from happening and in particular to stop Gladstone's obvious madnesses:

All our work is well done: our Debates carried on with dignity; and all Bills are discussed in a business like manner. Vide Irish Church [Bill], [Irish] Land [Bill] and Army [Purchase] Bill.

The only and chief charge agst us seems to be that we have a majority agst the Gov and so are able to check some of Gladstone's rash folly.

This I incline to think is advantageous to the Country.[23]

He had already had plenty of indications that complacency formed the best strategy. Indeed, simply looking around the empty benches must have persuaded Richmond that activism in the politics of the peerage held out a false hope. If he had clung to any optimism, the list of absent well-wishers who explained that they could not possibly come to London for a meeting at the Carlton Club to decide the leadership of their own party must have educated him. The correspondence is like a conversation with the halt, the lame, the very nearly dead. There was Lord Berners ('confined to my bed with gout'); there was Lord Rayleigh ('my age prevents me'). Lord Stamford and Warrington's 'sharp attack of bronchitis' kept him on his 30,000 acres in the Midlands and sounded less contrived than Lord Tweeddale's ever-conclusive 'weakness in my leg which frequently disables me from walking'. The Duke of Buckingham and Chandos made no bones about staying away, 'not being well', while Lord Churston's 'should any emergency arise' had all the vacuous philanthropy of the congenital backwoodsman. Lord Doneraile was apparently quite fit but marooned in Ireland and, '[l]iving so far away as I do', could hardly be expected to break his engagement with the foxes. The Duke of Buccleuch would have come, despite his

---

[22] Derby to Cross, 21 Mar. 1873, Cross MSS 51266 f.9.
[23] Richmond to Cairns, 20 Jan. 1972, Cairns MSS 30/51/2/ff.50–1.

distance from Westminster, if it had not been for the dogs: 'my hounds have been out only 24 times this season'.[24] And so it went on. Bishops in their nineties, minor unknowns, blundering farmers, recalcitrant aristocrats: it was not the stuff of a new model army to resist the democracy.

Perhaps their lordships' only ripple of dissent came over a technical issue – appellate jurisdiction and the role of the House of Lords as final court of appeal. A Judicature Commission established in 1867 with Cairns as its chairman had recommended a series of important adjustments to legal procedure and most of these Gladstone's government had embodied in the Supreme Court of Judicature Act of 1873.[25] The problem for Tory peers, when the Conservative government returned in the following year, lay in preventing any move to chip away at their privileges. For some the concern lay in maintaining the position of the House of Lords within the British legal system and resisting the transfer of judicial power anywhere else.[26] For others it amounted to making waves about a minor privilege that might swamp major ones in due course. 'That which is known to so few', Lord Ravensworth urged on his leader, 'may be disputed at every point, and any attempt to exaggerate the ?decline or enlarge the scope of a Privilege runs the risk of depreciating its importance, & may endanger its existence . . . Therefore for Heaven's sake let the Lion rest.'[27] But Cairns, who felt agnostic about where final appeal went so long as there were one, insisted on pressing forward with an amendment to the Liberal legislation, which plunged him into considerable unpopularity with his own party and which further alienated him from Disraeli who

---

[24] All this correspondence is in Goodwood MSS, file 862.

[25] Cairns had in fact wanted a good deal more than the Act proposed. He had hoped to get 'a very strong Ct. of Appeal *in* the Supreme Ct.', which would have the effect of 'gradually choking off' appeals beyond it. He even wanted to democratize the Inns of Court and 'roll them into a legal University' on the non-Tory ground that 'their public rights & privileges . . . are amply sufficient to justify public interference & control': Cairns to Palmer, 11 Oct. 1872, first Earl of Selborne MSS 1865 ff.88–90.

[26] This was Carnarvon's view, held on the ground that all past votes had been taken on that principle and could not be altered now: Carnarvon to Richmond, 3 Mar. 1875, Goodwood MSS 867 a 34–5.

[27] Ravensworth to Richmond, 12 July 1873, Goodwood MSS 866 w 222. Henry George Liddell, second Earl of Ravensworth (1821–1903). Eton and Christ Church, Oxford. Conservative MP for South Northumberland, 1852–78 when he succeeded to title. President Royal Agricultural Society (1891) and North of England Steamship Owners' Association. Seat: Ravensworth Castle, near Gateshead. His young widow married the footman.

had not forgotten the eruptions of 1869 and disliked lawyers anyway.[28] He was allowed to push his bill through but only by playing down any threat to the Lords' powers with a bland phrase about appeals needing to be held before 'the most skilled and experienced judicial minds that you could at any time procure the service of'. Salisbury lent a hand by soothing peers with a reminder that the bill contained a clause explicitly reserving discussion of the Lords' role until the following year.[29] The incident caused enough fretfulness and indigestion to suggest that the Lords still held some view of themselves as important ingredients in the constitutional system without providing any strategy for how to exploit their situation to maximize their impact. The second chamber could be used after 1880, Northcote thought, 'to afford a rallying point around which the Conservatism of the nation may make a stand'.[30] Beaconsfield, to whom he expressed this thought, could see that there were men in the Lords with the right qualities – those who, like Cadogan, 'c[ould] think on [their] legs & ha[ve] a good & never failing vocabulary'.[31] But neither the rallying point nor the vocabulary would have much power until someone identified a strategy consistent with Conservative views of political action.

Salisbury provided the strategy. He reached it quite early in his thinking, though he could hardly impose it during the 1870s, and it only became central, as Andrew Adonis perceptively remarks, in the civil war that Salisbury invented for himself in the 1880s and 1890s.[32] He demanded from the start that the party needed a doctrine about the House of Lords that was 'theoretically sound', 'popular', 'safe against agitation' and, just as important, would come into play comparatively rarely. The party ought 'frankly to acknowledge that the nation is our master, though the H of C is not: & to yield our own opinion only when the judgement of the nation has been challenged at the polls, & decidedly expressed'.[33] This view presented a

---

[28] Diary, 4 Mar. 1875, in Derby, *Diaries*, p. 198.

[29] *Hansard* (Lords), 9 and 16 Apr. 1875, ccxxiii, cols. 578, 1088 (Supreme Court of Judicature Act (1873) Amendment (No. 2) Bill).

[30] Northcote to Beaconsfield, 27 Aug. 1880, Iddesleigh MSS 50018 f.224.

[31] Beaconsfield to the Countess of Bradford (copy), 17 Feb. 1881, Cadogan MSS CAD/247.

[32] Andrew Adonis, *Making Aristocracy Work: The Peerage and the Political System in Britain 1884–1914* (Oxford, 1993), p. 111.

[33] Salisbury to Carnarvon, 20 Feb. 1872, Carnarvon MSS 60758 ff.98–9. This view requires situation because not everybody shared it. At a shadow cabinet in 1881, for example, Cairns had deemed it unconstitutional to stand against the 'will of the nation, as expressed through the representatives of the people in the House of Commons'. Salisbury preferred to envisage

Conservative constitution in which the Lords joined hands with the People to save them from manipulation by a short-sighted, self-centred and faction-ridden system of 'democracy'. The Commons could propose, certainly; but the House of Lords would reflect on the need to dispose in its 'drowsy but distinguished' way[34] with a lack of pecuniary interest, its regard for precedent and sense of safety and stability. If necessary it would act as a barrier against harm until the electors had the chance to comment more fully at a general election. This language had all sorts of uses: it could supply a ground for ignoring the House of Commons, for example, whenever it seemed to be trying to control the Lords in indirect ways. Salisbury took great care never to encourage any initiative by the Lords that might have the converse effect and he defended with some violence the view that no precedent should be set for permitting Commons' interference in the Lords' affairs.[35] It provided a way of rephrasing resistance to bills which the forced passage of Gladstone's proposal to abolish paper duties in his budget of 1860 had suggested the Lords would henceforth prove unable to delay or control.

It also required no change in the constitution of the House for its implementation. The unrepresentative character of the Lords became its purpose rather than its predicament: it strove to take the high ground of acting as a disinterested check on representative politics rather than another example of it. This meant that Salisbury could avoid dallying with any schemes of fundamental reform and did not feel embarrassed by the patently reasonable grievances of Scottish and Irish peers whose ability to serve in the House had always suffered from constitutional distortion. But in response to Lord Inchiquin's reform plan in 1874, Salisbury looked (or claimed to look) at the broader picture and frightened Richmond with a picture of jealousy, division and fundamental disturbance of the relationship between Lords and Commons.[36] Back in 1873 he had suggested privately that the House might be strengthened by making

certain conditions on which the Lords should press their own view. Gibson diary, 15 Aug. 1881, in A. B. Cooke and A. P. W. Malcolmson (eds.), *The Ashbourne Papers 1869–1913* (Belfast, 1974), p. 17.

[34] Derby to Cross, 22 Aug. 1880, Cross MSS 51266 f.64. Salisbury shared Derby's view about drowsiness. W. H. Smith reported the following story: 'Sir H. Holland left the House of Commons because he could not sleep. "Come up to our House," said Lord S. "We'll put you to sleep." ' Benson diary, 25 Apr. 1888, A10.

[35] E.g. Salisbury to Cairns, 23 Feb. 1882, Cairns MSS 30/51/6.

[36] Salisbury to Richmond, 20 Apr. 1874, Goodwood MSS 866 f 292.

judges in the Court of Appeal into peers *ex officio*;[37] and in later years he would offer modest support to the idea of life peerages and introduced a bill to that effect in 1888. But he remained permanently unimpressed by any 'great, flaring, dramatic reform of the House' and especially by any move to make its membership responsive to democratic impulses as in Lord Dunraven's proposal to have peers elected by county councils. '[I]t is difficult', the prime minister said in a tone at which we can now only guess, 'to understand the genesis of such an idea in any man's brain.'[38] He meant, as he often did, what he said; but he also thought instrumentally about the House of Lords as about everything else. Had he believed that he could gain his objectives by changing his mind, emotion and tradition would not have deterred him, which is why there remains just a glimmer of plausibility in Lord Kimberley's exasperated remark that Salisbury might propose abolishing the House of Lords altogether if he thought he could trump the Liberals by doing so.[39]

About the late-Victorian House of Commons Salisbury knew little. He recognized, as did all his colleagues, that its power had risen beyond all measure through the nineteenth century and that political leadership had tended increasingly to come from that House. It should be remembered, however, that Salisbury's ministerial experience while a member of parliament had been slight; that he sat for a pocket borough during the few years that he spent in the Commons; that his role as Lord Robert Cecil had always been pleasantly irresponsible; that he loathed in the deepest way having to kowtow to an electorate whose intellectual and moral qualities he despised. His contact with MPs came mostly through the cabinet or (as the opposition arrangement was coming to be called) the shadow cabinet. He did not care for those, either. Like Gladstone, he sought to reduce meetings of cabinet while in office and to avoid meetings when in opposition. 'I gravely doubt the prudence of "Shadow

[37] Salisbury to Selborne, 24 Feb. 1873, first Earl of Selborne MSS 1865 ff.241–3.
[38] Salisbury in Lords, *Hansard*, 26 Apr. and 18 Jun. 1888, cccxxv, col. 558 and cccxxvii, cols. 388–95.
[39] Kimberley to Dilke, 2 Sep. 1884, quoted in David Nicholls, *The Lost Prime Minister: A Life of Sir Charles Dilke* (1995), p. 143. This political, as opposed to constitutional, reading of Salisbury's intentions is what strikes me as insufficiently stressed in C. C. Weston, *The House of Lords and Ideological Politics: Lord Salisbury's Referendal Theory and the Conservative Party 1846–1922* (Philadelphia, PA, 1995) and inclines me, for once, to Gladstone's own opinion: 'It always appeared to him that Lord Salisbury was imbued with less [*sic*] constitutional principles than any other public man': Edward Hamilton's diary, 25 Jun. 1895, in Dudley W. R. Bahlman (ed.), *The Diary of Sir Edward Walter Hamilton, 1885–1906* (Hull, 1993), p. 304.

Cabinets"', he grumbled to Northcote at a bad time for the party in 1883: he thought they gave people the opportunity to stir up trouble and even blamed them for the trouble.[40] These perceptions require acknowledgement because Salisbury consistently worked with people who did not share them – who saw the Commons as the centre of political interest and took caucusing to be a necessity in modern party conditions. To a man like Richard Cross, Salisbury must have appeared sometimes grotesquely *de haut en bas*. Witness this moment of sublime pomposity when the Commons sent up to the Lords the Corrupt Practices Bill of 1883 to limit flagrant malpractice in elections. 'If the House of Commons insists on inflicting this severe flagellation upon itself,' said Salisbury, sounding more like Edward Gibbon or Horace Walpole than a modern politician, 'it seems ungracious to interfere with so edifying a penance.'[41] Similarly, Salisbury made no progress towards having cabinet records kept – a breakthrough that had to await Lloyd George's impatience at the absence of minutes in the middle of the First World War. The closest he came was at the very end of his career – 'We ought to have regular minutes' – but only because Selborne thought he had got a million to spend, which nobody could remember having given him.[42] In general, however, Salisbury imposed his dislike of cabinets and consultation without too much difficulty from colleagues. He even boasted about it in the House of Lords after Granville taunted him with the brevity of cabinets during the 1886–92 government, when, indeed, they could be made to meet at all:

I am bound to say that the fault with which the noble Earl charges our Cabinet is largely due to myself. Other Prime Ministers have possessed that wealth of language, that diffuseness, that abundance, that power of carrying every subject into the furthest detail, and adorning it with all the verbal decorations of a fervid imagination and an unlimited vocabulary; and, of course, if the Prime Minister possesses these qualifications, his adoring and listening Cabinet will enjoy the advantage of a succession of brilliant speeches of which the world knows nothing . . . But my poor hard-bound brains cannot produce these tremendous speeches, I am sorry to say, and the result is that we can get over our work in half an hour, an hour, or two hours.[43]

Bureaucracy left him equally agnostic. All Conservative ministers

[40] Salisbury to Northcote, 10 Jul. 1883, Iddesleigh MSS 50020 f.63.
[41] Salisbury to Cross, 12 Aug. 1883, Cross MSS 51263 f.76.
[42] Salisbury to Selborne, 30 Jun. 1901, second Earl of Selborne MSS 26 f.127.
[43] Salisbury in Lords, *Hansard*, 11 Feb. 1890, CCCXLI, cols. 30–1.

understood that the exponential growth of government as an activity meant that traditional systems of patronage could no longer sustain themselves. The archives are crammed with begging letters from people wanting a clerkship for a son or nephew, quite as much as in the days of Lord North or William Pitt. What is different is the late-nineteenth-century reply: terribly sorry, overwhelmed with requests, no chance in the near future, will place his name on the list, cannot really help. Everyone found this uncomfortable but Salisbury hated it with especial venom. And when he *did* interfere with 'normal' promotion, as he did in sending Lord Lytton to Paris or Lord Dufferin to Rome or Drummond Wolff to Tehran, he never heard the last of it from those who thought their claims stronger.[44] As usual, there was a contradiction: he loathed people who wanted favours but also loathed the system that made it impossible for him to grant them. Behind it all stood the Northcote-Trevelyan Report of 1853, which had introduced the idea of competition by examination for civil service posts, a 'reform' that Lord Robert Cecil had despised at the time. In a lifetime of reducing radical ideas to absurdity, he never performed better than over the need to make clerks pass formal academic examinations in order to do menial tasks in a government office, 'working equations, or rolling off the most exquisite iambics'[45] while filing documents or running errands. Instead of finding candidates who were 'tidy, neat, punctual, methodical, business-like, shrewd, ready-witted', the reformers had turned the civil service into a system of 'exhibitions for the schoolboys of the county', like entrance into an Oxford college. What joy when he finally got hold of one of the examination papers sat by these tormented proto-clerks. For a place in the Education Office: 'Write down the expansion of $(3x-4y)^9$, and by means of the binomial theorem approximate to $\sqrt[3]{31}$.' For a place in the Inland Revenue – he particularly liked the Inland part: 'On which side of the Himalayas are the source of the Indus, the Ganges, and the Brahmaputra?'[46] It is unlikely that anyone has ever been funnier in the House of Commons in making rubble of 'correct' opinions.

A final element in the state held a privileged place in the Conservative constitution: its means of self-defence. The army and

[44] Salisbury to the Queen, 19 Sep. 1886, RA VIC/A67/5a.
[45] Lord Robert Cecil, 'Competitive Examinations', *Quarterly Review*, 108 (Oct. 1860), pp. 569–605 at p. 578.
[46] *Ibid.*, pp. 586, 588. Cf. Cecil in Commons, *Hansard*, 8 May 1860, CLVIII, cols. 899–900.

navy established a close connexion with the Conservative view of the world if only for negative reasons since radicals of all colours wished to reduce their strength and resources in the second half of the nineteenth century. Officers appeared on the Tory backbenches regularly; the senior ones often had connexions with great families and the House of Lords and sometimes with the court, especially through the ubiquitous Duke of Cambridge whose indiscretions 'in general society' came to upset Salisbury.[47] Generals and admirals formed a staple of Tory influence and occasionally made themselves a self-parody of Conservative characteristics. Like the civil service, moreover, the armed services gave rise to serious political problems concerned with their recruitment and financing – problems that became more severe rather than less as the century progressed. Few issues caused more fury among Tory backwoodsmen than the Liberal government's decision in 1871 to abolish the purchase of army commissions, imposed by Gladstone's manipulation of royal warrant after he had failed to pass the bill through normal channels. Exactly as in the case of civil service places, the question concerned vested interests and patronage systems, but this time the victims of the reform were not clerks or schoolboys. The army scheme also touched, because of its mode of passage, every constitutional nerve and even brought the quiescent Marquis of Exeter out fighting on the street in Grosvenor Place. Allowing the bill to pass under duress would threaten not merely the army but the stature and credibility of the House of Lords as a vital facet of the state:

Having voted for, and carried the Amendment to the effect that the House of Lords declined to consider the Army Bill, until a complete scheme of Army reorganization was laid before Parliament, how can we with dignity now consent to pass the second Reading of the Bill, especially under the constitutional pressure put on us by Mr. Gladstone? To discuss the Army Bill at all after such an affront seems to me a great mistake, & one which will lower the House of Lords considerably in the eyes of the Country, while the vote of censure will be disregarded by Mr. Gladstone who will point with triumph to having coerced the Peers into obedience to his will . . . Mr. Gladstone has, by exerting the Royal Prerogative to abolish Purchase in spite of our vote plainly told the Country that he can do without the House of Lords. Let us bear in mind that that country is looking to us to know what our reply will be, hoping to see the Peers vindicate their authority as an Estate of the Realm.[48]

[47] Salisbury to the Queen, 7 Dec. 1888, RA VIC/A67/24.
[48] Exeter to Richmond, 25 Jul. 1871, Goodwood MSS 863 x 26.

His view did not persuade his colleagues, who felt the pressure irresistible, but it found a good deal of reflection in their private outrage over an action which had fitted Gladstone's conception of the constitution, and possibly Bagehot's, not their own.

The navy impinged for a different reason. Revolutions in the technology and scale of battleship and cruiser production placed unbearable strains on both the Exchequer's ability to pay and the state's willingness to accept burdens in other areas. Hardly any point in the chronology of Conservatism after 1874 escaped this pressure and its consequences dug deep into the nature of government by the 1890s. The narrative began in the vast hulk of George Ward Hunt (whom contemporaries deemed to weigh about the same as a light cruiser) at a time when few realized that a highly portentous story would unfold. But Hunt's demand at the beginning of 1875 for £200,000 to keep the Admiralty afloat proved only the start, for all the heartache to which it gave rise – 'where is the money to come from?'[49] – in an escalation of defence estimates that would climax in the Naval Defence Bill of 1889, which sought to introduce a 'two-power standard' under which Britain could rest secure that her provision of battleships and cruisers would equal those of the next two nations of Europe added together. Salisbury's figures dizzied the imagination quite as much as the prospect itself: £21.5 million over four and a half years to achieve the standard by 1894 with seventy-seven battleships and eighty-eight cruisers; and only the coaling capacity available and the difficulty of providing ordnance had made him stop there.[50] A point had to arrive, granted the nature of the current tax-base and the prolonged attack on indirect taxation since the repeal of the corn laws, when something would have to give. 'Black Michael' Hicks Beach wrote pages to this effect in his gloomiest mode amid the strains of the Boer War and threatened resignation unless there was action. 'The Estimates have risen from £18,700,000 in 1895/6 to £30,876,000 this year.' It was time to

---

[49] Diary, 12 Jan. 1875, in Derby, *Diaries*, p. 189: 'We cannot, without absurdity, put on the penny on the income tax which was taken off last year: nor without serious unpopularity begin raising taxes which our predecessors during the last five years have been occupied in reducing.' Cf. Hunt to Hardy, same date: '. . . I stuck to my guns supported by John Manners stoutly & by Carnarvon. Northcote not committing himself – & the others making no sign': Cranbrook MSS T501/260.

[50] Salisbury in Lords, *Hansard*, 27 May 1889, cccxxxvi, cols. 1059–65. He expected French totals in these categories by 1894 to be 48:14 and German 40:10. Russian and Italian provision caused less concern, respectively 27:3 and 19:17.

damn 'the wrath of such opponents as the Navy League, the "Service members" and the Daily Mail'.[51] He may as well have proposed taxing the London fog or Scotch mist. He certainly would need to tax someone, somewhere if the state were seriously to provide for the demands reaching it, not least from places where generals and admirals rarely went.

INTERFERENCE AND ITS LIMITS

The notion of 'state interference' in social or economic arrangements had a sustained airing in the last third of the nineteenth century. Partly it owed something to the expansion of population, to urbanization and the need to control what happened to the urban race in its unknown, hazardous or immoral environment. Partly it drew on a perceived urgency about responding to economic depression from the mid-1870s. But it also fed on a developing argument about what the state *was*: how it should be conceived or reconceived. The years from 1880 to the First World War became especially significant in this reconceptualization, which drew from both German thought and post-Darwinist ideas to argue for an organic link between state and people and allow the state forms of authority that would have troubled mid-Victorian writers.[52] When all these things melted together, a style of politics unknown to the 1850s and 1860s could take shape and Conservatives played an important role in stimulating or diverting the discussion. For Liberals, the problem became one of reversing a former language that recommended *laissez-faire* as the best way of securing individual liberty and constructing instead a new view of using the state in order to *create* liberties where few had existed before for the broad mass of the population.[53] Conservatives remained more preoccupied, as they always are, by the nightmares of the dead. Their own history since 1846 had taught them about the

---

[51] Hicks Beach to Salisbury (copy), 13 Sep. 1901, Balfour MSS 49695 ff.129, 131.
[52] For background to this important development, see among other studies G. B. A. M. Finlayson, *Citizen, State and Social Welfare in Britain 1830–1990* (Oxford, 1994), José Harris, *Private Lives, Public Spirit: A Social History of Britain 1870–1914* (Oxford, 1983); Michael Bentley, ' "Boundaries" in Language about the State' in Richard Whiting and S. J. D. Green (eds.), *The Boundaries of the State in Modern Britain* (Cambridge, 1996), pp. 29–56. For organicism in Liberal social theory, see Michael Freeden, *The New Liberalism: An Ideology of Social Reform* (Oxford, 1978) and Stefan Collini, *Liberalism and Sociology: L. T. Hobhouse and Political Argument in England 1880–1914* (Cambridge, 1979).
[53] See my *Climax of Liberal Politics: British Liberalism in Theory and Practice 1868–1918* (1987), pp. 74–95.

folly of changing their mind. They wanted to sound modern and relevant, certainly; but they expected to solve the new problems facing them within the constraints articulated by early-Victorian politicians – or they expected not to solve them at all. The latter option had many advantages and held little of the stigma attached to it that the twentieth century has inflicted on the inactive. Certain forces could not be controlled, any more than the weather. When Lord Beaconsfield got to his feet at the end of 1878 to announce that 'Her Majesty's Government are not prepared . . . with any measures which would attempt to alleviate the extensive distress which now prevails',[54] he merely added sauce to established doctrine and Conservatives mostly preferred to remain within that world. On the other hand, issues about the moral life of the working class, education and its support and the place of taxation in a Conservative state would hardly disappear with a few words of windy rhetoric. Conservatives had to face the question of what to do with the state and they decided that it would best be met with two incompatible arguments: one that said that the state should help the unfortunate, the vulnerable and the incapacitated, together with another that denied it the means of helping anybody.

Salisbury could offer both styles, but as his career came to maturity he showed more of the second than the first. Even in the early days, the fundamental ambiguity came through in his speeches. An attack on the health of the poor by those who adulterated basic elements of working-class diet such as tea or sugar won his sympathy at once. Not only was the practice criminal, but the state would have to 'step in and protect' the working man since he was 'unable to protect himself'.[55] Let anyone suggest, however, that the poor man would be helped best through state aid and his resistance to all forms of indiscriminate assistance led the argument. Either the law dealt with the situation, in which case it was the duty of the state to enforce it, or it did not, in which case it was the task of parliament to change it. Private individuals should not have to do the state's job and positive mischief would result from their trying to do so.[56] His language, never moderate, took on a lurid quality when considering issues of state power. The Whig/Liberal government brought in a Bill in 1861 to help rescue children whom the police considered

[54] Quoted in Paul Smith, *Disraelian Democracy and Social Reform* (1967), p. 304.
[55] Cecil in Commons, *Hansard*, 7 Jul. 1859, CLIV, col. 848.
[56] Cecil in Commons, *Hansard*, 8 Feb. 1861, CLXI, cols. 230–9.

might be at risk from a suspected association with criminals: they proposed that any such child be made a charge on the rates for its maintenance if two justices of the peace agreed. Cecil's mind moved away from the children and to the power – 'far too wide to be placed in such hands' – that the proposed legislation would give to the authorities. As for the suggestion that a JP could send a young person to an 'industrial school' if found begging, 'he could only characterize the Bill as worthy of the meridian of Paris and Berlin, and stated that it conferred on the police an entirely new power'.[57] Probably his firmness of view in this area hardened further in the aftermath of the reform act of 1867 with the power to manipulate the state that he held changes of this kind would present to the masses. If there were an exception to that attitude, it resided mostly in the field of education.[58] He objected to the state's incursion into the field of educating the nation's young; but, like Robert Lowe, he suspected that once the deed had been done, then both prudence and morality decreed that its consequences would have to be followed through in order to make the new structures work at all.

Of all Salisbury's excursions into the field of state intervention (and they were not numerous) few attracted so much attention or criticism as his contribution to the discussion on working-class housing in the 1880s that was reviewed in chapter 3.[59] Andrew Mearns's incendiary pamphlet of 1883[60] had presented a picture not only of sustained overcrowding and deprivation but, more tellingly, of vice and especially of incest. The argument bit so hard on late-Victorian reforming sensibility precisely because it joined together an account of damaging *laissez-faire* and a portrait of the moral consequences for vulnerable people. Salisbury knew a good deal about the subject already: he had always taken an interest in the problems caused by London's all-too-visible expansion. Faced by Mearns's revelations, however, the argument took on an urgency that overrode familiar cautions about the debilitating effect of state aid on the individual. In some ways he sympathized with the position of an extreme anti-statist such as Lord Wemyss, but while 'my noble

---

[57] Cecil in Commons, *Hansard*, 11 Jun. and 5 Jul. 1861, CLXII, col. 896 and CLXIV, col. 368. He failed to destroy the Industrial Schools Bill all the same.

[58] See below, pp. 205–19.

[59] Above, pp. 90–1.

[60] Andrew Mearns, *The Bitter Cry of Outcast London: An Inquiry into the Condition of the Abject Poor* (1883).

Friend may press as earnestly as he will upon us the necessity of leaving every Englishman to work out his own destiny . . . he must always bear in mind there are no absolute truths or principles in politics'.

We must never forget that there is a moral as well as material contagion, which exists by virtue of the moral and material laws under which we live, and which forbid us to be indifferent, even as a matter of interest, to the well-being in every respect of all the classes who form part of the community . . . After all, whatever political arrangements we may adopt, whatever the political constitution of our State may be, the foundation of all its property and welfare must be that the mass of the people shall be honest and manly, and shall have common sense. How are you to expect that these conditions will exist amongst people subjected to the frightful influences which the present overcrowding of our poor produce?[61]

Even then, the results proved less than radical and far from effective. A Royal Commission emerged under the chairmanship of Sir Charles Dilke; and Salisbury crowned the initiative as new prime minister in 1885 by propelling through the House of Lords a Housing of the Working Classes (England) Bill, albeit by stressing that 'there is nothing startling, sensational, or extreme in its provisions'. Nor, indeed, was there. Sanitary authorities gained some extra powers to enforce existing by-laws; the slum-clearance provisions of Disraeli's Artisans' Dwellings Act became compulsory on landlords rather than permissive; and they also acquired a liability to certify the healthiness of accommodation belonging to them.[62] It hardly amounted to an assault on the rookeries or promised to render Fagin fictitious.

Ideas, then, about vulnerability supplied one wing of the recommendation to enhance state power. Another derived from the size and complication of social mechanisms in a modern environment. Railways proved a case in point here – a topic which many Conservative landowners knew about through their encounters with companies wanting to lay track across their land or, as in Salisbury's case, from serving on their boards. Both he and Derby felt the wind blowing in the direction of state intervention, possibly even state purchase, by the 1870s. 'We both see the greatest objections to the

---

[61] Salisbury in Lords, *Hansard*, 22 Feb. 1884, CCLXXXIV, col. 1689. He was directing his remarks to Wemyss in Wemyss's capacity as 'head' of the Liberty and Property Defence League, which the tenth Earl chaired until his death in 1914. He had been a contemporary of Ruskin at Christ Church and retained a taste for water-colouring and sculpture as well as, seemingly, for some of Ruskin's individualism in politics.

[62] Salisbury in Lords, *Hansard*, 16 Jul. 1885, CCXCIX, cols. 890–2.

measure,' Derby wrote after a conversation in 1872, 'financial, as indefinitely increasing debt, and constitutional, as creating in various forms an enormous patronage.'[63] They and their colleagues produced a similar response to attempts to increase *dirigisme* over land itself, where threats came not only from compulsory purchase on the Irish model but also from the notion that there ought to be a 'ministry' of agriculture, a view that sounded bizarre or at least French. Salisbury got as far as asking what they actually did with their ministry in France, but no further. For agriculturists like Richmond, meanwhile, the whole discussion amounted to 'rubbish and nonsense'.[64] Lord John Manners pointed out with some violence to urban man in the form of W. H. Smith that if the government genuinely wanted to do something for agriculture then it wanted 'not a Department, not lectures, but duties on corn and cattle'.[65] There lay the rub. Give Tories half a chance to think about state intervention and they would immediately look to government to protect their interests with a reversion to pre-Peelite formulations that few among the leadership would now countenance. And they would do so with particular readiness once the economy took its apparent nose-dive in the 1870s and produced conditions in commerce and agrarian rents that only began to release their grip towards the very end of Salisbury's life.

Contemporaries saw this unhappy coincidence of Toryism and depression as simply that – a coincidence. Northcote's dwindling surpluses at the Exchequer by 1877 struck Derby as 'singular' and he mused in a disengaged sort of way about how recent Conservative administrations seemed to happen at times of depressed trade;[66] but there was no analysis that suggested the highly plausible argument that Conservative governments were *caused* by depression. It seems far more obvious from our distance than it did to contemporary commentators that Liberalism could be envisaged as a boom-economy formula: thriving when its sectionalism could find some

---

[63] Diary, 20 Jun. 1872, in Derby, *Diaries*, p. 110.

[64] Richmond to Cranbrook, 24 Feb. 1888, Cranbrook MSS T501/257. Salisbury's scepticism had doubtless been strengthened by Lytton's promising to send material from Paris on the French venture, while adding that 'the French themselves are thoroughly dissatisfied with the practical working of this Dept. of their Administration & would be glad to get rid of it if they could': Lytton to Salisbury (copy), 18 Jan. 1888, Lytton MSS D/EK 032 f.15. Richmond remained bemused. 'I cannot see what he [a minister] has to do': Richmond to Salisbury, 14 Mar. 1883, Salisbury MSS (Richmond, f.82).

[65] Manners to Smith, 24 Jul. ?1887, Hambledon MSS PS 14/62.

[66] Diary, 2 Apr. 1877, in Derby, *Diaries*, p. 387.

camouflage behind prosperity, falling apart when chill winds exposed its fundamental lack of consensus about what it wanted to achieve and whom it took itself to represent. At any rate a graph of Liberal misfortune superimposed on a picture of economic fluctuation would at least have proved suggestive to Tory strategists. As it was they saw themselves as victims of bad luck – a perspective that provided the gloss that all they could do was to wait for the cards to turn. Salisbury's rhetoric about it had more punch than Disraeli's throwing up of hands (and the sponge) but it came to the same thing. He began by reminding their Lordships of a piece of 'England' he knew well:

There is a great depression in a neighbouring country in the great wine-growing industry; but it would be of no use for them to discuss that depression, or bring it up as a matter of complaint against the Government, because it is depended upon well-known natural causes which no Government or Parliament can remove. I fear that the depression in England, though not depended [*sic*] upon such simple causes, is dependent equally upon great natural and economical causes, and the power of Parliaments or Governments to cope with it is very limited.[67]

Among the devices supposedly to hand one could count protective tariffs as the most penetrating and potentially helpful. They were in the air under the label 'fair trade' and not a few Conservatives followed the line of Sheffield's Sir Howard Vincent[68] in moving back to a tariff posture or at least joining in the mild sarcasm that Derby, for all his Lancashire roots, directed at the sanctification of Richard Cobden.[69] Opinion remained sharply divided among the leading lights. Derby felt comparatively relaxed about the prospect of duties. Northcote said, as always, that he needed to be persuaded.[70] Salisbury had his own sort of Lancashire root and he did not forget it.[71] He took particular trouble to squash tariffs because every fibre of his

---

[67] Salisbury in Lords, *Hansard*, 12 Mar. 1888, cccxxiii, col. 831.
[68] C. E. H. Vincent, MP for Sheffield Central through much of the period covered in this book until his death in 1908.
[69] Derby to Northcote, 26 Feb. 1877: 'I have never thought Cobden an oracle either on foreign or home affairs. He believed three things with all his heart – that the repeal of the corn laws would check the power of the landed aristocracy. That the example of England would bring about free trade all over the world. That great wars would never be made again, being incompatible with the ideas of an industrial age. In all these points he has been wrong. The landowners are stronger than before – Europe is showing more protectionist tendencies than 20 years ago, and America itself following suit – and all the world is armed to the teeth': Iddesleigh MSS 50022 ff.131–2.
[70] Northcote to Salisbury, 3 Sep. 1881, Salisbury MSS (Northcote, ff.430–1).
[71] Salisbury to Cranbrook, 6 Feb. 1879, Cranbrook MSS T501/267.

political being told him that, however desirable they might be for economic reasons, there was no possibility of introducing them without disaster to the state (and party) that made the attempt. In the same speech to the peers quoted above, he argued further:

> If we are to undertake the re-examination of that question it must not be done incidentally, by insinuation, by allusion, by hints. You must firmly walk up to the fortress that you have to attack and lay siege to it . . . In my belief, the economical arguments in favour of Free Trade are very strong; but they are not the strongest with which we have to deal. If he [Earl De La Warr] will look back upon the debates of 1846 and read the speech of Sir Robert Peel when introducing his great proposal, he will see that the political argument weighed more heavily than even the economical argument in his mind; and I believe that the political argument has lost none of its force. I utterly disbelieve that it is in your power to introduce Protection. If it were, I think it could be introducing a state of division among the classes of this country which would differ very little from civil war.

Having 'seen' what protection did to the Conservative party in 1847 and with what result, Salisbury ensured that the 'transformation scene' stood no chance of appearing in his time as a political leader. How prescient he was appears clear at once when one turns to the fortunes of his nephew after 1902 when protection and 'tariff reform' tore the guts out of Toryism and produced its worst electoral performance in living memory in 1906. Untune that string and discord would follow. But Salisbury and his generation had to re-tune some of its strings if the depression were to be endured at all, revenue retained intact and the navy kept afloat. They could hardly have recourse to a policy of progressive direct taxation since they would have no party at all in a fortnight if they did. But indirect taxation was unpopular, unfashionable and probably irreversible in its decline. By the 1890s Tories stood between an unstoppable force and an immovable object.

These intimations radically affected the Conservative understanding of what a state might do during an era of economic adversity. Indeed, Lord Robert Cecil had seen long before its onset that his party ought to set its face against the mood in favour of 'progressive' taxation, lest the stability of the state itself be endangered. The argument increased its austerity in 1860 when Gladstone as Chancellor of the Exchequer successfully sought to repeal duties on paper and prevented the House of Lords from thwarting him in an important constitutional precedent. For Cecil the point was not paper, though he scotched the 'tax on knowledge' rhetoric of the Liberals; he drew attention more aggressively to the relationship between taxation, property and the future of the state itself if the tendencies reflected in Gladstone's proposals continued to mask the fundamental vice of direct systems of taxation – not least in a climate which encouraged extending the franchise:

> There was an entire fallacy in the ordinary mode of dealing with the question of direct and indirect taxation. The proper way was to set the payments made by individuals in one class against the payments made by individuals in the other. The usual plan of estimating the amount paid by each class led to erroneous conclusions, and, moreover, exerted a mischievous influence by setting class against class. If you called upon one man to pay 8*d* in the pound towards the support of the State, while another man occupying a not very different station of life was made to pay only 4*d*, you were committing a great injustice. According to every principle of sound finance all classes ought to pay alike, and if that were done the indirect taxation of the country would be considerably increased and the direct taxation considerably diminished . . . [otherwise] progress seemed to consist in substituting direct for indirect taxes and in shifting the burdens from the poor to the rich. If such a policy were persisted in it would weaken the stability of the State and it ought least of all to be pursued just at this moment when they were going to hand over the government of the country to those who were not to pay for it. Such a plan of finance was really a plundering finance; it practically amounted to confiscation . . .[72]

Salisbury's view never deviated from this ideal position but the actualities of the moment led him to emphasize tax exemptions as his central concern. His worst case concerned a future world in which the masses would be let off paying tax altogether while the rich would be crushed in 'an attempt to "loot" the stockholders and the landlords'. He conceded that this moment had not yet arrived. But if the principle remained 'of slight operation now', it required little imagination to foresee the time in a democratized state when it could 'form . . . the most tremendous engine for loading the rich minority with the whole taxation of the country'.[73]

During the Disraeli government of 1874–80, this animus against direct taxation and exemption for the poor continued. Until the

---

[72] Cecil in Commons, *Hansard*, 12 Mar. 1860, CLVII, cols. 392–3.
[73] Lord Robert Cecil, 'The Income Tax and its Rivals', *Quarterly Review*, 109 (Jan. 1861), pp. 212–47 at pp. 216, 244. 'If the exempted classes come to power and find the Income-tax still in operation, it will be an evil day for the classes they supersede' (p. 246).

arousal of protectionist feeling at the end of the decade, however, it took the form of jacking up Northcote's resolve to keep the income tax low and constrict the exemption band. It was rather typical of Northcote's accident-proneness to rejoice about his surplus in 1874 – 'As regards the Revenue, I feel very cheerful'[74] – the day before Ward Hunt started his threatening noises about the navy. Thereafter it became a war of attrition, with Cairns and Derby agreeing with Salisbury that the exemptions originally conceived by Northcote ought to be confined to an income of £200 or below. Salisbury used his most pugnacious shorthand to penetrate the chancellor's consciousness. 'I feel strongly on reflection that you should not carry the exemption so high,' he wrote during the pre-budget flurry. 'Suggest £200 as limit of exemption.'

My fear is that whatever we do on these distinctly class issues will be the starting point for concession to the democratic party on the part of our adversaries hereafter: and will moreover give cause to the enemy to blaspheme at present. Don't let them have any reason for saying that we are bidding for Fred. Harrison:[75] & don't promote a graduated income tax to a place in the list of possible policies. Don't reply.[76]

Northcote contrived to hold together the navy and the cabinet on the basis of a 'fair surplus' (1877) and 'do[ing] without more taxes'.[77] But the double-bind of a deflating revenue and inflating navy drove him, like most others, to reconsider the fiscal base altogether and summon up the demons of state aid through bounties and tariffs. Beaconsfield could continue to proclaim that state aid remained 'out of the question'[78] since his distance from policy relieved him of the obligation to think about practical ways out of the mounting *impasse*. Men closer to the cutting edge knew that protection would win votes among those central to Tory politics. As early as the spring of 1877, Lord John Manners wore his miner's helmet to seek support from another 'industrial' aristocrat (and foreign secretary), Lord Derby. 'I feel so strongly on the critical state of our manufacturing and

---

[74] Northcote to Cairns, 14 Oct. 1874, Cairns MSS 30/51/5/f.13.
[75] Frederic Harrison (1831–1923), a well-known radical personality for his early involvement with the Positivist movement popular in his Oxford college, Wadham. Substantial private money: father lived in Lancaster Gate with a country house at Guildford. Harrison himself practised as a barrister and wrote widely for the better journals. Died a radical in his nineties at his unradical address in the Royal Crescent, Bath.
[76] Salisbury to Northcote, 25 Mar. 1874, Iddesleigh MSS 50019 ff.25–6.
[77] Northcote to Richmond, 2 Apr. 1877, Goodwood MSS 869 c 7.
[78] Beaconsfield to Cairns, 23 Dec. 1878, Cairns MSS 30/51/1.

financial prospect', he pressed, '. . . that I hope you will forgive me for again urging the importance of reserving . . . our right to impose an import duty on Coal. I would gladly see the right to impose low duties on the import of foreign manufactured goods likewise reserved; but perhaps that is beyond praying for.'[79] The same message appeared in the press, in the periodicals, in a widely remarked protection literature from the end of the 1870s.

Northcote's Gladstonian past and tremulous present argued against accepting this message without reservation. He seems, none the less, to have been affected by its virulence, which troubled one who could always see three sides to every question. Between 1879 and 1882, when the thickening climate of protectionism coincided with his last days at the Exchequer and his stepping away from office, Northcote persuaded himself that former aversions may no longer be sustainable. He worried about a 'trade war', to be sure, and could not bring his mind to countenance the 'commercial morality' of retaliation *pur et simple* and the 'very curious episodes' that would be bound to arise when fire fought fire.[80] If the policy could be made to seem a positive one, however, then he would not close his eyes to its possibilities, as he assured a backbencher with slightly less frankness than he probably would have deployed in cabinet. His starting point would have made a wonderful text for the next generation:

It will not do for the Conservative party to propose a tax on the food of the people. Even in a party sense we should soon find that such a proposal would recoil upon our heads. But, indeed, if we are to hold our own in the competition with the other manufacturing nations, we must take care not to handicap our people by raising the cost of the necessaries of life.

The same remark applies to the taxation of the raw materials of industry. If we are to bring those materials from the country of their production, work them up here, and sell them in the open markets of the World at a cheaper rate than the producing country itself can sell them at, we must impose the fewest possible restrictions upon their transport.[81]

This sounds more like a Liberal chancellor in 1860 than a strangu-

---

[79] Lord John Manners to Derby, 15 Mar. 1877, Derby MSS 16/2/5. Manners was, of course, heir to the serious coal-interest of the Dukes of Rutland, based at Belvoir. The family had nearly 30,000 acres in Derbyshire.

[80] Northcote to Balfour, 3 May 1879, Balfour MSS 49695 ff.3–4. The image of 'Hawkeye in the Prairie making fire fight fire' weighed with him and brought a momentary flight of literary fancy.

[81] Northcote to Maxwell, 28 Aug. 1881, Maxwell MSS 7043 HEM1.

lated Tory in the depths of economic depression. To Smith, however, he told a different story, 'disclaim[ing] Protection' as a sort of mantra but registering all the same a resentment against other countries and their flouting of the rules of free trade. '[W]e must not be squeamish', if such distortions indicated that British tariff policy ought to be reviewed.[82] The change of mood by publicists and now by close colleagues showed Salisbury clearly enough that his own position on free trade could not be read as a general one by the 1880s.

He reverted, therefore, to the *political* argument already identified: the case for protection failed in face of the fact (which he announced rather than proved) that it could never be introduced without a major offensive and would probably need both parties to agree to it, which they never would.[83] Meanwhile, he diverted discussion into two other channels. He appealed to the need for more indirect taxation and blamed Gladstone for his '1860' mood over the paper duties and in sending Cobden to Paris to negotiate the international treaty – a disaster because no 'advantage that was obtained by stimulating International communication in respect of gloves, silks, and wines at all meets or compensates the loss that the Chancellor of the Exchequer now has, when he looks over the resources of the country in a time of difficulty, in finding any item by which the Revenues of the country can be increased'.[84] Secondly, he did what he could to keep direct taxation, when it could not be avoided, away from the land. When discussion of 'succession duties' (i.e. death duties) had become current in both parties by the end of the 1880s, Salisbury attacked the idea, as seen in the last chapter, because it struck at his most cherished principle about landed property and the state: 'that it is dangerous to recur to realised property alone in difficulties – because the holders of it are politically so weak that the pernicious financial habit is sure to grow, especially if it be

---

[82] Northcote to Smith, 17 Jan. 1882, Hambledon MSS P58/21.
[83] e.g. Salisbury in Lords, 25 Mar. 1887, replying to De La Warr on the subject of the church tithe, which suggests that the position he adumbrated was adopted extempore. 'He was very anxious that his agricultural friends, with whose sufferings he had the greatest sympathy, should not imagine that it was within the range of practical politics that Protection could be restored in this country . . . Before Protection could be restored it would be not merely one Party, but both Parties in the State, that would have to be converted': *Hansard*, cccxii, col. 1463.
[84] Salisbury in Lords, *Hansard*, 9 Feb. 1888, cccxxii, col. 42. Silks and gloves he remembered from his rhetoric during the arguments of 1860 and 1861. Indeed, gloves deserve a place in the heritage of protectionist language over the past century: witness Baldwin's controversies over the importation of 'fabric gloves' after the First World War.

encouraged by a precedent of our own making'.[85] Of course, he failed in both projects. Direct taxation increased and the land continued to attract it. Death duties not only came about at the hands of the Liberal government of 1892–4 but Salisbury found himself driven into a rhetorical *impasse*, for he could neither accept them nor dispense with them. His private language about 'a law of grievous hardship and oppression . . . [which] would never have been permitted to pass, if it had been directed at a more numerous class' became the public avowal of the impossibility of 'part[ing] with a richly yielding source of revenue'.[86] Taxation had turned into a ratchet. Beach may have anticipated unrest after the South African War if the income tax stayed as high as 14d in the pound[87] (a basic rate of 5.8 per cent) but only Balfour of Burleigh would go to the wall for a reduction.

Frictions and contradictions of this kind in taxation and social policy reflected both the theoretical limits of state action and a recognition that the world had often moved beyond theory's ability to cope with the realities of a given world. State involvement in the life of the citizen had become an established reality by 1900, whatever Salisbury or Mallock or Maine thought about it. But different styles of intervention gave rise to varying forms of resistance. In the case of welfare and housing, the limits were set by libertarian doctrines in the intelligentsia and *laissez-faire* propensities within the party. Taxation dodged its theoretical constraints to become a headache concerned with practical administration: the timeless problem of revenue and how to raise it to carry on the business of government. Notions of degeneration and the need for a more disciplined society enticed Conservatives along the road of intervention during the Edwardian period. In the meantime, a gentle programme of turning permissive legislation into compulsory requirement marked the highest aspiration of Conservative politicians. Perhaps one issue more than any other ministered both to the need for action and the sense of limit in conceiving it. Once the radical Forster had forced through his educational reform of 1870, the

---

[85] Salisbury to Goschen, 3 Mar. 1889, in Cecil, vol. IV, pp. 191–2. W. H. Smith agreed with him: 'there is a great deal to be said against taxing a Class on the ground that they can afford it': Smith to Balfour, 13 Apr. 1889, Balfour MSS 49696 f.96.

[86] Salisbury to Beach, 7 May 1898 (transcript), Christ Church MSS; and in Lords, *Hansard*, 23 Jun. 1898, LIX, col. 1172.

[87] Beach to Salisbury (copy), 13 Sep. 1901, Balfour MSS 49695 f.128.

question how to organize British schools and how to find an appropriate role for the state in promoting that organization pressed on politicians and inaugurated a process of change that would not take acceptable shape until 1902. Both Liberals and Conservatives placed that problem, moreover, in a light particular to the late nineteenth century. They saw it as an issue that tested not only the range of state action but the relationship between state and church, which formed the preoccupations of most of those interested in the problem. In 1918 and 1944, Herbert Fisher and R. A. Butler would return to the contentious issues presented by the schools and their management; but their problems would prove strategic, technical and financial rather than denominational. Late-Victorians, on the other hand, took the full force of contention about the confessional character of the British state – something that Conservatives often cleaved to with some passion – and saw the discussion as continuous with an argument about the place of the churches in British society and politics that ran back to Richard Hooker's *Ecclesiastical Polity* in the sixteenth century.[88] Salisbury was not alone among Conservative voices in wanting to tell the British public that they still belonged to an ecclesiastical polity, notwithstanding Charles Darwin, *Essays and Reviews*, Bishop Colenso and Mr John Bright.

[88] See, for example, Bentley, ' "Boundaries" ', p. 30 and n. 6.

CHAPTER 7

The church

Throughout the second half of the nineteenth century, Salisbury defended the spiritual and secular claims of the Church of England. He did so, perhaps, in spite of religious feeling as much as because of it. That spiritual sentiments existed and mattered to him stands beyond argument. That he normally refused to talk about them makes their history speculative. His daughter reported in her biography that, when he went on his prolonged tour following his departure from Oxford, he took volumes of patristic writings with him;[1] this would have seemed natural to one associated with the 'Oxford movement' within high Anglicanism during its most heated phase. By the time he was thirty, Cecil held fixed and aggressive views about the need to defend the church against subversion from its 'low' wing and to hold the ground in particular from Nonconformists. This mood gave him a public reputation as (in descending order of plausibility) a high churchman, a spokesman for the clerical party, a covert Catholic, Monsignor Salisbury.

His personal religion appears, however, to have become an understated form of private practice in the chapel at Hatfield, when he became its owner, and to have resisted all attempts to intellectualize its character or significantly alter its formularies. At its centre lay Holy Communion and the language of Bible and Prayer Book. He took little interest in current theological debate and thought no better, as we have seen, of *Lux Mundi* in 1889 than of *Essays and Reviews* in 1860. He thought the clergy 'great fools' for running after Bishop Colenso as a doctrinal radical in the 1870s and wished everybody would 'be content to sit still till the passion for new ideas of all kinds [was] a little slaked'.[2] Yet equally he came to dislike some forms of ritualism dear to the hearts of Anglo-Catholic revivalists in

---

[1] Cecil, vol. I, p. 102.
[2] Salisbury to Hardy, 23 Feb. 1873, Cranbrook MSS T501/267.

the same decade, though he was later spotted on a couple of occasions at ritualist services when in London.[3] In no sense did he follow the path of his brother-in-law Beresford Hope, who became an icon of the ritualist offensive through his book *Worship and Order* (1887) and his support for practices that he deemed legitimated by the Prayer Books of 1549 and 1552.[4] Salisbury, by contrast, especially detested the idea of confession, which, he believed, encouraged women to confide in lascivious young priests about their unclean thoughts: its adoption would be 'fatal to moral vigour'.[5] Not that his own undoubted moral vigour had the rebarbative texture of Gladstone's or Bright's; one has a sense of a fairly relaxed conception of sin that harmonized with his fundamental view of the world as a place of mistakes and inadequacies. Eccentricities in matters of personal belief and his temporizing in bringing about reform in the church by legislation convinced his most bitter critic, his own archbishop of Canterbury, Edward White Benson, that Salisbury was an enemy with 'no limit apparently to his spite at anything clerical'.[6] But this merely showed that Salisbury did not confuse religion with the Church of England, a frequent mistake among archbishops, and that his reasons for lending support to the church did not commit him to thinking much of the opinions of bishops or theologians. What it did commit him to was defending an established and Erastian church against the forces of atheism and Dissent, a presumption that forms a crucial context for his entire political life. The violence with which he did so would doubtless have struck another, admittedly unbalanced, observer as further proof of an opinion he had long held: that '[t]he church is the creation of the upper classes who don't care a straw for religion – the Cecils and the lawyers . . .'.[7]

ESTABLISHMENT AND DISSENT

Salisbury believed in establishment as a force in human society. He espoused an established morality, he celebrated an established

---

[3] At St Alban's, Holborn, in 1882. See Nigel Yates, *Anglican Ritualism in Victorian Britain 1830–1910* (Oxford, 2000), pp. 162–3.
[4] For Beresford-Hope's role in the politics of ritualism, see *ibid.*, ch. 4.
[5] Salisbury in Lords, *Hansard*, 3 Mar. 1899, LXVII, col. 1177; Cecil, vol. I, p. 105.
[6] Benson diary, 17 Mar. 1891, A13.
[7] G. G. Scott Jnr, quoted in David Watkin, 'George Gilbert Scott Junior (1839–1897): "The History of a Narrow Mind"' in Michael Bentley (ed.), *Public and Private Doctrine: Essays in British History Presented to Maurice Cowling* (Cambridge, 1993), pp. 168–80 at p.177.

history, he subscribed to established ideas, he committed himself to an established church. Establishment provided a description or definition of the Church of England; but for Salisbury the fact of establishment also supplied a justificatory theory. It was his church *because* it had been established for three hundred years or, since Salisbury thought in round numbers and deemed the Reformation a local difficulty, a thousand years. 'He contended that the church has a claim upon the people from the mere fact of it having been established for ten centuries, and from it being held so fast as it was within the rigours and fetters of the law.'[8] Law and history and the state: Anglicanism was not only a religion but also a civic pact with previous generations and therefore a trust to be honoured. He believed in the truth of the Thirty-nine Articles of the church of England. But that was not why everybody should have to recognize them. Doing so reflected an act of citizenship in this ecclesiastical polity that he saw in England – whether one were a member of a university or a member of parliament. It explained why people should pay church rates, which he defended with something like fanaticism. It implied a view of why attacks on the Church of England must be resisted, for an attack on the church *ipso facto* damaged the state and social fabric. 'Theoretically', he conceded,' there is no reason why the secular position of the Church of Christ in any country should determine the precise form of its civil polity. But, practically, the spirit which abhors a national Church has been found also to abhor the institutions which give political predominance to the educated classes.'[9] No bishops, no clerisy.

Just as the church required defence from its detractors, secular life also needed protection when relations between church and state came into jeopardy. This was why Jews must remain out of parliament, for example. Their loyalty was not in question, nor their nationality, but the 'complicated relations which Church and State bore to each other' meant that to tamper with one side of the relation would affect the integrity of the other. When the first Jewish MPs did appear after Derby's minority Tory government altered the law in 1858, Cecil remained convinced that a major offence had been committed to the British state and its church, that the link between the two had been sundered, that all preaching would have

[8] Cecil in the Commons, *Hansard*, 17 Feb. 1858, cxlviii, col. 1563.
[9] Cecil, 'Church-Rates', *Quarterly Review*, 110, (Oct. 1861), p. 545.

to stop, that the church was dead. Never had he sounded *quite* so insane:

> there were four hon. Members who did not believe in the necessity of preaching the Gospel, and by those Gentlemen, whom recent legislation had admitted within the walls of the House, such discussions as the present, he contended, must be regarded as an insult. [*Cries of* 'Oh, oh!] He would repeat it, there was no longer any community between the Christian religion and the House of Commons, and all references to Christianity, and all quotations from the Bible, must now be not only out of place, but an insult to those four gentlemen.

This brought Sir Francis Goldsmid to his feet to utter a dignified and crushing reply, followed by Gladstone at his most prissy ('an opinion hardly worthy of his undoubted ability and high intelligence').[10] Here, as so often, Cecil's problem was logic: not too little but too much. It came into play less abrasively in other debates about the future of the church–state relationship, as when Salisbury crossed swords with Archbishop Tait in 1873 over the judicature bill that preoccupied some of the previous chapter of this book. Because the church owed its establishment to the state (and because Salisbury did not trust the wisdom of bishops), he argued that the final court of appeal even in ecclesiastical matters should be to lay judges and not clerics.[11] His position was open to misconception and both Tait and Edward Benson misconceived it. It looked as though he wanted the state to interfere in church matters, which was not his point at all. As he tried to reassure the Duke of Norfolk, whose Catholicism had been ruffled by a misreported speech of Salisbury's in 1891, he looked on ecclesiastical domination in secular affairs as almost as great an evil as lay domination in purely spiritual affairs.[12] He wanted critics to see that the two spheres overlapped and that an offence to one might bring about an offence to the other.

Many of these opinions and intimations Cecil had exercised before Gladstone set about disestablishing the Church of Ireland in 1869. But there can be no doubt that the raising of this issue sharpened the question of establishment for all Conservatives. If one section of the national church could go, why not others? Would the Church of Scotland lag far behind? And if that went, what price the Church of

---

[10] Cecil in Commons, *Hansard*, 14 Mar. 1860, CLVII, cols. 520 *et seq.*
[11] Tait diary, 12 May 1873, in R. Davidson and W. Benham, *Life of Archibald Campbell Tait* (2 vols., 1891), vol. II, p.123.
[12] Salisbury to Norfolk (copy), 20 Nov. 1891, Christ Church MSS, file E.

England itself? Faced with Disraeli's temporizing over the question, Salisbury's loathing for one whom he already regarded as cloven-hoofed since the parliamentary reform two years before reached new depths. Oddly enough, Disraeli believed in establishment, too; or at any rate he had agreed with Wilberforce that 'it [would be] all over with the Church of England, if she be disconnected from the State'.[13] As always with him, however, other things had to be equal and during the debates of 1868 it became clear that they were not. Some Conservatives worried about their seats if they persisted in too obstructive a stance against a popular measure and Disraeli began a quiet sliding away from commitment. Cranborne, as Cecil now had become, emptied his spleen on the entire party which he now regarded himself as having left. '[S]neering as regards us all', Hardy complained about him in his diary, 'venomous and remorseless against Disraeli.'[14] By working on Cairns, as low church as Cranborne was high, Disraeli moved toward the amendment of the disestablishment bill in the Lords in the spring of 1869 rather than its rejection – a position adopted also by the archbishops with only the high-church party of Marlborough, Bath, Harrowby and Redesdale holding out for rejection.[15] They and Salisbury, their new recruit to the peerage from the previous year, failed to persuade the forces of moderation or indifference. It was left to Salisbury with his rasping tongue and Magee, the bishop of Peterborough, with his mercurial Irish eloquence, to make the occasion of passage on 20 July 1869 at least a night to remember. Magee wrote to a close friend the next day his impression of events, leaving out of the account his own speech which many parliamentarians recalled decades later as the finest outburst of controlled invective they had ever heard in the House of Lords.

The Irish Church was last night – as I predicted from the first it would be – sacrificed to the Conservative party. . . . Salisbury stinging and goading the Ministry and Gladstone (who was present) to madness by his taunts, Hatherley even losing his temper and being fierce and indignant, the Lords

[13] Disraeli to Wilberforce, n.d., quoted in D. L. Edwards, *Leaders of the Church of England 1828–1944* (Oxford, 1971), p.102.
[14] Hardy diary, 1 Apr. 1868, in A. E. Gathorne Hardy, *Gathorne Hardy, First Earl of Cranbrook: A Memoir*, vol. I, p. 266. Cf. G. I. T. Machin, *Politics and the Churches in Great Britain 1869–1921* (Oxford, 1987).
[15] See Peter Marsh, *The Victorian Church in Decline: Archbishop Tait and the Church of England* (1969), p. 34. Salisbury had become concerned by July 1869 that 'one or two of the bishops' were appearing 'rather shaky': Salisbury to Cairns, 6 Jul. 1869, Cairns MSS 30/51/6/f.7.

generally emulating the Commons in violence and disorder, Winchilsea importing the element of simple insanity, which alone was wanting to the scene; and so amidst storm and fog, murky and stupefying and dirty, exit the Irish Church Bill.[16]

Perhaps that was the moment when Salisbury saw whom he should like to see advanced to an archbishopric. Certainly it was he who, when prime minister, recommended Magee's appointment to York for a poignant few weeks before Magee's unexpected death in 1891.

The disestablishment of the Irish Church has its Liberal location in the historiography: we are made to think of Gladstone resting on his axe at Hawarden and announcing his mission to pacify Ireland, or of the sheer usefulness of the device as a way of rallying discordant Whig, radical and Irish fragments around a single issue. The Tory location is left unspoken as so much sawdust beneath the axe. Yet it mattered. Behind much Conservative anxiety and strategy after 1869 stood the concern that disestablishment could no longer be seen as a chimera or goblin brought out by Salisbury and Hardy to frighten innocent churchmen. It had *happened* and might again. For a time in the first half of the 1880s, commentators thought that Scotland's turn had come. The Archbishop of Canterbury wrote woefully about it in his diary.[17] Salisbury recommended to colleagues that they 'work the question' when north of the border, for it had more power, he thought, than even the land agitation – almost certainly a misperception but a suggestive one.[18] Cranbrook, the former Gathorne Hardy and an important accession to the Lords' high churchmen, believed that disestablishment, if attempted, would lead literally to bloodshed.[19] And although none of these things happened, the politics of conserving the church against attacks from beyond its bounds took on a special urgency. Positively this had two facets: a serious attempt to remedy some of the patent inadequacies of church administration and its continuing corruption; and the development of the episcopal system to stem doctrinal deviations such as the ritualist movement of the 1870s and beyond. Negatively, it meant ignoring the Jews and the Catholics in order to concentrate on running a stiletto through the Nonconformists, whose 'attacks' on

---

[16] Magee to MacDonnell, 21 Jul. 1869, in J. C. MacDonnell (ed.), *The Life and Correspondence of William Connor Magee* (1896), p. 233.

[17] E.g. Benson diary, 12 Jul. 1883, A5: 'Dr. Sprott of Aberdeen. Thinks the disestabt. of the Scotch church is sealed . . .'

[18] Salisbury to Cross, 30 Oct. 1883, Cross MSS 51263 ff.77–8.

[19] Hardy reported in Benson diary, 7 Nov. 1884, A6.

the church mounted to crescendo in the tithe wars of the late-1880s; and it involved mounting a spirited rearguard defence of religious teaching in the schools and universities. Salisbury brought a political mind to the second of these objectives and a murderous relish to the first.

Bishops seemed to many Conservatives the key to church discipline and installing the right ones brought strain and anxiety to both Disraeli and Salisbury. Again, the location is traditionally Gladstonian: we know from his diary and daunting correspondence just how crucially Gladstone regarded these appointments and the hours he spent researching the competence and desirability of possible incumbents. But his was a nineteenth-century problem, not a personal one, and it affected Tory leaders too. The late-Victorian ones, apart from Northcote and to a lesser degree Richmond, were ignorant of churchmen: surprisingly so in the case of Salisbury, less so in one who, though baptized, had no particular reason to take an interest beyond the political. Neither Disraeli nor Salisbury chose the Primate with whom they were required centrally to work. Archibald Campbell Tait (archbishop of Canterbury from 1869 to 1882) was imposed on Disraeli by the Defender of the Faith who threw her weight around in this area more, and to more effect, than in most. So Disraeli found himself dealing with a Scottish Gladstonian in his attempts to avoid doing something about Anglican ritualism. Salisbury's equivalent was Tait's successor at Canterbury, Edward White Benson (1882–96), who ought in principle to have been acceptable, despite his having been Gladstone's nominee, since his father had always pretended a deep Toryism and Benson himself voiced Tory sentiments in his earlier years. In fact, Benson formed the view that Salisbury and his Conservatives cared little for the church and consistently failed to put ecclesiastical problems at the head of their political agenda. As he battled with Salisbury's second administration between 1886 and 1892 to effect helpful legislation, an innate (and probably clinical) depression joined hands with understandable disillusion to mould the sad and dyspeptic archbishop of the 1890s.[20]

Unlike some of his colleagues, Salisbury took no pleasure in

---

[20] Perhaps personal trauma had something to do with Benson's mood-swings. His wife deserted him, according to Stephen Pile, in order to live with Tait's daughter, Lucy. See introduction to E. F. Benson, *Secret Lives* (1985 (1st edn 1932)), p. 1. Among the six children of the marriage were A. C. Benson, future Master of Magdalene College, Cambridge, and E. F. ('Fred') Benson who was to write over a hundred works of fiction.

having bishops at his house[21] and dealt with them on the basis of reports of where they stood theologically, sometimes taking advice from churchmen, sometimes from friends such as Cranbrook, who was close to the eccentric firebrand J. W. Burgon, dean of Chichester, or from Richmond whose theological reading was no more extensive than any other but who sometimes had bishops to dine and sleep and shoot and fish, especially Claughton, bishop of Rochester (1866–77) and then St Albans from 1877 to 1890. If he thought the appointment an important one, Salisbury would think politically about it to the extent of reflecting on the kind of community into which the incumbent would be inserted – hence his tendency to find evangelicals for Norfolk in order to cope with Nonconformists and doctrinal primitives. He would also consider the balance between High and Dry and Low and Slow within the ministry at any one time. If he happened not to care much about a particular appointment, he was quite willing to pick up a tip from any passing churchman. When, for example, the bishop of Lichfield found himself in a railway carriage with the prime minister at the fag-end of the 1885–6 minority government, he found his brains picked about whom to appoint to Manchester, now that Fraser (1870–85) had died. Moorhouse of Melbourne, said Lichfield. Never heard of him, said Salisbury. But shortly afterwards Moorhouse received the call to Manchester where he remained until his retirement in 1903.[22] The churchmen genuinely known to Salisbury tended to be those such as H. P. Liddon with whom he had had an affinity from Tractarian days. In the context of ritualist controversy in the last quarter of the century, these were mostly unappointable, not least because the Queen would not have a ritualist at Balmoral, let alone Canterbury or York. In fact Salisbury could find himself ambushed by Benson and the Queen who, working together, prevented Liddon from becoming bishop of Oxford (as Salisbury would dearly have liked) and rightly insisted on

---

[21] A future exception was Cosmo Gordon Lang who lived long enough to recall that he 'used often to visit Hatfield in the old days and found the old man a most formidable & paralysing host': Alan Don's diary, 24 Feb. 1932. I am most grateful to Professor Philip Williamson for this reference. Rev. Alan Campbell Don (1885–1966); Chaplain and Secretary to the Archbishop of Canterbury, 1931–41; Canon of Westminster and Rector of St Margaret's, Westminster, 1941–6.

[22] Benson diary, 21 Jan. 1886, A8. James Moorhouse (1826–1915) was a son of a Sheffield master cutler. He married a daughter of the vicar of Sheffield and was consecrated bishop of Melbourne in 1876 shortly after becoming chaplain in ordinary to the Queen. He remained at Manchester from his translation in 1886 until his retirement in 1903.

Brooke Foss Westcott's getting Durham after the death of Joseph Lightfoot.[23] One way to avoid ambush was to proceed in secret. Benson was not amused when he saw one of his bishoprics gazetted without his knowledge. 'With his natural courtesy Ld. Salisbury communicates the choice of the Bp. of St Asaph to newspapers, so that . . . I first see it there. The contrast with Mr. Gladstone!'[24] Naturally, none of this could become public at the time. When Lloyd George did exactly the same thing in 1917, appointing Hensley Henson to Hereford without troubling to ask the Archbishop of Canterbury's opinion, insiders thought he was introducing a further damaging innovation into constitutional practice rather than doing what Salisbury had done without public reverberation some thirty years before.[25]

The need to strengthen the Church of England's weakening grip on this expanding society prompted the formation of new dioceses – Truro in 1871, four more in the 1880s, plus a number of suffragan bishoprics which enlarged for the politicians the problem of whom to appoint. And it was not just episcopal vacancies that bothered the heads of politicians: they had to find nominations for the clerical *Mittelstand* in the nation's deaneries without even the compensation of public acknowledgement for a job well done since most of the public knew even less about deans than about bishops. Disraeli's impatience with it all had a touch of majesty. ('Can you suggest a good High Church Dean, who is not a damned fool, and won't make himself ridiculous?'[26]) For Salisbury the process of appointment might drag on unconscionably as he thought through the impact on that balance in ecclesiastical politics whose mysteries had always bewildered his predecessor as Conservative leader. Key players during the Salisbury period would be the two Wordsworths, Christopher, bishop of Lincoln (1868–85) and John, bishop of Salisbury (1885–1911),[27] the irritating and seemingly immortal William

---

[23] The question of royal involvement and power in this area needs separate treatment: see Michael Bentley, 'Power and Authority in the Victorian Court', forthcoming.

[24] Benson diary, 18 Feb. 1889, A11.

[25] E.g. the report of Salisbury's son-in-law, Lord Wolmer, that a meeting had been held to discuss the constitutional propriety of Lloyd George's having made an episcopal appointment (Hensley Henson to Hereford) without consulting the Archbishop of Canterbury. Wolmer to Craik, 19 Jan. 1918, Craik MSS 7175 f.61.

[26] Disraeli to Salisbury, 28 Oct. 1875, Salisbury MSS (Disraeli, f.114).

[27] John was the elder brother. They were sons of the remarkable Christopher Wordsworth (1774–1846), brother of the poet, founder of the National Society and Master of Trinity College, Cambridge from 1820 to 1841.

Thomson, archbishop of York, and the coming men in Christopher Wordsworth's former chancellor, Edward Benson and Benson's own chaplain at Truro, Randall Davidson, later to become one of the major Primates of the twentieth century, playing Benson to Baldwin's Salisbury. Central in a different and disturbing sense, eventually, became Christopher Wordsworth's successor at Lincoln, Edward King, whose function was to rekindle in the 1890s some embers of the ritualism that Salisbury had hoped long since cold.

For all these churchmen the context of ritualism had dominated their strategic thinking during the Disraeli government of 1874 to 1880, culminating in the ministry's Public Worship Regulation Act intended to suppress wayward clerics playing fast and loose with the Prayer Book's stipulations. Derby's father, the fourteenth Earl, had set up a Royal Commission on the rubrics when prime minister in 1867, amid unease in London about the activities of high churchmen generally and in particular the eccentric style of celebration encouraged at St Alban's, Holborn, by the Rev. A. H. Mackonochie; and Cairns was far-sighted in seeing its report as potentially explosive for Conservatives whose high-church wing, represented particularly at that moment by Gathorne Hardy while Cranborne and Carnarvon were eating their locusts in the wilderness, would refuse to embark on any legislation controlling the affairs of churchmen.[28] They did not need to act, as events turned out, because they themselves were turned out. But further condemnations, particularly that in 1871 of an Anglo-Catholic priest, Father John Purchas of St James's, Brighton, who had apparently celebrated in medieval vestment, adopted the eastward position at the altar, used wafer bread, and mixed water with the wine ceremonially, heightened the agitation of the Church Association, founded in 1865, to put an end to unprotestant behaviour and stimulated yet further the loathing of the Queen for those who would undermine Her Church. Salisbury himself had to deal with an embarrassment of this kind at Hatfield in a living for which he was responsible.[29] The beauty of holiness attracted those who wanted a restatement of Laudian splendour at the altar. Edward Miall, acidulated leader of the former Anti-State Church Association (now usually referred to as the Liberation Society), preferred his own language for the process. He said the ritualists were 'decoying the

---

[28] Cairns to Disraeli, 5 Jun. 1868, Hughenden MSS B/XX/Ca/34.
[29] Salisbury to W. C. Talbot (transcript), 25 Mar. 1871, Christ Church MSS, file E.

people of England back to the depository of ecclesiastical rubbish which their forefathers had sturdily quitted'.[30]

Dean Burgon's intellectual refinement would not have permitted a phraseology of this kind; but it expressed pretty much what he thought. The ritualists, he believed, were every bit as bad as Nonconformists: indeed that is how they should be viewed and not, 'by the strange line my friend the Bp of Lincoln has taken', be allowed some sort of special tolerance for their indiscipline, as he explained to the ever-grave Lord Selborne in the summer of 1874. 'I look on with a kind of dismay,' he wrote, in agreement with a recent letter of Selborne's to *The Times*.

> Men are strangely forgetful of Church principles these days. I really can see *no* difference between the spirit of avowed Nonconformity & of this (so-called) 'Ritualism'. Amid the clamour also wh. is being raised for unbounded license in respect of *signs*, wh. are significant of *things* – there is an industrious putting out of sight of the growing indignation of the Laity – which I know to be excessive & which will at least result in as many secessions to Dissent if the 'Ritualists' are allowed free scope – as there are threatened secessions in another direction, if any effectual attempt is made to coerce them.[31]

Let them go to Rome, this meant: better to lose fainthearted churchmen in that direction than lose energetic men on the other side to Wesleyanism or worse. It all looked very intractable to the new Conservative cabinet. Disraeli's central position was that some legislation had to be attempted, if only to quieten the Queen, and that the bill devised by Archbishop Tait would at least allow them to take charge of the position and appear to lead rather than follow.[32] He took with him initially Cairns, Cross and Derby, for whom the 'Bishops Bill' remained an arcane but necessary contrivance, with Hardy and Hunt (whilst he remained afloat) on the other side. Salisbury's spirit undoubtedly lay with them; but Derby was surprised how conciliatory he became during the cabinet discussion of 11 July, as though he saw no alternative to a bill of some kind.[33] In

[30] Quoted in Marsh, *Victorian Church in Decline*, p. 115.

[31] Burgon to Selborne, 19 June 1874, 1st Earl of Selborne MSS 1866 ff.145–6.

[32] Tait himself hoped that the legislation would be used with discretion in cases 'where hearty work [was] being done' and favoured, predictably, the giving of more powers to bishops to regulate behaviour. Memorandum, 16 Dec. 1880, 1st Earl of Selborne MSS 1867 ff.142–7.

[33] Diary, 11 July 1874, in Derby, *Diaries*, p.175. This diary, which Peter Marsh did not see, casts great doubt on Marsh's identification of Derby as a spokesman for 'Protestant' politics. Derby loathed all forms of clerical politics and preferred a secular position on most issues.

fact a hybrid position probably reflected most precisely Salisbury's sentiments. He disliked the harm that the ritualists were bringing to the church; he disliked the bill because he thought that it ministered to an area in which interference from the state could only prove either tyrannical or redundant;[34] he sympathized with the Queen's difficulty. None of these qualifications led him to moderate his language in the parliamentary battle that ensued: few considerations ever did. But Tait got his law and a variety of inoffensive and sometimes pathetic clerics began the journey to prison for their disobedience.[35]

The impact of the Public Worship Regulation Act became considerable at the level of party politics for the redefinition it gave to the idea of a 'high church' party functioning inside the broader reaches of Tory support (with help from the English Church Union[36]), though it is arguable that the 'Protestant' accusations of Shaftesbury, Harrowby and the custodians of the 'low' conscience better deserve the title of fanatical, and for the role it played in isolating Gladstone in his own party: always a desirable objective. It impinged on Salisbury's future because it gave him a particular location at the very outset of his return to active political life after burying his blade in Disraeli. But the location was largely false. Certainly he did not abandon views on doctrine that approximated to a 'high church' position; but he saw even as the bishops' bill made its way through parliament that no future lay in perpetuating divisions of this kind; and he turned away to the problems of, first, India and then the Near East, hoping that the church issue would recede. It did not. In opposition again in 1881 he warned Tait that a mood had awakened which no archbishop could hope to end by edict. ' "Ritualism" is too strong to be "put down",' he argued; 'a serious attempt to do so would simply shatter the Church. . . . [I]t is odious to the majority of Churchmen, partly from habit, partly from dogmatic objection. The time is passed by when it was possible to

---

[34] Salisbury to Disraeli (draft), n.d. (Mar. 1874), Christ Church MSS, file E, ff.29–33.

[35] For an account of their often comical trials and wiles – especially those of the redoubtable Rev. Arthur Tooth who climbed into his locked church through the window to give clandestine services to his parishioners on his release from prison – see James Bentley, *Ritualism and Politics in Victorian Britain* (Oxford, 1978).

[36] Originally the Church of England Protection Society (1859). Changed its name almost at once and fought, under the leadership of its president, the Whig Charles Wood, later Viscount Halifax, for high-church principles and the rights of ritualistic priests. Amalgamated with the Anglo-Catholic Congress to become the 'Church Union' in 1934.

conciliate these rival bodies of opinion. If a fatal collision is to be avoided, the only thing to be done is to get them into different buildings.'[37] This made sense to the moderate Conservatives and Salisbury judged that they were the ones whose sympathies must be won.

How to accomplish this conversion seemed far from clear. For a Tory radical like Lord Randolph Churchill, the issue had become important but politically complicated. It was all very well for a low churchman like the bishop of Sodor and Man (Rowley Hill) to tell him that he should take up the evangelical line, repudiate the 'Puseyites . . . a fantastic and *now diminished party*' and go for a broad-based Protestant support, especially in the north of England where an earthy rejection of smells and bells persisted. Churchill was frank: he, as a politician, had to approach this issue from a party point of view and, seen from there, the outlook held more ambivalence, particularly when the leadership of the party had now become shared between Northcote and Salisbury. He wrote to the party organizer, Markham Spofforth, in 1884 that Disraeli had done great harm to the party by espousing Tait's cause of imposing discipline on the ritualists back in 1875.

At the General Election of 1880 the High Ch. party worked tooth and nail against us with damaging effect & it may be observed that the High Ch. Party, although a minority in the Church of England, are far more active & energetic at Elections than the Protestant Majority who are extremely apathetic on political matters & seem to exhaust their energy in the Ecclesiastical Courts . . . Further the Cons Party is already sufficiently divided. Lord S's High Church leanings are notorious & he has the support of Lords Carnarvon & Cranbrook in the H of L & of three University Members in the House of Commons. My own position in this matter is rather different. I have the greatest possible dislike of the Ritualist School & I feel sure that the more active of them are working for disestablishment. At the same time you are aware that all our political Actions have been in the direction of endeavouring to get Lord S recognized as the Leader of the Tory Party.[38]

Hatfield was worth a mass. For that reason, no high-political

[37] Salisbury to Tait, 5 Feb. 1881, in Davidson and Benham, *Life of Tait*, vol. II, p. 449.
[38] Spofforth to Churchill with encs., 23 Jan. 1884; and Churchill to Spofforth (copy), 27 Jan. 1884, Churchill MSS 9248/2. Quite which university MPs Churchill had in mind is hard to say with finality. Beresford Hope held one of the Cambridge University seats and he must obviously be one. The other Cambridge constituency returned Spencer Walpole and Oxford produced in 1880 J. R. Mowbray and J. G. Talbot. All three of these latter had been church commissioners.

challenge to Salisbury rested on low-church agitation: the latter's familiar names included men with peripheral power in the Commons or Lords, plus occasional bursts of bile from Lord Grimthorpe who, as Benson wearily noted, contrived to live up to his name. The most effective and respected of the band, the first Earl of Selborne, was not only a personal friend of Salisbury's of many years standing but also a Liberal until Ireland made him Unionist. Rather than become a serious force for destabilizing Conservatism, high-church antics merely entered the comic world of cartoon while their opponents likewise became caricatures of themselves. Liddon, Anti-Christ to all the Low and Slow, received in 1882 one of the *billets doux* that must by then have become familiar. 'Reverend Sir, I hear you have four cats which eat off your plate at dinner. How disgusting. Yours truly, A Protestant.'[39] It was not the stuff of radical politics.

Besides, Salisbury went out of his way when in power after 1885 to deny his supposed bias towards high-church appointments and to run a balanced ticket. Against the allegations of Bishop Marsden in 1889, he pointed out that only one position had gone to a ritualist (the Rochester deanery), counterpoised by a low appointment at Norwich. 'Bishop Jacque may be called a High Churchman,' he agreed, 'but he is not so decided in his colour as is the Bishop of Sodor and Man on the other side.' 'My appointments', he claimed to Hicks Beach, 'generally have been of moderate men – neither Ritualist nor ultra-Protestant: because I am convinced that the mass of English Churchmen are moderate men – caring little for a man's views so that extremes are avoided.'[40] Some eruptions he could not avoid. But when in the following year the bishop of Lincoln came to trial at Lambeth Palace for his toleration of ritualistic practice, the passions raised tended to be provincial and ecclesiastical rather than forming a coherent assault on the establishment or the prevailing understanding of relations between church and state. Little optimism existed during the 1890s that the 'discipline' problem had been cured – Salisbury himself brought a bishop to his feet in dudgeon after telling the House of Lords in 1898 that '[w]e have no discipline in the

[39] Benson diary, 6 May 1882, A4.
[40] Salisbury to Beach, 24 Oct. 1889, St Aldwyn MSS PCC/69/86–7. He conceded all the same in 1891 that high-church appointments in the church had preponderated in recent years, so that he felt obliged to look for evangelicals to restore the balance. 'But the difficulty is to get a good Evangelical in the present state of Church feeling': Salisbury to Cross, 30 ?Nov. 1891, Cross MSS 51264 ff.82–3.

Church of England'[41] – but the focus had by then moved away from
liturgical practice to the latitude given the church in its patronage
and its bases of finance.

Salisbury believed in patronage almost as strongly as had Disraeli,
not because it suggested inward and spiritual grace but because it
ensured that power stayed in the right hands. Presenting to livings he
took seriously, and he probably supposed that everyone else did, too.
In fact, numerous scandals concerning inappropriate incumbents
and the difficulties faced when patrons wished to be rid of them
forced his government's hand and prompted a patronage bill in 1887
along the lines of one drawn up 'with much vigour and unanimity'
by the archbishops and four bishops at the end of 1885. Gladstone
had given facilities for introducing it in his 1886 government but it
had not survived the press of business in the Commons.[42] Salisbury
'half blessed half banned' the bill of 1887, according to the bishop of
Peterborough, but swung behind it on second reading in the Lords
where it had been introduced.[43] All the same, the failure of the
government to push a patronage bill through the House of
Commons when other matters occupied its attention and parliamentary time persuaded the Archbishop of Canterbury that Salisbury's heart was not in the exercise and that his much-vaunted
commitment to the Anglican Church contained more rhetoric than
zeal. It was the same with Benson's own discipline bill. Through the
sessions of 1888, 1889 and 1890 it bounced from one House to the
other: entering the Lords with a passionate appeal from Benson for a
critical reform of church abuses, finding the usual opposition from
the ultra-Protestants headed by the implacable Grimthorpe[44] and
worries from churchmen such as Cross (now Viscount Cross as a sop
for only getting the India Office in 1886) and Halsbury who had
succeeded Cairns as lord chancellor and who brought to the defence
of church and state a level of manic emotion that only the events of
1911 would fully reveal to the public. It would struggle through the
peers' House and then fall into the abyss of Commons business,
during which Salisbury would regularly promise that he would make

[41] Salisbury in Lords, *Hansard*, 7 Jul. 1898, LXI, cols. 125, 127.
[42] Benson diary, 28 Dec. 1885, A7. The bishops were London, Peterborough, Carlisle and
    Durham.
[43] Magee to MacDonnell, 3 Mar. 1887, in MacDonnell, *Magee*, vol. II, p. 241.
[44] Cranbook had come to think of him as 'quite a power in his own line . . . his terse emphatic
    language tells': Cranbook to Salisbury, 2 Apr. 1886, Salisbury MSS (Cranbrook, ff.271–2).

it a government measure and see it through, only to withdraw the bill at the end of the session when there seemed no hope of including it in the programme.

At first this to-ing and fro-ing appeared the result of a temporary hitch. After three sessions it did not. And yet, Benson argued to the Leader of the Lower House, '[f]or the good of the Church [the discipline bill] is simply vital. The cases it would affect may not be many, but they are *monstrous*, and they supply endless material to our worst adversaries, and are a grievous offence to the best dissenters.'[45] Benson's depressions became deeper during this period, as his diary makes plain, and his sense of marginality plainly played no small part in accentuating them. He has been criticized for responding 'with petulance' when his proposals regularly ran into the sands.[46] Perhaps a sunnier disposition would have felt some frustration, however, as Salisbury's promises repeatedly failed to result in action. When Benson was told yet again in 1890 that nothing could be done during that session, his catalogue of grief contained evidence as well as emotion. 'Thus . . . year after year is our time wasted', he railed in private. 'What has this Govt done in pursuance of its promise to "stand by the Church they love" (Ld. Salisbury)[?] Has passed the Extraordinary Tithes [Act] . . . That is all: has scotched the patronage bill, the Discipline Bill in 3 forms, and dares not pass the Tithe Bill.'[47] In 1891 it happened again, this time because the Liberal Unionists (now co-operating with the Conservative government) cowered before Nonconformist demands to resist. Only in 1892 did the government make church reform a government measure and put a discipline bill on the statute book. The 1895 government proved no more willing to help. Exactly the same tale of deferral and indifference attached to a revived attempt at patronage legislation in a benefices bill. Benson's language from several years before re-emerged unchanged. 'The instances of corruption which it would stop *may* not be serious, but they are *awful*,' he intoned – to Balfour this time since he was now leading the Commons after Smith's death. He added a new element, however: the electoral vocabulary that spoke of mandates and threatened defections. 'You know that all Conferences . . . have produced resolutions in favour

---

[45] Benson to Smith, 17 Aug. 1888, Hambledon MSS PS13/65.

[46] Peter Marsh, *The Discipline of Popular Government: Lord Salisbury's Domestic Statecraft, 1881–1902* (Hassocks, 1978), p. 167.

[47] Benson diary, 30 Jun. 1890, A12.

of the Bill with scarce a reserve . . . I am sure that if it is not passed the Church could not possibly stand at another election as it did at the last . . . Are we not bound to redeem a pledge which I can bear witness was given everywhere . . . [?]'[48]

After two parliamentary sessions of this third Salisbury government, cynicism had grown like a fungus among churchmen both on their conception of the Conservative party but also on their understanding of the political process as a whole. There was 'that most blatant and factious of all vestries, the House of Commons'.[49] There were the Lords with their absent or vacuous bishops, the logic-chopping of Halsbury and Selborne, the groaning Grimthorpe. But for Benson the entire performance, rather than individual personalities within it, made his heart sink: 'having to shoot the roaring mocking querulous fantastic wilful rapids' that made white-water of the Thames across from Lambeth Palace.[50] Nor did damage restrict itself to the episcopate. Members of parliament felt the tug of ecclesiastical sympathies and observed the Conservative government's treatment of the church, sometimes with deep regret and sometimes incredulity. Few did so to greater effect than two of Salisbury's own sons. Hugh, the youngest, had always suffered from nervous instability and a certain hysteria about church issues, rather like his father during his younger days. James ('Jem'), the eldest, had appeared less volatile. To find them both ranged against their own father suggested that they saw fault in the government as well as in the political ineptitude of the Archbishop of Canterbury. At the end of 1896, Hugh Cecil wrote to Balfour's sister-in-law, Frances:

To this day it remains a mystery to me why they did not find time last session for the Benefices Bill . . . [T]hey would have stopped the damaging accusation wh: now can and will be made against them of total indifference to the Church's interests. Besides they wd. probably have stopped Jem and me voting ag'st them on the Land Bill & the consequent suspicion that the Prime Minister sympathized with the landlords. Altogether it seems to me an astonishing blunder – only accountable by supposing a total contempt for the power of Church men to harm or serve them. I rejoice therefore when I read in the papers that Ld. Cranborne & his brother are embarrassing the Govt & I hope we may carry that embarrassment to an acute point.[51]

---

[48] Benson to Balfour, 5 May 1896, Balfour MSS 49788 ff.6–7.
[49] Magee to Grier, 5 Dec. 1885, in MacDonnell, *Magee*, vol. II, p. 218.
[50] Benson diary, 22 Dec. 1887, A9.
[51] Hugh Cecil to Frances Balfour, 15 Dec. 1896, Balfour MSS 49830 ff.223–4.

Over ritual, over discipline, over tithe (to which we shall return), the sustenance that Salisbury's party offered to the established church appeared more virtual than real. In part the failure followed from the weakness of church – and especially high-church – sentiment within the forces of Conservatism as a whole. Derby's fear in the 1870s that the 'clerical party' – the *parti prêtre*, as he liked to call it – might take over its direction proved a passing perception resting on a particular constellation of forces in the later stages of Disraeli's period of power. During Salisbury's period of dominance, what he could achieve for the Church of England turned out to be modest, and what he attempted to achieve not much greater. As always, Salisbury showed himself better at resisting what he personally disliked than at producing the consensus required for a popular and sustainable policy.

DISSENT AND EDUCATION

Of all the elements in political life that threatened relations between church and state, the one that Salisbury most disliked was Nonconformity. A negative attitude hardly made him unusual among Conservative Anglicans. One of the problems facing the young Benson when he went to Truro lay in its location amid Cornish Wesleyans and he came away from the experience with a clear sense that ' "conversion" à la Methodists . . . is . . . wretchedly poor', that 'the number of Lunatics in Bodmin asylum who [came] there in sequence on revival manifestations' was startlingly great, 'that its success was owed entirely to its mode of organization' and that its social and theological harm was unconscionable:

John Wesley's work has been done [in Cornwall] in the most complete manner . . . I am obliged to own that those earliest principles of his which he repudiated afterwards with much contempt are the principles which have here taken most root, and that his own system is already decaying before its worst characters, and that it invaded regions where good & wholesome work was being done, and that still it leaves neglected hapless regions which the Church does not touch, and starts into rural organization wherever new Church work begins with vigour, and that, worst of all, it has eliminated the marked doctrines of the Catholic Church wherever it has come; all sacramental teaching and love; abandons the Christianity of the soul until the moment of conversion comes, and recognizes no pervading results of the Incarnation, and has extraordinarily abused the doctrine of the Judgement. The result of this has been a very widespread immorality of a very dark character, and a disregard of truth and honesty.[52]

If the future archbishop of Canterbury could adopt so vibrant a tone about Nonconformists, there seems at first blush nothing distinctive in drawing attention to the animadversions of a future prime minister. Yet Salisbury's rationale had its own flavour. He, too, thought Dissenters inspired no trust, that their parliamentary representatives were 'restrained by no ordinary scruples', that they were driven by a lust for looting the church and that their language about rights was mischievous and that they had to be kept out of Anglican institutions at all costs.[53] What drove the engine of resentment in Salisbury's mind, however, was history and a particular view of Dissenting origins.

Possibly his mental equanimity when discussing Nonconformity might have appeared firmer had not the bicentenary of the ejections of clergy in 1662 come round at just the moment when he needed journalistic material of a pronounced polemical kind in order to justify his present posture by citing past iniquity. 'The Bicentenary' appeared in the *Quarterly Review* in July 1862 and is important to understanding not so much Cecil's level of passion, which was partly contrived, as the style of his reasoning about Dissent and its claims to equality. His argument began not with the ejections of ministers by the Restoration church but with the anti-Laudians of the 1630s, whom he regarded as the source of trouble in the first place; and his sympathies rested not with those ejected but with their predecessors who in 1644 had suffered usurpation, disgrace and starvation for the crime of loyalty to their church:

> The middle of the night was often chosen for the execution of the sentence; and no circumstances of sickness or infirmity, however piteous, availed to stay the course of the rude soldiery who were charged with the execution. The pregnant, the newly-delivered, the bedridden, the infirm, were thrown out at midnight into the street or road, sometimes with the snow on the ground, and left to shelter themselves as best they could under hedges or in barns, and feed themselves on crab-apples or turnip tops until they could obtain some scanty alms from the pity of a concealed adherent.[54]

Six or seven thousand clergymen and their families ate their turnip tops and slept under hedges, according to Cecil, the victims of

---

[52] Benson diary, 25 Jul. 1877, 29 Jul. 1877, 6 Jan. 1878, A3 ff.202–3, 206–7, 238–9.

[53] e.g. Cecil in Commons, *Hansard*, 17 Apr. 1861, CLXII, col. 678.

[54] Cecil, 'The Bicentenary', *Quarterly Review*, 112 (Jul. 1862), pp. 236–70 at p. 269.

baseless allegations.[55] This placed the great martyrs of 1662 under a new light, of course. 'Before we commemorate the great wrong they suffered in being ejected from their parsonages, it is material to inquire how they got into them.' Cecil added a nicely turned parable that he sometimes reused: 'If a pick pocket has possessed himself of your handkerchief, and yields it up to you again under the gentle pressure of the police, his most admiring and enthusiastic friend would not think it necessary to preach a sermon in his honour, upon the next anniversary of the event.'[56]

Once he had sorted out the narrative to his own satisfaction, Cecil had an excellent platform from which to launch his missiles against modern Nonconformists as true heirs, in every unpleasant sense, of the looters of 1644, heirs who lacked none of their forebears' vindictiveness if not their strength, which is why it is no accident that 'they should grasp at every available means for rekindling the fire which they fear is dying away'.[57] This made them dangerous – the more so for using the tactics of accommodation and subversion rather than confrontation. 'They do not wish to give up to indiscriminate pillage a land flowing with milk and honey. They are too anxious to partake of the vintage to desire to open the vineyard to the trampling hoof of the secular wild boar . . . They have no conscientious objections to an Establishment. The only change they would suggest is, that they should be the Establishment themselves.'[58] This knock-about journalism had no intellectual substance but made good reading for beleaguered vicars and rectors and perhaps reinforced the spirits of those who had joined Cecil in resisting the abolition of church rates during the previous year. It was a call to arms. 'There is a motley throng of religionists crowding outside the door of the church, anxious to force their way in, in order to divide the treasure which is stored inside. As long as the door is kept shut, they cannot reach even the smallest objects of plunder. They have made the effort recently, with at first some prospect of success, and have been in the end bitterly disppointed.'[59] Virtually all the positions that Salisbury would ever adopt in his dealings with Dissent find some reflection in this article; and while so much of his

---

[55] Modern estimates of the dispossessed are more scholarly and consequently more cautious: perhaps 2,500 ejections out of around 8,600 clergy for the entire period of the civil war and protectorate.
[56] Cecil, 'Bicentenary', p. 238.   [57] *Ibid.*, p. 237.
[58] *Ibid.*, p. 269.   [59] *Ibid.*, p. 262; cf. pp. 268–70.

journalism presents a precipice from which to retreat when faced
with the realities of practical life, he never pulled back from the edge
when considering Nonconformists, for whom he nursed and cultivated a perfectly genuine hatred. In some ways they probably struck
him as similar to the Whigs in the political environment: Whigs were
worse than Radicals and Socialists because at least one knew what the
latter wanted and saw the sense of it from their own point of view.
Whigs, on the other hand, were class traitors who would not be able
to hold onto a foot of their land or a whit of their wealth if their
radical friends and other *bien pensants* had their way. Nonconformists
were worse than atheists. At least Charles Bradlaugh and his atheistic
associates took a clear position about religion and the church. The
Dissenters wanted to destroy the church from inside while professing
friendship. They sought to despoil its historicity, trivialize its majesty
and transfer its authority to weird covens of Muggletonians, Ranters
and Shakers – names that Salisbury loved poisonously to declaim.

Preparing for war, therefore, became Salisbury's sole mode of
peace when he turned his mind to Dissent. And the enemy, so
powerful was the organization of Nonconformity, had ranged itself
throughout the nation, ideally placed to undertake the subversion it
envisaged in order to gain its central objectives.

[T]he Dissenting chapels scattered over the country are not merely
institutions for propagating and preserving the faith of Brown, or Fox, or
Muggleton; they are earthworks and blockhouses for the maintenance of an
untiring political guerilla. A large proportion of the Dissenting ministers are
ready-made electioneering agents. They are natural adepts at all the lower
strategems of political warfare, and are unequalled in the art of dressing-out
grievances and manufacturing discontent.[60]

This is why they lied about their numbers, of course – to make
themselves sound like representatives of a mighty phalanx rather
than a modest cell. The religious census of 1851 had suggested a
Nonconformist adherence that could not possibly be right, Cecil
said: many of the chapel returns implied a congregation that
physically would not fit into the building.[61] It was the same with
resistance to paying church rates. Local Anglicans found themselves

---

[60] Cecil, 'The Conservative Reaction', *Quarterly Review*, 108 (Jul. 1860), pp. 265–302 at
pp. 270–1.
[61] Cecil in Commons, *Hansard*, 11 Jul. 1860, CLIX, cols. 1722–3. Estimates of the larger
denominations in 1851 suggest just under half a million for Methodist membership of all
persuasions and 140,000 Baptists. Cf. Alan D. Gilbert, *Religion and Society in Industrial England;
Church, Chapel and Social Change 1740–1914* (1976), pp. 31, 37.

confronted by Dissenting fanatics determined 'to manufacture a martyr by daring the churchwardens till they sold up the shop fittings of some peculiarly aggravating Quaker'.[62] Yet the provocations always presented themselves as the language of equity and common sense. He could not even agree that the only good Dissenter was a dead one, since dead ones provided relatives with endless opportunity for creating mischief over where to bury them. Where Salisbury and higher friends such as Carnarvon and Cranbrook emphatically did not want them was in Anglican churchyards: the deep end of the wedge, as it were. Nor did the bishops, at least at first, in an argument that lasted decades. What service should be read over the coffin? What about repairs to the fabric of the churchyards? Would live Dissenters claim exemption while their dead colleagues cumbered Anglican earth? Salisbury expected, as always, the worst and resolved to resist it – remembering that no concession would ever satisfy a Dissenter, 'so long as there is more to be got'.[63]

He could maintain a truly regal hysteria through controversy on church rates, Anglican trusts and charities, and the doomed attempt to hang onto the Thirty-nine Articles in the universities against the reforming enthusiasm of Gladstone's first government. After 1874 the context shifted, however, because ritualism upstaged the Free Churches in 1875 and because by the time burials came on in earnest, in 1877, Salisbury had his mind deeply preoccupied by events in Russia and Turkey. From 1886 his location made warfare yet more circumspect, whatever his private feelings may have been. For in dealing with the great Nonconformist contentions of the late 1880s and 1890s – tithes and schools – he had to deal for the first time as prime minister and with a fist tied behind his back by Liberal Unionists whose Dissenting constituency made policy more of a no-trump bid than Salisbury would have preferred in a purely Conservative configuration.

Richmond's attempt, as lord president of the Council, to consolidate the legislation on burial practice in a Conservative direction showed the width of feeling about the matter in some directions, the degree of non-feeling about it in others, and the capacity for

[62] Cecil, 'Church Rates', *Quarterly Review*, 110 (Oct. 1861), pp. 544–78 at p. 548. For a history of the question, see J. P. Ellens, *Religious Routes to Gladstonian Liberalism: The Church Rate Conflict in England and Wales, 1832–68* (University Park, PA, 1994).
[63] Salisbury to Palmer, 31 Jul. 1870, 1st Earl of Selborne MSS 1864 f.69.

obstruction still present in the aged second Earl of Harrowby, whose determination to destroy Conservative policy on burials was only outdone by his son's passive genius for preventing the formation of a Conservative policy on education. Derby from the start thought Richmond's bill 'harmless & useless', which fully indicated his depth of commitment to the cause of Anglican burial.[64] More disturbing and less predictable were the bishops, several of whom seemed to want to meet Dissenters more than half-way by allowing burial on Anglican ground, provided that the curate could refuse those who had displayed an impure character when alive. Even Beaconsfield's squabbling and petty-minded cabinet thought this proposal absurd. But Richmond failed to persuade the archbishops, the House of Lords and the Lower House of Convocation toward a policy of simple resistance – a failure which 'much mortified' Salisbury, Carnarvon and Gathorne Hardy.[65] Behind all the shiftiness hobbled Harrowby, a year short of his eightieth birthday and still an active member of the Society for the Prevention of Cruelty to Animals. He thought Tory attitudes to Nonconformists *unfair*. Now there are many objections to their policies for which Conservatives tradition-ally voice a ready reply, but this one always causes difficulty, since it is not the point of being a Conservative to make the world *fair*. Conservative bishops such as Rochester and Peterborough under-stood this and expressed their support for Richmond's keep-them-out line. Others wavered and succumbed to Harrowby's excruciating reasonableness in an amendment so cringingly worded that Laud himself might have surrendered. Relatives of deceased Nonconfor-mists should be able to request burial in the churchyard without the rites of the Church of England provided that . . .; and the list of warnings and prohibitions filled a paragraph. When it came to the vote on 18 June, Richmond decided to go down fighting like a man. '[I]f this Amendment was carried,' he brayed, 'the Church of England would be the only body in the country which could not set apart a portion of ground for exclusive interment of persons of their communion. Were the Nonconformists the only body of men who were to have liberty of conscience?'[66] The majority of peers plainly found this prospect deplorable but irrelevant and voted themselves

---

[64] Diary, 10 Mar. 1877, in Derby, *Diaries*, p. 381.
[65] Cross to Richmond, 28 May 1877, Goodwood MSS 869 c 10; diary, 9 Jun. 1877, in Derby, *Diaries*, p. 407.
[66] Harrowby and Richmond in Lords, *Hansard*, 19 Jun. 1877, ccxxxiv, cols. 1929–30.

content with Harrowby's amendment by 127 to 111. Salisbury voted in the minority.

In the biography of her father, Lady Gwendolen Cecil did not waste much space on burials: her index goes from Bulgaria to Cabul. But she should have been more patient. The controversy made its mark in persuading Salisbury that the church had become its own worst enemy with a streak of gutlessness in its thinking. It therefore helped him resist the church's wilder claims about tithe which, for the whole of his 1886 government, formed a continuo of Dissenting protest. Just half a century had passed since the Whig government of Lord Melbourne had attempted to meet and assuage the perpetual complaints of farmers about tithe owners confiscating, as they saw it, the historic tenth of their produce as a contribution to clerical upkeep. The Tithe Commutation Act of 1836 rightly received great plaudits, for, by allowing tithe to become a money payment determined by the price of corn, it imposed an imaginative solution which kept the clergy from starvation while removing the more visible signs of unrest and resentment. During the years of 'high farming' after 1852 the scheme worked fairly well, though no provision would ever dilute the acid of Nonconformist farmers who saw no reason to support a church they despised. Where it all toppled into difficulty, like so much else that turned on property relations, was when depression hit the countryside at the end of the 1870s. The index that produced a figure for any year's tithe raked back over a seven-year period to produce an average which, multiplied by the size of the holding, gave the amount to be paid to the tithe-owner. And that bill went to the occupier of the land, not its owner, so tenant farmers dependent on the sale of their produce frequently found themselves in the front line, with tithe operating as a first charge on their income. The system more or less worked when the present year's crops and profits ran in rough harmony with those of the previous six years because farmers knew what to expect and knew that they would generate the resources to pay. But when prices collapsed and profits with them, they faced a bill resting on an average that took no account of their current difficulties but rather ministered to a situation that no longer existed. Egged on by Dissenting churches that pointed to the manifest injustices of the system anyway and the depravities of an established church whose indiscipline the government had shown itself too feeble to correct, farmers (especially in Nonconformist Wales) began to refuse payment, claiming that they could barely pay rent, let alone an unfair tax. But curates in country parishes often had little income outside their annual tithe; so clerical letters of complaint and panic poured into the offices of rural deans, into Lambeth Palace, even into Hatfield. 'Things are indeed becoming most serious', the vicar of Ruthin reported in 1887. 'Unless something is done speedily tithe rent-charge [its technical description] will cease to exist as property and the clergy will have no official incomes whatever . . . The farmers & others know that distraint [the legal penalty for non-payment] costs the tithe-owner more than the value of the tithe and so pay nothing! I have been applied to as Rural Dean by clergy having no private incomes & in great distress.'[67]

Faced with increasing protest of this kind and pressed hard by his archbishop to bring in urgent legislation, Salisbury both claimed and demonstrated a certain degree of ignorance. His only idea was to shift the burden from the occupier to the landowner, unaware that in many regions it would be the work of eternity to establish who the 'owner' of a particular parcel of land might be.[68] He did know that distraint had become very unpopular; he also knew that English landowners were not amused by his proposals to transfer the burden from the tenants to themselves – a point not lost around the cabinet table on landed but encumbered ministers such as Sir Michael Hicks Beach. Salisbury knew that Wales was a long way away; he knew that it was not a Conservative place; he knew that he had not an inch of land there. Everything argued the need for delicacy and forethought, all the same, if only to damp down noise from 'the disestablishers'.[69] Even Cross's harmless-looking bill to allow clergymen to sell off unwanted glebe without reference to their bishop drew thunder from the Earl of Hardwicke after Salisbury had offered his support. 'The doctrine of the Noble Marquess' was apparently 'the most monstrous he had ever heard enunciated in their Lordships' House, and he was astonished that a Conservative Government should have brought forward a proposal so subversive of Conservative principles with regard to land'[70] – not the sort of remark the prime minster wanted to hear from behind him. In fact he treated the problem as he treated ecclesiastical discipline: best to take one's time and educate parliament and public slowly toward the objective

---

[67] Bulkeley R. Jones to Salisbury (copy), 5 Feb. 1887, Benson MSS 171 f.33.
[68] Benson diary, 31 Jan. 1887, A9.
[69] Salisbury to Hartington, 20 Jun. 1888, Devonshire MSS 340/2181.
[70] Salisbury and Hardwicke in Lords, *Hansard*, 10 Mar. 1887, cccxi, cols. 1708–9.

of improving the law. He vetoed a select committee because he did not trust its party composition and wanted to retain control. He mistrusted Smith's line that they should get a bill through 'for the sake of Wales and peace',[71] for the issue could hardly be expressed so simply. Hartington and his Unionists did not feel peaceful about tithes and their lack of peace arguably mattered more than the pacification of Welsh curates. The church would have to make 'concessions' – perhaps by offering to accept only a half of the amount theoretically due, perhaps by abandoning the seven-year averages for three-year ones that would better reflect current conditions. It amounted to a style of 'support' from this most Anglican of prime ministers that Canterbury and York could well do without. 'He is not much of a friend,' muttered Benson to himself in the small hours.[72] To visitors at Arlington Street he may have seemed energetic in his hopes to help the church through a difficult problem over tithe.[73] It is not how Salisbury struck the churchmen. Bill after bill foundered or was withdrawn. Only in 1891 did a tithe act emerge, leaving Hicks Beach furious that Salisbury still did not know any more about the subject than he had done when the controversy started. Some of the churchmen felt anxious even for the stability of rural property now that the transfer of tithe to the owners had been effected. In the south of England, particularly, worries came to light for the future. Rev. David Lamplugh of Maidstone reflected such concerns when he wrote to Lambeth Palace in the wake of the Act: 'Tithe Rentcharge now becomes for the first time a real burden upon Landowners and a charge on the inheritance: it is like a mortgage with strict priority, to be paid in many cases out of scanty rents. We have never been in this position before; and having regard to the prevailing temper of men, it is a hazardous experiment . . .'[74] This does not sound like a triumph of Conservative policy; but then the mounting of political resistance in an expanding democratic system left little room for unmitigated victory. The best Salisbury could achieve was to delay the intolerable by welcoming the unpalatable.

In the schools – an area of greater concern to him than tithe – he

---

[71] Smith to Akers-Douglas, ?28 Jul. 1887, Chilston MSS C/25.
[72] Benson diary, 4 Apr. 1888, A10.
[73] Typical of the embarrassments was Cranbrook's when he had Benson staying at Hemsted Park in 1887. The latter asked him whether there was going to be a tithe bill this session. 'I believe that there will,' Cranbrook had replied. Cranbrook to Salisbury, 7 Jan. 1887, Salisbury MSS (Cranbrook, f.361).
[74] Lamplugh to Benson, 3 Apr. 1891, Benson MSS 171 f.283.

found himself with a similar predicament and ultimately negotiated a parallel outcome. Without question, Salisbury wanted to protect denominational education, resist the advance of state schools and avoid the twin evils, for him, of free and compulsory education. Until the Liberal education reform of W. E. Forster in 1870, the march of the state had been held in check. The church's National Society remained a significant agency for the distribution of government grants to Church of England schools and thus retained a national provision for a national institution in the eyes of Lord Robert Cecil.[75] He had spoken in the 1850s with his usual hyperbole against any idea of using local taxation to fund schools and the arguments remained in his mind over the next half century even when he could not enforce them. He could point, in the first place, to 'manifest injustice' in imposing local education rates to address national objectives: the responsibility rested with the centre if it lay anywhere. There was the 'religious difficulty': how would the localities deal with divergent needs of parents in regard to denominational teaching? And there was the connexion between state involvement and compulsory attendance:

the liability of rate-payers to build schools would probably have to be accompanied with a power to compel attendance of children. The State, having entered into a compact with the rate-payers, would be bound to take care that their money was not wasted, and that could only be effected by obliging the children – at whatever cost to their parents – to frequent the schools. The injustice of such a proceeding was palpable . . . Suppose a labouring man had 12s a week, of which two children earned 4s a week[;] by sending them to school he would lose one-third of his income.[76]

We have seen that he also deprecated the introduction of competitive examinations for public office and sought to stop the secular tide from reaching Oxford at all costs. Over the next thirty years he lost every single battle. The schools became a secular instrument

---

[75] The National Society for the Education of the Poor in the Principles of the Established Church (1811) represented Anglican opinion in education, a rejoinder to the largely Nonconformist British and Foreign Schools Society (1807). The National Society played a significant part in maintaining the 'National' schools after 1870 until they received state aid under the Balfour act in 1902.

[76] Cecil in Commons, *Hansard*, 13 Apr. 1856, XCLI, cols. 824–6. He remained very taken with this argument against compulsion and used it long after Sandon's act of 1876 had brought it about. 'At present, a parent living in a threepenny school parish [i.e. one charging a threepenny education rate] . . . and having three children of school age, pays 30s a year on an income of about £60 – an income tax of sixpence in the pound over and above what his neighbours have to pay': Salisbury to Cranbrook, 10 Dec. 1889, in Cecil, vol. IV, p. 157.

between 1870 and Balfour's comprehensive reform of 1902. The universities lost their religious tests in 1871. But at least he prevented a Dissenting take-over, the outcome he perhaps perceived as worse than the encroachment of the state, precisely because the state could not help but act in some degree as the church's secular arm. If he lost the battles he at least prolonged the war.

The 1870s proved the crucial theatre. Salisbury could do nothing to prevent the passage of radical legislation in Gladstone's government of 1868–74. Nor could he then affect Conservative thinking significantly because of his own choice of purdah following his resignation over reform in 1867. What he could and did do was to work hard for the National Society, for the future of the endowed schools and for the University of Oxford's role as an Anglican seminary. He spent a good deal of his own time trying to help individual schools whose endowment might be threatened, as in the case of Emmanuel Hospital, Westminster, or which might face assault from a local school board under the Forster act, as with Emmanuel School, Camberwell.[77] He wrote clever, courteous, well-modulated letters and memoranda to the Whig minister envisaging reform in Oxford, representing himself as trapped in a vice quite as much as the cabinet:

If I were to consult my own peace of mind I should get rid of this University Tests Bill & its Committee at any price. Its [*sic*] a perfect nightmare. But the difficulty of which on reflection I cannot get rid is this. I have promised to do my utmost to get a thorough enquiry – both publicly & to those whose views I represent. I could not muddle the affair up – and assent to the passing of the Bill, unless I got for them a substantial concession. I should not think the Headship of Colleges issue could be resolved without the concession either of some punitive power against Anti-Christian teaching – or of some control over the election either of fellows or at least of Tutors.

He could not abandon his enquiry motif without attracting to himself 'a flavour of Dizzyism', which God forfend.[78] Disraeli's own sympathies lay far distant from those of Salisbury, Carnarvon and Hardy, and he put the main burden on his new leader in the Lords, the Duke of Richmond, who seems not to have inflamed the clerical imagination in his oratory. 'I am glad you liked what I said upon Education,' he replied to a kind note from his friend Hardy. 'It was

---

[77] See Marsh, *Victorian Church in Decline*, p. 69. For Camberwell, see the lengthy correspondence with Ripon in March–April 1872, Ripon MSS 43519 ff.50–66.
[78] Salisbury to de Grey, 1 Aug. 1870, Ripon MSS 43519 ff.5–7.

heavy work speaking as the House was very empty. I do not think more than *one* Bishop remained. I shd. have thought it was a subject that wd. interest them.'[79] But then Richmond, quite apart from his normal talent at emptying the House, had already made a fuss about the need for a Department of Education which would allow the state to sort it all out – an idea he had got from Lord John Manners and one not calculated to keep bishops in their seats.[80]

But of course the divisions in Conservative opinion about the role of the church in education became more pressing when Disraeli's government took office in 1874 with Salisbury as an uneasy and contemptuous colleague. Richmond had the overview of policy with Harrowby's son, Lord Sandon, directly responsible for education as vice-president of the Council – the constitutional position until the Board of Education finally came into being as a ministry in 1902. Richmond did not hope for much. He thought that if some church teaching happened in church schools, that would be acceptable to Tory parents and ought to do for anybody. Salisbury and Sandon wanted more but they did not want the same thing. Salisbury wanted, and failed to achieve, an Endowed Schools Bill in which a battery of 'church clauses' would protect the place of denominational teaching. His clauses were stripped out of the bill by the cabinet with the help of so-called friends. 'Hardy blustered a good deal about his attachment to the Church,' Salisbury explained to Carnarvon who had not been able to come to cabinet, 'but voted with Derby on all points.'[81] And Derby thought the issues less than gripping; his diary does not even mention Salisbury in the accounts of these meetings. It does mention Sandon; and what *he* wanted was compulsion, the very outcome that Salisbury supported least. By the end of the 1874 session, Cairns – furthest of all from Salisbury in education as in everything else – saw real trouble on the horizon with the cabinet breaking up over a Salisbury attempt to relaunch the Endowed Schools Bill in an Anglican direction.[82] He ought to have worried rather about Sandon whose mental wiring Derby failed to isolate until a cabinet in February 1875 that Sandon was allowed to attend.

A discussion followed on educational matters. Sandon being called in: he is very strong for compulsory schooling, I did not at first see why: but he is

[79] Richmond to Hardy, 23 Jul. 1870, Cranbrook MSS T501/257.
[80] Richmond to Marlborough, 2 Feb. 1868, Marlborough MSS 9271/3/22.
[81] Salisbury to Carnarvon, 24 Jul. 1874, Carnarvon MSS 60758 f.137.
[82] Diary, 22 Sep. 1874, in Derby, *Diaries*, p. 179.

against school boards, and thinks that if more children can be forced into the existing schools, they can be kept up as at present on the voluntary system, to the great content of the local clergy. Hence his zeal.[83]

That was the strange twist. Sandon felt quite as strongly as Salisbury about church schools but believed that compulsion would save them. He knew, moreover, that only he could save England – always a trying conviction in a colleague – and carried about with him 'the heavy responsibility . . . that the Country attaches to me in these matters'.[84] Sheer persistence won the day, and Sandon's education act in 1876 put an end to another of Salisbury's lines of argument by making school attendance compulsory.

India, the Afghans, the Turks, the Zulus and Gladstone put paid to any further lines of argument for a decade; and by the time Salisbury returned to study the schools issue he was a changed man with different priorities and entrenched accommodations. He had also missed the point of what some churchmen were saying. Among thinking men such as Benson, Westcott and Lightfoot, the campaign waged by Salisbury and his colleagues on behalf of the church against board schools misrepresented the priorities of those who led the church. 'If a tenth part of [the misplaced energy] had been thrown into the expanding and perfecting of Training Colleges,' the distinguished trio had agreed, 'there wd. have been no fear. Board Schools are inevitable. And the difference in the school is made not by the subjects of education, but by the religious or irreligious character of the teachers.'[85] This was a clearer-headed judgement than the one provided by Salisbury and his colleagues, with their fears that the new education code's proposed inspectors would have ' "tremendous" powers' or the suspicion that Matthew Ridley could not be given the education portfolio in 1885 because he was 'somewhat advanced' in his religious views.[86] Sensible views inside the church could and should have been encouraged; but the bunker attitude merely led to further bombardment. In the 1874 government it had been compulsion. In the 1886 ministry it was Salisbury's other

---

[83] *Ibid.*, 10 Feb. 1875, p. 195.

[84] Sandon to Richmond, 25 Nov. 1875, Goodwood MSS 867 a 80. Richmond found him 'really the most touchy, suspicious man I ever saw [who] seems to have a great opinion of his own importance': Richmond to Cairns, 5 Jun. 1876, Cairns MSS 30/51/3/f.96.

[85] Benson diary, ?30 Apr./1 Mar. 1879, A3 f.304.

[86] Smith to Cranbrook, 24 Apr. 1889, Cranbrook MSS T501/260; Salisbury to Cranbrook, 13 Aug. 1885, Cranbrook MSS T501/267. Cf. Salisbury to Hicks Beach, 19 Aug. 1885: 'Ridley would give us trouble with the clergy': St Aldwyn MSS PCC/69/23.

phobia, free education, pressed and passed by his colleagues over his live body in 1891. All he managed to do was corrupt the logic of the proposal by denying the appropriateness of beginning with a principle at all, along the lines that Cross had suggested;[87] and then to grumble sulkily, when the bill went through, about 'clergymen in the towns' who, he thought, were the act's main critics and about how the church schools were not worth saving anyway because their teachers were '*culture-people*, and little else', persons better able to discourse on Matthew Arnold, presumably, than St Matthew's gospel.[88]

There were some better moments in the 1890s – supporting the Bishop of Salisbury's attempt to reintroduce denominational education in board schools if parents requested it and were willing to pay for it; or making the earnest Liberal minister, A. H. D. Acland, sound like a ravening beast who ate Christians for breakfast.[89] He could still rubbish the rhetoric of wet Liberals more readily than anyone on the red benches. Witness his artfully bad definition of undenominational education:

> It means without teaching the divinity of Our Lord. That is the real point on which, in the long run, all these regulations will turn . . . Now we say that to do that is really to put out of gear religious teaching altogether; that religious teaching is not possible in this hypothetical way . . . The notion that there is a religion expunging that upon which men differ, and leaving nothing but that upon which all men can agree, is the wildest chimera that ever entered the brain of a politician.[90]

But it became glaring, especially through the unhappy attempts to draft and put through an education bill in the 1895 government's lifetime, that Salisbury neither had the confidence of the broad mass of Conservative support for further reform of the state sector, nor the allegiance of the die-hard element, which included members of his own family, who sought to dig their church into a defensive rampart that might prevent further loss of ground. By the end of the second session, Hugh Cecil no more believed in the government's credentials on education that he did on discipline or patronage. 'The real

---

[87] Cross to Cadogan, 4 Jun. 1891, Cadogan MSS CAD/455. Cross had wanted a statement from cabinet 'that there should be public school accommodation available without payment of fees for the children over 5 and under 14 of all parents who desired it', a moment of Enlightenment rationalism that brought immediate demur from the centre of the table.

[88] Salisbury to Harrowby, 9 Jul. 1891, Cecil, vol. IV, pp. 159–60.

[89] Salisbury in Lords *Hansard*, 4 May 1893, XII, cols. 37–9, 31 Jul. 1893, col. 866.

[90] Salisbury in Lords, *Hansard*, 4 Sep. 1893, XVI, cols. 1850–51.

truth', said one who always saw himself in possession of it, 'is of course that neither the Govt. nor the party as a whole really cares about religious education. If they did there are ways of saving the schools.'[91]

They did and they didn't. Salisbury retained to the end his hostility to the secularization of the young: it was no accident that thorough-going educational reform had to wait until he had retired from public life. But his appointment of a Liberal Unionist, the Duke of Devonshire (formerly Lord Hartington), to the post of lord president in 1895 marked clearly enough both his acceptance that party politics would have much to say about what happened in education and his willingness to bend when necessary. The Queen's overriding of his views about episcopal appointments – especially over Durham in 1889 – had done nothing to strengthen his determination to save the church, just as his difficult relationship with Benson until the latter's death in 1896 had provided a less than stable platform from which to do so. It remained the case that Salisbury had instincts about the church's *politics* that were foreign to Gladstone and that this would make him the last prime minister of Britain to construct his view of what should be done from a position inside the mind-set of a senior Anglican churchman, with the possible exception of Baldwin. Whether he were speaking about the establishment or Dissent, Oxford colleges, theological colleges or elementary schools, his positions turned on an understanding of the place of religion in the conduct of public affairs. As public affairs expanded their geography as well as their social scope, he addressed imperial perspectives in the same way. Perhaps he had never heard of the Bishop of Melbourne. Perhaps he clenched his tongue in his cheek when he pretended to apologize to the Bishop of Calcutta.[92] He recognized all the same the place of the church in a wider world and took seriously the claims of those who defined his nation's sensibilities and mission in language drawn from three centuries of Protestant experience.

[91] Hugh Cecil to Frances Balfour, 15 Dec. 1896, Balfour MSS 49830 ff.221–2.
[92] Salisbury to Bishop of Calcutta, 4 Jun. 1875, Christ Church MSS C/2/125.

CHAPTER 8

The empire

'Moorhouse of Melbourne': the phrase spans half a world. During the years of Salisbury's maturity, say from 1860 to 1900, the fact of empire (sometimes erupting in war and the waving of flags, always present as an unspoken context of dominion, colony and dependency) developed in its urgency and relevance to political action, not infrequently at Salisbury's own bidding. Imperial ideas and doctrines saturated the higher journalism of the clerisy and acted as grounds for propositions and recommendations in both Houses of Parliament. Victoria's ascent from Queen to Empress of India in 1876 merely decorated a movement of popular enthusiasm and universal awareness. Defending India, the jewel in her crown, was no longer enough. Wider still and wider should her bounds be set. From Venezuela to Zanzibar, from Sierra Leone to Herat, from Bombay to Weihaiwei, Greater Britain made felt her imperial weight – never more so than during the decade and a half when Salisbury dominated the metropolitan polity. It affected his everyday thinking; he responded to its pressures and challenges, if only to raise an eyebrow or make a cool and empty parliamentary statement. As in most other Conservative environments, the world of empire refracted a spectrum of views and emphases, with a language of mission and destiny spoken by a Lytton or Milner at one end of the range and the anxious whispers of a Northcote at the other. Salisbury himself did not tremble at thoughts of war, though he deemed bloodshed better avoided. Neither did he join the wild-eyed visionaries in their march to glory. He rather reflected and manipulated the instincts of his generation in favour of a strong and peaceful empire with India at its core and the great white Dominion of Canada and Commonwealth of Australia framing its periphery. He developed his own style of imperial argument resting on race,[1] about which he remained unsentimental, commerce, whose demands he took seriously and for which he saw an imperial role, and strategy in whose subtleties he delighted and whose nuances he came to despair of teaching to those around him. Between his becoming secretary of state for India in 1866 and presiding over the opening of the Boer War in 1899, he brought that style of speaking to bear on issues raised by the future of India and Africa quite as much as on concerns closer to home.

THE WHITE MAN AND HIS BURDENS

Salisbury shared the prejudice of his generation and culture in believing that white people possessed a special pedigree and played a privileged part in the world order. He was a 'racist' in the terminology of the late twentieth century, which often slaps the label on anybody who believes that races have any specific characteristics at all or who countenances using race as a ground for stating any proposition, negative or positive, about modern society. But he went far further than that. He felt instinctively that races could be precisely ordered in a familiar nineteenth-century pattern of descent from superior to inferior: Teuton, Celt, Latin, brown (Christian), brown (Muslim), black, yellow – a decline widely reflected with minor variations in the political literature of Britain between 1870 and 1900. Unlike Disraeli he brought little romance to race: he saw no mystique in the East, no genius in the Latin races and thought the future Teutonic without any of Disraeli's wistfulness.[2] Certainly there could be bad white men – he retained for many years his dislike of the Boers he had met on his South African tour, 'as degraded a set of savages as any white man in the world'[3] – but in general the whites seemed to him to enjoy a rightful priority in the

---

[1] To the modern ear a term such as 'ethnicity' may seem both more accurate and (for a post-Holocaust sensibility) more comfortable. It needs to be faced, however, that when late-Victorians talked about race they frequently meant a constellation of alleged characteristics that they deemed unchangeable, inevitable, biological, *intrinsic* in some ultimate sense. I retain their word because I seek to retain their world.

[2] See Disraeli's concern in 1870 that 'the Latin races are worn, and that the future of Europe is Teutonic': Derby diary, 18 Aug. 1870, in Derby, *Diaries*, p. 67. Cf. Paul Smith's recent emphasis on Disraeli's Jewishness and his racial imagination: *Disraeli: A Brief Life* (Cambridge, 1996).

[3] Quoted in J. F. A. Mason, 'Lord Salisbury: A Librarian's View', in Lord Blake and Hugh Cecil (eds.), *Lord Salisbury The Man and his Policies* (Basingstoke, 1987), pp. 10–29 at p. 17.

world's deliberations. Indeed, when the time came to go to war with the Boers in 1899, he warned his cabinet to expect trouble. Degraded the Boers may have been, but they were still white men. 'We must remember', he told colleagues, 'this is the first time we have gone to war with people of the Teutonic race';[4] and the implication was that they would prove harder to beat than people of inferior ones.

Throughout his forty-year commentary on world affairs, Salisbury consistently assumed this sense of superiority. Black slavery was, he thought, a bad thing though he opposed, as we have seen, North American attempts to outlaw it by force and retained his outright opposition after the Civil War to any attempt to strip owners of their slaves without compensation.[5] White slavery seemed to him far worse simply because its victims were white. That was what most appalled him about the social system in Poland: 'the depth of the degradation to which the Polish nobles had reduced their slaves'. For, of course, 'these were no negroes, men of an inferior race imported from a barbarous land and incapable of the acute and sensitive feelings of the white man'.[6] They were like *us*. Exactly the same sentiments permeated his imperial thought. The empire began at home and began, therefore, with the race that made it. Here domestic policy fused with a conception of empire; so when Salisbury argued for urgent reform of working-class housing in the 1880s, he did so partly because 'it [was] by the character of the English race and the nature of those produced from generation to generation' that all public functions could continue to be carried out.[7] And when he turned his attention to the colonies themselves, the white ones attracted special attention and care. He felt as grateful as the Liberal government to the Indian princes for supporting British efforts in the Sudan in 1885. But, when the Australians of New South Wales offered military assistance, he could not repress the degree to which 'of course, we feel still more strongly such indications of good feeling when they come from our own blood . . . They are true Englishmen, and have behaved in a manner worthy of the race from which they

---

[4] Reported by Lord Ashbourne in A. B. Cooke and A. P. W. Malcolmson (eds.), *The Ashbourne Papers 1869–1913* (Belfast, 1974), p. 31.
[5] It was a case where contract overrode sentiment: '[p]hilanthropy does not justify bad faith': Salisbury to Beach, 31 Dec. 1896, St Aldwyn MSS PCC/69/138–41.
[6] Lord Robert Cecil, 'Poland', *Quarterly Review*, 113 (Apr. 1863), pp. 448–81 at pp. 477–8.
[7] Salisbury in Lords, *Hansard*, 16 Jul. 1885, CCXCIX, col. 897.

have sprung, and the splendid Empire of which they form so important a factor.'[8] The Teuton remained the tortoise on whom the empire reposed: independent in his liberty, transparent in his honesty, fortunate in his family, slow to anger, slow to thought, inevitable in the righting of wrong and punishment of evil.

Blacks had failed, according to the Conservative vision, to acquire these virtues thus far in their development. They had to be educated towards a future in which they, too, could acquire them, but in the meantime part of the point of an empire lay in providing a secure framework, a well-fenced garden, in which they could grow in safety and receive the kindness that children deserved and required. This theme – family, children, love, education, responsibility – ran through tracts of imperial rhetoric, Conservative and Liberal, and Salisbury subscribed to some of it, though not the parts that he considered emotional cant. Prudence, not sentiment, underpinned his recommendation of protectorates as appropriate when dealing with 'inferior' races, but even that concession so worried Hicks Beach by its generosity that, when asked by Gwendolen Cecil for his recollections of Salisbury in 1913, the letter containing Salisbury's cautious meditation remained the one closest to memory. 'Ever since I recommended the restoration of Mysore [near Bangalore in southern India] thirty years ago,' Salisbury had written to him in a relaxed letter from Walmer in 1896, 'I have always been of opinion that the condition of a protected dependency is more acceptable to the half-civilised races, & more suitable for them than direct dominion. It is cheaper, simpler, less wounding to their self-esteem, gives them more careers as public officials, & spares them unnecessary contact with white men.' This he took to be true generally, but felt it especially valuable when dealing 'with Moslems, with Arabs, who hate us & our religion & our special notions with a particular hatred'. It was not that he '*fear[ed]*' the discontent that dominion brought in its wake; but repression meant bloodshed and that seemed both unpleasant and unnecessary.[9] This side of Salisbury's presentation of the racial issues became stronger in the mellowing of old age when he looked to principled imperial feeling along these lines rather than to the rabid xenophobia and triumphalist

---

[8] Salisbury in Lords, *Hansard*, 16 Mar. 1885, CCXCV, col. 1222.
[9] Salisbury to Hicks Beach, 2 Sep. 1896, St Aldwyn MSS PCC/69/117–18; memo by Hicks Beach, n.d. (Dec. 1913) in which he remembered this 'long and admirable exposition', *ibid.*, 207.

tendencies of the Jubilee culture. There seems no reason to doubt
the genuineness of this letter to Northcote's son in India at the turn
of the new century:

It interests me to find that you are struck with the 'damned nigger' element
in the British society of Bombay. It is bad enough in official and military
circles here. I look upon it as not only offensive and unworthy but as
representing what is now, and will be in a highly magnified proportion, a
serious political danger. But I preach in the wilderness. It belongs to that
phase of British temper which in the last few months [of the South African
War] has led detachment after detachment of British troops into the most
obvious ambuscades – mere arrogance. But it must become formidable as
the increase of communication presses its existence more upon the
consciousness of the subject races . . . We have tried in vain here – with the
Queen to back us – to obtain some military honours and grades for the
native princes. It is not conceivable that they should bear for two more
generations this ostentatious mark of contempt: that those of their race are
not allowed to fill any high command. It is the fashion in which Turkey
treats her Christian subjects . . .

It is painful to see the dominant race deliberately going over into the
Abyss.[10]

Too much unmelted butter should not be placed in Salisbury's
mouth. He moved in an environment within which race functioned
as a daily ingredient of conversation – often as a significant style of
joke, as though he and his friends were trying to leave offensive
material in the archives over which their po-faced successors can
shake their heads. Resolving an inter-departmental confusion of
administration with the Foreign Office in the 1870s, Salisbury used a
favourite phrase in advising Derby that he should wallop his own
niggers.[11] The problem could have been sorted out in less acerbic
language. That it was not says something about Salisbury, but
politically outraged researchers are likely to get wrong what it says,
which is something to do with Salisbury's inability to employ neutral
language (to which we shall return), something to do with the framework of humour within which all participants lived and worked, and
somehow connected to a system of near-universal reference within
Conservative conversation. It does not imply that Salisbury sought to

---

[10] Salisbury to Sir Henry Northcote, 8 Jun. 1900, Christ Church MSS, no file. Cf. Disraeli's
outburst to Salisbury in 1875: 'Nothing is more disgusting, than the habit of our officers
speaking always of the inhabitants of India – many of them descended from the great races
– as "niggers". It is ignorant, & brutal, – & surely most mischievous': Disraeli to Salisbury,
13 Dec. 1875, Salisbury MSS (Disraeli, f.118).
[11] Salisbury to Derby, 24 Jan. 1876, Derby MSS 16/2/72.

own slaves whom he wished to beat, as earnest authors from the West Coast are likely to allege, far less does it follow that he countenanced a style of imperial policy that saw the way forward in genocide in the fashion advocated by the great Liberal James Anthony Froude. At dinner with the latter in 1879 the Tory Lord George Hamilton felt so compelled by Froude's table-talk that he felt obliged to write it down. 'He pointed out to me', Hamilton wrote, 'that there was a virile and intelligent race, physically stronger than the average European, who were [*sic*] multiplying and increasing faster than white men under the influence of civilization, and that the Zulus and Kaffirs would ultimately demolish the white race. I asked him what was his policy, and in a gloomy tone he informed me that there was no policy but to exterminate them. I pointed out to him the extreme difficulty of such a policy in these days of sentiment and humanitarianism. He replied: "If you do not adopt that policy, they will exterminate you." '[12] Salisbury would have seen in such talk the ravings of a madman, just as he would have rejected his friend Carnarvon's impatient absolutism in face of racial difficulty in the West Indies as both undesirable and politically unworkable.[13] For him, race presented itself as a reality with which policy should deal, peaceably if it could, forcibly if it must. It was not the only context of imperial argument and it often was not the most important one.

Historians of various national styles of imperialism – British, Dutch, Portuguese, Belgian – build models in their minds of what made empires tick. A familiar and rather tedious aspect of those models often lies in the area of commerce: did trade follow the flag and thus supply the explanation for wanting to plant the flag in the first place? Early critics of imperialism, among whom the British social democrat John Hobson stands prominent in his intellectual ability and literary grace, argued for this position as a fundamental truth. Discovering new investments and markets abroad for capital saved by a *rentier* class at home functioned as the 'taproot' of empire.[14] Since Hobson's treatise on imperialism at the turn of the century, the argument has veered between 'economic' explanations

[12] George Hamilton, *Parliamentary Reminiscences and Reflections, 1886–1906* (2 vols., 1922), vol. I, p. 156.

[13] 'Long talk with Carnarvon on W. Indian affairs: he alleges that parliamentary govt. works badly in these communities of mixed race . . .', diary, 14 Jul. 1876, in Derby, *Diaries*, pp. 309–10. Derby thought him 'by nature inclined to absolutist as against parliamentary theories of govt.': *ibid.*

[14] See J. A. Hobson, *Imperialism: A Study* (1902).

of this kind and 'strategic' or 'ideological' concerns that various writers have taken to provide a more telling context. Salisbury shows traces of all of these things; but he comes as a particular godsend to the more tired end of the 'economic' position. Certainly he had (if anyone finds the term helpful) an ideological position about race and responsibility. Yet, overwhelmingly, his lack of sentimentality about empire rested on the thought that the *point* of acquisitions lay in helping British commerce at a time of economic difficulty. Strategic concerns played often a signal role in his thinking, as one would expect in one of the century's most masterful foreign ministers. And his private thoughts did not always present the same emphases as his public statements on the platform or in the House of Lords. So far as public argument went, however, the empire mattered for what it brought home and what it brought home made its way into the balance-sheets of the nation.

Replying to Lord Granville in the debate on the Queen's Speech when parliament opened in November 1891, Salisbury made an unambiguous public defence of the imperial frame of mind and rejected any doubts that commerce benefited from the possession of an empire:

[T]he doctrine that the flag draws the trade is covered and supported by the documents which are annually laid before us . . . [I]f we look at the trade of this country with India, and compare it with the trade that we carry on with other countries quite as rich and quite as vast, I think [Granville] will see that the political connexion with that country is a very powerful factor in the enormous commerce which we are enabled to derive from it. Although it is lamentably true that some of our colonies, not following our Free Trade example, have interposed the obstacles of tariff between us and them, which hinder our trade, yet I think it is the fact that our trade is increasing more rapidly with the Australian Colonies than with any other part of the world. I do not, of course, say that the trade of Africa will be an immediate compensation for what we may lose in consequence of the existence of Protectionist beliefs in America, but it is a motive for preventing territory from falling into the hands of other Powers, that those Powers will probably use the dominion which we concede to them for the purpose of crippling the trade that we otherwise should possess; and that seems to be a legitimate motive for the accession of territory which might otherwise be wanting.[15]

Here the two arguments of economy and strategy blend together in a highly characteristic mix: trade demands annexation and annexation

---

[15] Salisbury in Lords, *Hansard*, 25 Nov. 1891, CCCXLIX, cols. 24–5.

stops other powers from annexing, which is not immoral as a motive because Britain will allow other powers to trade with their colonies whereas they, the rival imperialists, will build trade barriers. Ergo, the expansion of Britain is in everybody's interest – a sort of public benefaction. He said it all again in 1894 with exactly the same defence of empire against charges of ambition and vainglory:

There is a much more solid reason: to keep our trade, our industries alive we must open new sources of consumption in the more untrodden portions of the earth, and we are the only nation that can occupy those countries without shutting them to all the world besides. If we occupy a distant, large and uncivilized country and attempt to make it subservient to the purposes of commerce, we injure no others, because all others are as free to use it for commercial purposes as ourselves. But there are other countries which, if they occupy any of these regions shut it out from British commerce, as though the access to it was physically impossible.[16]

This flavour in Salisbury's public rhetoric never faded. However much he may have diluted the racial account of imperialism in the later years, he continued to react strongly against '*quasi*-sentimental language' about empire and to remind his audience constantly of 'what I might call the business side'.[17]

Behind the scenes his tone could become distinctly more cautious and from exactly the same chain of reasoning. For the forces of economic change that could lead to expansion could also prompt a refusal to expand when the circumstances of the case threatened to turn advantage into encumbrance. Disraeli's over-quoted irritation about 'millstones around our necks' – a dismissive outburst against small and useless acquisitions – made an important point, after all. If the purpose of taking a piece of territory lay in making it economically worthwhile, then many such tracts of Africa and Asia promised a return of worse than zero, taking into account the costs in men and money involved in annexing it and the still greater cost of policing it. This consideration often made Salisbury a most reluctant imperialist on the grounds of *cui bono?* Take the case of Sierra Leone in 1878. The British and French had broadly followed a live-and-let-live policy in West Africa for a generation, but local tensions sometimes

---

[16] Salisbury in Lords, *Hansard*, 1 Jun. 1894, xxv, col. 151. For an admixture of the racial tinge, too, cf. his speech in the following session lamenting the failure to build commercial infrastructures in 'these new countries'. '[O]ther outlets for the commercial energies of our race are being gradually closed by the commercial principles which are gaining more and more adhesion': *Hansard*, 14 Feb. 1895, xxx, col. 698.

[17] Salisbury in Lords, *Hansard*, 20 Jul. 1900, LXXXVI, cols. 617–18.

arose over threats to ports. Something of the kind urged the British governor of Sierra Leone to declare himself in favour of appropriating a particular piece of coastline from the French in 1878; and Hicks Beach (colonial secretary and already deeply disturbed by the Zulus on the other side of the continent) asked his foreign secretary for advice. He ought to have remembered this reply more vividly than the later one that he retained, for it was a superbly judged tug on the bit:

My hesitation arises from this cause. We have now on our hands a Transvaal war: & probably an Afghan war. We may at any time be called on to vindicate the Treaty of Berlin by force of arms. To add to all these burdens a nigger war for the sake of settlements which commercially represent but little profit, & financially only represent deficit, would not be creditable to our wisdom.

But will the appropriation of these strips of Strand produce war? Who can say? The wars of 1864 and 1873 [the so-called Ashanti wars] arose without any definite intention on our part to go to war. In those parts it is I believe the custom of every bit of land to have six claimants to its ownership: & if one sells, it is the duty of the other five to shoot the purchaser. Can you be quite certain that the people who have sold to you are the only claimants?[18]

The empire was a place where money could be made. It was also a sink down which, as in Uganda, 'great sums of money have been risked and lost'.[19] In order for the commercial motive to dominate, therefore, clear and secure gain had to present itself as a realistic prospect. If it did not, annexation might happen anyway but the ground would be different and the objective usually strategic.

Very often the strategy in question would have a domestic face because colonial policy, in a supposed democracy, had to be represented as also Conservative policy. The fate of Governor Eyre in Jamaica or General Gordon in the Sudan gave rise to issues that impinged on domestic policy at Westminster as well as on discussions about the substantive issues raised in either case. Whether Tory imperialists or Liberal Unionists would subscribe to a particular initiative could have a major effect on whether policy were allowed to run in one direction or another. In so far as disembodied colonial strategies could emerge (and they rarely did), Salisbury sought to

---

[18] Salisbury to Hicks Beach, 10 Oct. 1878, St Aldwyn MSS PCC/69/7–8. The latter is partially quoted in Lady Victoria Hicks Beach, *Life of Sir Michael Hicks Beach, Earl St Aldwyn* (2 vols., 1932), vol. I, p. 72.

[19] Salisbury in Lords, *Hansard*, 1 Jun. 1894, xxv, col. 147.

keep a cool head and see the width of ramification that always followed from an overseas *démarche*. He never allowed imperial concerns to obscure the path of foreign policy more generally conceived and preferred to avoid pointless fights rather than provoke them. In many ways this reticence made him less combative than Disraeli, who liked the verbal violence of Lytton, say, for its avoidance of masterly inactivity that allowed the electorate, which preoccupied him far more than ever it worried Salisbury, to go to sleep.[20] And for a certain style of Gladstonian Liberal, Salisbury's apparent inactivity seemed insufferable – a mere capitulation to supine instincts and a failure to see that great bullies, like the Turks, will always need to have their bags and baggage cast into the ocean by righteous Powers. Mr Gladstone, went the refrain, had seen all this when he supposedly seized Smyrna in the autumn of 1880 in order to chastise the Sultan.[21] 'The contrast to this action supplied by Lord Salisbury's inaction over Crete', raved Lord Rendel in 1896, 'often, I feel sure, occurred to Mr. G. He was, even in the most intimate conversations very slow to judgement on rivals or men who held his old offices. He would use, however, such expressions as "Grasp your nettle" in commenting on Lord Salisbury's nerveless, passive habit of shifting all responsibilities on subordinates and shirking all definite action . . . To my mind, of all the countless popular delusions, none is more absurd that the idea that Mr. G. could "funk" where Lord Salisbury would fight.'[22]

Rendel's remark shows that he no more knew how to construct a cool-headed overseas policy than did his master and that he failed to distinguish inaction from intelligent refusal to act. All strategic decisions came from Salisbury himself: subordinates ultimately did what they were told notwithstanding the weight that he might place on the opinion of his able under-secretaries in the Office: Julian Pauncefote, Philip Currie, even Thomas Sanderson when he thought

---

[20] 'With Lytton's general policy I entirely agree. I have always been opposed to and deplored masterly inactivity': Beaconsfield to Cranbrook, 17 Sep. 1878, in A. E. Gathorne Hardy, *Gathorne Hardy, First Earl of Cranbrook: A Memoir* (2 vols., 1910), vol. II, p. 97.

[21] In fact the threat of seizing Smyrna, to deny the Porte customs duties until after Greek territory negotiated away at Berlin had been effectively ceded, proved sufficient; and the Turks had climbed down. John Morley, *Life of Gladstone* (3 vols., 1903), vol. III, pp. 8–9. Gladstone later came to think the Greeks ungrateful and unsatisfied. But he supported Rosebery when the latter, as foreign secretary, tried a 'forward' policy there in 1886: see Gladstone to Rosebery, 10 Mar. and 28 Apr. 1886, printed in M. R. D. Foot and Colin Matthew (eds.), *The Gladstone Diaries* (14 vols., Oxford, 1968–94), vol. XI, pp. 507, 541.

[22] Stuart, Lord Rendel, *The Private Papers of Lord Rendel* (1931), pp. 129–30.

that his ideas would not get back to Derby. Sometimes the strategic complexion of a given area would demand, in his eyes, an urgency of action that would shock and chill. 'I think you will have to take Burmah' is not the command of a nervous colleague[23] and protecting India called alternately for resolution and realistic withdrawal. His own side frequently made Rendel's mistake and found 'Olympian neglect' no way to run an empire.[24] But they, too, saw opportunity where Salisbury (often vastly more informed about context than backbenchers and *frondeurs* such as Lord Randolph Churchill) saw difficulty and ground for caution. He repressed, for example, Canadian aspirations to make her own treaties with British backing, as the wayward governor-general had been urging in 1879 – a prospect to fill the Foreign Office with alarm. 'The real difficulty', Salisbury told the colonial secretary, 'is that we are called on to defend with English blood & money States over whose actions we have no control, & whose well-being interests us only sentimentally. In a treaty we make with foreign States, in which Canada is interested, it is our influence that gets the Treaty made, it is our strength that has to enforce it, it is we who must bear the brunt if Canada breaks it on her side . . .'[25] It was not a question simply of what Britain would do or a colony might do but what would happen when third and fourth parties made their presence felt with their own networks of patronage and Great Power reverberations. He felt the same when prime minister about giving Suakin, on the Sudanese coast, to the Turks, as they demanded in 1888. Turkish weakness, the bane of Salisbury's diplomatic existence for a quarter of a century, meant that one had to look ahead. There would be 'evils . . . and we should be held responsible for them all. Worst of all, if the Turks were kicked out by the Soudanese we should have to put them in again: and Bulgaria would be nothing to the Soudan as it would be portrayed by Gladstone's eloquence whenever we tried to do it.'[26] So he squashed that, too. Further south, in the hinterland of Zanzibar's

[23] Salisbury to Cranbrook, 3 Sep. 1879, Cranbrook MSS T501/269. Cf. Marvin Swartz (ed.), *The Politics of British Foreign Policy in the Era of Disraeli and Gladstone* (Basingstoke, 1985), p. 16.

[24] Lord Eustace Percy, *Some Memories* (1928), p. 33, referring to Salisbury's attitude to American pressure over Venezuela in 1895. The point was rather that Salisbury regarded the pressure as 'Cleveland's electioneering dodge' about which no immediate action was required: Salisbury to Goschen (transcript), 23 Dec. 1895, Christ Church MSS, no file.

[25] Salisbury to Hicks Beach, 8 Aug. 1879, St Aldwyn MSS PCC/69/9–10. J. D. S. Campbell, Marquis of Lorne, later ninth Duke of Argyll, was governor-general of Canada from 1878 to 1883.

[26] Salisbury to Smith, 27 Dec. 1888, Hambledon MSS PS13/89.

mainland coast in modern Tanzania, he had had occasion a few months earlier to rebut Lord Harrowby's allegation of dwindling British influence in the area. Salisbury's justification for letting the Germans share in the territory turned on the need for flexibility and seemed to him far preferable to the alternatives, not least the likely encroachment of Portugal or the return of the area to wilderness. 'What advantage does my noble Friend think could be derived by humanity, civilization or commerce', he asked rhetorically in the House of Lords, 'from leaving the vast tracts of territory which he has described to be simply wandered over by naked savages or to be the hunting ground of slavers?'[27]

Racial licence, commercial advantage and strategic vision never operated independently: like colour-filters on a lens, they tinted the imperial vision of the white man's Great Powers. Sometimes the moral case for resisting slavery could have its outing, as over Zanzibar or the Red Sea.[28] Or the 'Conquest' argument could be got out over the Sudan – 'I lose no chance of referring to [it]' – in order to evade the complications that followed trying to make the case from having held Egypt.[29] Or perhaps simple trade or naked power-politics would do. Normally, however, one thing would lead to another and the forms of argument would blend into a composite case. The British presence in Weihaiwei on the Shandung peninsula in north-east China supplied a case in point toward the close of Salisbury's final administration. Originally a German intervention there had supplied the stimulus for 'a political measure in order to balance and compensate that which had been done by another Power'. But imperial advantages soon became obvious. The place could be used both as a coaling and naval station. Moreover, certain wider concerns recommended a presence. In particular the anxious neighbours of China, especially Korea and Japan, needed reassurance that Britain had no intention of abandoning the area.[30] Each local argument developed into a vortex that brought other localities, other powers, into its swirl.

Two places made bigger swirls in London than anywhere else on

---

[27] Salisbury in Lords, *Hansard*, 6 Jul. 1888, cccxxviii, cols. 545–9.

[28] Thus Salisbury briefed Cairns to speak in the Lords about the deleterious effect of Liberal policy in north-eastern Africa on the suppression of the slave trade: Salisbury to Cairns, 7 Feb. 1884, Cairns MSS 30/51/6/f.137.

[29] Salisbury to Cadogan, 4 Feb. 1892, Cadogan MSS CAD/521.

[30] Salisbury in Lords, *Hansard*, 17 May 1898, liii, cols. 1518–20.

the planet. For the whole of Salisbury's life as a statesman, the holding of India and the defence of her north-west frontier never lost their immediacy. The acquisition of a place in the African sun, meanwhile, consumed the energies of the Colonial Office after 1880 and killed various politicians quite as certainly as it killed General Gordon.

THE JEWEL AND ITS SETTING

India provided Salisbury's earliest administrative experience and helped form the presuppositions about ministries, offices, responsibilities and 'experts' on which he often rested his judgements about other sectors of his life. Part of the deep etching of India on his mind is explained by the disaster over which he presided on first entering the India Office in 1866. He recalled it in a letter to the viceroy, the Whig Lord Northbrook, when he returned to the department in 1874:

When I took office in February [1874] my mind was full of a personal experience of my own in the year 1866. The day I took office in that year Lord Ellenborough wrote to me warning that there were indications of a terrible Famine, and urging me to take measures in time. I was quite new to the subject – and believed that if any precautions were necessary the local Government was sure to take them. I did nothing for two months. Before that time elapsed the monsoon had closed the ports of Orissa [in eastern India, south-west of Calcutta] – help was impossible – and – it is said – a million people died. The Governments of India and Bengal had taken in effect no precautions whatever . . . I never would feel that I was free from blame for the result.[31]

In fact Salisbury had bowdlerized his memory of the incident. Rather than merely expect that precautions would have been taken, Cranborne (as he then was) had told Sir John Lawrence that Lawrence's telegrams about impending famine had left him puzzled and that he 'fear[ed] that you must look in the present state of things for little help from here'.[32] The pain of responsibility stayed with him, always mixed with recrimination over poor lines of authority when dealing with Indian affairs. He greatly disliked having an Indian Council as an intermediate agency standing between parliament and the minister in charge: indeed, he tried to get rid of it.[33]

---

[31] Salisbury to Northbrook (transcript), 29 Jan. 1875, Christ Church MSS C/2/97.
[32] Cranborne to Lawrence, 16 Oct. 1866, Christ Church MSS C/1/6.
[33] See David Steele, 'Salisbury at the India Office' in Blake and Cecil, *Lord Salisbury*, pp. 116–47 at pp. 139–40.

He came to hate, too, the way that politicians often intrusively talked about India, when they they could raise the interest, in the way that hunters would resort to a 'bagged fox, only turned out when there [was] no other'. And when politicians did get round to considering the affairs of a vast continent of which they knew next to nothing, what possible good could they do? 'It is of no use', he told the Viceroy with whom he had become increasingly out of sympathy,

> to ignore the enormous difficulty under which we work in having to rule such an Empire as India in subordination to such a Parliamentary Constitution as that of England. I am intensely impressed – as you have probably discovered – with the untrustworthy character of the House of Commons as to all matters which it has not been compelled to study carefully. It is not that they wish, consciously, to take the Government of India into their own hands. But on Indian subjects they have so little genuine knowledge or conviction that they vote like women – on the impression or whim of the moment. A clever appeal to sentiment – the invocation of some English commonplace or clap-trap – will swing round into the wrong lobby a sufficient number to make a decree by which the whole Government of India might be thrown into confusion.[34]

Uncertainties of this kind made the secretary of state no better than useless in Salisbury's eyes: he lacked expertise himself and the Council that was supposed to guide him was worse than useless.[35]

The language Salisbury deployed when discussing the future of India turned on his conquest argument and showed conclusive impatience over any mutterings about greater participation or democracy. People like Northbrook failed to see, he would allege, that sweetness and light made no sense in a country that had been taken by force and must for the foreseeable future be forcibly restrained. For 'no one believes in our good intentions' and no amount of rosewater would conceal the blood on the sword. 'We are often told to secure ourselves by their affections – not by force – our great-grand-children may be privileged to do it – but not we.'[36] To his greatest blockhead in the Indian administration, Sir Philip Wode-house, he used shorter temper and shorter words. 'As to action the

---

[34] Salisbury to Northbrook (transcripts), 5 Feb. 1875 and 10 Dec. 1875, Christ Church MSS C/2/98 and C/2/180.

[35] As early as 1867, following his resignation from Derby's government over the provisions of the reform bill of that year, he warned his successor, Stafford Northcote, of the need to find his own way: 'study the subject thoroughly for yourself, consult the Cabinet afresh, & take your own line . . . Don't let yourself be guided by any one in the office, for there is no one competent to guide you' (22 Mar. 1867): Iddesleigh MSS 50019 f.3.

[36] Salisbury to Northbrook (transcript), 29 May 1874, Christ Church MSS C/2/19.

matter is simple: India is held by the sword: and its rulers must in all
essentials be guided by the maxims which benefit the Government of
the sword.'[37] From this stark starting-point a number of deductions
followed. First, no hope should be given to the struggling millions of
ryots that their lot could improve other than by emigration. If it were
to be given, they would drift toward some form of 'tenant right', like
the Irish, and that would be a very bad thing. Second, the *bien pensants*
whose opinions shaped Indian administration should stop trying to
give higher education to the natives. All it did was to turn them into
literate, and therefore more effective, subversives – filling Calcutta
with newspaper contributors, pundits and agitators. Primary education was fine, particularly if it could introduce 'new ideas into a
Hindoo's brain',[38] which he rather doubted. Third, the native
princes ought to be kept sweet. Happily, they 'attach so much
attention to form that it is often possible to pay them in shadows for
the substantial power of which we are increasingly compelled to
deprive them'.[39] Fourth, Indians should pay taxes like everybody else
and that meant widening the possible base of taxation by stimulating
railway construction and other enterprises. Meanwhile they ought to
pay at least for the water that the imperial authorities provided,
whether or not they chose to use it. Salisbury could not understand
why they might refuse. 'It would be as reasonable to allow any one
who chose to walk blindfold to abstain from paying the Lighting rate
in London.'[40] Fifth, the Indians should be made to reduce their
cotton duties for the sake of Lancashire industry, despite the declared
intention of Northbrook in the opposite direction – '[t]he Viceroy is
tiresome, of course'.[41] Sixth, the intrusion of elective provisions in
Indian administration by liberal hotheads at home should be
resisted. When Dufferin tried this in his Indian reform bill in 1888,
Salisbury reacted against the thought of Indian 'lawyers, agents,
newspaper-writers' getting themselves elected to positions of power –
'the class among whom disaffection is the strongest'.[42] Besides, the
whole idea of representation was not, he said a couple of years later,

[37] Salisbury to Wodehouse (transcript), 4 Jun. 1875, Christ Church MSS C/2/126.
[38] Salisbury to Sir Richard Temple (transcript), 5 Feb. 1875, Christ Church MSS C/2/99.
[39] Salisbury to Northbrook (transcript), 20 Apr. 1875, Christ Church MSS C/2/118.
[40] Salisbury to Temple, 8 Jan. 1875, Christ Church MSS C/2/92.
[41] Salisbury to Carnarvon, 20 Sep. 1875, Carnarvon MSS 60758 f.160; cf., Richard Shannon,
     The Age of Disraeli, 1868–1881: The Rise of Tory Democracy (1992), p. 273.
[42] Memo by Salisbury, 31 Dec. 1888, Cross MSS 51264 ff.27–31.

'an Eastern idea' at all; 'it does not fit Eastern traditions or Eastern minds'.[43] Nor did it fit imperial objectives, as Salisbury defined them.

These purposes formed part of an internalization of 'India' within the political system. If it provided jobs for the boys who went there, it offered also jobs for boys at home, in the dedicated schools who trained up the Indian civil service, in the considerable infrastructure required in London to service so vast an administration and, at the top, posts of senior responsibility which provided dignified and efficient posts for aspiring statesmen. Salisbury held the Indian bureaucracy in great admiration – 'a first-rate service, well accustomed to deal with Orientals' – and thought it quite unlike the Colonial Office where all a man could expect was 'broken down political hacks & people "who have deserved well of the party"'.[44] The work also supplied lessons for home consumption, especially in the case of the closest colony. It is well known that Salisbury used images of Africa in order to frighten Conservatives over the dangers of conceding representative government to Ireland, never more unpleasantly than in his notorious 'Hottentots' speech in 1886 at the height of the fever over Gladstone's Home Rule proposals, when he made the Irish sound as incapable of self-government as African tribes, the Russians and the Greeks.[45] Yet India was never far away when thoughts turned to Ireland. Both places felt the lack of Teutons. Both rested on a peasantry desperate for land. Both had incipient and insidious nationalist movements with which the imperial state would need to cope. And the last thing Salisbury wanted to see in Calcutta was a collection of 'Anglo-Indian Butts' intent on destabilizing British rule.[46] The process of 'simianization'

[43] Salisbury in Lords, *Hansard*, 6 Mar. 1890, cccxlii, col. 98.

[44] Salisbury to Cross, 12 Jul. 1878, Cross MSS 51263 f.43.

[45] At St James's Hall, 15 May 1886. 'When you come to narrow it down you will find that this – which is called self-government but is really government by the majority – works admirably when it is confined to people who are of Teutonic race, but that it does not work so well when people of other races are called upon to join in it.' Quoted in Cecil, vol. iii, p. 302. This speech also fulfilled a distinctive *party* function at a critical moment in the repercussions of the Irish controversy: see the brilliant location of the speech within high politics by A. B. Cooke and John Vincent, *The Governing Passion: Cabinet Government and Party Politics in Britain 1885–86* (Brighton, 1974), pp. 79–82. But gut as well as brain interfered with Tory appreciation of South Africa in these years, with its spectre of 'vast areas peopled by Savages and adjacent to independent States which are not influenced by the public opinion of civilised people': W. H. Smith to Salisbury, 9 Dec. 1888, Hambledon MSS 1868 f.881.

[46] Salisbury to Lytton, 20 Apr. 1877, quoted in Steele, 'Salisbury at the India Office', p. 137.

in the representation of Irish Celts during which Irishmen were made more and more to resemble monkeys,[47] fitted easily into a typology of imperial characteristics grounded in African and Indian perceptions and brought the empire to the doorstep.

As well as considering 'India' (the icon) and its various representations, Salisbury and his colleagues faced more substantive work in thinking about external elements that no rhetoric could control and which arose from India's geography rather than her races or religions. In the late-Victorian period Conservatives confronted two important contiguities. In the east, India bordered on Burma and raised thereby potential difficulty with France, because the French saw a role for themselves in Burma; the nexus also held out promise of increased security for trading links with China, which British policy sought to develop. In the north-west (present-day Pakistan) Indian policy shaded away into questions about Afghanistan and what to do with it. More especially, it concerned Russian intentions in the area and the residual fear that someday, somewhere, in one way or another, the Russians intended invading India.

Originally Salisbury had thought that the French could be kept out of Burma by diplomatic finesse. It seemed a short-sighted idea to make a defensive, military alliance with the Burmese: one never knew where that would lead, it 'might be embarrassing' and would almost certainly prove expensive because of the policing involved. 'The country itself [was] of no great importance', after all. Best, then, to keep the commitment small so long as the central objective could be secured, that of ensuring 'easy communication with the multitude who inhabit Western China . . . an object of great national importance',[48] while ensuring the neutrality of Thailand for the same reason. But the French proved more persistent and perceptive than Cranborne himself had foreseen in 1866 and by the time he returned to the India Office in 1874 clouds had gathered on the horizon. Strategy remained as before, the creation of 'a large and most lucrative trade [that] might be drawn from Rangoon to China

---

Isaac Butt (1813–79) had led the Home Rule party at Westminster since his election for Limerick in 1871, following impeccable credentials from Trinity College, Dublin, and early years as a Liberal-Conservative.

[47] See Perry Curtis Jr, *Apes and Angels: The Irishman in Victorian Caricature* (Washington, DC, 1997 (1st edn 1971)). But see, too, the cautionary remarks of Roy Foster about this style of analysis: R. F. Foster, *Paddy and Mr. Punch: Connections in Irish and English History* (1993), pp. 171–94.

[48] Cranborne to Lawrence (transcript), 10 Dec. 1866, Christ Church MSS C/1/8.

– to the great benefit of Indian Finance'.[49] But his confidence that diplomacy would be enough had weakened. The apprehension that the French would establish themselves in Burma, he told Derby in May, had become reality,[50] though his perception seems in retrospect hard to substantiate. The authorities in Calcutta continued to believe that Burma posed threats that ought to be removed militarily, but few in the metropolitan power wanted another Burmese War. Undoubtedly the coming to the Burmese throne of King Thibaw in 1878 and the arrival of Lytton as governor-general of India in 1876 played their role in destabilizing the situation. What also gave it a great press forward, however, was another impetus in neither Burma nor India. For when Salisbury became prime minister of his minority government in June 1885 the annexation-party received a boost for the first time from a powerful and sympathetic personality in a position of great power and with honed political instincts. It may well be that French pressure on the region *decreased* in the immediate months before the annexation of January 1886. It is equally clear, however, that Conservative pressure for action – 'I think we shall have to take strong action with the French'[51] – had impinged on Salisbury's parlous regime for some time and equally clear that the annexation of Burma during Salisbury's own government was no accident of external manufacture. In building models of 'core and periphery' in order to explain empire, we have to recall that core *politics* matter as well as peripheral economics and that the record of party-political argument will frequently not be found in official papers and diplomatic despatches. This consideration affected Thailand no less strongly, though, like Persia, it seemed doomed to fall

---

[49] Salisbury to Northbrook (transcript), 17 Apr. 1874, Christ Church MSS C/2/1. This remark sits uncomfortably with Cain and Hopkins's certainty that policy toward China was 'essentially reactive' and that '[s]trategic motives played little or no part in Foreign Office thinking because China was not on the route to anywhere of importance to Britain': see P. J. Cain and A. G. Hopkins, *British Imperialism* (2 vols., 1993), vol. I, p. 445. The strategic imagination of *Salisbury*, as opposed to the wooden-headedness of officials in the Foreign Office, likewise makes little appearance in D. K. Fieldhouse, *Economics and Empire 1830–1914* (1984 (1st edn 1973)), pp. 173–85. For a helpful recent survey of the historiography, see Nicholas Tarling, 'The British Empire in South-East Asia' in Robin W. Winks (ed.), *The Oxford History of the British Empire* (5 vols., Oxford, 1998–9), vol. v, pp. 403–15.

[50] Salisbury to Derby, 11 May 1874, Derby MSS 16/2/7.

[51] Churchill to Smith, 23 Aug. 1885, Hambledon MSS P59/65. Salisbury had informed the Queen ten days before that Burma had become 'sensitive'; '& that any attempt on the part of the French to obtain any hold in Burmah would render measures of precaution on our part in that country necessary': Salisbury to the Queen, 10 Aug. 1885, RA VIC/A63/41.

under foreign influence and by 1895 Salisbury had moved toward the idea of sharing sovereignty there with the French.[52]

Whatever the strength of Salisbury's preoccupation with Burma, however, it became a minor irritation in comparison with the Afghan difficulty. This one he did not solve but his failure leaves him in exalted company among those who took charge of policy from the first Afghan War in 1842 to the Soviet withdrawal almost a century and a half later. Then as now, Afghanistan presented to the world a fractured, near-tribal polity dominated by local allegiances and underpinned by some of the most formidable territory on the globe. Overcoming the mountains, either through the Khyber Pass at the eastern end or by going around the western end via Herat presented the Russians with their major strategic headache and gave the British their central defensive anxiety. For both sides the relevant maps had a line of towns running around the base of the mountains: Kabul, Kandahar, Quetta, Herat and further north Merv, now Marv in Russian Turkmenistan. On the British side of the frontier, three provinces abutted the Afghans: Kashmir, Punjab (which, under the inspiration of Sir John Lawrence, pursued policies of coexistence rather than aggression) and Sind whose Baluchi people and officials, under the guidance of the militant Sir Bartle Frere, saw the advantages of a 'forward' policy to establish a buffer zone against possible Russian ambitions. The combination of Northbrook and Lawrence promised a peaceful approach to the difficulties during Salisbury's first two years in the London office under Disraeli (1874–6). It was the coming of Lytton in 1876 that altered everything. He had been fourth choice, behind Lord Powis, Lord John Manners and Lord Carnarvon. And in accepting 'the superb, but awful, post',[53] he raised questions in the minds of future colleagues about his suitability, not merely on the grounds of his fragile health but also because of the 'dreamy and undecided' character that convention ascribed to the sons of romantic novelists.[54] Few, in fact, brought to India less dreaminess and indecision: Lytton's problem was quite the reverse. He conceived the threat from Russia to be real rather than

---

[52] Selborne to Chamberlain (reporting Salisbury's views), 7 Sep. 1895, in D. George Boyce (ed.), *The Crisis of British Power: The Imperial and Naval Papers of the Second Earl of Selborne, 1895–1910* (1990), p. 20.

[53] Disraeli to Derby, 23 Dec. 1875, Derby MSS 16/2/1.

[54] Diary, 12 Jul. 1874, in Derby, *Diaries*, p. 175. Their editor, *hors du texte*, wonders whether Derby might have had in mind 'the widower – druggie – poetaster – Second Secretary side of his character'. Private communication.

rhetorical and decided that occupation and defence of the Afghan lands demanded urgent action. His belligerence, which reversed Northbrook's policies, placed the British cabinet in a quandary and left Salisbury in a difficult position through his last two years at the India Office. In some respects the appointment of Lytton suited him, for perpetual battling with the Indian administration had been wearisome. Like Disraeli (and unlike Derby, the foreign secretary) he felt that Lytton would at least take a grip on the situation and have the fibre to confront aggression on the north-west frontier if it should arise, though Carnarvon, for one, had the sense to warn Salisbury at the outset to be aware that 'you may find yourself committed to some fatal act of Lytton's'.[55] Where trouble in fact emerged was in the definition of necessity and the means of meeting it. Lytton had a virtue that Salisbury always mistrusted – enthusiasm – and the realistic evaluations of options that forever dominated Salisbury's strategic concerns sometimes made his understanding of what was possible diverge from that of his ranting friend at the other end of the telegraph. Direct friction between the two was eased by ministerial reshuffling. Although Salisbury remained Indian minister until 1878, his last two years thrust him increasingly into the role of extraordinary mediator and ambassador in the resolution of conflict between Russia and Turkey. As foreign minister between 1878 and 1880, in the wake of Derby's resignation, he saw Lytton's pyrotechnics against a wider context of embarrassment into which Beaconsfield's administration had allowed itself to slide.

Salisbury began with the clear view voiced by his new leader that Northbrook placed far too much weight on the 'broken reeds' of Afghanistan and Persia as bastions against possible Russian designs. The implications of that belief included a refusal to leave those countries to internal management. At the very least a European representative would have to be imposed at either Herat or Kandahar.[56] By the spring of 1875, he had come to differ from both Northbrook and his own colleagues. The latter he deemed often insufficiently alive to the problems caused by annexing territory as a

[55] Carnarvon to Salisbury, 23 Jun. 1877, Salisbury MSS (Carnarvon, f.307). But Disraeli remained committed to Lytton precisely because of Lytton's determination to do something. 'It is a moment when what is called prudence is not wise. We must control, & we must create, events': Beaconsfield to Salisbury, 20 Sep. 1878, Salisbury MSS (Disraeli, f.316).

[56] Disraeli to Derby, 15 Oct. 1874, Derby MSS 16/2/1; Salisbury to Northbrook (transcript), 7 Jan. 1875, Christ Church MSS C/2/91. Herat was chosen ultimately. The government deemed Kabul unsafe for any such individual.

punitive act for disloyal behaviour. In particular he thought their proposed attack on the Gaekwar of Baroda quite misconceived, for all the Gaekwar's uppity behaviour.[57] He took the lesson to be that Britain should foster relations with potentates of a different stripe. 'The kind of Native Prince whose existence is most compatible with our policy', he explained, 'is a Prince of the Rajpootana type: big enough to form a substantial rivet in the Indian social structure: not big enough to give us the anxiety with which we watch the Courts of Hyderabad, Gwalior and Indore.'[58] But he differed still more sharply from his viceroy over where boundaries must be drawn against the Russians. Persia was a lost cause: the Russians would take it; the British could not stop them. Afghanistan he saw quite differently and recognized at once, as usual, the centre of the issue. 'We cannot conquer it; we cannot leave it alone.'[59] Strategies for confronting that paradox oscillated in the 1874–80 government. Originally Salisbury hoped to secure Herat – 'rightly or wrongly deemed the key to India'[60] – and hang onto Merv. Increasingly, however, he despaired of the Afghan Amir, Sher Ali, and came to feel that no intermediate position made sense between renouncing the country and occupying it. On the other hand, Salisbury as foreign secretary from 1878 placed the Afghan problem in a matrix of elements concerned with the restraining of Russia; and he felt by no means certain that the Afghans headed the order of priority. For Lytton himself he felt considerable personal esteem: they were long-standing friends and neighbours in Hertfordshire. Lytton's bellicose, self-righteous tone through 1878 – 'personal, grandiloquent and offensive'[61] – caused much worry all the same through its lack of balance and left the prime minister suspecting that the Foreign Office and the India Office were playing blindman's buff with each other: 'the seeds of precipitation and disaster!'[62] No one in the cabinet felt more fury with Lytton when the viceroy went beyond all instructions to send troops into Afghanistan during November.

Salisbury's thinking is well caught in a long letter to Cranbrook in

---

[57] Literally the 'cow-keeper', the Gaekwar was the traditional title of the ruler of Baroda or what is now Vadodara in Gujarat, western India.

[58] Salisbury to Northbrook (transcript), 12 Feb. 1875, Christ Church MSS C/2/100.

[59] Salisbury to Northbrook (transcript), 5 Mar. 1875, Christ Church MSS C/2/106.

[60] Cranbrook to Salisbury, 16 Aug. 1879, Salisbury MSS (Cranbrook 1868–85, f.141).

[61] Maurice Cowling, 'Lytton, the Cabinet, and the Russians, August to November 1878', *English Historical Review*, 76 (1961), pp. 59–79 at p. 59.

[62] Beaconsfield to Salisbury, 12 Sep. 1878, Salisbury MSS (Disraeli, f.309).

September 1878. It shows more than most written statements his chess-playing mentality as he looks deeply into the possibilities and considers the role of the Amir:

The proposal to guarantee his territory appears to me unwise, because it will lead to an ambiguous position, & expose you to constant charges of bad faith. The position is ill-defined: & you may be called upon to fight for a disputed question of title over a piece of Central Asian sand which is claimed by some one of Russia's numerous allies. Again, Russia is not likely to attack Afghanistan herself: but is very likely to poke up some Toorkoman Khan to do it. In that case will your guarantee hold good? If so you are likely to be engaged at the shortest possible notice in a war with the wild tribes, who require no vote of credit to put their force on a war footing. If not, your guarantee will be of no value: for these tribes will fight on Russia's behalf, armed through her agency, & will conquer (if they conquer) for her profit. Again – if you guarantee Afghanistan against Russia – will the guarantee be claimable if Shere Ali loses his throne – or if his kingdom should be divided on his death: or if the war should be caused by his fault – or by any conduct which you may think unwise? If so, your future is not enviable. If not, then it must be accompanied with a demand that he will submit himself in every thing to your counsils [*sic*]. Such an offer of guarantee would not only be no bribe in his eyes but a ?tendered insult.[63]

How great the change from major to minor in the modulations of Salisbury's thought since the confident days of the 1860s. But here is his mind at the height of its analytical power, doing what Gladstone could never come close to doing, ratiocinating almost like a computer in a series of 'If . . . Then' statements while bringing, as a chess-computer cannot, psychological insight to bear on an opponent's frailties. It seems the more powerful for its uniqueness among colleagues on his own side. Beaconsfield was happy to leave it all to Lytton; Northcote bleated that everybody had to think ahead, without himself quite being able to manage it; Richmond, refreshed from the grouse-moors, thought the Amir a troublesome rogue and decided the Afghans would have to be taught some manners.[64] Amid these reflections, Lytton drove forward for Kabul despite his limited orders and despite Salisbury's clear view that he must rest content

---

[63] Salisbury to Cranbrook, 17 Sep. 1878, Cranbrook MSS T501/269. Something depends on the character one accords to the so-called Penjdeh incident of 1885 when Russia either did, or did not, intend invading Afghanistan. Seen one way – the way most historians now see it – Salisbury showed prescience beyond that of many contemporaries. Seen in the other, he was more optimistic than most.

[64] e.g., Northcote to Cairns, 26 Sep. 1878, Cairns MSS 30/51/5/ff.34–5; Richmond to Cranbrook, 27 Sep. 1878, 21 Sep. 1879, Cranbrook MSS T501/257.

with taking and holding Kandahar. When Lytton met with military
disaster the reflections became yet more painful. Salisbury did not
waste his notepaper on calling the Amir a cad but did find his own
cynicism hardening over the future of these territories that had
already claimed too much British blood. The problem, after all, lay
in deciding what to *do* to keep the Russians out:

> The question – shall we lean on the Persian or the Afghan leg – is still
> perplexing. The Persian Shah is frightened of Russia, no doubt: & is
> therefore inclined to betray us. But the Afghan Amir (if not a traitor) is so
> weak that his good dispositions, supposing them to exist, are perfectly
> useless. To which, then, shall we confide Herat? The Shah may sell it: the
> Amir will certainly lose it. We have a certain hold on both i.e. we can do
> both a certain amount of harm. But that species of influence though it may
> overcome ill will or self-interest, is perfectly useless with impotence. I lean
> therefore to the belief that the Shah will serve us better than the Amir . . . If
> he [the Amir] retains any kind of value, I should be inclined to transplant
> him to Candahar – & leave the Cabrolees to cook in their own gravy.[65]

Lytton's policies ran into calamity, not because of the Afghans
(according to Lytton) but because of Gladstone. Before he had time
to develop his ideas or vindicate his campaign, he found himself,
rather like Churchill in 1915, made responsible retrospectively for a
military and political *débâcle*. Undoubtedly the return of Little
Englandism at the 1880 general election did nothing to weaken the
British government's determination to pull out of 'forward' situations
on the north-west frontier. All Lytton could do on his return to
Britain was to inveigh at his customary length and with his usual
persistence against his detractors. 'I must show', he told the former
prime minister, his greatest supporter, 'that from 1870 down to the
death of Sher Ali, the Russian authorities, notwithstanding the
engagement of their Government to regard Afghanistan as "entirely
beyond the sphere of its influence" were incessantly and successfully
moving heaven & earth to establish a Russian alliance with that
Country . . .'.[66] With Salisbury he both preached to the converted
but met a wall of incredulity that Afghanistan could be held if the
Russians proved serious in their intention and if the defensive

---

[65] Salisbury to Northcote, 24 Sep. 1879, Iddesleigh MSS 50019 ff.176–7.
[66] Lytton to Beaconsfield, n.d. (1879–80) (copy), Lytton MSS D/EK 035. He later accused the
Liberal government of cynically abandoning Kandahar and publishing for its own purposes
an account of policy which paid no attention to what Lytton's Indian government had
contended throughout the crisis of 1878–9. Cf. Cranbrook to Lytton, 26 Jan. 1881 and reply
(copy), 28 Jan. 1881, Lytton MSS D/EK 035.

posture on which Lytton seemingly placed his trust remained all that stood in their way. Looking back, towards the end of his life, Salisbury came to think that either Peel's government or Beaconsfield's should indeed have grasped its nettle. Had Afghanistan been fully conquered, suppressed and militarized in 1842 or in 1879, then the Bear could have been kept out.[67] As it was, he placed no faith in the treaty with Russia to which observers from Lord Randolph Churchill to Sir Robert Morier looked as the way forward in the 1880s. By 1884 the Russians had taken Merv, as predicted. They caused a flurry of fear in 1885 by threatening Penjdeh. They would continue to roll forward, it seemed, and no treaty would persuade them to change their minds. 'You can have an *entente* with a man or a Government,' Salisbury explained to the British ambassador in St Petersburg, 'but no one, except Canute's Courtiers ever tried to have it with a tide. The tide is constantly advancing – not because of the ambitions of Courts or the schemes of Statesmen – but moved by the forces which cause vast, rude populations to overflow their borders . . . [Russia] can promise nothing with respect to Affghanistan [*sic*] except that she will eat Constantinople first. When it is eaten she must go forward . . . in the direction of India.'[68] Meanwhile all was difficulty. 'We have practically to defend a position which our soldiers cannot reach: we have made ourselves in effect responsible for the good conduct of a potentate whom we cannot control: & we have led him to believe that we shall secure a delimitation of boundary by our diplomacy, which in reality we have no means of exacting.'[69] In public he spoke the vocabulary of Beaconsfield: uplift and optimism.[70] In private, he thought the best chance lay in obstruction and delay to give the Russian empire time to fall apart, like the Turkish,

---

[67] Salisbury to Cranbrook, 1 Sep. 1897, Cranbrook MSS T501/269.

[68] Salisbury to Morier, 2 Oct. 1886, in Agatha Ramm, *Sir Robert Morier: Envoy and Ambassador in the Age of Imperialism, 1876–1893* (Oxford, 1973), p. 236.

[69] Salisbury to Cross, 2 Jun. 1887, Cross MSS 51263 ff.167–8.

[70] E.g. at the Mansion House, 9 Nov. 1885: '. . . so far as our knowledge and information goes there is nothing to prevent us from heartily re-iterating those celebrated words of Lord Beaconsfield that "there is room in Asia for Russia and for England." (Cheers)': *The Times*, 10 Nov. 1885, p. 6e. Cf. his language in defending the Queen's Speech in 1898 when he defined a 'forward' position as one simply of 'converting to our ideas in matters of civilization these splendid tribes': *Hansard*, 8 Feb. 1898, LIII, col. 42. It should be added that Beaconsfield had lost his private uplift long before it became public: he looked forward morosely at the end of 1880 to walking into the House of Lords to address the peers 'on a falling Empire': Beaconsfield to Salisbury, 29 Dec. 1880, Salisbury MSS (Disraeli, f.553).

under the weight of its own incompetence and intractability. History has not proved him wrong.

THE DARK CONTINENT

Salisbury had no first-hand knowledge of India. His long tour in the early 1850s had taken him to the Cape for a while, however, and about that region he claimed, dangerously, to know whereof he spoke. Not surprisingly, some sense of the South African problem came through his early speeches as a member of parliament. He resisted attempts from Palmerston and Gladstone to reduce expenditure on defending colonial territory in South Africa by reminding the House of a few coarse realities. 'It was true, indeed,' he readily conceded, 'that the Dutch needed hardly any assistance to keep the Caffres [i.e. Kafirs] at bay; but then that was because they shot them as they would wild beasts, which our feeling would not permit us to do. Again, it had been our policy to plant two Republics which were rapidly growing in power to the north of Cape Colony, presenting a constant source of danger . . .'[71] His low view of the Dutch settlers never left him and contributed to an atypical willingness to envisage confrontation in this sector and override the Colonial Office with its 'traditional view which it continues to impose on every successive Secretary of State – & that is that every thing must be sacrificed & risked in order to keep the Dutch population of the Colony in good humour'. This letter to Cranbrook in 1885 continues in a sentence that looks forward ominously to 1899. 'I feel that a mistake is being made in trying to govern these outlying acquisitions through a High Commissioner at Cape Town. He is too distant – & he is too much under the influence of men whose sympathies are not wholly British.'[72] By 1885 Salisbury looked back at a past configured by two signal disasters: the crushing of Sir Bartle Frere's misguided expedition against the Zulus in 1879 and the Boers' demolition of British forces at Majuba Hill in 1881 after the government had persisted in attempts to annex the Transvaal on the quaint assumption that this was what the Boers wanted.[73] The setting up of a Transvaal republic

---

[71] Cecil in Commons, *Hansard*, 30 May 1860, *Hansard*, CLVIII, col. 1834.
[72] Salisbury to Cranbrook, 11 Sep. 1885, Cranbrook MSS T501/267.
[73] There is a chapter of graphic exculpation in John Morley, *Life of Gladstone* (2 vols., 1906 (1st edn, 3 vols., 1903), vol. II, pp. 263–86. 'That horrid Transvaal business is now uppermost in political thoughts': Hamilton diary, 13 Mar. 1881, in Dudley Bahlman (ed.), *The Diary of Sir*

struck Salisbury as no less purblind and became the more so as his pessimism deepened in the retrospect of the 1890s. 'I thought it was a policy', he explained to the Lords, 'tainted with the fault, which is a virtue in many men's eyes but in my eyes is almost the most dangerous fault a policy can have – it was an optimistic policy. It was an undue belief in the effect of amiable acts not supported by requisite strength.'[74] The suspicion that it would all go wrong helped him sweep aside palliatives. The suggestion that universal suffrage among the whites of the Transvaal would redeem the situation only persuaded him, as so often, that its proponent had gone off his head.[75] The Jameson raid at the end of 1895 caused him more embarrassment than moral pain: he was relieved when it 'fizzed out' as an issue.[76] When the Boer War arrived in earnest under his premiership in 1899, he was too old and ill to take much grip. But it is interesting that even in its latter days, he held that the 'unhappy war' had been 'forced upon us' and that 'the nation ha[d] in no way changed its view with regard to it'.[77] He took to the grave a view of South Africa as a British preserve which the Boers could not be allowed to sully – a view easier to hold because the Boers had no Great Power behind them and in particular had no call on the French.

Finding an accommodation with the French in western and, more particularly, north-eastern Africa seemed to Salisbury an issue of considerable moment – perhaps one more pressing than keeping the Russians out of Afghanistan. Ever since Disraeli's resolution of the Canal purchase in 1875, which implied a permanent French presence at Suez, the options had become stark when constructing policy toward Egypt. 'You may renounce – or monopolize – or share.'[78] His famous pronouncement concealed a preference for sharing in

---

Edward Walter Hamilton (2 vols., Oxford, 1972), vol. 1, p. 114. On the Tory side, Lytton found these justifications hard to bear. 'Mr. Gladstone has the impudence, I see, to boast about clearing the country from "blood guiltiness". But for my part, I shall always hold that hoary but shameless old head of his guilty in no small degree of the blood shed in vain at Majuba, and the premature death of one of England's noblest & ablest soldiers [General Colley]': Lytton to Cadogan, 16 Apr. 1881, Cadogan MSS CAD/257. Lytton had known Colley especially well: the latter had been his military, later private, secretary before succeeding Sir Garnett Wolseley as governor and commander-in-chief in Natal. Rifle bullet through the forehead on Majuba Hill.

[74] Salisbury in Lords, *Hansard*, 28 Jul. 1899, LXXV, col. 662.
[75] Salisbury to Knutsford (draft), 14 Sep. 1891, Christ Church MSS, file E.
[76] Salisbury to Wolmer, 2 Jan. 1896, 2nd Earl of Selborne MSS 5 f.34.
[77] Salisbury to Cranbrook, 22 Dec. 1901, Cranbrook MSS T501/263.
[78] Salisbury to Northcote, 16 Sep. 1881, Iddesleigh MSS 50020 ff.22–3.

the Egyptian case because he saw little choice, granted French ambition in the area. Northcote had veered to a degree between monopolizing and renouncing; but Salisbury had warned him that there could be little hope of 'cut[ting]the towrope':

> we have a pecuniary interest in the payment of the [Egyptian] tribute & of the Suez Canal shares: & our capitalists have an interest in Alexandria harbour which we could scarcely afford to disregard. But above all these 'entanglements' is the apprehension, which freed us to accept them, that if we stand aside France will become as dominant there as she is in Tunis.[79]

Neither did he share Derby's feeling that Egypt could go because, like India, it did not really pay.[80] Even if it cost Britain to stay there, Salisbury would have urged caution about leaving when the French were so eager to move in, for he who turned the valve at Suez controlled the flow of trade and arms to India. The corollary was that, as in Afghanistan, Britain could neither take nor renounce Egypt. As the partition of Africa advanced, moreover, the issue moved beyond Egypt itself into the Sudan and the question of how best to stabilize the situation there once the famous Mahdi had roused his people to rebellion and *jihad*. Gladstone's decision to allow the bombardment of Alexandria in 1882 caused Liberals much heartburn. Salisbury and most of the Conservative opposition felt only that the action came as too little, too late. 'We must beat other nations fairly,' Salisbury said in private, 'but henceforth we must be the first in Egypt.'[81]

Between the disaster of Majuba Hill in 1881 and news of the death of General Gordon in the Sudan at the beginning of 1885, Africa presented the Conservative opposition with a fertile ground for criticism. Indeed, Salisbury rediscovered a strain of parliamentary violence, if only to cover the mess he made of leading the Lords through the Irish land bill and its aftermath. With Ireland and the coming reform bill on his left side, he punched with his right against Gladstonian mismanagement of the Egyptian campaign, the failure to see the importance of the Sudan and even to countenance its separation from Egypt – '[i]t was impossible to conceive a more stupendous blunder than that'[82] – while laughing privately at Gladstone's inability to understand that there was no point in

---

[79] Salisbury to Northcote, 4 May 1879, Iddesleigh MSS 50019 f.149.
[80] Diary, 28 Jun. 1877, in Derby, *Diaries*, p. 412.
[81] Salisbury to Northcote, 29 Jul. 1882, Iddesleigh MSS 50020 f.43.
[82] Salisbury in Lords, *Hansard*, 26 Feb. 1884, CCXCIV, col. 1314.

threatening the Mahdi with anything other than steel. 'The Govt.', he told Cairns, 'have made the enormous mistake as to Egypt of omitting to examine into the condition of their teeth before commencing to bark.'[83] Then, of course, their teeth began to fall out. In the light of a century's retrospect one feels a certain sympathy for Gladstone's government as it became blamed for the death of a great popular hero; it is quite apparent that Gordon would have sunk any government trying to control his actions and that his actions in the autumn of 1884 went far beyond his instructions and should be regarded as more misguided than noble. But in the popular mind his death made a martyr of him and marked like a stain the government's integrity for its failure to help him. Conservatives joined in the vilification, naturally – not least because Gordon had at least had a policy in the Sudan[84] – but Salisbury remained thoughtful about alternative paths to follow. He veered between two objectives: externally one of keeping the French out and internally of avoiding an expensive and pointless attempt to turn Egypt into a British enclave. He found his mind running back to the north-west frontier of India and the lessons learned there:

I take the general objects of our own policy to be to keep Egypt from European interference on the one side, & from anarchy on the other . . . But I do not believe in the plan of moulding Egyptians to our own civilization. As long as they are Mohometans that is impossible: & we must not forget that though we have often ruled mixed creeds . . . we have never yet ruled Mohometans alone. The only place in which we have tried it, is Afghanistan, & there it was not precisely a success.[85]

His starting-point in the new conditions created by the French and the Mahdi was that a new treaty ought to be negotiated with the help of the Germans, who would delight in restricting the French, and thus find a *via media* between annexation and an international policing of the territory, with a right to occupy Alexandria at will and control the railways.[86] Yet new conditions had also been created by an imperialist electorate at home and he underestimated the degree

---

[83] Salisbury to Cairns, 1 Jun. 1882, Cairns MSS 30/51/6 f.87.
[84] Before Gordon's death, Salisbury had recognized that the government was 'in a hole': Salisbury to Churchill, 20 Sep. 1884, Churchill MSS 9248/4. In the Lords, he expressed his firm support for Gordon's insubordination, for 'we have very little doubt that his policy is much better than that of the Government . . .': *Hansard*, 23 Oct. 1884, CCXCIII, col. 18.
[85] Salisbury to Cairns, 20 Feb. 1885, Cairns MSS 30/51/6/ ff.155–6.
[86] Cf. Cecil, vol. III, p. 235.

to which he could ignore the popular lust for annexation and planting of the flag.

In fact Egypt became a millstone. The financial aspect of the problem of governing that territory had turned urgent from 1883 when dual control of the finances with France had ended; and in many ways Cairo, under the tutelage of its remarkable agent and consul-general, Evelyn Baring, later first Earl of Cromer, drew money and resources away from where Salisbury would rather have had them. 'I heartily wish we had never gone into Egypt,' he had come to think by 1887. 'Had we not done so, we could snap our fingers at all the world. But the national, or acquisitional feeling has been aroused; it has tasted the fleshpots and it will not let them go.'[87] Some of the diplomatic headaches were eased by the signing of a convention with Turkey over the future of the Suez Canal in 1887. It also offered hopes that British troops might be pulled out of Egypt in three years' time, but only if there were to be no threats from outside or corrosions from within – an unpromising condition in view of the state of Egypt's turbulent politics and fragile Exchequer. Cromer achieved much in these awkward circumstances. A £9 million loan agreed among the Great Powers in the summer of 1885 had helped to put the economy on a better footing and by 1888 Cromer had almost got the accounts to balance. But the inability to raise taxes across a wide enough base raised the same problems as Indian experience had shown. So when the threat of starvation fell on the Sudan in 1890 appeals went to London for subventions and were curtly resisted by the Prime Minister. ('We have no right to impose on the British taxpayer . . .'[88]) The pressures became worse, of course, as north-east Africa turned into a prime territory for scrambling. Holding Egypt of itself guaranteed little, after all. Any force that could control the upper Nile had the means of subduing the entire country by turning off its water. Not only did this mean retaining control of the Sudan, but also preventing hostile powers from obtaining adjacent territories. Like an advanced knight on the chessboard, the Sudan looked doomed for capture unless the square upon which it sat could be protected by other pieces. Hence Rosebery's need to annex Uganda in 1894 to prevent encroachment from the south in the direction of the White Nile. Hence Salisbury's

[87] Salisbury to Sir Henry Drummond Wolff, 23 Feb. 1887, *Cecil*, vol. IV, pp. 41–2.
[88] Salisbury in Lords, *Hansard*, 17 Mar. 1890, CCCXLII, col. 978.

perception that '[t]here are four, if not five, Powers that are steadily advancing towards the upper waters of the Nile' in 1895 and his prediction that '[t]here will be a competition – I will use no stronger word – for the advantages which predominance in that region will confer'.[89] But to win that coming conflict and forestall undesirable annexations meant investing men and money, adding greatly to the already intolerable level of defence expenditure at home and possibly curtailing the effort in Egypt itself. In a campaign to send forces to Khartoum in 1896, for example, Salisbury reluctantly decided to halt the mission at Dongola, despite the efforts of an imperialist optimist such as Lord Halsbury to carry it on:

> I carefully considered your objection to the policy of stopping for the time at Dongola which we had previously announced . . . [M]y own judgement is unaltered. Egypt cannot pay for a campaign to Khartoum, because she is forbidden to borrow: & even if we paid that bill for her, the cost for several years of administering these desolated provinces would upset her financial balance. It is safer, therefore, to make good the advance we have made.[90]

So much for withdrawing the troops. It had become a taunt of the Liberal party by the 1890s that the occupation seemed as permanent as ever, for all the Tories' whining about its 'difficulties & dangers'.[91]

Indeed, the temperature of conflict with France rose higher through the decade, just as the likelihood of conflagration in South Africa increased almost annually. In the one case a resolution would only come in 1904 with the entente reflecting a very different constellation of European forces from that faced by Salisbury's governments. To persuade the French towards harmony required a decade of dissonance. In West Africa, Salisbury decided by 1897 that patience had finally lost all virtue after the French had filched successive slices of British territory: it was a moment for gunboats to encourage them to 'behave decently'.[92] In the Sudan tension finally

---

[89] Salisbury in Lords, *Hansard*, 14 Feb. 1895, xxx, col. 699.
[90] Salisbury to Halsbury, 5 Oct. 1896, Halsbury MSS 56371 f.63.
[91] Gladstone to Rosebery, 1 Feb. 1893: 'Balfour made a singular declaration last night, undoubtedly in direct concert with Salisbury. It was that the *difficulties & dangers* of the occupation had been increased; but that this did not mean it ought to terminate sooner.' Printed in Foot and Matthew (eds.), *The Gladstone Diaries*, vol. xiii, p. 195.
[92] Salisbury to Beach, 3 Oct. 1897, St Aldwyn MSS PCC/69/151–2. The situation was not helped, he decided, by the enterprises of Sir George Goldie and his Royal Niger Company. 'Goldie is a great nuisance – his knowledge of foreign relations must have been acquired in a music-hall': to Wolmer, 26 Aug. 1897, 1st Earl of Selborne MSS 5 ff.49–50. The Company, originally the United African Company (1879), represented the crown until 1900 in what became Nigeria.

reached the point of war when French and British forces found themselves chin-to-chin at Fashoda in 1898. In South Africa the fizzling out of Jameson's raid did nothing to improve relations with the Boers and the promise of some form of war between the Cape and the Transvaal darkened Salisbury's horizon for the next four years. There was one silver lining, he thought. At least the contestants could not join forces and establish a United States of South Africa – a prospect too horrible to envisage.[93] Yet such comfort seemed small enough when contrasted with the many pains that empire now brought to those responsible for administering it. Perhaps what had most altered Salisbury's own perception of these difficulties was his changing responsibilities at home. He had first encountered empire in the India Office and had retained some of its perspectives while foreign secretary during the last two years of Beaconsfield's government, serving a master whose own imperialism remained obvious and unquenchable. When he became both his own master and his own foreign secretary, Salisbury saw the force of rather different considerations. Some of them stemmed from the need to marry the demands of empire to the realities of European foreign policy in which appeasing Germany or repelling Russia might play a greater role than any enforced by the Mahdi or Amir of Afghanistan. Some of them came from closer to home – from the Houses of Parliament and a nest of party hacks and advisors. One of them came closer to home more literally. For the Carlton Club stood only yards from Salisbury's front door in Arlington Street; and it stood, as though trying to make a political statement, with its back turned to him.

---

[93] Salisbury to Wolmer, 24 Mar. 1896, 1st Earl of Selborne MSS 5 ff.39–40.

CHAPTER 9

The party

Salisbury's thought and behaviour had a party dimension but often not the one that observers imagined. He liked those around him to reflect a collection of 'decently Conservative' attitudes that educated people ought to arrive at by instinct. And he undoubtedly believed that the Conservative party should be the party for such people. If he was not 'intellectually a fusionist',[1] he certainly failed, throughout a long career, to act like a 'party man' in any simple sense: the Cecil temperament got in the way, rather like the Churchill one. He was often the despair of his managers and could not understand the enthusiasms of supplicants for party favours. Party had to act as a vehicle for persuasion and no politician can allow squeamishness to override necessity in convincing an electorate of what it must be made to think. For Salisbury, however, it also had to accommodate personal honour defined in his own highly-defensive, occasionally self-defeating way and the two imperatives came into conflict. He could always retire to Hatfield if challenged over what he took to be honourable courses of action and did so early in his political career. On the other hand, he could take the *idea* of party very seriously out of a Burkean respect for tradition and a view that properly constituted and conducted parties had a crucial role to play in the parliamentary system and the constitution generally. This produced apparent contradiction. He might take endless trouble to assert a favourable party balance on a Royal Commission, as on the Oxford Commission in the 1870s, while pursuing a party line in the House of Lords of which most of his colleagues disapproved and in complete disregard of Carlton Club sentiment. He would express disgust with party hacks wanting jobs, yet insist on appointing to important constitutional positions from a party slate. His own sense of history

---

[1] Robert Taylor, *Lord Salisbury* (1975), p. 187.

seems to have supplied the resolution of these attitudes – an 'unwritten law' imposed by past practice. That is why he would not allow Halsbury to have his way over the mastership of the Rolls in 1897:

It is at variance with the unwritten law of our party system: & there is no clearer statute in that unwritten law than the rule that party claims should always weigh very heavily in the disposal of the highest legal appointments. In dealing with them we cannot ignore the party system – as you do in the choice of a General or an Archbishop. It would be a breach of the tacit covenant on which politicians & lawyers have worked the British Constitution together for the last two hundred years. Perhaps it is not an ideal system. Some day no doubt the M[aster of the] R[olls] will be appointed by a competitive examination in Law Reports. But it is our system for the present: and we shall give our party arrangements a wrench if we throw it aside.[2]

This is the deeper aspect of Salisbury's party mind, expressed in the language of contract with the dead, tacit covenants, which stood at the heart of his being. Sadly, he rarely taught others about it but tended rather to assume that they shared his inner visions. That he did not, and that they did not, may help to explain why his relationship with the Conservative party, far from being one of reciprocal admiration, frequently dissolved in distrust and only solidified when Home Rule for Ireland supplied the solder.

THE END(S) OF THE CONSERVATIVE PARTY: 1867

Every decade or so, someone announces the end of the Conservative party. Personal failure, pique, depression or the politician's ultimate weakness – impatience – may inform Tory pessimism. A bad election, an embarrassing war, an economic downturn, a sexual or financial scandal, a leadership contest: there are always 'objective' reasons for gloom. But among Conservatives the rot goes deeper than temperament or situation. Perhaps it has its fundamental cause in the kind of doctrine that Conservatism recommends. Like the Ranters and Shakers of the seventeenth century, against whom Salisbury ranted and shook in the nineteenth, Conservatism has a close and necessary relationship with the end of the world. That everything slides from a better condition to a worse is not merely the

---

[2] Salisbury to Halsbury, 29 Sep. 1897, Halsbury MSS 56371 ff.76–7.

Tory's allegation, after all; it is an important reason for his existence. Each battle in the Westminster chamber, every lost vote, brings nemesis a step closer. Liberal and Labour politicians argue about their respective futures, of course, but they tend not to assume that the fundamental malevolence of the world is waiting to strangle their respective parties and loot their national heritage if the wrong decision be made or if their leader should have an off-day. They do not suffer the sheer weight of change as a form of personal reproof for having somehow connived at it. They think, in their cheerful way, that some changes bring improvement. They do not see how much pain there is in the cosmos of the much-remarked Oxford don who reduced English Conservatism to the heroic, if unforgiving, observation that all change is for the worse, *even change for the better*.[3] No wonder Conservatives take their task so seriously and revile those among their number who cannot see the train until it hits them. In recent memory the end of the Conservative party has come with the accession of Mrs Thatcher, with the subversion of Mrs Thatcher, with the platitudes of Mr Major, with the tonalities of Mr Hague. In the 1860s it came about when the irresistible force of Benjamin Disraeli met the immovable object of Lord Robert Cecil.

Ostensibly their collision occurred in 1867 over the reform bill that Disraeli and his leader, the fourteenth Earl of Derby, wished to impose on the party. It is a famous and familiar story.[4] The narrative brackets those three years during which Cecil was Lord Cranborne (1865–8) and for many students of the nineteenth century the lesser title is better known than the major one he acquired in 1868. Having reluctantly taken the India Office in Derby's minority government, formed after Gladstone's reform bill had brought down the Russell government in June 1866, Cranborne developed increasing indigestion as Conservative plans for a similar turn towards democracy came to the cabinet table in February 1867. What frightened Cranborne and Carnarvon was numbers: the same bogey that had made Gladstone so timid with his failed proposal of the previous year. Once they discovered that the new electors might amount to

[3] A favourite observation of the late Dr R. A. Sayce. I owe this dispiriting anecdote to Professor James Campbell.
[4] For the party-political background stimulated by the first centenary, see Royden Harrison, *Before the Socialists: Studies in Labour and Politics 1861–1881* (1965); Robert Blake, *Disraeli* (1966); F. B. Smith, *The Making of the Second Reform Bill* (Cambridge, 1966) and especially Maurice Cowling, *1867: Disraeli, Gladstone and Revolution: The Passing of the Second Reform Act* (Cambridge, 1967).

200,000, they dug in their heels against so great an increase, especially when they expected that 'the contingent so introduced would fight against us'.[5] Within days it became clear to colleagues that 'Cranborne w[ould] not long act with Disraeli, that w[as] the bottom of it';[6] and before the week was out he was drafting his letter of protest to the party leader:

I find on closely examining the scheme wh. Mr. D. brought to the notice of the Cab. 5 days ago that its effect will be to throw the small boroughs almost and many of them entirely into the hands of the voters whose qualif. is lower than £10 . . . I find that in almost every case those of our friends who sit for boroughs with less than 25,000 inhabitants (a majority of boroughs) will be in a much worse condition in consequence of our bill than they would have been in consequence of Mr. G's . . . I am convinced that it will, if passed, be the ruin of the Conservative party.[7]

The drama came to its head on 2 March, as Lord John Manners confided to his diary that evening. 'For two hours we discussed it,' he reported, 'the rest of the Cabinet urging every consideration we could think of on Cranborne . . . It all turned on Cranborne, who remained immovable. At last, Lord Derby, seeing it was useless to persevere, said, rising, "This is the end of the Conservative party." '[8] Both sides thus adopted the same language and both were wrong. For the discussion had not been about the end of the Conservative party so much as its ends. The resignations of Cranborne and Carnarvon ended neither Disraeli nor his policies; but they illustrated a divergence of purpose and outlook that began long before the reform bill and did not end there.

Disraeli was a Peelite in at least one respect: he spent the thirty years after 1845–6 marked by the experience of Conservative catastrophe; those events remained the base-line of his political thinking until he discovered the Holy Grail of an election victory in 1874. The party existed to reassert 'Tory' values, within limits, but its primary ambition had to be that of regaining power for those who worked on its behalf. Parties were instrumental for Disraeli quite as much as for Salisbury, but their goals lay in very different directions. Principles and the character of public men mattered to Disraeli – it is

[5] Cranborne to Carnarvon, 22 Feb. 1867, Carnarvon MSS 60758 f.34.
[6] Hardy diary, 26 Feb. 1867, in Nancy E. Johnson (ed.), *The Diary of Gathorne Hardy, Later Lord Cranbrook, 1866–1892* (Oxford, 1981), p. 32.
[7] Cranborne to Derby (draft), 27 Feb. 1867, Christ Church MSS E20.
[8] Manners diary, 2 Mar. 1867, in Charles Whibley, *Lord John Manners and his Friends* (2 vols., 1925), vol. II, pp. 125–6.

absurd to picture him drained of belief – but he saw the inappropriateness of party politics for acting as their vehicle. The task for a party lay in acquiring the best minds for immediate purposes at hand: it did not greatly concern him where they came from. Hence his disappointment that Gladstone had not come into the Tory administration of 1858. 'It was not my fault that he did not. I almost went on my knees to him,' he believed in foggy retrospect.[9] About issues and contexts there was the same latitudinarianism. If the problem of the moment were the church, then the Conservative party should become a church party. If the topic of the moment was guano, then the party ought at least to take an interest in fertilizer. ('Can't you do anything about Guano?'[10]) And the power of the people rarely interested him until the reform debates after 1864 made the issue a runner. He had been far more exercised by the coming of the Second Empire in France as a decisive moment – one that would dominate the rest of his career, as he thought.[11] What he found hardest to understand was inflexibility, though he had roasted Peel for his retractions. He dispensed with protection quite as passionately as he had defended it; he became a radical when doing so seemed opportune for Tory reasons. How to make an impression on the pudding-like electorate of the 1850s and early 1860s became the critical question. To look for a way of making it different from his own – that he could understand. Having no interest in whether one made an impression or not seemed not merely a luxury he could ill afford but a sort of category error: a place from which no politician could begin.

Yet Robert Cecil began there out of background, temperament and his view of the human condition, to which party had somehow to accommodate itself. This is why it makes sense to consider his party affiliation as a peripheral segment of his situation. Given that his father held office in Tory administrations,[12] Salisbury's affiliation could only have been Conservative: he had none of the casting around for a platform that so preoccupied Disraeli in the 1830s. He chose, it is true, to enter parliament when the Burghley-dominated seat of Stamford became available in 1853, when he could make the

---

[9] Disraeli to Wilberforce, 28 Oct. 1862, Wilberforce MSS c13 f.190.
[10] Disraeli to Malmesbury, 2 Sep. 1852, Derby MSS 1749/51.
[11] Disraeli to Derby, 7 Dec. 1851, Derby MSS 1749/51.
[12] He had been Lord Privy Seal in the first Derby government (1852) and Lord President of the Council in the second (1858).

transition to Westminster without the expense and inconvenience of an opponent. But he did so with little zest. During the previous autumn he had told his father that he saw only three possibilities for a career – parliament, the church or the Bar. He found them all impossible and all undesirable, 'for all modes of life are equally uninviting'.[13] The maiden speech had none of Disraeli's spectacular sensationalism. It commented critically on the idea of university reform (a continuing concern, as noted earlier) and brought a loyal encomium from Gladstone, who must have recalled the baby boy he had seen long before at Hatfield, perched on an ottoman and wearing a frock.[14] Disraeli did the proper thing and wrote a kind letter to Cecil's father, though the reply suggests that his son's intervention had hardly reconfigured political life:

> It is a very great satisfaction to me that Robert's first attempt has met with your approbation. I am afraid that your praise may be a little increased by the friendship which I hope you entertain for his father. However I thought his speech read tolerably well in most of the papers except the Times and he tells me that it was delivered in a very thin House which makes it the more formidable a performance.[15]

In fact Cecil's impact remained very limited until the end of the decade. We have observed his harrying of governments over church rates and the need to conserve religion in the universities. He did enough for Disraeli to wonder about giving him an under-secretaryship in the minority Tory administration of 1858 and for his father, with whom he was still on terms, to consider jobbing him into a clerkship of the Council of which he held the patronage.[16] None of it suggested stardom.

Only with his marriage, the rift that followed with his father and the need to write extensively to make his living did Cecil develop his sense of polemic to levels at which he could not be ignored. Yet his polemic was rarely deployed directly in the service of party. He disliked the public platform and seldom appeared on one. When he spoke in the House after 1859 – and his writing commitments constrained what he could do – he could as easily deplore parties of

---

[13] Cecil to Salisbury, 2 Sep. 1852, in Cecil, vol. I, pp. 36–7.
[14] Gladstone declared Cecil 'rich with future promise'. His admiration did not last long. *Hansard*, 7 Apr. 1854, CXXXII, cols. 711–14.
[15] Salisbury to Disraeli, 10 Apr. 1854, Hughenden MSS B/XXI/C/135.
[16] Cecil to Salisbury, 12 Jul. and 4 Aug. 1858, Christ Church MSS E34; Salisbury to Disraeli, 23 ?Nov./Dec. 1858, Hughenden MSS B/XXI/C/136.

all kinds as encourage his own. When he pressed Palmerston's new government in 1859 to set up a commission to enquire into electoral bribery, his loathing of 'those low party agents, the necessity and disgrace of every party' bit into friend as well as foe, just as his daring accusation of an 'organized system of bribery which emanated from associations and clubs in London' brought its inevitable taunt from across the swordlines: 'the Carlton Club!'[17] In his writing, party trailed behind the issues of the moment in foreign policy – Poland, Russia, Prussia, but above all what he insisted on calling the 'Confederate War' in America, an unwinnable 'mere war of revenge' against the southern slave-owners, those 'natural allies of this country'.[18] When he turned his mind to democracy in the burgeoning reform context of 1864, his thoughts similarly began far from the Carlton Club and the need of Derby and Disraeli to dish Whigs. They began, perhaps, in south Australia during his tour in 1852 as he watched how the police commissioner had kept gold diggers in check. '[T]he government', he wrote to an English correspondent, 'was of the Queen, not of the mob; from above, not from below, holding from a supposed right (whether real or not, no matter) and not from "the people the source of all legitimate power," and *therefore* instead of murders, rapes and robberies daily, Lynch law and a Commitee of Vigilance, there was less crime than in a large English town, and more order and civility than I have myself witnessed in my own native village of Hatfield . . . [T]here it stands, a last protest against the principles of modern squeezability.'[19] Even in his early twenties, before party politics infested his mind, Cecil resisted the squeeze and it would take more than the Conservative party to smooth his prejudices into the shape of loyalty, let alone servility.

These were the years of acidity, culminating in his immortal gibe at Gladstone's behaving like a country attorney in 1861,[20] but the corrosions little benefited the Conservative party. Even when he drew up the balance sheet for Palmerston's government in 1864, his passage on the opposition (one of his best and most recalled) used a metaphor that his own leadership cannot have found complimentary.

---

[17] *Hansard*, 1 Aug. 1859, CLV, cols. 750–1.
[18] 'The Confederate Struggle and Recognition', *Quarterly Review*, 112 (Oct. 1862), pp. 535–70 at p. 537; *Hansard*, 30 Jun. 1863, CLXXI, col. 1819.
[19] Cecil to Rev. C. L. Conybeare, 11 Jul. 1852, in Cecil, vol. I, pp. 31–2.
[20] See below, chapter 10, p. 302.

Whenever its fate shall come, [this Parliament] will pass from existence with a fair title to the gratitude of Englishmen. It has done that which it is most difficult and most salutary for a Parliament to do – nothing . . . But though it has produced little, it has extinguished much . . . The House has opposed to its attacks . . . the stolid and . . . effective resistance of a sandbag. Liberalism has vainly buried its shafts in that impenetrable mass . . . [T]he Speaker's duty might almost have been performed by an automaton constructed to articulate the sounds, 'The Noes have it.'[21]

He did resort to a rubbishing of the Whigs in a piece on electoral politics in 1865, but for reasons that had more to do with class solidarity than Tory tactics. He always hated them more than the Radicals because the Whigs had sufficient advantage in education, culture and property to know what they were betraying; and as people like Lord John Russell trifled again with democratic recommendations, there seemed no need to refrain from reminding him and them that their party amounted to 'an accidental compromise due to the matrimonial arrangements of a few great families, with the peculiarity that many of them are willing to sacrifice the interests of their class, in order to promote the personal ambition of those who belong to their family connection'.[22] But there was none of the earnestness of Lord John Manners, who always saw the world through the lens of his party, as he looked back on the reform debate in 1864 and rejoiced that 'the government . . . have little cause to congratulate themselves. Every important able man spoke against them, and after Lord Palmerston's removal, their present political position is untenable. The poor old man failed dismally in his speech and obviously cannot manage a new House of Commons.'[23]

Palmerston did not manage; he died. His death in October 1865 removed a personality for whom Cecil had more time than many on the government side and brought forward Russell and Gladstone, both of them known to Hatfield as dangerous men in their different ways. There had been another death over the summer which also shifted Cecil's perspective. He had been sitting in his place in the Commons on 15 June when a messenger called him from the Chamber to deliver the news that his elder brother, James, had died suddenly. 'A great change in his position and future,' Gathorne Hardy had written in his diary that evening, 'which affects our party

[21] 'The House of Commons', *Quarterly Review*, 116 (Jul. 1864), pp. 245–81 at pp. 245–6.
[22] 'The Elections', *Quarterly Review*, 118 (Jul. 1865), pp. 280–95 at p. 295.
[23] Manners to Blackwood, 11 Jul. 1864, Blackwood MSS 4191 ff.70–1.

much.'[24] The effect lay, of course, in the future when Lord Cranborne, as he now became, would succeed to the marquisate when the
elderly second Marquis died. For the next three years that event
hung over Cranborne's head and must have coloured his thoughts as
the reform issue deepened. Perhaps he seriously contemplated
refusing to go to the Lords, as he later claimed, and only accepted
the elevation because he 'was so disgusted with the course the Tories
had pursued in respect to Dizzy's Reform Bill'.[25] More probably he
recognized the inevitability of a transformed status which would
make even less demands on his party loyalties than he allowed his
position as a member of parliament to make. 1867 mattered greatly,
of course. Had the issue not been accelerated so stridently by
Disraeli, then Cranborne/Salisbury could have looked forward to a
ministerial career in a purely Tory government. The reform bill
shifted the ground of his unease from democracy to a concept that
weighed on him far more – that of personal honour.

Something of this mood had already marked his dealings with the
Liberals over their own reform proposals. In April 1866 a violent
letter to Gladstone, which even Cranborne appears not to have sent,
accused him of having made 'a reckless and injurous imputation to a
number of gentleman (your adversaries) of odious opinions which
they never expressed & which they never gave you the slightest
ground for believing that they had entertained'.[26] But after his
resignation from Derby's government the high ground became his
constant place of retreat. He did not blame his colleagues for this
exile; he blamed Disraeli. Carnarvon, who went with him, together
with the ever-aghast General Peel, became close to Cranborne for a
while and received his confidences. By the beginning of April he had
learned that Cranborne had lost any hope that the government

[24] Hardy diary, 15 Jun. 1865, in A. E. Gathorne-Hardy, *Gathorne Hardy, First Earl of Cranbrook: A Memoir* (2 vols., 1910), vol. I, p. 173.

[25] Salisbury to Wolmer, 7 Feb. 1893, second Earl of Selborne MSS 5 ff.13–14. He says that the plan had been to instruct his solicitor not to search for proof of his father's marriage in order to tell the House of Commons that he had no corroboration that he held the entitlement to a peerage, apparently believing that they could not have done anything about it without new legislation. It all sounds very far-fetched, though contemporary evidence suggests that the idea was at least broached and that Cranborne ultimately rejected it on the ground that the Tories in the Commons would in the future have to work with Liberals of one stamp or another, a situation which he could not bring himself to confront and which provoked the well-known remark: 'Pure "squire" Conservatism is played out.' See Cecil, vol. I, p. 294.

[26] Cranborne to Gladstone (draft: not sent), 11 Apr. 1866. It is not obvious which remarks had so annoyed Cranborne.

stood for anything. 'No powers can extract . . . any public avowal of what they mean to stand by & what they mean to fall by.'[27] It was the refusal to draw lines – thus far and no further – that appalled him in Disraeli's management of the reform bill. Seen from a party point of view, that refusal not only made complete sense but could be portrayed as a situational requirement since only a willingness to run down the hill without brakes would enable the minority administration to keep itself alive by dividing the opposition into its many fractions. So, for Disraeli, Cranborne's resignation rested on as obscure a set of doctrines as had Gladstone's from Peel's government over the Maynooth Grant; it was a case of 'a very clever man' having made 'a very great mistake'.[28] Cranborne's own perception reversed this diagnosis. Disraeli had shown himself – as another Salisbury would famously describe a Tory colleague a century later – as too clever by half.[29] He had compromised integrity and honesty in order to advance a political stratagem. And Cranborne's utterances would bear the mark of that conviction for the next few years, rising in their shrillness once Disraeli assumed the party leadership in February 1868 and Cranborne went to the House of Lords following his father's death in April.

He and cousin Exeter had already fallen out over the bill. 'I am sorry I am quite unable to take your view,' Cranborne told him and rehearsed exactly the same argument in private that he had presented to his colleagues and the party. 'We have struggled against concessions much smaller in amount mainly because we feared they would lead to this very measure of Household Suffrage we are now proposing. My opinions on the subject remain what they were. I think that to admit to the register such multitudes of poor & ignorant men would be dangerous to the Constitution.'[30] He had also wondered, more prosaically, whether Exeter would withhold his patronage at Stamford at the next election, a contingency which his succession made irrelevant. He dealt with the party hierarchy in the same tone. When Northcote appeared on the day of Derby's resignation, to offer him, on Disraeli's behalf, the India Office once again, 'I told him that I had the greatest respect for every member of the

---

[27] Cranborne to Carnarvon, 1 Apr. 1867, Carnarvon MSS 60758 f.39.
[28] Disraeli at Edinburgh, 29 Oct. 1867, quoted in Richard Shannon, *The Age of Disraeli, 1868–1881: The Rise of Tory Democracy* (1992), p. 24.
[29] See above, p. 13, n. 12.
[30] Cranborne to Exeter (draft), n.d. (March 1867), Christ Church MSS E2.

Govt, except one – but that I did not think my honour was safe in the hands of that one.'[31] It is not recorded whether Northcote reported this formulation back to his leader. Even with people he did not know, he chose to refuse collaboration with the party in its Disraelian mould by using language which could only become the talking point of local constituencies and county society.

> . . . I cannot blind myself to the fact that the aims and objects of the heads of the Conservative party have changed very much in the last two years. On the subject of distribution of political power they have become democratic. On the subject of the Irish Church their views are enigmatic & uncertain. As far as I can judge the one object for which they are striving heartily is the Premiership of Mr. Disraeli. If I had a firm confidence in his principles, or his honesty – or even if he were identified by birth or property with the Conservative classes in the country – I might . . . work to sustain him in power. But he is an adventurer: &, as I have good cause to know, he is without principles and without honesty . . . [And] for all practical purposes Mr. Disraeli for the time being at least, is the Conservative party.[32]

Of course this had its disingenuous side in implying that Salisbury had never questioned Disraeli's personal desirability before, despite having known and worked with him over many years. Nevertheless, as he turned to his new enthusiasm of a railway directorship, the compulsive reflections on personal honour became, if anything, more rigid. When he discovered an inadvertent conflict of interest while undertaking his commercial work, the subject had no political embarrassments lurking within it and he could have ignored the matter without penalty. His letter to the Lord Chancellor begged advice at once, none the less. How could he acquit himself honourably?[33] It had become the refrain of his entire correspondence.

And of course Salisbury was not alone. A serious movement of opposition to Disraeli's leadership inevitably arose once he had lost the 1868 election. It felt as though a painful operation had been endured only to find that the complaint had not been cured. Disraeli, for his part, withdrew from active politics to write *Lothair*,[34] seemingly oblivious of the grumbling and conspiring. Salisbury did not play an active part in the resistance – his views were sufficiently well known

---

[31] Cranborne to Carnarvon, 27 Feb. 1868, Carnarvon MSS 60758 f.55.
[32] Salisbury to R. W. G. Gaussen (draft), 11 May 1868, Christ Church MSS E2.
[33] Salisbury to Cairns, 9 Oct. 1869, Cairns MSS 30/51/6/f.15. Salisbury had learned that he held shares in a company that had gone into liquidation.
[34] The novel appeared in May 1870 and immediately ran through eight editions: see Paul Smith, *Disraeli: A Brief Life* (Cambridge, 1996), p. 154.

– but his name along with that of the new Earl of Derby became mentioned in dispatches as a possible replacement in the event of Disraeli's being forced out. Meanwhile, the Lords vented their own concerns about the quality of recent leadership when Cairns gave way to Richmond as Conservative leader in the House of Lords, none more so than the Duke of Northumberland. In formal terms he could not be described as a major force within the party structure. But no duke lacks prestige; and to hear the holder of one of the most ancient titles in the country snarling that, 'after the events of 1867–68, [he] could never again submit [his] political action to the guidance of any individual' gave some sense of the depth of personal injury. He would support Richmond, needless to say, but 'according to [his own] conception of true Conservative principle'.[35] What helped Disraeli was the fission among his critics. Salisbury and Derby could hardly act together – less for political reasons than personal ones. The death of his father had opened the door for Salisbury's stepmother to bring her relationship with Derby out of the closet and the stepson found little pleasure in that. By the spring of 1870 some sort of reconciliation seems to have evolved[36] but a corner had been turned all the same and divergent paths, widened by policy differences, would take them to very different places before 1878 when Salisbury turned Derby into 'Titus Oates'. Carnarvon remained close to Hatfield's heart but he lacked a certain weight and resolution as a political figure and, like Derby, wound up less instinctively Conservative than Salisbury preferred in a close collaborator. This isolation made Salisbury happy to fire guns randomly and go down with all flags flying if the government proved too strong. 'I think there are many cases', he announced, rejecting a compromise with his friend and political opponent Roundell Palmer, 'in which it is better to be openly beaten than to accept a merely nominal compromise. The legislative effect of the two processes is of course exactly the same: but in the one case your friends are indignant with the enemy, in the other case they are indignant with you.'[37]

---

[35] Northumberland to Richmond, 28 Feb. 1870, Goodwood MSS 862 v 15.

[36] 'Dined Travellers, with Carnarvon. I had walked up from the House with Salisbury, between whom and myself friendly relations are being re-established: but we shall never, I think, be on intimate terms again': diary, 29 Mar. 1870, in Derby, *Diaries*, p. 56.

[37] Salisbury to Palmer, 31 Jul. 1870, 1st Earl of Selborne MSS 1864 f.69. Palmer had been looking for some flexibility over the issue of religious tests in the universities.

Only with Disraeli's re-emergence in 1872 did any stability return to the upper echelons of the Conservative party. Looking through the miasma of the *Alabama* dispute at the opening of the year, Disraeli thought he had never seen 'public feeling so agitated & so ?dark'.[38] His response has become celebrated. Two major speeches, at Manchester and the Crystal Palace in 1872 had the objective of giving the party a national rather than a sectional agenda and sought, historians contend in retrospect, to give the message an imperial twist. At the time, however, these performances seemed far less significant than posterity wants to make them. Derby certainly saw no grounds for optimism, when '[Disraeli] had nothing to tell his friends that was either new or important'.[39] Indeed, for those who, like Derby, thought the party's lack of unity and focus the central issues, no amount of speechifying would improve matters. In a sense the worst outcome might be that the government fell, in which case an election would reveal all their divisions and the party would become a joke. As threats of dissolution travelled the corridors of Westminster during the summer of 1872, Derby reflected on the difficulties in his own House:

It is clear to me that we cannot go on permanently as we are doing now: Richmond, though sensible by nature, has never studied political matters, and his want of knowledge is painfully apparent in debate: Salisbury destroys by violence the effect of his undoubted ability: and Cairns, whose character and capacity make him the proper Conservative leader, if he would accept the post, is rather too much disposed to dwell at length on details . . . But besides all this, there is no concert or communication, and each of the three takes a line of his own.[40]

Perhaps that predicament impressed itself also on Salisbury. Certainly his return to writing, following the railway interlude, did not display the venom that a piece calling itself 'The Position of Parties' would have called forth a couple of years before.[41] Even so, the revival of Tory fortunes in the constituencies during 1873 – giving the

---

[38] Disraeli to Northcote, 27 Jan. 1872 (MS torn), Iddesleigh MSS 50016 f.114. A Confederate warship, the *Alabama*, had been allowed out of Liverpool in 1862 and had begun preying on Northern ships. After Gladstone had succeeded in persuading the parties involved to consent to arbitration after the war, the American government was awarded over £3 million in damages against Britain.

[39] Diary, 4 Jul. 1872, referring to the Manchester speech: in Derby, *Diaries*, p. 110.

[40] Diary, 7 Jul. 1872, in *ibid.*, p. 111.

[41] *Quarterly Review*, 133 (Oct. 1872), pp. 558–93. Richard Shannon astutely notes that for the first time since the rupture over reform, Salisbury, 'who had not printed a civil word about Disraeli', contented himself with ignoring the leader: Shannon, *Age of Disraeli*, p. 145.

lie to die-hard mantras that the coming of the secret ballot would mean the end of the Conservative party[42] – pressed on Salisbury's conscience painfully by suggesting that the moment of decision might be thrust on him sooner than he would have preferred.

It came in February 1874 as Salisbury returned from a holiday in Sorrento. Carnarvon made it plain that he wanted to accept office under Disraeli but wanted also to act with Salisbury; and Salisbury himself discovered nothing beyond his personal hatred of the prospect on which to ground a refusal. Yet in returning to the India Office he could not expunge those seven years of resentful reflection that had shown him that the ends of the Conservative party were various and not all to his liking. All Conservatives enjoyed the thought that their party had become electable again: it was as rich a moment as 1841. On the other hand, many must have shared the Earl of Malmesbury's suspicion that the result had little to do with them and much to with the Liberal voters' 'dislike & *fear* of Gladstone's *reforms*'.[43] It followed that Conservatives would feel comfortable only if they followed Salisbury's instinct of doing as little as possible. And the world was not made this way. Already the economy had begun its downturn that would make every administration for the next twenty years feel the emptiness of its treasure-chests. Already the questionable Liberal expedition to quell the Ashantis had brought Africa into the centre of political discussion. Already the crumbling of the Turkish will to govern and the emerging Russian will to expand threatened to turn the prism at home and present another facet through which the perceptions of party might refract, colour and disperse.

RUSSIANS AND TURKS: 1874–1881

Foreign policy often leaves party politics alone and can be approached by the historian as an arcane craft practised by an eccentric *cognoscenti*. One recalls the undergraduate who brazenly announced that British history required no knowledge of Europe because one

---

[42] Even Richmond noticed '[h]ow curious it is, that we seem to be so successful in all sorts of constituencies under the Ballot': Richmond to Hardy, 6 Aug. 1873, Cranbrook MSS T501/257. He had in mind in particular the experience of Greenwich, where the Tory candidate beat his Liberal rival into second place after the death of Gladstone's partner in the constituency. In the autumn he expressed similar pleasure over the prospects for Taunton, which his party just failed in the event to win.

[43] Malmesbury to Richmond, 10 Apr. 1874, Goodwood MSS 866 w 278 (emphasis in original).

could always pass an examination paper while knowing nothing about it.[44] The effrontery works better for some periods than others. It makes the 1930s unintelligible. It drains the 1980s and 1990s of much Tory argument. In the nineteenth century, it cripples any conception of George Canning's politics in the 1820s and it turns Disraeli's only government – that which held power from 1874 to 1880 – into a shadow of itself as the future of Europe became its obsession. 'Europe' during these years focussed only indirectly on France or Italy, or even on Bismarck's new Germany. The concern lay further east and fed on anxieties that had preoccupied the chancelleries of European capitals ever since the Crimean War of 1854–6 had propped up the Turkish state and made it look as though it were a serious power. The so-called Black Sea clauses of the Treaty of Paris gave the western powers a text that many wished to preserve, just as it presented St Petersburg with a consuming grievance.[45] Russia had used the embarrassment of the French in 1870–1 to force through the abrogation of the clauses' most disagreeable features in the Treaty of London of May 1871. How long this 'solution' would hold water in the other capitals of Europe remained one question. How long the Turks could perpetuate their empire without internal revolution or financial collapse posed another. Policy produced two salient thoughts in London which would find coded expression in many sectors of political discussion over the next thirty years. Everything should be done to prevent another Crimean War;[46] and, secondly, in the event of its becoming inevitable, Britain must not fight it alone. Salisbury added his own persistent rider. '[W]e went to war to prevent the expansion of the Russian empire in a manner that would be most dangerous to our interests.' We did not do so to sustain 'the most oppressive and rapacious of all governments' and its sultan in Constantinople.[47]

Why did Russia and Turkey so powerfully disturb domestic politics? Religion and strategy both contributed, the more so for

[44] The undergraduate in question thrived and now holds a senior position teaching history in one of Britain's best schools, which rather proves his point.

[45] Articles x to xiv forbade the closing of the Bosphorus and Dardanelles, neutralized the Black Sea and opened it to commerce, required Russia and Turkey to admit consuls to their ports and prohibited their establishment of military arsenals on the coast.

[46] By November 1876 Beaconsfield thought it 'wise . . . to assume that there will be an invasion of Turkey by Russia' but did not see why 'that would necessitate any declaration of war against Russia on our part'. Beaconsfield to Salisbury, 29 Nov. 1876, Salisbury MSS (Disraeli, f.183).

[47] Cecil in Commons debate on the Danubian principalities: *Hansard*, 4 May 1858, CL, col. 77.

their mutual intertwining. Russia sent confusing messages in its autocracy (offensive to radicals), its Christianity (attractive to Dissenting radicals), its Slavic character (offensive to Conservatives) and its lack of impact in the west (attractive to Conservatives). Strategically it threatened, for some, Constantinople, for others merely an eastward expansion that would not signify. For those looking beyond the north-western frontier of India, it sometimes promised a Mongol invasion and the end of civilization. Turkey, on the other hand, offended virtually all churchmen even before it attracted the reputation of having put to death Bulgarian Christians in 1876. A salient exception was the Prime Minister who had not quite shed his Young England mythologies about the east and continued to see a certain nobility in the Porte. But it could be seen, too, as a necessary evil whose toleration was dictated by the need to keep Constantinople in the hands of a client state. All of these conflicting positions would find some voice between 1876 and 1878 when the Conservative cabinet found the Near East dominating its discussions (perhaps, as Derby thought, because domestic issues had become so low-key) to the point that Lord Beaconsfield, as Disraeli had become, complained that his cabinet seemed in 'permanent sitting' – 'all of us absorbed in the critical state of our foreign affairs'.[48] One consequence, critical in the history of international relations, was the Treaty of Berlin in 1878. Others, deeply relevant to the history of the Conservative party, were that the Earl of Derby showed himself a failed Peelite, even a closet Whig, who needed to change parties, that the Earl of Carnarvon displayed tendencies so unsound as to remove him from the centre of party thinking and that the Marquis of Salisbury displaced Derby at the Foreign Office and implied, through the strength of his handling of the Russo-Turkish war, that he had become Beaconsfield's heir.

If Disraeli had always been a Turk, Salisbury had been a Russian since at least the Polish crisis of 1863. Liberal sentiment screamed at the brutal suppression by the Russians of the Polish rising of that year. Cecil did not scream. He saw the eighteenth-century partitions of Poland as understandable and necessary acts and he saw, when he looked at a future Polish state, another Turkey. Behind this vision one can see a particular view of the nature of international relations and an early indication of cold-blooded intelligence.

---

[48] Beaconsfield to Marlborough, 16 Feb. 1878, Marlborough MSS 9271/4/43.

Influence, if it be excessive and constant, is veiled conquest. The intense anxiety which the Great Powers have displayed to warn each other's reigning families off such new thrones as those of Greece and Belgium arises from that unquestionable fact. The remonstrances which the Western Powers thought themselves at liberty to address to Austria against the secret treaties by which she retained the small Italian States under her influence rest upon no other basis . . . The truth is, that in a carefully-balanced structure like the European system of nations, each State has a vested right to the complete and real independence of its neighbour . . . If, from any internal rottenness, that independence shall have become an absolute impossibility . . . [the neighbours may impose] . . . a tutelage of ambassadors such as that which is established at Constantinople, or . . . a partition. It cannot be said that the Turkish arrangement has been eminently successful in averting war. And it is very doubtful whether it would . . . have even been practicable with a people who were not gifted with an Oriental facility of submission. But as a matter of self-preservation, neighbouring powers must exact one of these two securities from a State which has become permanently anarchical and defenceless.[49]

The Tsar had his vices, no doubt. But he presided over a *state* and one that constituted little threat to British interests. Even during his tenure of the India Office in 1866, Cranborne had dismissed worries that Russia had designs on Afghanistan and India.[50] He thought that Persia would fall, but nothing could be done about that.[51] And even when colleagues had become consumed with anxiety about the prospect of a Russo-Turkish war in 1878, Salisbury calmly pointed out that the dangers to Britain came from powers closer to home and that, even if Russians did take Constantinople, the consequences for Britain had little of the seriousness that tremulous ministers supposed.[52]

These instincts remained entirely consistent. For Salisbury's colleagues, however, the demonstration of instinct at one remove through its application to a series of complicated events left them confused about what he wanted. If he resisted war with Russia, his

---

[49] 'Poland', *Quarterly Review*, 113, pp. 450–81 at p. 470. Cecil reviewed in this article Heinrich von Sybel's *Geschichte der Revolutionszeit* (Düsseldorf, 1860), which explains the breadth of reference.

[50] 'When there is so much room for her to the eastward of Bokhara, it would be a sheer wantonness on her part to provoke a powerful antagonist by turning to the South': Cranborne to Lawrence (copy), 27 Aug. 1866, Christ Church MSS C/1/2.

[51] Salisbury to Derby, 1 Aug. 1874, Derby MSS 16/2/7.

[52] E.g. Salisbury to Lytton, 16 Feb. 1877, in Cecil, vol. II, p. 129; Derby diary, 16 June 1877: Salisbury 'said two things [in cabinet] which are more decided than any former utterance of his: that Russia at Constantinople would do us no harm: and that we ought to seize Egypt' (in Derby, *Diaries*, p. 411).

message said one thing; if he agreed with it then his attitude seemed self-contradictory. In fact he maintained an undertow of argument that found no difficulty with fighting or not fighting Russia so long as the object were not the shoring up of a decrepit Turkish empire; and as the object repeatedly shifted so did his response. Others within the Tory elite sought their own consistency in precisely the opposite sense: they wanted a war at once if Constantinople looked as though it might fall. Until the Turkish atrocities in Bulgaria made Russian action likely, the position could be held together rhetorically. Thereafter pressure increased on politicians to say what would happen if the Russians chose to attack; and any declaration involved taking into their confidence the new Tory electorate whose vote in 1874 had put the government in place but which had since had the Gladstonian 'bag and baggage' message thrust down its throat that the evils of Turkey licensed action by any civilized power.[53] For some, such as Gathorne Hardy, this popular dimension seemed urgent. 'Russia . . . never occupied a position for mischief as she does now,' he wrote to Cairns, who shared his concerns, in September 1876. 'If she decides upon open action public feeling (I won't call it opinion) would tie our hands.'[54] Carnarvon trembled, too. But *his* concern was by-elections, especially the forthcoming one at Buckinghamshire, and he nagged the prime minister for reassurance. Beaconsfield told him, in effect, to take an aspirin,[55] but he did resolve on one masterstroke: that of sending his major strategic critic, Salisbury, as British representative to an international gathering in Constantinople aimed at resolving the Russo-Turkish dispute without a war. This achieved nothing beyond the 'sea-sickness, much French and failure' that Salisbury had characteristically foreseen,[56] but it got the Indian Secretary out of the country from November 1876 to February 1877 and gave

[53] Gladstone's pamphlet on *The Bulgarian Horrors* had sold in remarkable numbers and his campaign, originally orchestrated by W. T. Stead, Bishop Fraser of Manchester and the historian Edward Freeman, had turned into a popular rage against the heathen Turk. Cf. Richard Shannon, *Gladstone and the Bulgarian Agitation* (1975), esp. pp. 50–112. For the prosaic R. A. Cross, now a Tory minister, it was hard to 'imagine how any public man c[ould] so wholly have lost all sense of responsibility as Gladstone . . .': Cross to Derby, 13 Sep. 1876, Derby MSS 16/2/75. 'I cannot understand any man', raged Richmond, 'who has any responsibility acting as he has done; and ?solely for party purposes': to Salisbury, 26 Sep. 1876, Salisbury MSS (Richmond, f.36) [MS damaged].

[54] Hardy to Cairns, 14 Sep. 1876, Cairns MSS 30/51/7/f.10.

[55] 'I think he considers me rather an alarmist . . .': Carnarvon to Cairns, 15 Sep. 1876, Cairns MSS 30/51/8/ff.108–9. Disraeli was quite right. When he went to the House of Lords in 1876, his seat was retained by the Conservative party and held again in 1880.

[56] Cf. Cecil, vol. II, p. 91.

slower minds time to take stock when Beaconsfield's prediction that it would all be over by Christmas turned out to have been optimistic.

Constantinople was vile. It reminded Georgina Salisbury, who went with her husband to give moral support in the English language, of a small county town with none of its compensations. Her husband thought it vile because it reflected Turkish dilatoriness and moral corruption but also because it still contained Sir Henry Elliot. Salisbury had been trying to have him recalled from the Embassy for some time on account of Elliot's pro-Turkish stance. 'No advantage can result from such a policy now,' Salisbury had seen back in September. 'The Turk's teeth must be drawn: even if he be allowed to live . . . I hold that all our troubles come from Elliot's stupidity and laziness: and I have been preaching against him privately & in Cabinet for the last two years.'[57] Unlike Lord Stratford, Elliot's predecessor, who could draw on a certain strength in his period from the Turks' remembering how the British fleet had sunk the Turkish at Navarino in 1827, Elliot's appeasement made the Turks brave at precisely the moment when Salisbury wanted to 'squeeze' them by threatening the cancellation of the Treaty of Paris.[58] He failed to extract either usable threats from the cabinet at home or any sense from the Turkish representative in Constantinople. If he thought 'the position of Britain ha[d] been improved'[59] by his visit, he must have had in mind the recall of Elliot: there was nothing else to celebrate. Indeed, his modest attainments drew criticism from colleagues. He had not kept them sufficiently in touch (Hardy, Cairns, Richmond). He had not been nice enough to the Turks (Carnarvon). He had been too bellicose with the Russians (Derby, Beaconsfield). When he left Constantinople for a rest in Naples on his way home on 22 February 1877, he knew he would return to a subdued welcome, for all his colleagues' disingenuous letters of appreciation.[60]

[57] Salisbury to Carnarvon, 13 Sep. 1876, Carnarvon MSS 60758 f.181.

[58] Cecil, vol. ii, p. 122. Cf. Salisbury to Carnarvon n.d. ?25 December 1876 (decrypt), Carnarvon MSS 60758 ff.191–2. He saw the refusal as an opportunity missed, as he told the foreign secretary. '[L]iberate yourselves from the Treaty of Paris, which imposes heavy responsibilities, & gives no corresponding advantages. It was signed under the belief that English counsels would always be listened to at the Porte: but this condition ceased to exist when Lord Stratford left': Salisbury to Derby, 26 Dec. 1876, Derby MSS 16/2/7.

[59] Salisbury to Richmond, 6 Feb. 1877, Goodwood MSS 869 c 3.

[60] Richmond played the game, as ever, and blamed the other side. 'I feel certain if it had been possible to convince the Turk you would have done so': Richmond to Salisbury, 2 Feb. 1877, Salisbury MSS (Richmond, f.38).

Possibly it would have helped Tory harmonies if domestic legislation had been either improving or popular. But the Public Worship
Regulation Act had not only stretched the church but also length-
ened the axis from Salisbury to Cairns; the labour legislation of 1875
struck observers as more prudential than far-seeing and the parliamentary scene appeared quiet to the point of boredom: 'no great
debates, . . . no explosion of party zeal, . . . no danger to the govt,
and no victory to its opponents . . .'.[61] Perhaps a little adrenalin
would have taken some attention away from Salisbury's misson.
Another problem appeared in personnel. The Commons management was safe enough in the hands of Hardy, with Cross and Smith
helpful. The Lords were still reeling from poor Richmond whose
equanimity seemed no more expansive than his knowledge and who
would be heard ranting at those around him ('I have no patience
with Huntly airing his ridiculous opinions'; 'I thought Elcho very
mischievous the other night') or being moved to explosions which
raised him to the same height as the late Sir Robert Inglis in
proclaiming memorable *doubles entendres*.[62] But embarrassment in
cabinet went beyond the sage of Goodwood. The enormous George
Ward Hunt became so impossible at the Admiralty that he had to be
dropped. Richmond's brother, Lord Henry Lennox, tried unilaterally
to declare independence for the Office of Works until the Chancellor
of the Exchequer prevented it and provoked a spirited resignation.[63]
Sir Charles Adderley, 'a charming fellow', turned out to be too
brainless to understand the documents that the officials at the Board
of Trade kept bringing to him and would have had to go if Disraeli
could have found someone else.[64] That he could not speaks volumes
for a central Tory difficulty. Rather like the Whigs a generation
earlier, the Conservative party found itself caught between generations, with few to bridge the gap save those of disturbing middle-class
backgrounds such as Cross and Smith – Lord Randolph Churchill's
celebrated department-store – and few of the old guard young
enough or capable enough to hold down a ministerial post. The Old

---

[61] Derby diary, 17 Aug. 1875, in Derby, *Diaries*, p. 238.
[62] Richmond to Cairns, 12 Jul. 1874, Cairns MSS 30/51/3/f.49; Richmond to Hardy, 22 May
1875, Cranbrook MSS T501/257. His most sublime inadvertence comes in this latter letter.
'It seems to me that in [the] Ho. of Lords all the *pokes* I get are from behind.'
[63] He withdrew it with less spirit and hung on grimly until forced out by financial scandal in
1876.
[64] For Adderley see Derby diary, 25 Jul. 1874, in Derby, *Diaries*, p. 176.

Gang satirized by the 'Fourth Party'[65] after 1880 was already mildly ancient.

Salisbury had learned in Constantinople a lesson of great future importance. It did not concern the weakness of the Turks – he knew that already. What he came to appreciate was the usefulness of acting alone. Both Beaconsfield and Derby had given him a free hand in the discussions, subject to cabinet approval; and once he became his own foreign secretary after 1885 that is how he chose to arrange foreign policy. On coming home in 1877, the contrast felt overwhelming. He no longer had to cope with Elliot, certainly. But he now had the dithering Carnarvon, the alternately warlike and hesitating prime minister, the coolly pacifistic Derby and all the intervening shades around the cabinet table. His Russian sympathies combined with his mistrust of Shuvalov (confidant of his stepmother, Mary Derby) led him to invite Ignatiev – sometime ambassador to Turkey, Berlin, London, Paris and Vienna – to Hatfield in March and he did what he could to move events forward. How determined he felt about doing so emerges from his correspondence with Lytton who, for all his wild imaginings about Russian expansion in Afghanistan, remained someone whose fundamental instincts Salisbury trusted. Ideally, an accelerated policy would require tackling the Russians directly while aiming a diplomatic charm-offensive at Austria who could then be relied on to prevent Russian excesses. But no one would play: 'these are dreams'. His next melancholic sentence is often quoted out of context to make him recommend precisely what he was seeking to avoid. 'English policy is to float lazily downstream, occasionally putting out a diplomatic boat-hook to avoid collisions.'[66] By the end of March the prime minister's thin patience had dissipated in an open attack on Salisbury and Carnarvon in cabinet for rocking the boat.[67] In the Commons, too, the mood of absorption in Austria, Bulgaria, Rumelia and strips of earth unknown to most party men from the Carlton threatened to connive with Gladstone's mission to make the Near East the test of party. 'Since I have known parliament', Derby reflected in his diary in

---

[65] See below, pp. 275–7.
[66] Salisbury to Lytton, 9 Mar. 1977, in Cecil, vol. II, p. 130. He returned to the theme in May in a letter to Carnarvon castigating Beaconsfield and Derby for their 'emasculate, purposeless vacillation': *ibid.*, p. 141.
[67] Carnarvon to Northcote, 30 Mar. 1877, Iddesleigh MSS 50022 f.210.

April, 'attention has never been so fixed on foreign policy.'[68] The
Queen wanted war: the one consistent strand in politics.[69] Derby
started to tabulate the cabinet ministers' changing policy positions:
in April he has the prime minister and Cairns hot for intervening
militarily if the Russians were to approach Constantinople, with
Salisbury and Carnarvon against; at the beginning of May he has
Carnarvon wanting to take Egypt as a defensive precaution with
Salisbury cheerfully adding Basra and the Gulf to the list of areas
requiring protection; by the end of May either Disraeli and Cairns
will resign or Salisbury and Carnarvon will. By the middle of June
Austria has become the key to the situation for Salisbury and Derby
who stumble into a *rapprochement*. By the end of July Manners and
Hicks Beach want a war, Disraeli nearly does, Salisbury, Cairns,
Richmond and Northcote are less persuaded and Derby has now
joined Carnarvon in the peace camp. The defeat of the Russians at
Plevna provided a pause for thought while the aggressors regrouped.
But by October the familiar faces were back at the table and now all
sitting in different places: for war – prime minister, Cairns, Richmond, Manners, Hicks Beach; against – Salisbury, Carnarvon and,
more or less, Derby; undecided – Northcote, Hardy, Cross, Smith.[70]
And so on. Derby gives a kaleidoscope of cabinet discussion in which
no one seemed to say the same thing twice.

Yet Salisbury's own tune in this game of musical chairs had a
theme and a rhythm. He wanted Britain to have her share of the
spoils when Turkey fell to pieces,[71] but he wanted to do nothing that
would indirectly help Turkey out of a wish to conserve Constantinople. Once it became clear, Plevna notwithstanding, that the Turks
would indeed be crushed, he came out of his tent and recommended
as much violence as the next man. The cold realization of Turkish
doom in fact accelerated policy in November and December far
more than Salisbury had been able to effect in March. Carnarvon
was swept towards decisiveness:

As regards war itself I think it is difficult to exaggerate the folly of it. We sd.
go into it not only with inadequate resources and without allies – and
perhaps even with serious opposition to expect from Germany and Italy if

---

[68] Diary, 18 Apr. 1877, in Derby, *Diaries*, p. 391.
[69] 'She is ready for war, says that rather than submit to Russian insult she would lay down her
Crown,' etc., etc. Carnarvon to Salisbury, 25 Mar. 1877, Salisbury MSS (Carnarvon, f.295).
[70] Derby, *Diaries*, pp. 392, 397, 404, 410–11, 425, 442.
[71] Hardy diary, 6 Dec. 1877, in Gathorne Hardy, *Memoir*, vol. II, p. 36.

not Austria – but we should certainly open the door wide to European disturbances of every kind . . . Nor have we the miserable excuse of being able to restore even to its former position the Turkish Empire. It is breaking to pieces past all remedy and we are simply shutting our eyes to facts that are as clear as noon-day.[72]

Derby, more significantly, began from November to note privately that his own disagreement with the prime minister was becoming fundamental. When Beaconsfield finally insisted on sending a naval force to Constantinople in January 1878 both Carnarvon[73] and Derby sent in resignations, though Derby was prevailed upon to withdraw his – temporarily as events showed. Northcote wrung his hands in habitual anxiety – 'chaos . . . overthrow of the government . . . peace of the world', etc., etc.[74] – and then threw them in the air with relief when Derby came back. The moment of decision came in March when Beaconsfield would no longer defer declaring a state of emergency and sending forces. This time there was no bringing Derby back. It was a decision that propelled Salisbury, no less inevitably, into the Foreign Office as though Derby had been merely keeping its seat warm for the past four years.

Of itself this did not portend a great deal. Beaconsfield held the public eye as the architect of the Congress of Berlin and it was as his assistant that Salisbury accompanied him there, striking the normally shrewd Bismarck as having the appearance of a country attorney – an attractive *bouleversement* when one remembers what Robert Cecil had called Gladstone back in 1861 – in comparison with 'the old Jew', whom he deemed far more formidable. Salisbury was to hold the Foreign Office for less than two years. During that time his master-plan (if anyone had one) of capitalizing on Turkish weakness and Russian compliance by imposing a new Turkish treaty with financial help in return for various reforms died on the desk of the Chancellor of the Exchequer who prosecuted the Gladstonian finance of his youth, whatever the service departments wanted.[75] With the Afghans and Zulus in the headlines, the Foreign Office cut

---

[72] Carnarvon to Northcote, 15 Dec. 1877, Iddesleigh MSS 50022 ff.229–30.

[73] The policy dispute took a personal turn when the prime minister delivered a public rebuke in cabinet. Carnarvon wanted retraction and apology; Beaconsfield demanded submission and apology. It was one of those moments when tired, vain and overworked men become little boys.

[74] Northcote to Derby, 27 Jan. 1878, Derby MSS 16/2/6. Salisbury had had 'Chaos' and 'war': Northcote to Salisbury, 14 Dec. 1877, Salisbury MSS (Northcote, f.123).

[75] See Salisbury to Northcote, 22 Aug. 1878, Iddesleigh MSS 50019 f.106.

no great figure in the later days of the government as economic depression oppressed some rural areas in particular and Gladstone ran rings around the government for the benefit of his bemused Midlothian farmers, retirement all forgotten and the years rolling away. 'Gladstone is amazing!', wailed Beaconsfield. 'I believe he is possessed of a devil, & as the age of miracles is past, I hope the evil spirit will remain where it is.'[76] Party politics had once more become head-to-head, even though its fields of reference now traversed the globe. Salisbury had no part in that and not much of one in reconfiguring the post-Derby Foreign Office, merely 'picking up the china that Derby had broken', as he modestly said.[77]

But one could look deeper into the situation and argue a different case in two senses. Salisbury's accession gave notice that Conservative foreign policy would one day cease to function as a product of party politics and lapse into a technical discipline controlled largely in private by one overarching intellect with the administrative help of a very small number of professional assistants. Disruption overseas, imperial disputes, threats of war would naturally continue to disturb equanimity. As a defining element in party identity, however, these would appear in the record of the 1880s and 1890s as largely *Liberal* problems. By making foreign policy in his study at Hatfield (often keeping it from even the cabinet until he had to secure approval), Salisbury invented his personal mode of splendid isolation. He learned what the 1870s had to teach and made sure that Britain's interests could not be made a plaything of party by abstracting party from its processes, except where a public encouragement or rebuff might serve national purposes. The party also learned from these years of Russians and Turks and what they learned constitutes a second dimension of significance in Salisbury's emergence. He left the 1860s in retirement with no party; he rejoined it in 1874; he became its de facto deputy-leader in 1878. His pre-eminence in the Lords, once Cairns had refused to lead and Richmond had accepted, had become apparent quite early. Indeed Granville, from the Whig benches there, felt some relief when Disraeli accepted his earldom because he would no longer have to face 'so formidable an opponent' as Salisbury.[78] But from 1878 it seemed unlikely that Salisbury's

---

[76] Beaconsfield to Richmond, 2 Jan. 1879, Goodwood MSS 865 w 80.

[77] Cecil, vol. II, pp. 231–2.

[78] Granville to Delane, 9 Feb. 1877, quoted in Marvin Swartz (ed.), *The Politics of British Foreign Policy in the Era of Disraeli and Gladstone* (Basingstoke, 1985), p. 57.

stature within the party could be confined to the Lords. Northcote had had some successes in the Commons and was by no means always the perplexed nonentity that legend would later invent. But his melancholic thoughtfulness led him to see both sides of a question – and many, many more besides. For the young bloods roused by the lacerating voice of Lord Randolph Churchill, who had entered parliament in 1874, he seemed dilatory and without purpose. Salisbury, too, they sometimes disdained in private. Yet they tempered their sarcasm with fear, for behind the perfect manners and stylish cynicism they rightly detected *malice*: a critical constituent of effective party management in an age when the rules of engagement were unspoken.

TOWARDS LEADERSHIP: 1881–1887

None of this made the party Salisbury's when Beaconsfield eventually died in April 1881. Nor did it become clear for some years that Salisbury would establish the mastery he came to practise over his party. In the autumn of 1882 he almost lost the House of Lords.[79] In 1884–5 he faced major difficulty with Churchill. In 1886 his party could have flowed into a fusion with Unionist Whigs. It took a fortnight over Christmas of 1886 and New Year of 1887 to recast his relationship with Conservatism in a form that would become permanent. That is why a narrative of Conservative politics in these years looks very different from a *Salisbury* narrative. From the point of view of the electoral historian, the election of 1885 and the 'hung' parliament that the Irish contingent produced, the minority government that Salisbury ran until January 1886, the disastrous Gladstone government that attempted a Home Rule bill in the spring of 1886 and the election that Salisbury won, though without an overall majority, in July form the critical nodes of argument. For the historian of policy, the coming of Gladstone's declarations in favour of Home Rule for Ireland and the unwillingness of his party to follow him demand great weight in any account. But from Salisbury's vantage point the focus has to be high-political because his was; it turns on the need for resolution of issues relating to party fusion, the need to discard Northcote, the imperative to bring to centre-stage

[79] Above, pp. 116–20.

Balfour and Smith and, above all, the necessity to do something with Churchill, whose trajectory had become his own in negative: the story of a man whose rise required Salisbury's fall. The *dénouement* loses none of its significance through familiarity: county ball at Hatfield just before Christmas 1886; Salisbury sitting on the sofa with the future Queen Mary in the early hours of the morning; in comes the special messenger bearing Churchill's resignation from the Exchequer. All changes and changes utterly.

How implausible it would surely have seemed after the defeat of 1880 that Churchill would ever become Chancellor of the Exchequer at all and most certainly not in a Salisbury or Northcote government. His father, the Duke of Marlborough, had become used to writing letters of apology to leading Conservatives for the excesses of his son since his entry to the Commons. Lord Randolph Churchill was already a name associated with wild instability plus a certain rhetorical brilliance and ungovernable temper. He and his associates in the Tory party soon became better known as the Fourth Party – Churchill, Henry Drummond Wolff, John Gorst to a lesser degree and, far more remotely, Arthur Balfour who acted as a useful conduit to his uncle. The attacks mounted by that group in the lower House concentrated on the Leader there, for since the loss of Beaconsfield an uncomfortable duumvirate of Northcote and Salisbury had emerged through the lack of any convincing alternative. For Northcote the Fourth Party felt nothing so generous as contempt. There was positive, personal hatred. 'I saw the Goat more Goaty than ever,' Drummond Wolff spat in 1881. 'He is a loathsome creature, full of small spite & destitute of virility except in its lowest germ development, a kind of earthworm.'[80] Salisbury came out better, not least because no one could write comments of this kind to his nephew; but the attack on Northcote over the next few years directly impinged on Salisbury's sense of personal honour. He did not agree with the criticisms that Churchill and his friends made so publicly, though his reason for rejecting them turned on a different matter. He felt that his sense of collegiality – 'a tie, not of expediency, but of honour'[81] –

---

[80] Drummond Wolff to Balfour, 17 Nov. 1881, Balfour MSS 49838 f.101. 'All this nonsense at not being "personal"', another sympathiser wrote to Churchill in applause of his speeches, 'requires to be put down. All the harm in the world is done by "persons" & it is persons and not principles or parties that have to be put in the pillory for the warning and encouragement of others': T. Gibson Bowles to Churchill, 4 Dec. 1881, Churchill MSS 9248/1.

[81] Salisbury to Churchill, 28 Aug. 1885, Churchill MSS 9248/5.

made it impossible for him to lean on or repudiate Northcote, while his own constitutional doctrines rendered it inconceivable that the Leader in the House of Lords would try to tell the House of Commons its business. Eventually the Fourth Party discovered its error in pressing Salisbury to do so and transferred its lack of affection to Cross and W. H. Smith, who upset Churchill on class grounds as well as policy matters. Their collective achievement never matched their claims.[82] But Churchill had proved able, through the power of his public language and willingness to confront his own leaders as unpleasantly as he savaged Gladstone, to formulate a challenge not merely to Northcote and Salisbury as leaders but to the entire orientation of the Conservative party. As the coming man burning with radical electricity, he closely resembled Joseph Chamberlain, a personal friend and admirer through whom Churchill threatened to destroy two Old Gangs simultaneously by doing away with 'Conservatives' altogether – he disliked the term and tried never to use it[83] – and invigorating centre-politics with the 'Democratic Tory party which was always Dizzy's dream'[84] – a Tory Democracy which would share more characteristics with Chamberlain's Unauthorized Programme on the Liberal side in 1884–5 than with anything expected from a possible Salisbury leadership.

After his bruising encounter with Tory resistance over the arrears bill in 1882, Salisbury 'led' with a discretion that sometimes seemed the same as inertia. If he thought Northcote 'not generally in favour of over-violent action',[85] he himself treated the three great issues of Ireland, Egypt and the reform bill of 1884 as areas suitable for quiet management rather than histrionics. None of the eschatological remarks of 1867 reappeared in 1884; the franchise extension and redistribution became the fruitful results of deals struck in private with the government. Salisbury's purposes had much to do with cementing Tory strength in a redistribution that would carve up towns in the 50,000 to 150,000 population range into single-member constituencies and seek in the countryside to bring about 'the

---

[82] '. . . we have destroyed the Central Committee [nominated by Salisbury and Northcote]: we have revolutionised party management: and defeated the leaders in their attempt . . . to suppress us': Gorst to Churchill, 27 Jul. 1884, Churchill MSS 9248/4.

[83] Churchill to Smith, 5 Feb. 1886, Hambledon MSS P59/120. He was writing in the context of a possible Salisbury–Hartington fusion and writing to an enemy: so *cum grano salis*.

[84] Gorst to Churchill, 10 Sep. 1882, Churchill MSS 9248/1.

[85] Salisbury to Cairns, 7 Aug. 1882, Cairns MSS 30/51/6/f.167.

adequate representation of the agricultural population'.[86] Egypt
largely looked after itself: Tories simply threw sarcasm over the
bombardment of Alexandria in 1882 and contumely over the neglect
of General Gordon in 1884. Ireland proved intractable as a property
issue, as we saw earlier in this study, but the Liberals seemed no
better at discovering a solution for its difficulties and the land act of
1881 made a good whipping post. Beyond parliamentary requirements, Salisbury reduced quietude to complete silence. Indeed the
party managers, among whom Aretas Akers-Douglas, later Viscount
Chilston, became significant after 1883,[87] suffered considerable
frustration in trying to stimulate Salisbury into speaking at all on the
platform. Partly his reluctance was temperamental and counter-
Gladstonian; but it also reflected an intelligent appreciation of when
to shut up. 'We shall do no good,' he told Balfour: better to say
nothing.[88] In opposition this strategy can work well if the government is making much noise and much mess. Salisbury noted
privately that Churchill's spectacular performances had begun to
turn against property; and that once they did that he would dig his
own hole.[89] He noticed that Chamberlain's famous attack on his
own Whigs for neither toiling nor spinning would divide the Liberals
in the same way. Allowing someone close to the Tory soil like
Richmond, who had joined his mentor Cairns in the attack on
Salisbury in 1882, to direct his splutterings elsewhere brought some
comfort and peace; and Richmond became so upset about Chamberlain in January 1885 that he wrote to Cranbrook about him, when he
ought to have been on his horse, and concentrated on the sheer

---

[86] Northcote to Dilke, 13 Mar. 1885, Dilke MSS 43893 f.23; Salisbury to Dilke, 25 Nov. 1884,
Dilke MSS 43876 ff.23–4. Some Conservatives had worried about single-member
constituencies, though Smith reported less anxiety by January 1885: Smith to Akers-
Douglas, 20 Jan. 1885, Chilston MSS C/25. The second issue continued to worry landlords.
'[B]y professing to add 68 members to what are called "counties"', Hicks Beach had
complained in November, 'it makes a show of fairness to the interests it swamps': Hicks
Beach to Northcote, 21 Nov. 1884, Iddesleigh MSS 50021 ff. 240–1. For exhaustive analysis
of the high-political twists, see Andrew Jones, *1884: The Politics of Reform* (Cambridge, 1972).

[87] Opposition Whip from 1883; at the Treasury from 1886–92. 'No one knew better the
changing mood of the lobby, the exact value of the frondeur, or the extent of an intrigue'
(J. S. Sandars).

[88] Salisbury to Balfour (from France), 22 Sep. 1881, *Salisbury–Balfour Correspondence*, p. 83. He
refused the Dover Conservative Club's invitation in the New Year in similar terms: 'while at
some periods it is prudent to speak, at others it is expedient to be silent . . .', Salisbury to
G. Fielding (copy), 7 Jan. 1882, Christ Church MSS file T. The point is not that he made no
speeches: he plainly made many. But he edited out many more that the machine would have
liked him to deliver.

[89] Salisbury to Northcote, 2 Apr. 1884, Iddesleigh MSS 50020 ff.71–2.

iniquity of it all for three complete sentences: 'Did you ever read such speeches as those made by Chamberlain and Dilke? It seems to me undisguised Communism. I do not understand Gladstone allowing them to remain in the Cabinet. Notwithstanding a great number of foxes I have killed a great many pheasants this year.'[90]

Richmond's alarm had none of its normal eccentricity, for the first three months of 1885 filled Conservatives with a genuine and general depression. News of Gordon's death in Khartoum pointed to one end of the world; black threats from the powers of Europe and the brooding presence of Russia over the Afghan frontier suggested other routes to perdition. Salisbury himself suffered an epigrammatic moment in March which has gone into the history books as evidence of his unshakeable pessimism:

Matters are gloomy – I never saw them gloomier. We have differences amounting to very serious tension with France, Russia & Germany which carries Austria. Add to that Egypt, Ireland, a crushing Budget in prospect, & trade which will not revive. I cannot be thankful enough to those fourteen gentlemen who stand between us & such an inheritance as that. But can the Govt. go on?[91]

Three weeks later the Duke of Northumberland exclaimed 'What a terrible mess we are in!' and the heir to the dukedom of Rutland declared on the same day: 'The state of affairs at home and abroad is perfectly appalling.'[92] So Salisbury seems to have caught a mood. He was prescient about future trouble also. Among his catalogue of evils was the coming budget and that proved the cause of the government's defeat on 8 June when Gladstone's second administration crashed in the House of Commons. Those who did not have to pick up the pieces naturally felt some exhilaration. Salisbury did not feel any. Indeed he went to considerable trouble to avoid having to form a minority government while new electoral registers were prepared to reflect the changes instituted in 1884–5. Drawing on the precedent of May 1832, when attempts to make first Wellington and then the nonentity Charles Manners-Sutton prime minister turned to farce, he hoped to persuade the Queen that it would only bring ignominy for him to take over unless he had assurances from Gladstone about

---

[90] Richmond to Cranbrook, 24 Jan. 1885, Cranbrook MSS T501/257.
[91] Salisbury to Cairns, 3 Mar. 1885, Cairns MSS 30/51/6/ff.170–1.
[92] Northumberland to Maxwell, 23 May 1885, Maxwell MSS 7043 HEM2; Lord John Manners to his brother, 23 May 1885, in Sir Charles Whibley, *Lord John Manners and his Friends* (2 vols., 1925), vol. II, p. 233.

Liberal behaviour that Gladstone could hardly claim to control.
Undoubtedly the monarch's own appeal to him was decisive.
Perhaps he also found his mind cleared to an extent by an old friend
on the other side of the House. The Earl of Selborne had written to
his son a letter which plainly had been passed to Salisbury and
whose logical force must have pushed the leader of the opposition
down the uncongenial road:

I am sorry for what you say about Lord Salisbury's intention to insist on the
pledges, which Mr. Gladstone cannot give . . . [E]ven from Lord S's view of
the situation I think he ought to go on.

Let me suppose him to take office, having done what he could to obtain
the assurances which he thought it his duty to ask for, & not having
obtained them. One of two things must happen. *Either*, without these
assurances, the new Opposition would act reasonably, & throw no
difficulties in the way of the necessary business of Government, *or* they
would do the reverse. In the former case, Lord S. would be, practically, in
the same position, as if he had obtained the assurances he asked for. In the
latter, it is conceivable, that . . . he might . . . be forced to retire. This is far
from certain: there is a great body of reasonable & moderate Liberals in the
House of Commons, whom violence & obstruction would disgust & who
might turn the scale . . . But, supposing it *did* happen, Lord S. & his friends
would be morally strengthened, with all the moderate & patriotic men in
Parliament & in the country, at every step of the struggle . . . [93]

Of course, Salisbury was more concerned about the reaction from
his own party and there the combination of grasping and hungry
Tories looking for a job, which sickened him, and the imponderable
behaviour of Churchill, who would have to be brought in to head off
his resentments as a thwarted genius, left him dismayed and
depressed. Carnarvon, sent to Ireland, had already revealed his
softness to Salisbury and begun a summer of humiliations for the
prime minister.[94] 'Do not let my colleagues be alarmed,' he bleated

---

[93] Selborne to Wolmer, 22 Jun. 1885, second Earl of Selborne MSS 96 ff.121–3. Salisbury
wrote to Wolmer on the following day, claiming that Selborne's letter 'has been one of the
chief causes of my taking the course I have, with much hesitation, taken': *ibid.*, 5 f.1.

[94] He had written from Porto Fino in February to say that he agreed with a recent piece by
Gavan Duffy and that 'our best & almost only hope is to come to some fair & reasonable
arrangement for Home Rule . . . what other alternative or chance is there? . . . a mere
policy of indefinite repression is . . . impossible': Carnarvon to Salisbury, 5 Feb. 1885, 'very
private', Salisbury MSS (Carnarvon, f.505). Hardinge quoted the first part but softened the
second in bland paraphrase: Sir Arthur Hardinge, *The Life of Henry Howard Molyneux Herbert,
Fourth Earl of Carnarvon 1831–1890* (3 vols., 1925), vol. III, pp. 151–2. Salisbury worried that
such things should be put 'on paper' and wrote a holding letter. But why did he then hand
Ireland to Carnarvon when he came to power in the summer? Did he think a dose of
Dublin would change his mind? Did he *intend* the chalice to be poisoned?

to Ashbourne, but he wasted ink on the thought. Churchill, now installed in the India Office which had also been, of course, Salisbury's first ministerial appointment, plied his chief with memoranda of strident tetchiness about impending Russian aggression against Persia and Afghanistan.[95] At the cabinet table Churchill found Cross 'a bigger fool than ever'[96] and picked a fight with anyone who might remotely want one. 'He has been giving me such a dance lately,' Salisbury groaned by mid-August.[97] It did not augur well for the party's direction. Come the election in November, Salisbury struck Carnarvon as the reverse of enthused. 'He looked very ill,' he reported of a conversation on the 20th, '& with little of his old nerve, energy & incisiveness.'[98] All of this means two things. First, 1885 should be seen, from a Tory point of view, as a continuum of perception rather than a period hinging on the June collapse of Gladstone's government. Secondly, Salisbury ran into the crisis of Gladstone's 'conversion' to Home Rule when already very low in spirits and judgement and under bombardment from Churchill. It was the steadier mind of Smith who reminded waverers like Balfour that the revelations required Conservatives to keep their nerve. He wrote to him on Christmas Eve:

> One word. I do not agree that we *must* break up.
> We may be broken up, but it would be treason not to make an effort to give the Country a strong Government.
> An appeal has been made to Hartington [Gladstone's likely successor but a Whig opposed to Home Rule] . . . If he will not take office then we must go on bravely until we are beaten, and with those who beat us will rest the responsibility of preserving or destroying Parliamentary Government in England.[99]

It was going to be the most political Christmas of the last forty years.

The Marquis of Hartington (soon to become eighth Duke of Devonshire) played an important though negative role in Tory party strategy over the next six months. His resistance to Home Rule on what were taken to be principled grounds attracted the admiration of the Queen, who made no secret of it, and caught the imagination

---

[95] Salisbury to Churchill, 19 and 21 Jul. 1886, Churchill MSS 9248/6.
[96] Note by Churchill on Downing St paper, 6 Aug. 1885. Ascription by Ashbourne in A. B. Cooke and A. P. W. Malcolmson (eds.), *The Ashbourne Papers 1869–1913* (Belfast, 1974), p. 103.
[97] Salisbury to Richmond, 17 Aug. 1885, Goodwood MSS 871 d 47.
[98] Memo of conversation, 20 Nov. 1885, Carnarvon MSS 60759 f.77.
[99] Smith to Balfour, 24 Dec. 1885, Balfour MSS 49696 ff.8–9.

of those who hoped that he might bring the Whig families into a fusion with Salisbury's party. Doing so would involve breaking with Joseph Chamberlain, his radical co-resister, but there were grounds for believing that Hartington might contemplate doing so: they were, after all, implausible allies. But much of this had to wait not only for Gladstone's combining with the Irish vote in parliament to dismiss Salisbury's minority administration in January 1886 but also for the Home Rule bill itself and Liberal reactions to it. Tory reactions needed no great foresight to predict what would happen. Salisbury had left office uttering a warning – 'The disease is not in Ireland. The disease is here – in Westminster'[100] – and little more could be done until Gladstone had brought in his bill. George Joachim Goschen on the Liberal benches began immediately to look for an 'understanding' with Akers-Douglas's electoral organization on behalf of those who supported the Union, the beginning of a drift that would bring 'Göschen', as Smith originally disparaged him, into the centre of Tory politics within a year.[101] Most observers waited to see whether the bill would survive the Commons, which it failed to do, despite Gladstone's monumental speech in its favour, 'a supreme effort', as one Tory presciently remarked, 'to make words dominate facts and high-flown phrases settle incurable differences of rival races, religions and interests'.[102] Chamberlain, having resigned minor office on the presentation of the bill, stage-whispered in the corridors that the prime minister was 'a dangerous lunatic' and Hartington 'an old idiot': both perceptions helpful to Tory morale.[103] In the election that followed Gladstone's parliamentary defeat, the Unionist camp legitimately hoped both to win at the polls and to win over the old idiot, perhaps even to make him prime minister at a moment when no one else relished the position.

---

[100] Salisbury in Lords (debate on the address), *Hansard*, 21 Jan. 1886, CCCII, col. 68. The government was beaten on the 26th. 'Out!', noted Cranbrook the following day. 'We have a good report to show, and Salisbury has established a European reputation': Gathorne Hardy, *Memoir*, vol. II, p. 239.

[101] Goschen to Akers-Douglas, 9 Feb. 1886, Chilston MSS C18.

[102] Lord George Hamilton, *Parliamentary Reminiscences and Reflections* (2 vols., 1917–22), vol. II, p. 24. Liberals had not been much kinder. Selborne thought Home Rule would bring 'Rebellion', financial ruin and the patent breaking of a promise made at Midlothian that nothing would be done without consensus. 'A man would have been out of his senses, who thought that all Liberals would agree in setting up an Irish Parliament': Memo by Selborne, 28 Dec. 1885, 1st Earl of Selborne MSS 1869 ff.105–8.

[103] Cranbrook to Ashbourne, 3 Apr. 1886, in Cooke and Malcolmson (eds.), *Ashbourne Papers*, p. 105.

Least of all did Salisbury relish it. His attempts to make Hartington take first place, egged on by imperatives from Windsor, had nothing rhetorical in them: he genuinely preferred to keep out of it, partly to drive wedges deeper in the former Liberal camp, no doubt, but centrally because he found the prospect of another crippling period of responsibility for Irish and European affairs, pecked at constantly by Churchill, dispiriting at best. It was a good moment *not* to be prime minister. For the party managers, of course, any intimations of this position would have struck them as culpable weakness. They had won the election handsomely.[104] And the prospect of a period of majority government, the first since 1874, had its force with the lowly and outcast. 'Beach tells me', Akers-Douglas confided to Smith, 'he found a strong feeling existing at the Carlton & among your old colleagues that Salisbury must again be Prime Minister & I am sure the Party in the Country would not stand Hartington . . .'[105] Happily, Hartington felt the same way. Even Salisbury had come to see that his saviour's 'foolish tone' of late had done nothing to commend him as Tory leader, though he held out some hopes that the next Duke of Devonshire might be persuaded when Salisbury came back from France and his post-election siesta.[106] All he got, in the event, was a promise of 'independent but friendly support'. The Liberal Unionists, as they now called themselves, would keep their own counsel; there would be no fusion. In the festive judgement of 'Black Michael', as Sir Michael Hicks Beach was justifiably known, the Tories would be forced into taking office and would fail to do anything worthwhile with it.[107]

Salisbury set out slowly, tentatively, indecisively. When he met parliament he struck a sympathetic observer as 'mov[ing] as if on ice or among eggs'.[108] His major appointments had been intended to broadcast a sense of balance. Instead they suggested fumbling. He had wanted to extract Lord Lyons from the Paris Embassy for the Foreign Office; but this safe pair of hands belonged to a man of nearly seventy and he had the good sense to refuse.[109] So Salisbury turned to his senior adjutant, Sir Stafford Northcote (now Earl of

---

[104] Conservatives 316; Liberal Unionists 79; Liberals 190; Irish Nationalists 85.
[105] Akers-Douglas to Smith, ?17 Jul. 1886 (MS blotted), Hambledon MSS P59/156.
[106] Salisbury to Alfred Austin, 12 and ?19 Jul. 1886, Austin MSS.
[107] Hicks Beach to Salisbury (transcript), 15 Jul. 1886, St Aldwyn MSS PCC/31/unfol.
[108] Cranbrook diary, 19 Aug. 1886, Gathorne Hardy, *Memoir*, vol. II, p. 260.
[109] Lord Redesdale, *Memories* (2 vols., 1915), vol. I, p. 159.

Iddesleigh) and made him foreign secretary, while boxing the
compass in appointing Lord Randolph Churchill to the Exchequer.
He quickly regretted both decisions and so did many in his party.
Richmond, who had indicated no wish to serve and then taken
umbrage when not asked, haughtily remarked that the foreign
minister ought at least to be able to speak French and have 'a certain
amount of back bone'. Churchill, meanwhile, struck the Liberal
Unionist intellectual Goldwin Smith as 'like a low newspaper
reporter' whose appointment to high office was 'dangerous, disgrace-
ful and an ominous proof of the weakness of Lord Salisbury'.[110]
Within a month Churchill was leading Salisbury the dance of the
previous November. Every item of evidence suggests that he could
not help it: the illness that would kill him had plainly taken hold and
affected his sense of proportion and reality. Faced by the heavy
demands of the Exchequer, his highly-strung personality began to
snap almost at once. Salisbury's reports to Cranbrook in September
tell a tale of impending collapse.[111] The prime minister took a
personal role, meanwhile, in the crisis of Alexander's deposition from
the Bulgarian throne and fended off endless rantings from the
Queen. Yet in carrying so much he could not also carry party
colleagues. On the backbenches there were few worries since
Gladstone had given his own party more trouble than had Salisbury
the Conservative party '[T]he G.O.M. ha[d] succeeded in utterly
smashing up the Liberal Party for the present!' and that seemed
good enough.[112] Close colleagues held a different view. Salisbury
simply did not *lead* enough.[113] When Smith went to see him about
disagreements in cabinet over the details of Poor Law reform, he
came away shocked:

I went to see Salisbury today and found him as I thought very low indeed
. . . But behind all I could see there was a great depression which he said in
a joking way partook of the weather (we have the vilest fog I ever

---

[110] Richmond to Cranbrook, 2 Aug. 1886, Cranbrook MSS T501/257; Goldwin Smith to
Selborne, 31 Aug. 1886, 1st Earl of Selborne MSS 1869 f.209.

[111] 'I am sorry to say that Randolph who has much more to do – & is exciteable [*sic*] besides –
shows signs of ?giving out. Yesterday he had to go to bed with a feverish attack' (2 Sep.
1886). 'He has been overworked & knocked up – and sees things *en noir*' (5 Sep. 1886):
Cranbrook MSS T501/263. The Queen 'expressed much anxiety at some of the sayings of
RC' during the following month: Cranbrook to Salisbury, 29 Nov. 1886, Salisbury MSS
(Cranbrook, f.331).

[112] Walter Long to Maxwell, 3 Nov. 1886, Maxwell MSS 7043 HEM2. Maxwell sat for
Wigtownshire, Long for Devizes.

[113] Cranbrook diary, 23 Nov. 1886, in Gathorne Hardy, *Memoir*, vol. II, p. 263.

remember) and a sense that the most important member of the Cabinet was at issue with himself and the other members of the Cabinet on many if not on most questions.

The upshot is that there will be no meeting of the Cabinet for the present.[114]

Avoiding cabinets would become a habit, but out of a wish to act on his own rather than from a fear of the bullying that Churchill administered. Salisbury had brought Balfour into the cabinet in November and that offered one element of protection, albeit junior. But the prime minister's physical condition continued poor and there is no evidence that he had a solution to the difficulties with Northcote and Churchill before the latter picked his famous and last fight. Ostensibly the chancellor refused to countenance Smith's naval estimates and then refused to budge from the refusal. In fact, Smith's view – that the estimates controversy came at the end of a long series of provocations intended to wear down Salisbury – remains hard to gainsay. Churchill's loathing for Smith probably had more to do with it than the chancellor's zeal for retrenchment, coupled with an irrational drive to bring matters to a crux between himself and the prime minister. 'It was really Salisbury or Churchill,' Smith said on reflection, 'and if S. had gone, none of us could have remained . . .'[115] Churchill's excuse for his mistake in resigning – his assumption that he could not be replaced – invests an irrational act with strategy. The file that Salisbury had amassed on his chancellor's impending collapse persuaded him towards the more plausible view that Churchill's nerves were shot and that his judgement had gone. Whatever the reason, Churchill's departure was a godsend and this time Salisbury neither dithered nor weakened. Within a fortnight he had brought party colleagues into positions he wanted and used the need to accommodate other people's opinions as cover for his own objectives.

Certainly he did not mean to crush Iddesleigh by taking him out of the Foreign Office. He blamed Goschen (his Liberal Unionist brainwave for the Exchequer) who had insisted on the change – part, perhaps, of his Liberal 'prudery'.[116] Iddesleigh remained high-minded, though the family were very bitter and Devon society rang

---

[114] Smith to Cranbrook, 24 Nov. 1886, Cranbrook MSS T501/260.
[115] Smith to Akers-Douglas, 24 Dec. 1886, Chilston MSS C/25.
[116] Salisbury to the Queen, 27 Jan. 1887: 'the difficulty is in satisfying his scruples – one might almost say his prudery – about his Liberal character': RA VIC/A65/33.

with rumour of betrayal; but he saw clearly enough that Salisbury was registering 'his dissatisfaction with my administration of the F.O.'[117] Taking the Foreign Office himself, as well as the premiership, was a bold move but one that he plainly wanted (despite public language that a chain of necessary shuffles made it unavoidable) in order to insulate policy from his party and parliament. His other masterstroke, apart from inserting Goschen, lay in making W. H. Smith leader of the Commons, for Smith was a strong Conservative with a good mind, excellent administrative qualities and much energy until his heart condition caught up with him in 1891. The signing-up of Goschen sent helpful signals both to Hartington, who again refused to come in,[118] and to Chamberlain, whose attempts to rejoin the Liberal party were about to end in ignominious exclusion. The major offices of state and the two chambers at Westminister were in capable and trustworthy hands. In a very real sense the years of Salisbury's domination of the Conservative party began in January 1887.

MANAGEMENT: 1887–1898

In party matters, as opposed to policy questions, Salisbury managed from afar, unless an issue had serious strategic importance such as whether the Liberal Unionists should be brought under the Conservative wing. He managed foreign policy himself – to a degree inconceivable a hundred years later – and he took a hand in resisting domestic proposals that promised more democracy (no way to run an empire, as he said) or seemed ill thought-through. He kept in close touch with senior Conservatives in the cabinet; he found himself in closer touch than he could have predicted with Hartington

---

[117] Iddesleigh to Smith (copy), 10 Jan. 1887, Iddesleigh MSS 50021 f.61. The bitterness at The Pynes became so much greater when Iddesleigh collapsed and died in the ante-room to Salisbury's office in Downing Street. It was the first time Salisbury had ever seen a dead body. He was never forgiven the bluntness of his treatment of the former co-leader. The previous correspondence makes it quite clear, all the same, that Salisbury acted under the genuine impression, with which Iddesleigh had explicitly presented him, that the latter would gladly stand down if any difficulty in reforming the ministry should arise. He may not have meant it – he plainly did not – but he *wrote* it and Salisbury marked the passage with pencil (either at the time or in self-extenuation afterwards). Northcote had played the same card during the negotiations to form a new government in June 1885 and Salisbury had immediately begged him not to stay out. Doubtless Iddesleigh expected a repetition.

[118] Salisbury did his best on Christmas Eve to press Hartington towards 'junction of any kind' . . . [I]nterests very much larger than those of any one party in the State are at issue': Salisbury to Hartington, 24 Dec. 1886, Devonshire MSS 340/2070.

and Chamberlain. He allowed Akers-Douglas and his colleagues to help plan his public diary for speeches and receptions. Georgina Salisbury continued to run the domestic calendar. If he allowed his name to be used in association with constituency activities such as those run after 1883 by the Primrose League, 'something of the combined character of a music hall, a harvest supper and women's institute', as their historian describes them,[119] he did so with considerable repugnance and he maintained his uninterest in how 'the party' felt about a problem unless Smith or Akers-Douglas taught him otherwise, when he would reassure himself and the Queen that the party organizers had the situation under control.[120]

Largely it was a matter of how to expend the limited energy available. Disraeli had solved the problem by spending little time on policy, which he left to subordinates, and devoting much of his time to what nowadays might be called man-management. Salisbury thought this perspective short-sighted and he reversed it, spending most of his day working on the details of legislation or diplomacy, coping with the Queen when and how best he could, and with the party hardly at all. Because time and energy were at a premium when Salisbury ran two Departments of State, moreover, it should not be forgotten that, like Gladstone, he stood the pressure only for the early years of his two major ministries. Over the Christmas of 1890 he went down with an influenza virus whose effects he still felt the following spring and from which he claimed his legs never recovered: observers noticed the slower pace. Three years into the 1895 government, when he was sixty-eight, he suffered the breakdown that marked the end of his primacy, for all his continuing in office at the Queen's insistence. These obvious constraints need integrating into any sketch of Salisbury's activities.

Keeping out of war with France and restraining the ambitions of the Portuguese occupied much of Salisbury's time in the first majoritarian ministry of 1886–92. But these did not become party concerns. Russia did to the extent that Churchill became obsessed by it, but the questions raised by Russia after Penjdeh did not become so spiky as they had appeared in the 1870s, not least because Britain's

---

[119] Martin Pugh, *The Tories and the People 1880–1935* (Oxford, 1985), p. 29.
[120] E.g. Salisbury to the Queen, 18 Oct. 1889: '[E]very effort at preparation [for elections] is made by the Central Conservative Office. But we have been unlucky. It was impossible to foresee that one gentleman would break his neck by tumbling off his horse . . . or that another would suddenly cut his throat': RA VIC/A67/93.

interests in south-eastern Europe had lessened and Russia's had turned eastwards.[121] Oddly, Russia mattered more in a party sense than it did to framers of policy since it had become so draped in the tapestries of status. When relations cooled in 1896 over a new bout of Turkish atrocities in Armenia, Salisbury quickly saw that the effect of a confrontation with Russia would raise all the party ghosts of the 1860s and 1870s, those 'critical phases of opinion on foreign policy'; and he did not want to go down a road whose electoral consequences seemed unpredictable.[122] Germany dominated the European agenda in Bismarck's last years of power before 1890. It did not dominate Salisbury's in the sense that he knew what he did not want from Germany. Like the next generation of Chamberlains, but not the present one, Salisbury cleaved to a French sympathy before a German and felt instinctively that a German alliance would take the country down a wrong turning. Besides, the Home Rule controversy of 1886 had castrated British government in its dealing with all Great Powers, he thought, and made policy less a matter of action than response – the sin of which he had once accused Beaconsfield. 'The prospect is very gloomy abroad,' he counselled the Queen, 'but England cannot brighten it. Torn in two by a controversy which almost threatens her existence, she cannot in the present state of public opinion interfere with any decisive action abroad. We have absolutely no power to restrain either France or Germany . . .'[123] These early days of real leadership thus bifurcated between a privately conducted diplomatic programme and a public excoriation of Gladstone for having gone mad and brought the country to the edge of dissolution.

An anxiety that Gladstone was now out of his mind preoccupied all Unionist society as a real possibility. How terrifying that he seemed 'prepared to *see*, as well as *call*, black white & white black, and to sacrifice *everything* to his own political objects'.[124] How absurd that he seemed to believe all his opponents evil. His personal relationship with Salisbury went sharply downhill. Gladstone did not think much of the prime minister's constant allegations and con-

---

[121] 'We do not desire to establish any special influence of our own,' Salisbury told the peers at the opening of the 1887 session; 'we should have no use to make of it if we possessed it.' But Russian influence 'must not be expanded into dominion': *Hansard*, 27 Jan. 1887, cccx, col. 37.

[122] Salisbury to Austin, 17 Aug. 1896, Austin MSS.

[123] Salisbury to the Queen, 24 Jan. 1887, in Cecil, vol. IV, p. 15.

[124] Selborne to Wolmer, 11 Apr. 1887, second Earl of Selborne MSS 97 ff.5–6.

fessed in private that Lord Salisbury had 'behaved very ill to him'.[125] His adversary certainly had lost any sentiment he had ever had; the kindnesses shown in refusing to attack Gladstone when the latter heard the news of Lord Frederick Cavendish's murder in Phoenix Park, Dublin, in 1882 belonged to a better age governed by gentlemen. Gladstone had not merely 'behaved ill': he had, in the universe inhabited by Salisbury and his circle, betrayed the trust of government, just as Peel on their own side had betrayed it in 1846. Fascinatingly, Gladstone's mind went back to the same year as he decided that Salisbury would never have the stomach for a fight to the death over Ireland. Lord George Bentinck would have done so, possibly, but not he.[126] It was a curious eruption of Peel and the corn laws in a world beyond both. The same unwillingness or inability to face the real world led Gladstone to feel during his last government that the opposition had made fools of themselves in obstructing Home Rule – a strategy he thought 'suicidal' now that the country had become converted to his ideas and the parties divided, as Sidgwick put it, 'on Union-Disunion lines till further orders from destiny'.[127] Once he had retired and died, Gladstone receded in Salisbury's demonology. By the time of Salisbury's own departure from politics in 1902, Gladstone had become in memory nothing more disturbing than 'that marvellous mixture of talent and blind optimism'.[128] But in the late 1880s and through the first half of the next decade the loathing was real enough.

Both Hartington, now Duke of Devonshire, and Joseph Chamberlain were to outlive Salisbury and both played a role in his sense of where the Conservative party ought to go. The first supplied little difficulty: his class, his acres and the great palace at Chatsworth might have made him a Tory in any case had the creeper of cousinhood not entangled him. He played his game cleverly when Salisbury made overtures, refusing involvement for many years and sitting lightly when he did join the Conservative cabinet in 1895. Never persuaded that politics ought to feel more urgent than his stable or the Duchess of Manchester, Devonshire remained as ungovernable among Salisbury's colleagues as he had among

---

[125] Conversation with Rendel in Jan. 1889: see *The Private Papers of Lord Rendel*, p. 67.
[126] *Ibid.*, p. 94.
[127] Gladstone diary, 8 May 1893, in M. R. D. Foot and Colin Matthew (eds.), *The Gladstone Diaries* (14 vols., Oxford, 1968–94), vol. XIII, p. 235.
[128] Salisbury to Cross, 23 Jul. 1902, Cross MSS 51264 ff.133–4.

Gladstone's and the only surprise about his resignation in 1903 is that it took so long to come about. The Tories got nowhere with Rosebery (the other senior Whig prospect for conversion), despite his dislike of Home Rule and who, in a sense, might have done more for them as a potentate with the common touch. 'I wish we had him on our side', Blackwood, the Edinburgh Tory publisher said in 1890, 'with all his *superficial* talk, as the *masses* believe in him somehow, as they do in Gladstone's verbiage.'[129] But Rosebery could not see himself in a Conservative government after 1895, less because it contained Salisbury or Devonshire, perhaps, than because it would mean working with Chamberlain.

The former radical's decision to place his future in Conservative hands by accepting the Colonial Office from Salisbury in 1895 presents a well-known narrative told from Chamberlain's side.[130] Seen from Salisbury's it looks even stranger. Why an established Conservative Anglican aristocrat should want to bring into this government an (at best) Unitarian screw-salesman from Birmingham with a record of radical destructiveness does not seem obvious. Before 1885 Salisbury had watched his career with a sort of repelled curiosity. He had seen him as a self-promoting gambler: thin on ideas, thin on beliefs, thick with Churchill. So when Chamberlain made his stand on 'principle' in 1886 and resigned from Gladstone's government when the Home Rule bill came on, his gesture did nothing to raise his stakes on the Tory red benches. Salisbury retained his opinion that 'the personal element' played too great a role in Chamberlain's behaviour for him ever to succeed. 'He w[ould] never make a strong leader. He ha[d] not yet persuaded himself that he ha[d] any convictions.'[131] Once Chamberlain had cut his ties with the Gladstonians in 1887, however, the tone began to change – sufficiently for Salisbury to offer Chamberlain the chance, with the Queen's blessing, of a special mission to sort out a fisheries dispute with the French in Newfoundland. He also made an effort to avoid upsetting Chamberlain's Liberal Unionist allies in parliament.[132] By the end of the following year, Lytton – now ambassador

---

[129] Blackwood to Maxwell, 9 Jun. 1890, Maxwell MSS 7043 HEM3.
[130] For versions of Chamberlain's trajectory after 1887, see Richard Jay, *Joseph Chamberlain: A Political Life* (Oxford, 1981) and Peter Marsh, *Joseph Chamberlain: Entrepreneur in Politics* (New Haven, CT, 1994).
[131] Salisbury to Balfour, 29 Mar. 1886, *Salisbury–Balfour Correspondence*, p. 138.
[132] In March 1887, for example, he commended Cadogan for having introduced an Irish land bill (the one that so offended Lord Waterford) without, as Salisbury believed, 'frightening

in Paris – was informing Salisbury of the impression Chamberlain had made with his new wife when they called for lunch at the embassy:

He appeared to be very earnest in his loyalty to the existing unionist party, not distinguishing between the Conservative and Liberal wings of it – spoke of you as 'our Leader', and, I am bound to say, in terms of apparently cordial admiration & respect – of Goschen, with reserve & politely and no approval, of G. Balfour with unbounded praise, of J. Morley, Trevelyan & his former political friends with great bitterness & contempt; I think he is obviously reckoning on the leadership of a reconstructed Radical party at some period, which he deems still remote, after Gladstone shall have been removed to another world & Hartington to another House.[133]

If this were Chamberlain's vision then prosecuting it would ruin all the good he had achieved through networking over lunch. In the spring of 1895, when Gladstone had truly gone and Rosebery looked as if he would be departing shortly, Salisbury had grave doubts over any rapprochement with Chamberlain despite their developing regard. It did not turn on class: Salisbury had learned to loosen over that, unlike Gladstone, not least by applauding the success of men like Cross and Smith. And it is not as though Chamberlain came to the table with hands reeking of muck or brass; he had become an accepted part of the Westminster scene over the past two decades and could converse directly and energetically in a way that Salisbury found attractive.[134] He liked people with money so long as they were not vulgar. No: *policy* proved the problem, compounded by Chamberlain's rejection of Goschen.[135] Chamberlain's attempt simultaneously to proclaim himself an ardent imperialist with Tory qualifications and a devoted radical with advanced views on church and land, simply left too many Conservatives suspicious. Salisbury almost felt sorry for him when the Tory press sank in its teeth:

the landlords' yet 'satisfy[ing] Mr. Chamberlain and his friends . . .': Salisbury to the Queen, 31 Mar. 1887, RA VIC/A65/68.

[133] Lytton to Salisbury, 5 Dec. 1888, Lytton MSS D/EK 032.

[134] Balfour did not, somehow. Not quite a social thing – Chamberlain knew which fork to pick up – but Balfour probably found too little cultural content in one who thought too much about politics. '[W]e all love[d] him', of course; but 'Joe . . . does not absolutely and completely mix, does not form a chemical combination with us. Why? I cannot tell . . .': Balfour to Lady Elcho, 15 Mar. 1892, Balfour MSS SRO GD433/2/68. Balfour was failing to regret that lumbago would keep Chamberlain from attending a dinner to meet the Salisburys, Londonderrys, Grosvenors and Rayleighs – a prospect to give lumbago to the most accomplished *haut bourgeois*.

[135] Salisbury to the Queen, 29 Mar. 1889, RA VIC/A67/48, reporting an opinion he had got from Herbert Bismarck, who had got it from Dilke.

Many thanks for your most interesting account of Chamberlain's emotions. I sincerely pity him – if that is not too big a word to use – for he has got himself into a peck of troubles. That unlucky letter on the Welsh Church – & his speaking in favour of the death duties last year – were proceedings better suited to the innocence of the dove than the wisdom of the serpent. If he wishes for a following – which is purely a question of taste – he has no choice now except to put as far into the shadow as he honestly can his anti-Church and anti-land opinions. I think he has got himself into trouble largely from a very common defect of earnest men – he cannot believe in earnestness on the other side. He does not really believe in a convinced Churchman, or a squire who retains his opinions honestly: & he does not – or rather did not – realise that they would be impervious to his powers of persuasion.[136]

Perhaps the change of tense marked a change of heart. Once he had become a member of Salisbury's government in 1895, Chamberlain threw himself into imperial schemes with his innate energy and his congenital lack of judgement, culminating in his complicity in Jameson's unauthorized and farcical activities in the Transvaal in December. Salisbury seems to have felt a genuine affection for his minister in these years and the respect was returned. It is certainly not without significance that Chamberlain never revolted against Salisbury's leadership. He waited for the easier target of Arthur Balfour after 1902.

For all that, Salisbury worried about the politics of fusion and understood its implications for language inside the Conservative party – particularly when a general election loomed, as in 1891–2. He had said from the start that 'the path of a man who attempts coalition is beset with pitfalls';[137] and nothing in the experience of the years since 1886 had undermined that opinion. He also understood the fragilities of Conservative politics rather better than many of its historians. What looks like an insuperable dominance between 1886 and 1906 in the perspective of the late twentieth century did not feel so at the time. Indeed, all the lessons of Salisbury's generation insisted that Liberalism had a powerful undertow within the British electorate. So when a former radical and current Liberal Unionist, Jesse Collings, announced in a strategic circular, 'we are sure of the

---

[136] Salisbury to Wolmer, 13 Apr. 1895, second Earl of Selborne MSS 5 f.21. Writing to Akers-Douglas on 16 April, Salisbury used a party tone rather than a familial one (Wolmer was his son-in-law): 'To sit upon the fence for nine years is an unprecedented achievement: but he can hardly complain because we will not hold his legs to prevent him tumbling upon either side': Chilston MSS C/18.

[137] Salisbury to Smith, 23 Jan. 1887, Hambledon MSS PS 12/27.

Conservative vote', Salisbury pounced on the confidence at once. 'There is just as much susceptibility on our side as on the other,' he wrote in a memorandum, 'and great tact and circumspection in both wings will be necessary in order to secure Liberal votes without losing Conservative votes.'[138] There was the rural vote, for example, which could well collapse in view of economic depression, disappearing rents and trifling with tithe. (The self-appointed county guru, Henry Chaplin, reassured colleagues that the Tory voters in the countryside 'are naturally better disposed to us than they are to Schnadhorst' and would rally round if someone showed a shred of sympathy for their plight.[139]) There was the urban villa-owner whose support Salisbury self-consciously sought. How would such a person react to a party that moved in the direction of Chamberlain and his politics of class envy? The thought oppressed the Conservative leader when he came to draft his programme for the election. '[T]hough we may use phrases which will please Joe – we must in doing so alarm many people who have always been with us. I fear these social questions are destined to break up our party – but why incur the danger before the necessity has arrived: & while the party may still be useful to avert Home Rule[?]'[140] Everybody shared some of this anxiety. No one could have expressed it with the same depth of realism or matched its majestic pessimism of tone.

The cause led the message and the institution had to fit in wherever it could. Probably the main use of the Conservative party to Salisbury was as an instrument for coercing loyalty. Here he differed sharply from Peel, who also saw his party as a weak and broken thing but who turned on it with a special kind of sourness. Salisbury accepted brokenness: it was part of the human predicament. He accepted the broken people with whom he had to deal. From all those involved in Conservative activism he wanted nothing more than loyalty which he repaid with a loyalty of his own. The demand was for 'something more necessary than ability – & that is the general confidence that the party can rely on you to stand by

---

[138] Memo by Salisbury, 29 Jun. 1891, Christ Church MSS file E (Palmer).

[139] 'I am not of the opinion that it is too late': Chaplin to Balfour, 25 Dec. 1891, Balfour MSS 49772 ff.73–4. Francis Schnadhorst was a leading Liberal organizer and secretary of the National Liberal Federation.

[140] Salisbury to Balfour, 26 Jul. 1892, *Salisbury–Balfour Correspondence*, p. 430. This recurrent motif in the private Conservative correspondence, that 'the repeal of the Union' was still at stake after Gladstone's first bill had failed, argues a pervasive and genuine concern. See, for example, Smith to Salisbury, 27 Jun. 1890, Salisbury MSS (Smith, f.390).

them at a pinch'.[141] That is why Gorst would not do, for all his noise about being clever and irreplaceable. If the party system were 'in a rickety condition', or could be made out to be so, colleagues had to realize that they could not resign now, lest it became 'difficult to see the Queen's Government carried on at all'.[142] That is why Hicks Beach had to stay in 1899. The very party that Salisbury privately derided and often caricatured became a public icon before which others were made to pay their respects. It was one of Salisbury's many dialects and one of his more effective. He managed his party as he managed his correspondence, his friends, his peers, his cabinet, his administrators and his public – with words. And his ability to do so compellingly and through a striking range of registers stands as the first of his legacies to a less literate century.

[141] Salisbury to Gorst (copy), 7 Sep. 1891, Christ Church MSS, file E.
[142] Salisbury to Hicks Beach, 18 Oct. 1899, St Aldwyn MSS PCC/69/180–1.

CHAPTER 10

The legacy

LANGUAGES

Salisbury's voice endures in his journalism, his speeches, his letters and an assortment of reported remarks. It is a voice with several registers, however, and they have survived neither in equal volume nor with consistent authenticity. The journalism attracts attention for its accessibility and also for its polemical quality. It gives a picture of Lord Robert Cecil's posturings between 1859 and 1865. Yet he disowned in private every page of it, refused to discuss it and regarded it as the necessary frothing of a man made poor. Earnest students who examine it for the 'ideology' of Conservatism or in a search for the inner man thus begin in the wrong place. The texts present a valuable and unusual resource; but they always demand situation and contextual understanding rather than excerpting as the pronouncements of a Carlylean sage. His public speeches, when he could be made to give them, now appear mostly flat and desultory. Compared with the brilliance of a Randolph Churchill or a Chamberlain, they seem ponderous and awkwardly modulated to their audience. Follow him into the House of Lords, on the other hand, and he becomes transformed into the maestro of the red benches: the register shifts appreciably as the intimacies of the chamber he best understood loosen Salisbury's language and tone. Follow him still further to Hatfield and the leather-topped desk, and his voice eases still further in his favourite medium, the private letter to a friend or colleague in which he can play with expression and deploy not only the humour, but also the *charm*, which other registers sometimes concealed. He was not Baldwin's tutor, assuredly, though he must have come across his father, who was a backbench MP in the 1890s. All the same, he often feels like one making a model for those among his successors who could learn how to rule by cultivating a variety of dialects.

For the private in Salisbury one has to go not only to the correspondence but to certain restricted segments of it. He knew how to make a personal letter convey nothing beyond calculated rhetoric, dipping his pen in semolina to smudge out any opinions:

Dear Lord Randolph,

I am very much obliged to you for sending me the statutes of the Primrose Tory League. Its objects are most excellent. I quite agree with you as to the supreme importance under present circumstances of volunteer effort at and between elections. Any undertaking which results in the supply of this want will be of great service to the party in that respect.

Yours very sincerely,
Salisbury[1]

This little exercise in *politique* was not 'very' sincere, but it certainly deserves Drummond Wolff's description as judicious. It no more represents Salisbury's opinion of the Primrose League than his *Quarterly* articles had revealed his inner feelings about policy. Sometimes the performance becomes toe-curling, especially when the 'lower' races have to be kept sweet.

My honoured Friend,

I have received with great satisfaction the bag of sugared Tilli seeds which you have forwarded to me in token of your friendship and regard. I pray you to accept the assurance of reciprocal sentiments of esteem on my part. Hoping that your Highness may enjoy prosperity & a long life

Believe me,
Your sincere friend,
. . .[2]

So a certain discrimination within the correspondence becomes necessary. Read sensitively, though, the letters can breathe conviction when Salisbury has settled in his opinion about a matter and when he writes to someone he trusts. On occasion they define policy with rapier precision, especially in disposing of the Great Powers or when he was controlling hotheads in India. They did not have to be set-piece arguments filling side after side of Hatfield stationery. They might take the form of a paragraph's demolition with the characteristic bite and acid, as when the Prime Minister deeply disbelieved in rumours that the French were about to become bellicose again in

---

[1] Salisbury to Churchill, 23 Dec. 1883, Churchill MSS 9248/2.
[2] Salisbury to Maharajah Holkar of Indore (draft), 6 Apr. 1884, Christ Church MSS, file E. It was an imperial *topos* as much as a Salisbury device, of course. The Duke of Devonshire declared himself no less delighted by his own bag of tilli seeds when some arrived from *his* 'sincere friend', the same Maharajah, in 1888: Devonshire MSS 340/2168A.

1901. '[T]hese scare rumours', he told the Admiralty, 'are too foolish to be noticed. The French cannot go to war without obtaining the assent of their Parliament. Can we fancy that assent being obtained, if no kind of cause for war be alleged? What have the French to get by going to war in this piratical fashion? The utmost they could do would be to confiscate a couple of P&O steamers.'[3]

Yet for the most part what strikes the reader of these hundreds of letters is their ease of statement, combined with an atmosphere of authority, as though articulateness brought no pain and responsibility no fear. Salisbury could be pompous, as in the famous remark about cabinet having to wait until Hartington had watched one quadruped run faster than another. Normally he was not. If he used literary gloss, the source would often turn out to be the Bible or Book of Common Prayer, which, like so many of his generation, he plainly knew by heart. His oblique remark to Hicks Beach in 1887 – 'I am afraid your Balaam has not answered your expectations – & has altogether blest Holmes when he was sent down for to curse' – makes less sense to a secular generation than to its recipient who, as Salisbury well understood, read his Bible as regularly as the premier.[4] He had felt no less safe in bombarding the bourgeois home secretary with the Book of Common Prayer after New Street Quarter Sessions had failed to remunerate their Clerk of the Peace. 'They send the rich empty away', which was bad enough; 'but they don't fill the empty with good things'.[5] Neither text implied piety or affectation: the point lay in a gentle humour within the network of common experience that suffused both religious worship and family life and infected composition with the inevitability of the common cold. Without gloss, the notes sent to colleagues could sound both short and sharp. It is revealing to compare, for example, the length of Salisbury's letters to Balfour with Balfour's to Uncle Robert in their published correspondence.[6] But there would usually be a twist of lemon or at least a sense that the writer enjoyed the act of writing. When he regretted to Carnarvon the leaking of an appointment by the person appointed, he smiled over the thought that 'when a man

---

[3] Salisbury to Selborne, 18 Jun. 1901, second Earl of Selborne MSS 26 ff.124–5.

[4] Salisbury to Beach, 25 Jan. 1887, St Aldwyn MSS PCC/69/58. Cf. Numbers 22:12.

[5] Salisbury to Cross, 12 Oct. 1874, Cross MSS 51263 f.5. He had in mind the Magnificat from the Book of Common Prayer: 'He hath filled the hungry with good things/And the rich he hath sent empty away' (cf. Luke 1: 53).

[6] See *Salisbury–Balfour Correspondence*. Except for statements about policy written to ministers, he probably wrote most at length for the Queen.

goes about asking what the climate is like & what the expenses are – the secret is pretty sure to leak out', rather than merely reporting the fact through pursed lips.[7] Likewise when a respectable bishopric (Salisbury) was refused 'in terms which would be unnecessarily strong if he had been asked to go to Sierra Leone',[8] or when he told a colleague that Ashbourne should be kept away from the Irish land bill of 1896, and the more diplomatic Lansdowne fronted in the second chamber instead. His language gave no hint of the rebuff. Like an inspired captain of cricket telling an unsafe pair of hands that third man represented the acme of defensive positions, Salisbury advised Cadogan that Ashbourne 'w[ould] be more usefully employed in lying in wait for any discontented Ulster peer, & overwhelming him with legal thunder'.[9] It changed no substantive point but the formulation preserved dignity, smoothed feelings and kept the team together. One sees the same strategy when Goschen's secretary left a page out of his long letter to the prime minister in 1895, at which the overworked leader might have been forgiven for curtness in his reply or for not replying at all. This is what actually came back to Goschen:

> I think it a rude thing to send a man's letter back to him. But through some secretarial mistake your note has arrived in a condition from which only the Higher Criticism of Germany could extract a continuous meaning . . . Your fourth page ends with the inchoate question 'Will you let me know your views at once on the "Narcissus" ' & there it breaks off . . . [10]

Courtesies: lubricated by pleasantries and perhaps a dash of bitters. Most of Salisbury's colleagues had supplies of one of these ingredients but none – not even Disraeli – could emulate the tone and effect of one of their leader's better cocktails.

The same cannot be said of his performances on the platform. He lacked Disraeli's skills in delivery: the gestures, the pauses, the carefully timed sniff for which *cognoscenti* waited. Salisbury's addresses raised cheers at predictable points and he could work in a certain amount of heavy-handed humour. Distance remained, all the same. Someone once said that when Lloyd George spoke on the platform he lurked simultaneously among the audience, testing response and looking for advantage. The third Marquis of Salisbury stayed where

---

[7] Salisbury to Carnarvon, 11 Dec. 1875, Carnarvon MSS 60758 f.155.
[8] Salisbury to the Queen, 3 Aug. 1885, RA VIC/D13/16.
[9] Salisbury to Cadogan, 20 Feb. 1896, Cadogan MSS CAD/837.
[10] Salisbury to Goschen, 19 Dec. 1895, Christ Church MSS, no file.

he was. At no point did he become other than the third Marquis and it showed in the content and form of his public utterances. He could be pedestrian enough even for the Duke of Richmond – 'Salisburys [*sic*] was a good speech at Bournemouth'[11] – and often found it hard to establish a wavelength with the audience he so cordially loathed. Perhaps that was the point. It becomes difficult for a violent anti-democrat to take the people to heart and convey the sense of 'sharing' that the Grand Old Man had a genius for implying in his great, outdoor speeches to vast audiences. Salisbury never really *wanted* to talk to those standing patiently beneath him; and the more that Gladstone turned politics into a language of popular inclusion, the more Salisbury deepened in his resentment.[12] If Gladstone always accepted 'addresses' from loyal activists (the original family home in Scotland, Fasque, has a room virtually wall-papered with them) and responded with one of his short and cheerful lectures, Salisbury refused them on the ground that they 'w[ould] look like plagiarism on the statesman who has invented these wayside orations',[13] as well as out of a native disbelief in cheerfulness. Not that he proved unpopular or unsuccessful: constituencies queued to invite Salisbury to speak and he always accepted a few – a very few – of the invitations pressed on him by party managers. Often, however, his language itself conveys awkwardness in dealing with a mass public. 'Confidence and prosperity', he told a Manchester audience, 'are convertible terms. (Hear, hear.)'[14] One wonders, despite the in-formed cheer, how many Mancunian people understood such for-mulae. There was always 'splendid isolation', of course, following the Disraelian model of rousing people to an awareness of their own greatness. Yet, even when he announced that famous and misleading doctrine at the Guildhall in 1896, his language suited an elevated audience with its reference to the 'emotional and philanthropic spirit with which you, in your splendid isolation, are able to examine all the circumstances' surrounding the recent Turkish atrocities in Armenia.[15] Other references to 'splendid' or 'abundant' isolation occur more naturally in the House of Lords than on the stump and

---

[11] Richmond to Hardy, 3 Dec. 1872, Cranbrook MSS T501/257.
[12] He once told the Queen that 'making political speeches is an aggravation of the labours of Her Majesty's servants which we owe entirely to Mr. Gladstone': Salisbury to the Queen, 16 Dec. 1887, RA VIC/A66/61.
[13] Salisbury to H. Dobinson (draft), 27 Sep. 1884, Christ Church MSS, file T.
[14] Salisbury at Manchester, 16 Apr. 1884, *The Times*, 17 Apr., p. 6a.
[15] Cecil, vol. IV, p. 86.

he went out of his way to retract when writing to one of the less isolated monarchs in Europe.[16]

Best among his various ploys for winning over an audience we may rate the satire on which he had cut his teeth as a young man; and best among the possible victims of satire was Gladstone himself, especially once he had shown his true colours over Home Rule. Unionism gave all Conservatives an easy ride in ways that an advanced social policy and electoral reform had not. They believed in their message and it was one simple enough to sell on any platform. Salisbury particularly liked to rubbish Gladstone's claims to consistency and he became shriller as the architect of Home Rule decided that he had always been in favour of it. Inevitably there appeared a pamphlet in the Gladstonian mode – this time called *Genesis of an Idea* – and Salisbury took it with him to Edinburgh in 1888 in order to dismember it before his audience. It was, he said:

an account of how, 15 years or more ago, Mr. Gladstone had conceived the idea of giving Home Rule to Ireland, and how, during many years, he had gone on nourishing, and nurturing and developing this idea in his own brain. (Laughter.) He had somehow or other entirely omitted to inform any of his colleagues of what was going on (laughter), and during the whole of that time, I have no doubt with the most absolute sincerity, he used language and made eloquent speeches which conveyed, unfortunately, to the world the exact reverse of the truth. (Laughter.) . . . Now, I cannot help thinking, by certain external appearances, that another idea is generating in the recesses of that teeming brain. (Laughter and cheers.)[17]

'That teeming brain' was a favourite expression and a very good one; the speech as a whole reads well and its reception, so far as one can judge, seemed effective. Stripped of its verbal devices, on the other hand, the structure of what Salisbury had to say did not go beyond reaction to the initiatives of others. He found two or three points,

---

[16] For the Lords, see the Queen's Speech in January 1897 when Salisbury depicted British action in Egypt as a moment of ('if I may so express myself') abundant isolation; or his regretting the 'splendid isolation' imparted by Britain's constitutional controls over the executive and military in 1900: *Hansard*, 30 Jan. 1900, LXXVIII, col. 31. 'Lord Salisbury has no reason to think that England runs at present any special danger of being isolated': Salisbury to the Queen, 25 Aug. 1888, RA VIC/A66/129.

[17] Salisbury at Edinburgh, 30 Nov. 1888, *The Times*, 1 Dec., p. 8e. Henry Sidgwick sensed the distinctive register when the Salisburys came to stay at the Sidgwicks' home in Cambridge where the prime minister was to be awarded an honorary degree. Salisbury seemed 'particularly attractive in private life – one recognises the style of his public speeches in his humorous observations; otherwise I should describe his manner as simple, gentle and unassuming': diary, 11 Jun. 1888, in A. and E. M. Sidgwick, *Henry Sidgwick: A Memoir* (1906), pp. 490–1.

said them as clearly as he could, injected humour if some was available and stopped with the job done so far as he conceived it. Neither explicitly nor in the interstices of what he said can one find material to suggest that Salisbury was a *theorist* of the public statement at a time when many among the Churchill/Chamberlain/ Balfour generation had come to see real problems about the direction of modern democratic politics and the changing nature of the messages that had to be argued from the platform. Here Salisbury far more closely resembled Disraeli or the elder Derby than his preoccupied juniors.

Contrast, for example, the fate of Salisbury's nephew. Balfour suffered from a powerful mind and a theoretical temperament: he saw and acted upon the implications of democratic advance with sufficient acuity to worry about them; and he lacked his uncle's *dix-huitième* dismissiveness that might have allowed him simply to reject modernity. Where Salisbury used speeches to achieve an occasional rhetorical objective, the platform plagued Arthur James Balfour and became, eventually, his gibbet in the days of tariff reform. He had told Alfred Austin as early as 1891 of his fears for the future in this respect as he reflected on the problems of persuading the men of Huddersfield towards constitutional argument. 'What I feel most acutely', he wrote, 'in these days of government by the Platform is that the things which most require saying are either too dull, or too difficult, or too unpalatable to be fit matter for popular oratory: – hence we are all apt to lapse into smooth platitudes edged with personalities. This cannot be the proper way to work democratic institutions . . .'[18] But of course he was part of the first generation to try to work them. He recognized, too, the role of language as a medium of some opacity whose very murkiness he himself would put to use so sublimely after 1903 when he had protectionists gnawing one of his legs and 'free fooders' the other. One of the latter predators was his cousin, though Hugh Cecil never wasted time on family loyalty; and in defending his own speeches on tariff reform, Balfour held off the attack by saying that, although he meant what he had said, his speeches only represented what he thought in so far 'as is possible to most of us in working, on the spur of the moment, with such a difficult instrument as language'.[19] Salisbury felt the

---

[18] Balfour to Austin, 12 Dec. 1891, Austin MSS.
[19] Balfour to Hugh Cecil, 16 Jul. 1903, Balfour MSS 49759 f.37.

opposite. Language was so clear a vehicle of meaning that one had to exercise the greatest reticence in using it on a public platform. The most effective way of ending these troubles was to oppose them altogether: speak sparingly, speak in generalities, keep your own counsel.

His strictures applied in part to parliamentary work, at least in the cockpit of the Commons. But Lord Robert Cecil had used language there that he never would have employed beyond Westminster and in doing so had done himself considerable harm. In the absence of his peerage, he might never have achieved a significant career because of his refusal to play the parliamentary game and curb his tongue, whether in speaking to his own side or about the other one. Gibes and flouts and jeers had been there from the start, never so pointedly as in his celebrated apology to Gladstone in 1861, which proved so much worse than his original offence. The context lay in Gladstone's growing confrontation with the House of Lords. Cecil regarded the position adopted by the Chancellor of the Exchequer as a sort of 'legal chicanery' that would lead the two Houses into dangerous conflict with one another, a constitutional development he opposed until it suited him. In the course of his criticism of Gladstone's conduct, Cecil compared him to an attorney, which many in the House thought an offensive simile, and he was called upon to withdraw his remark. He did so in a carefully-judged provocation that brought the House to its feet in an uproar that even the reported speech of *Hansard* cannot suppress.

He had been very much taken to task for an expression he had ventured to use the other night to the effect that the course taken by the Chancellor of the Exchequer was worthy rather of an attorney than a statesman. That expression was thought to be too violent . . . he ought to take the first opportunity either to apologise or to retract. Therefore he felt that he was only doing justice to his own feelings when he avowed that on that occasion he did a great injustice, [Hear, hear!] to the attorneys. They were a very honourable set of men and he was sure – [*Cries of* 'Oh, oh!' *frequently repeated, so that the noble Lord was unable to conclude the sentence.*][20]

This had more to do with the winning of a parliamentary reputation

---

[20] *Hansard*, Customs and Inland Revenue Bill, 13 May 1861, CLXII, col. 2030. The manner left some positive impressions behind as well as negative. When Gladstone sat through one of Disraeli's more oblique performances in 1868, he groaned to Robert Lowe, 'Oh! For one hour of Cranborne!': Lowe to Lady Salisbury, 6 May 1868, in Lady Burghclere (ed.), *A Great Lady's Friendships: Letters to Mary, Marchioness of Salisbury, Countess of Derby, 1862–90* (1933), p.187.

than the assertion of conviction; and he certainly won one. Translated to the Lords, however, this form of attack would not do at all, as Salisbury well knew. He developed a style through the 1870s, behind the lead of Richmond and Beaconsfield, which married some of this aggression to a more expansive humour and a sense of intimacy to which peers would respond irrespective of party. Once he had survived the party disaster of 1882 over the arrears bill, when he manifestly misjudged Conservative feeling in both Houses, he became known for interventions which his opponents claimed to dislike for their 'tone of levity' (Granville), or 'that agreeable flow of irony and sarcasm to which we are all accustomed.' (Rosebery).[21]

Granville coped with Salisbury like a tolerant aunt, perfectly well aware that rings were being run around her by her petulant nephew. Rosebery did better: he was no more afraid of Salisbury than was Churchill of Gladstone in the Commons and he could return Salisbury's sharpness in kind, at least before the insomnia got him. More vulnerable were middle-rankers among the peers, such as Ripon and Kimberley, who could not think fast enough on their feet and found themselves nonplussed by Salisbury's feline mischief. We have a few of these one-liners.

THE MARQUIS OF RIPON: For my part, I give honour to the late Lord Carnarvon and his Colleagues. In 1885 they set us an example. The only difference between them and us is that they have withdrawn their hands from the plough and we have gone forward.

THE MARQUIS OF SALISBURY: What plough?[22]

That time it was Ireland. During the following year Ripon tried to make out that his allotments policy was no more radical than Chamberlain's had been in his Unauthorized Programme.

THE MARQUIS OF RIPON: The provision that an allotment of pasture land may be as much as three acres recalls the fact that a few years ago a right hon. Gentleman proposed to establish universally allotments of three acres and a cow. This extension of the quantity of land which may be allotted under the [local government bill] is a step in the direction of three acres and a cow, and I do not expect, therefore, to hear any objections on that point from my noble Friends opposite.

THE MARQUIS OF SALISBURY: Do you propose to insert the cow?[23]

---

[21] Granville in Lords, *Hansard*, 23 Oct. 1884, CCXCIII, col. 24; Rosebery replying to the Address on the Queen's Speech, *Hansard*, 5 Feb. 1895, XXX, col. 35.

[22] *Hansard*, 6 Sep. 1893, XVII, col. 295.

[23] *Hansard*, 25 Jan. 1894, XX, col. 1574.

Occasionally he would reduce a critic to violence by acting pre-emptively with a piece of studied offence that would turn an opponent into a loose cannon. Here he is winding up Kimberley in 1898:

THE MARQUIS OF SALISBURY: I heard the noble Lord say that he did not believe that any Government would do it, and that always means that you believe the Government has actually done it.

THE EARL OF KIMBERLEY: I quite join issue with that meaning. It is not in the least what I intended.[24]

Whereupon, of course, a speaker would lose his thread and stumble resentfully toward incoherence – as could Salisbury himself during these later years as age and illness told.[25]

In the mature peer of the 1890s one often sees in Salisbury a form of effortless superiority among the members of his House, relying less on these barbed devices than on humour, even goodwill, to make his mark. Hobby-horses still presented an attractive mount from time to time. The violence of his reaction to civil service examinations in his Commons days had not disappeared, for instance, but rather had turned by now into a sardonic playfulness. He toyed thus with Lord Playfair in 1893. 'As this appears to be an occasion for obtaining miscellaneous information,' he observed in the routine, procedural manner that often betokened trouble, ' I wish to ask the noble Lord opposite what he intends to do with the Merchant Shipping Bill? It is a most strange Bill. It was got secretly through the House of Commons – I believe at 12 o'clock at night – and was introduced as secretly into this House. As far as I can gather, it is a measure for subjecting the men engaged in the herring industry at Yarmouth and on the East Coast to a literary examination.'[26] Raising a laugh amid earnestness requires skill and judgement; and Salisbury's sense of the boundary seems far surer in the 1890s, as one might expect, than the 1850s. During the Boer War, when grievous matters depressed the agenda, Salisbury as an aged and ill premier contributed to a

---

[24] *Hansard*, 8 Feb. 1898, LIII, col. 38.

[25] ' . . . in the middle of his speech the other day we saw him furtively fumbling in various pockets: finally he discovered his purse; a great big purse: this he unwound and turned out a lot of rubbish from which he selected a morsel of crumpled paper. This he flattened out and read to the House: it was about the coal trade of Genoa, quite irrelevant': Lord Crawford's diary, 28 Jul. 1897 in John Vincent (ed.), *The Crawford Papers. The Journals of David Lindsay Twenty-seventh Earl of Crawford and Tenth Earl of Balcarres, 1871–1940* (Manchester, 1984), p. 42.

[26] *Hansard*, 8 Aug. 1893, XV, col. 1531.

tricentenary discussion on the erection of a statue to Oliver Cromwell in the palace of Westminister, one carried out, critics alleged, without the consent of parliament and indeed in the teeth of a recommendation from the Commons in 1895 that no such statue should be placed there. What Salisbury dwelled on was not so much the procedural problem as the aesthetics of placing the statue in a so-called 'sunken garden', the kind of expert-speak on the part of the architects that would always appeal to his sense of the ridiculous. 'I am no adorer of Oliver Cromwell,' he said to the peers, 'but if I wished to hand down an unfavourable view of his policy and history, I could devise no more outward and visible sign of it than to put him at the bottom of a hole.'[27] Moments of this kind contributed to recollections of Salisbury as a *presence* in the second chamber: a figure defying replication but leaving his mimics with memories of lunges and ripostes for display at the dining tables and in the drawing rooms of Conservative society.

MEMORIES

Conservative society values memory because its members accord experience a particular weight and pedigree. Joining the past's lessons to present predicaments and reviewing the later event in the light of an earlier forms part of the texture of Tory practice; and throughout this study we have seen Salisbury deploying that prejudice – pointing to an historical precedent, rejecting courses of action that might encourage unwanted ghosts to revive, urging his friends towards objectives that correlated with his image of his country's traditions and his party's past. The past, on the other hand, never functions as an open book waiting to be read: the book itself has to be found among many such books and its text has to be given a reading that makes for comfort and mutuality. When, in our own

---

[27] *Hansard*, 21 Jun. 1900, LXXXIV, col. 594. For the centenary and the statue, see Blair Worden, 'The Victorians and Oliver Cromwell' in Stefan Collini, Richard Whatmore and Brian Young (eds.), *History, Religion and Culture: British Intellectual History 1750–1950* (Cambridge, 2000), pp. 112–35. Salisbury could fuse this second chamber register with his epistolary manner as in this delicious moment of 'humble duty' to Her Majesty: 'Lord Northbrook [Gladstone's First Lord of the Admiralty] then defended himself against the charge of having been nearly a million sterling wrong in his accounts. As far as it was possible to follow the explanation . . . [i]t did not amount to much more than this – that he could not be wrong in his accounts, because he never kept any . . .': Salisbury to the Queen, 14 Jul. 1885, RA VIC/A63/21.

day, the Conservative sympathizer takes up the *Sunday Telegraph* on the day of rest, he or she does not seek some sort of crystalline truth and feels no disappointment when not provided with it. The point lies rather in re-entering a shared world of 'common sense' – one common among Tories – and relishing a sort of vicarious fellowship that turns on an unspoken instinct that many others in all parts of the country are doing the same with the same, common purpose – a sort of secular communion. Historically, too, the construction of an agreeable and usable sense of past experience has formed the 'common sense' of Conservative generations. Salisbury's proved important in that process during the second half of the nineteenth century by creating an environment in which *le parti conservateur* of Lord Liverpool and the Duke of Wellington could be remembered and the pollutions of Peel forgotten. As we narrate nowadays the demise of Tory leaders, the story becomes an evenly paced succession of deaths: Peel, 1850; Disraeli, 1881; Salisbury, 1903; Balfour, 1930. Yet within its own internal account, late-Victorian Conservative history made a past with a different rhythm that suppressed Peel in order to rediscover those who had gone before, leaving his grave to be tended by the Liberals he had encouraged.

Even before his death, of course, Peel's former colleagues had felt the tug of Liberalism and given signs of 'going over' if the time were right. For Sir James Graham – he of the 'Derby dilly' of 1834, which had already made the crossing once in the opposite direction – going Whig amounted to little more than going home. Derby himself adhered gamefully to the Tory cause through disastrous years and left it to his son – the fifteenth Earl – to wander back to the Whigs again when Salisbury and his supporters drove him out of the Foreign Office. It made good material for an historical 'tendency'. Perhaps Peel could have done more about it had he left behind a formidable political dynasty of his own. Like Gladstone he failed to do so, missing the trick of Randolph Churchill and Joseph Chamberlain who between them contrived all unknowingly to stitch up Conservative politics in the 1930s through the warfare of their respective genes and surnames.

The Peels had five boys, four of whom made a public impact, so all should not have been lost. But Robert, the eldest, lounged around Oxford and left without a degree for the diplomatic service, prompting the fastidious G. C. Boase later to complain about his 'want of moral fibre', 'volatile character', 'absence of dignity' and (worse, seemingly) 'an inability to accept a fixed political creed'.[28] Perhaps Sir Leslie Stephen's *Dictionary of National Biography*, generated under the shadow of Irish separatism and Gladstonian betrayal (and in which Boase was writing) took these derelictions more seriously than it might have done in sunnier days. The second son, Frederick, had a political career of sorts and entered the House for Leominster in the year before his father's death. He received an under-secretary-ship from Russell *before* the emergence of the Aberdeen coalition in 1852, whose Peelite members so outraged Tory opinion, and spent a peaceful six years as Palmerston's financial secretary to the Treasury – not a device for winning over Conservative sympathies. William, the third boy, went respectably but irrelevantly into the navy where he rose to some prominence, just as his uncle Jonathan had done in the army before retiring in apoplexy from Derby's cabinet with Cranborne and Carnarvon over the reform proposals of 1867. It was the youngest of Peel's sons, Arthur, who came closest to claiming a political role, though hardly one to cheer his father's former party. Gladstone gave him an under-secretaryship in 1880 – he had long been returned consistently as a Liberal by Warwick and Leamington – but he had to resign through ill-health and accept the post of speaker of the House of Commons through Salisbury's heyday after 1884. What a wry comment: that Peel's son should wind up defending the Lower House against Salisbury's ramparted chamber.

While Arthur busied himself with the Gladstonian present, an Oxford contemporary of his began baptizing the Peelite past and revealing it to have been incipiently Liberal all along. Charles Stuart Parker was not the first to try, for several others had imposed a shape on the history of Peel since 1850. George Henry Francis, the earliest, had backed his horse each way in a biography of 1852, offering first a Tory reading of Peel's character and then a Liberal one before declaring both of them right. 'In acts he violently oscillated; in mind never.' This gave Peel the gift of moderating the passions of whatever party he was in. 'His memory will live', Francis said, 'not in his public acts alone, but by the spirit of moderation, and the love of safe and steady progress, which he instilled into the national character.'[29] Others in the 1850s felt uncomfortable about going even so far. The secretary of the Northern Political Union admitted readily enough

---

[28] *Dictionary of National Biography sub* Peel, Sir Robert, third Baronet.
[29] G. H. Francis, *The Late Sir Robert Peel, Bart: A Critical Biography* (1852), pp. 106–7.

that he found Peel hard to make out but predictably moved toward seeing him as one of the enemy. For 'if Toryism be defined to be merely a general resistance to change, and a preference to [*sic*] government by a few persons, as the least liable to change, such change include[d] Sir Robert Peel, without excluding his high Tory colleagues, Perceval, Eldon, and Liverpool'.[30] Doubtless the Crimean War and its embarrassments reinforced rejections of sclerotic elites of the kind radicals thought Peel had embodied. The perspective of Jellinger Cookson Symons, whose name was perhaps his most impressive feature, differed as that of a barrister whose mind-set differs from that of an agitator. A vicar's son with a Cambridge degree, Symons felt less constipated by oligarchy than did radicals and disliked Peel, not so much because he symbolized an elite as because he gave rise to suspicions that he had not been up to the demands of membership. 'He evoked no new light from the darkness he dispersed, and left us in the weakness of disruption.' 'It will take perhaps another generation', Symons concluded, 'to restore the tone and dignity of statesmanship; and to teach us the truth, that great ministers must be great men.'[31] All the same, he conceded that Peel had convinced his public 'that he was destined to be *the people's minister*'; and Symons played with the fantasy of a Peel who would have gone on, had he lived, to introduce spectacular reforms before expiring in a blaze of *Liberal* glory: 'the latest act of his official life would have been perchance to resign the Premiership to the Right Honourable Richard Cobden, then and long previously a member of his Cabinet'.[32] It was all fiction but fiction is often suggestive.

The mood gained some plausibility when Cobden became signifi-cant enough to refuse the Board of Trade from Palmerston in 1859 and look Gladstone in the eye as an equal. Here was a moment when public memory could catch up with Gladstone's own private recol-lection of his former leader and make Peel into the Peelite that he had always resisted becoming. The first task for the sculptors of memory lay in transcending Peel's apparent incoherence and his failures of management; and the family came to the rescue through Peel's nephew, Sir Lawrence, who had retired from his post as chief

---

[30] T. Doubleday, *The Political Life of the Rt. Hon. Sir Robert Peel, Bart.: An Analytical Biography* (2 vols., 1856), vol. II, p. 485.
[31] J. C. Symons, *Sir Robert Peel as a Type of Statesmanship* (1856), p. 196.
[32] *Ibid.*, p. 189.

justice of Calcutta in 1855 and began to reflect thereafter on his uncle's shade. His message was about forgiveness and taking the long view:

Every man understands that, as there are shadows cast on the brightest day of sunshine, so we must take into account, in every estimate of human character, some little outbreaks of temper, of vanity, of unseemly triumph, some excesses of the spirit of advocacy, some undue tenacity of opinion, or of sway, some occasional lack of courtesy, spots and freckles which will at times disfigure the fairest face which the world can show. We think not of such things as these when the dead lies in his vault, in the old church-yard 'with his face up to heaven', we feel then what a loving spirit stirs in us, and that in our charitable thoughts God is visiting us, we judge then as we would be judged, and can feel how human errors may fade away before mild and pitying though unerring eyes.[33]

He protested too much, possibly, but this deeply felt and moving passage underscored the work still to be done among those confronting living memory – not so much among those for whom Peel had already become sanctified but as a salve for those still smarting over the reverses of 1846, even of 1829: events within recall of a man born with the century. George Barnett Smith recalled neither event: he was born in the year that Peel won his first election and became a national leader. By the time he came to write books about great figures in history during the 1870s and 1880s, Smith drew both on the created 'memory' of Sir Lawrence Peel's generation and his own committed Liberal position to see in his hero someone who self-consciously spoke to a later generation, which would understand his actions better than those who witnessed them. 'Charged by his former friends with consistency and dissimulation,' Smith said of Peel at the beginning of Gladstone's second ministry, 'this distinguished political leader fell back upon posterity for his vindication.'[34] And Gladstone's politics were, one assumes, precisely that vindication. Smith's other biographical subjects in the same period turned out to include Shelley, Gladstone, John Bright and Victor Hugo.

Enter Charles Stuart Parker. He was born in the year of Catholic Emancipation in Liverpool out of which his father, an Ayrshire Scot, traded sugar from the West Indies. (The Gladstonian echoes begin early.) Thomas Chalmers was his godfather. He must have overlapped briefly with Lord Robert Cecil at Eton, but his formative

---

[33] Sir Lawrence Peel, *A Sketch of the Life and Character of Sir Robert Peel* (1860), pp. 302–3.
[34] G. B. Smith, *Sir Robert Peel* (1881), p. 1.

influences emerged at Oxford, both in his own college – University College – through Goldwin Smith and the future Dean Stanley, and elsewhere among friends such as T. H. Green, G. C. Brodrick, G. J. Goschen and, as we have seen, Arthur Peel. Against this neutral texture of acquaintance Parker then began to do Liberal things. He married Edward Cardwell's daughter. He climbed mountains with Willy and Stephen Gladstone. He stopped writing for the *Saturday Review* because he disapproved of its cynicism even before Lord Robert Cecil's ink blackened it. He became Liberal MP for Perthshire – and later Perth City – at Gladstone's instigation. He inherited a considerable amount of money. When, after nearly a quarter of a century in the House of Commons, he retired from politics in 1892, the task into which he threw himself was continuing the biography that Speaker Peel had asked him to write and whose first volume had appeared in the previous year. He completed it through the last, desperate and unavailing struggle of Peel's *soi-disant* pupil, Gladstone, to consolidate Peel's work and confer justice on Ireland. Those three volumes[35] became the Liberal embalming of Peel and the starting-point for historians until the 1920s. Whatever else he had once been, Peel no longer looked like a Tory by the 1890s but appeared an apprentice Liberal confronting heroically his generation's lack of insight and humanity – a visionary seen in contrast to those around him rather than figuring among their accomplices. For the Tories themselves he had frozen into memory as the man who tried to make two and two make five.[36]

All of this made Salisbury's generation into heirs and turned their experience into its own form of legacy. For Disraeli and his contemporaries, a frontier of memory lay across the magical year 1832 with a crucial mile-post in 1846. Gladstone's stupefying longevity confused the picture by making him appear a contemporary of Salisbury's when he had been born only four years after Disraeli and had served in the famous Peel cabinet. Few others had his reach of memory. Certainly no one on the Tory front bench after 1880 could match it. Salisbury knew these dates as historical moments, but nothing burned into his personal experience until 1867. Disraeli, on the other hand, was sixty-two by then and his mind was still fixated

[35] C. S. Parker, *Sir Robert Peel, from his Private Papers* (3 vols., 1899).

[36] 'I can hear you saying that bit about 2 & 2 making 5 acc. to Sir R. Peel': Lavinia Talbot to Balfour, 25 Dec. 1879, Balfour MSS SRO GD433/2/62. Presumably she thought Balfour found such goodwill appealing at Christmas.

on the far-earlier events that had shaped him. When he won his only majority in 1874 his mind went back at once to Peel's only majority. 'We have gained more than Peel did in 1841.'[37] When he stopped during that summer to water his horses between country houses, he realized after a while that the place was a *lieu de mémoire* stimulating recollections beyond the reach of any member of Salisbury's future entourage:

I . . . wandered about for ten minutes. It was not even a street but detached dwellings embowered in gardens and a boulevard of linden. I asked its name and was told it was Hindon. It returned two members to Parliament before the Reform Act of 1832, and in 1830 I was in negotiation to be its member paying 1,000 per annum; and having at that time no other income but a little pocket money from my Father. Bulwer [Lytton] was trying at the same time for St Ives and succeeded. I was so disgusted that I went abroad. Bulwer remained but his first effort at a Parliamentary career was soon cut short by ruthless fate. So we were both dancing on a volcano little dreaming that the old system was so near its extinction. The scene forced one to moralise. I recalled with vividness my bitter pang of disappointment at not representing these Cottages in the House of Commons and then thought of greater Reform Acts than Lord Grey's, and all that had happened since.[38]

Perhaps reminiscence – constructed as much as retrieved – received further stimulus from the appearance that autumn of the first instalment of Greville's memoirs which so upset the court through its depictions of George IV and William IV.[39] In reading Greville's description of Peel, Disraeli could not but recall his own, etched for posterity in his biography of Lord George Bentinck. He certainly produced a flurry of catty remarks about Greville's vanities and misrepresentations.

By the 1890s Disraeli had himself become a reminiscence and the trajectory of Toryism that he had done so much to establish had become a dotted line drawn by others. Those who joined up the dots could not be described as Conservative friends: an important point

[37] Disraeli to Lady Bradford, 12 Feb. 1874, in Marquis of Zetland (ed.), *The Letters of Disraeli to Lady Bradford and Lady Chesterfield* (1929), vol. 1, p. 53.
[38] Disraeli to Lady Bradford, n.d. (Aug. 1874), *ibid.*, p. 135. Why Disraeli thought Bulwer Lytton had been the victim of cruel fate is hard to discover. He did move from St Ives, Huntingdonshire, in the reformed parliament but did so voluntarily and was elected at Lincoln as a progressive protectionist where he remained until he lost the seat in 1847.
[39] Henry Reeve, *The Greville Memoirs: A Journal of the Reigns of King George IV and King William IV* (8 vols., 1874–87). A less expurgated, but more condensed, two-volume edition appeared in the United States in 1927, edited by Philip Whitwell Wilson, but the seminal selection by Lytton Strachey and Roger Fulford, published as a limited edition, did not appear until 1938.

about the framing of a public 'memory' among the educated classes. Spencer Walpole might have seemed an exception, since he had been the elder Derby's home secretary and had written a much-remarked *History of England* from 1815 to 1861. He carefully avoided the Disraelian period and its sequel, though Walpole began composing the text through the Disraelian high-point after the mid-1870s. He completed it while he was governor of the Isle of Man – a Gladstonian appointment with its own message, suggesting that Walpole had attached himself to the Derby dilly in its return to Liberalism. His history instigated a long-running feud with the Herries family when its author alleged that J. C. Herries should never have been given the Exchequer by Lord Goderich in 1827 as 'he had acquired no Parliamentary distinction which justified his promotion'.[40] He then went on, with the zeal of a Liberal convert, to identify Peel's as 'the name of greatest mark'[41] in his period, with only one possible implication for Disraeli who had destroyed him. With friends like this, Disraelian Conservatism wanted no enemies. It was the same with other public diarists and historians. Three who come to mind at once are Justin M'Carthy, whose *History of My Own Times* became a pillar of 'public' history, Peter Clayden who wrote a survey of the Beaconsfield government and Sir Henry Lucy whose parliamentary diary appeared in the press throughout the late nineteenth century and was collected into a number of volumes.[42] One element in their separate biographies brought these men together: they had all worked on the *Daily News*, a significant and increasingly Liberal organ and each brought radical (or in M'Carthy's case Parnellite) sympathy to the task of dismantling the house that Disraeli and Salisbury built.

No one put it back together again in the lifetime of either man. There were editions of speeches but no sustained effort at constructing an historical memory to match that of the Gladstone industry. Neither Disraeli nor Salisbury found himself a Morley to produce the three-volume Life and Times within a few years of the subject's demise; and once Morley had done so in 1903 (the year of

---

[40] Spencer Walpole, *A History of England from 1815* (5 vols., 1878–86), vol. II, p. 461.
[41] *Ibid.*, vol. V, p. 552.
[42] Justin M'Carthy, *A History of My Own Times* (7 vols., 1881–1905). Peter Clayden, *England Under Lord Beaconsfield* (1880); *England Under the Coalition* (1892). Sir Henry Lucy, *A Diary of the Salisbury Parliament, 1886–92* (1892); *A Diary of the Home Rule Parliament, 1892–5* (1896); *A Diary of the Unionist Parliament, 1895–1900* (1901).

Salisbury's death) all public figures had to face measurement against a superhuman model of political correctness and each, inevitably, fell short. Even William Flavelle Monypenny, once an assistant editor of *The Times* with a later Milnerite period in Johannesburg, found the comparison daunting. As an unreconstructed, undefected Tory, Monypenny had no squeamishness over Peel: '*His* weakness as a statesman lay in his failure to understand the significance of a great historic party as an organ of government not easily to be created, not lightly to be destroyed.'[43] Enough said. But Disraeli, too, lacked something crucial to greatness. George Eliot had said at the time that the party missed 'some solid, philosophical Conservative to take the reins'.[44] In retrospect Disraeli did not satisfy his biographer that he had repaired the omission. In a meditation later printed by George Buckle, Monypenny sadly concluded that 'Disraeli's place is not among the greatest of all, the supreme statesmen who lay the foundations of many generations . . . the supreme teachers who awaken the conscience and elevate the mind and are an inspiration to mankind in every age.'[45] It was as though the very act of writing up Disraeli had turned Monypenny into a Gladstonian. Salisbury, too, had to wait for tides to change. Only when his daughter began to reconstruct the narrative, deep in the death of Gladstonian optimism after 1914, did a different public message become available and new Conservative futures make their appearance on the horizon.

POSTERITIES

'Salisbury', the historical figure, became the creation of several kinds of future after the death of Salisbury the man in 1903. The original and central creation took place entirely at the hands of the Cecil family. In the *Dictionary of National Biography* the entries for both Salisbury and Balfour were written by Algernon Cecil, Salisbury's nephew. Gwendolen's brother, Hugh, meanwhile relocated the Hotel Cecil in his much-admired account of *Conservatism* in 1911, which followed the anti-Peelite path to the extent of leaving him out of the

---

[43] W. F. Monypenny and G. E. Buckle, *The Life of Benjamin Disraeli, Earl of Beaconsfield 1804–1881* (6 vols., 1910–20), vol. II, p. 310.

[44] Eliot to Blackwood, 1873, quoted in Neil Roberts, *George Eliot – her Beliefs and her Art* (1987), p. 51. I am grateful to my pupil Hilde Jakobsen for this reference.

[45] Monypenny and Buckle, *Disraeli*, vol. VI, p. 645.

discussion altogether. But none of these re-creations had the status or longevity of Lady Gwendolen's account of her father. This had all the making of a family disaster: it threatened to be apologetic, distorted and amateur in a world of increasingly sophisticated biography. Instead it became a triumph of personality and intelligence on the part of an author who knew one big thing: that the memory of the late nineteenth century provided by Gladstone's voluble disciples was *wrong* in its worship of an icon and denigration of Salisbury's tenure of power. Isolated in her garden house at Hatfield, surrounded by unclimbable piles of paper barely visible through the smoke from her Woodbines, this magnificent woman sat beneath her brown felt hat and made her own sense out of the chaos of late-nineteenth-century politics whose relics lay about her. Ultimately it turned out to be too much to ask; her four volumes took the narrative only to 1892 and she had to leave out many aspects of policy where she lacked the knowledge to proceed effectively. Her biography nevertheless made available to the inter-war public a different understanding of Tory continuity from that currently peddled by the Liberals and would have given many helpful hints to her contemporary statesmen had they had the patience or wit to acquire them. The biography fell in fact into the Baldwinian abyss. People admired Lady Gwendolen's pleasant turn of phrase, her commitment to the project and loyalty to her father's memory but the intelligentsia did not see how important her account might be for standing history on its head. The reasons for this myopia had nothing to do with her or her subject. Rather they derived their force from a cultural climate that would have made any life of Salisbury a non-event.

It was not that Baldwin and Salisbury chased Toryism in different directions: one can argue with some plausibility that one echoed the other in significant respects.[46] But neither of them was like Disraeli and it was *his* shade that had once again come to protect Conservative memory in the 1920s, reinvigorated by a dose of Peel. From the first days of peace, when George Kitson Clark gained entry to the newly opened Peel papers in the then British Museum, this scion of a Liberal–Tory family from Yorkshire strove to relocate Peel in a stream of civilized Conservative values, a task taken forward after

---

[46] See Michael Bentley and Andrew Jones, 'Salisbury and Baldwin' in Maurice Cowling (ed.), *Conservative Essays* (1978), pp. 25–40.

the Second World War by Norman Gash. Baldwin helped the process from the Disraelian side by appealing to one-Englandism in an age of industrial strife, appropriating both Peel's sense of service as a major element of his language and Disraeli's pretended compassion and his role, convincing then if not now, as an educator of the public. 'Salisbury' was no use in a General Strike or a National Government. Nor, as his son discovered, was 'Randolph Churchill'. Peel/Disraeli pointed the way forward in their blend of fairness and inspiration and Baldwin twisted them together like twine. He did not do so mechanically or derivatively, for Baldwin had his own quiet genius. But nothing that Salisbury had ever said or done seemed likely to find its way into the post-war condition of England via Baldwin or anybody else – least of all through his surviving and famous nephew. Balfour lived on until 1930 but he was no longer what he had been. His function for the 1920s was to act as a sort of constitutional megalith – advising King and cabinet of what might be done and what were best avoided, recalling the days of his uncle in his writing but aware always that he himself had never made the grade as an heir, with the disastrous election of 1906 an inextinguishable fact in his biography and his ultimate worsting by the boring and infinitely less able Bonar Law in 1911 a hurtful permanence.[47] Magnifying Salisbury merely made Balfour's diminution the more marked.

Nor was it a moment for ideological assertion of the kind Salisbury had enjoyed. The Left, which he had begun to confront in the 1880s, became a parliamentary presence after 1922 and a sensitive handling of it demanded a certain false modesty which Baldwin cultivated to perfection and which Neville Chamberlain never came close to understanding. Those who wanted to turn politics into an outlet for doctrinal comment, none more so than Oswald Mosley, had a difficult time of it in the post-war decade; and even when capitalism seemed to run onto the rocks in 1931, an ecumenical message of togetherness in the face of the storm seemed far more appropriate than a Salisbury sneer at the antics of the socialists who had caused it. Rather than advertise one's prejudices and judgements as a Tory, the pressures of the moment required dissembling of a kind Salisbury had never been able to maintain for long. Those imperatives became

---

[47] A recent biography of Law asserts the latter's unboringness and intellectual grasp: R. J. Q. Adams, *Bonar Law* (1999).

still stronger, moreover, as MacDonald's doomed administration of 1929 gave way to the National Government in the summer of 1931. It responded to royal request, as Salisbury had done in 1885, but the prospect for the Conservative party held none of Salisbury's potential then. Before it lay a decade of management-politics with Baldwin de facto national leader until 1937 amid a 'Toryism' of *The Next Five Years* and *The Middle Way*:[48] not volumes one could anticipate Salisbury commissioning, let alone writing. Party politics only partly explain this shift. It had more to do with a transformation of the idea of the state and its role in society – a role already altering in Salisbury's period but one greatly transformed by the experience of the First World War and the economic depression and unemployment that followed. Perhaps it fitted this context that the only Cecil who achieved national prominence after the collapse of the Lloyd George coalition was Lord Robert, later Viscount Cecil of Chelwood and that he did so as a quasi-Liberal accomplice of Viscount Grey in championing the League of Nations.[49]

What else could one champion in the international situation faced by Baldwin and Chamberlain? Rearmament held few attractions given the nature of public opinion. Winston Churchill found himself driven towards it – later than he retrospectively asserted – after the failure of either 'socialism' or 'India' to bring him back to office: it was an outsider's issue. The alternative to the League was a sort of isolation, though there appeared little splendid about it and it stretches credibility that Salisbury would have allowed foreign policy to drift into the mess that Chamberlain inherited in 1937. There was no Naval Defence Act: there was next to no navy, a crippled army and a fragile air force. Isolation betokened not strength but vulnerability in the shadow of the bombers that Hitler claimed to possess. As Hitler's intentions tended progressively, within the British public's mind, toward an evil determination to dominate, so the response to him called up memories of the nineteenth century that excluded Salisbury's sedate experience and turned more to Gladstone's moralizing against international Wrong. It is no accident but instead a

---

[48] See *The Next Five Years: An Essay in Political Agreement* (no author, 1935) and Harold Macmillan, *The Middle Way* (1938).

[49] The fourth Marquis, James Cecil, retained respect and authority within the Conservative party, especially during discussions over the desirability of breaking away from Lloyd George's coalition government in 1921–2; but he was a party figure more than a national one.

concealed lesson that the version of 'Gladstone' that came to dominate twentieth-century views of him until the appearance of the Gladstone diaries after 1968 was created against the image of Hitler and the need to expel him bag and baggage from his European dominion.[50] It hardly seemed an appropriate time for Salisbury's icy cynicism or insular judgement: one was fighting the devil and all his works and Churchill brought Marlborough to his aid more than anyone from the nineteenth century, least of all his father. These were the years during which Salisbury receded – years when, as the Oxford History of England educated a generation of undergraduates to believe, he dwindled to the status of a second-rate politician.[51]

Another future stretched away from 1945, full of Attlee's millenarian promise and heralding the arrival of The People in government. Its word was not 'socialism', of which there was little, but 'consensus' as though an enlightenment had dawned which only the foolish or perverse would wish to resist. Salisbury's grandson, the fifth Marquis, kept the flag flying in his appalling, non-consensual remarks; but for Conservatives these were lean years waiting for Churchill to go and finding little help from his successor, whose handling of Nasser during the Suez crisis of 1956 recalled his handling of Mussolini when he had been minister for League of Nations affairs during the 1930s and owed nothing to the coolheadedness of Hatfield. Another 1930s product, Harold Macmillan, brought to the situation his insight that Tories had to be led by their left hand; and both he and later Edward Heath tried to engineer a Toryism that understood the demands of a consumer economy and found something friendly to say about Europe: glad-handing until their left hand hurt. In confronting the rise of Harold Wilson they played a kind of Baldwin to his Lloyd George[52] – at least Wilson was no Gladstone – with the single confusion that the Labour leader thought he was the new Peel with his Hundred Days of reforming zeal and executive energy. But one other situation helped 'Salisbury' indirectly. From the second half of the 1950s Britain entered a period

---

[50] I argue this case in Michael Bentley, *The Climax of Liberal Politics: British Liberalism in Theory and Practice 1868–1918* (1987), pp. 129–32.

[51] Sir Robert Ensor, *England 1870–1914* (Oxford, 1936) put Salisbury under a Fabian illumination and found insufficient radicalism: 'a very great foreign minister, he represented in home affairs the merely anti-progressive section of his party' (p. 90).

[52] A. J. P. Taylor told me in 1970, in one of those impromptu addresses to individuals that made the Beaverbrook Library so entertaining a place, that Wilson was transparently Lloyd George *redivivus* and Roy Jenkins an aspirant Asquith.

of imperial difficulty associated with Macmillan's wind of change; and the reconsideration of imperial commitments had an historical undertow, first in the work of Dame Lillian Penson and later that of others engaged in reworking the history of empire, especially Ronald Robinson and John Gallagher.[53] It marked the beginning of a turning to Salisbury as a figure of greater status than the inter-war period had allowed and the start of a revaluation. A. L. Kennedy's account of 1953 was too weak to provoke an overt revision[54] but when the future Conservative historian Maurice Cowling began in these years his serious reading of late-nineteenth-century politics by following Lytton's correspondence with Salisbury about India, he perhaps helped along a movement greater than he could have realized at the time.[55]

Overwhelmingly, however, the threshold for a revival in late-Victorian Conservatism came with the Conservative party's own reaction against the self-conscious Disraelianism of Macmillan and Heath. It appeared most noticeably in a Powellite right-wing and the rise to prominence of Keith Joseph, Norman Tebbit and their public voice, Margaret Thatcher. Who could claim paternity for such people? Certainly not the constructed 'Disraeli', who had been made to wring his hands over the plight of the dispossessed and whose writings had turned into the Torah for the 'civilized' and 'decent', who believed things had reached a pretty pass when the Tories could become the party of commercial travellers and nasty young men got up in styling mousse and red braces. Baldwin could not be used, either, in the then state of his reputation as a collaborator in the appeasement of Hitler and as a leader led by his followers.[56] The cave of Tory radicals seeking to impose a new future in the 1970s found little to help them in the apparent centrism of the 1920s. Nor

---

[53] R. Robinson, J. Gallagher with Alice Denny, *Africa and the Victorians: The Official Mind of Imperialism* (1965) made a lasting impact on the historiography. Dame Lillian Penson (1896–1963) had been professor of modern history in the University of London and the first female vice-chancellor. A collaborator with G. P. Gooch and, in particular, Harold Temperley in her earlier years, she was best known to Salisbury scholars for her Creighton Lecture of 1962, *Foreign Affairs under the Third Marquis of Salisbury* (1962).

[54] A. L. Kennedy, *Salisbury* (1953).

[55] See Michael Bentley (ed.), *Public and Private Doctrine: Essays in British history presented to Maurice Cowling* (Cambridge, 1993), pp. 4–5.

[56] A partial academic reversal of this view appeared in 1969 in Keith Middlemas and John Barnes's flawed assessment of Baldwin. But a fuller appreciation of Baldwin's weight as a generator of Conservative messages across a broad range of matters has taken another thirty years to mature. See Philip Williamson's important biography, *Stanley Baldwin* (Cambridge, 1999).

would Churchill do, for all Thatcher's upturned gaze toward his public, iconic past. Churchill had his own forms of radicalism but, like his father's, they ran across the seams of party and often pointed in a continuing New Liberal direction with implications for the place of the state that hardly fitted Thatcherite plans. He offered a model during the Falklands War in 1982 when patriotism became more than enough to hold Conservatives together. He offered little else in a *party* sense. Better, then, to look forward rather than back and lay claim to one of those New Conservatisms that the previous century, which few Thatcherites and fewer of her critics knew about, had also produced.

The novelty foxed many commentators into thinking that 1980s Thatcherism was not a Conservative politics at all but rather a sort of inverted liberalism. It is easy to see why. A language about rolling back the frontiers of the state and shrinking the public sphere seemed to have more to do with John Stuart Mill and Herbert Spencer than with Peel and Disraeli. But then those who followed this train of thought found themselves perplexed by a concurrent commitment to a 'strong state' in a series of assertions by the government after 1979 in favour of a powerful defence policy and expanded police force. The confusions were genuine enough but the frame of reference that had given rise to discerning them also had its confusions, not least in failing to see that Margaret Thatcher's style of argument had deep Conservative roots, even if she and her partners did not fully appreciate from whence the sap was rising.

Needless to say, the third Marquis of Salisbury did not inspire the Iron Lady. The tortured retrospect we have been considering makes it plain that he inspired nobody because no one gave him the future that Gladstone and Disraeli received from their apostles. But one can point to a certain sense of rediscovery. Robert Taylor's political biography, which appeared in 1975 (when the Lady ascended), made one statement.[57] When Hugh Cecil and Lord Blake (biographer of Bonar Law and Disraeli) collaborated in commissioning some new studies of Salisbury at the beginning of Margaret Thatcher's premiership they made a deeper one, catching the new mood and producing a volume full of fresh perspectives on the unremembered

---

[57] Robert Taylor, *Lord Salisbury* (1975) gives no hint of current context other than to note that 'there is a modern ring about Salisbury, even if most of the political issues of the time have long since vanished' (p. 193).

prime minister.[58] Some of his contexts also became livelier, especially the economic one that compelled rethinking and, as we have noticed, a refusal to rethink the role of the state.[59] The picture of a magisterial figure in foreign policy – an old and familiar image – widened to encompass the broader treatment that Salisbury brought to domestic British politics as he moved on from the rudderless moments of Beaconsfield's last years and the everlasting anxieties of Northcote. For the notion that Conservatism consisted in believing as little as possible in order to ensure flexible response – Disraeli's insight of the 1850s and 1860s – Salisbury substituted an overt and abrasive ideological position. Toryism was *about* something and the point of political behaviour lay in telling sympathizers what they ought to think about its content. This content modulated its tone as need demanded, of course: it could only be 'situational', in Maurice Cowling's *bon mot*. But the content, whatever it was, had to hurt opponents as well as console friends. Rather than blur the edges of discord in order to sound moderate, Salisbury had seen the need to polarize and divide the British public into those who had something to lose on one side and the rest on the other. He reduced the self-government of a *soi-disant* democracy to the self-interest of a self-conscious class. And it is here that Lady Thatcher became his inadvertent echo. Her content differed from Salisbury's because her situation differed from his. She demonstrated, all the same, an assumption about the inevitability of capitalism, a commitment to tooth and claw, a contempt for sentimental cant and a predisposition to divide and rule that recalled the 1890s more forcefully than the Conservatisms of her own century.

By the 1990s this Tory tradition had became nostalgic in the light, the very subdued light, of John Major and the catastrophe of the election that followed his departure from office in 1997. The world of Blair and Hague will not help Salisbury's longevity any more than it offers Lady Thatcher any grounds for encouragement. It takes the mind back rather to an image of a young Ramsay MacDonald facing an even younger apprentice Baldwin. Both aspire to be good at the

[58] Lord Blake and Hugh Cecil (eds.), *Lord Salisbury: The Man and his Policies* (Basingstoke, 1987).
[59] E. H. H. Green, *The Crisis of Conservatism: The Politics, Economics and Ideology of the British Conservative Party 1880–1914* (1995). Cf. Green (ed.), *An Age of Transition: British Politics 1880–1914* (Edinburgh, 1997). The thoroughness of the former study made a treatment of the theme here less pressing than it otherwise would have seemed and readers are guided to it especially for discussion of Conservative understanding of the currency issue (and bimetallism in particular) that preoccupied some politicians throughout this period.

thing that Salisbury loathed, the projection of low, hard cunning as though it were the Sermon on the Mount. One of them has already proved adept at seeming a sandalled saint.

Salisbury was not a millennial person. Indeed a few of his cynical remarks would not go amiss amid the Uplift in which we currently hover as though lost in one of Sir Richard Branson's balloons. Yet the last quarter of the twentieth century has played an important part in his reconstitution as a political mind of extraordinary weight and vision. Many of the disasters he anticipated have never happened. The class war, in particular, never acquired the violence he assumed it would; instead it dwindled into the reproduction of a placid underclass more stirred by the National Lottery than a General Strike. The German problem on which he expended some of his energies became all too real, on the other hand, and made war the cosmic terror that he never had to confront in his more confined world of 'theatres' and 'spheres'. His sense that the state would expand and loot all in its path seemed likely by 1919, all too true by 1949, less clear by 1999. His temperamental quirk that nothing matters very much is now shared by two-thirds of the western world, though for entirely different reasons. In the long run Salisbury is quite as dead as everybody else. The long run from 1815 to our own day gives us, none the less, an important sense of situation for his life, ideas and politics, one better understood on the cusp of the millennium than those around him could have appreciated. It becomes possible to see lines of force running behind Salisbury's emergence and extending beyond him into a world of which, inevitably, he could know nothing. Will the Cranbornes and the Salisburys have anything to say about the place of Britain in the next thousand years as their ancestor so frequently did about the previous thousand? It seems as unlikely now as it did when the second Marquis deployed his undeniable testosterone. But then, Britain's is a more intractable culture than Mr. Blair and his accomplices understand and a Conservative life after death seems no less inconceivable at the end of the twentieth century than it did at the beginning. Meanwhile, for the Cecils of Hatfield, the clock continues its slow and even tick.

Sources and further reading

Unless otherwise specified, books are published in London.

ARCHIVAL SOURCES

It will have been evident that this book rests mostly on archival sources. The dependence owes something to the purposes lying behind this particular project but also much to the simple dearth, after 1865, of primary printed sources comparable to those left by Gladstone and some others in the political system – with all the consequences commented on in the last chapter of this study. Salisbury's own collection of manuscripts at Hatfield House was closed throughout the preparation of the volume to accommodate Andrew Roberts's research for his official biography, mentioned below, and items mentioned here from that collection relate solely to incoming letters seen after the reopening of the archive. Many transcripts of Salisbury's letters in the Hatfield House material were made, however, when the collection was housed at Christ Church, Oxford, and (at the instigation of the late Professor Colin Matthew) I made a good deal of use of these for outgoing material not recovered from the archives of other politicians. In order to distinguish the two types of source, I have adhered throughout to the description 'Christ Church MSS' to refer to the transcripts and 'Salisbury MSS' to letters at Hatfield. Granted that the subject of this book is not so much Salisbury as his world, recourse was made to a number of archives reflecting his political contacts of which the following list contains the most immediately helpful or significant for the questions posed here. Locations of depositories relate to where the author happened to see the material in question. These sometimes alter over time and researchers should check before visiting.

Royal Archives	Papers and Journals of Queen Victoria, Windsor Castle
Austin MSS	Papers of Alfred Austin, Bristol University Library
Balfour MSS	Papers of Arthur James Balfour, British Library

Balfour MSS SRO	Formerly the Whittingehame collection, now housed in the Scottish Record Office
Benson diary	Diaries of Archbishop Edward White Benson, Trinity College, Cambridge
Benson MSS	Lambeth Palace Library
Cadogan MSS	Papers of the 5th Earl, House of Lords Library
Cairns MSS	Papers of 1st Earl, Public Record Office
Carnarvon MSS	Papers of 4th Earl, British Library
Chilston MSS	Papers of 1st Viscount, Kent Record Office
Churchill MSS	Papers of Lord Randolph Churchill, Cambridge University Library
Craik MSS	Papers of Sir Henry Craik, National Library of Scotland
Cranbrook MSS	Papers of 1st Earl, Suffolk Record Office
Cross MSS	Papers of 1st Viscount, British Library
Derby MSS	Papers of fifteenth Earl, Liverpool Record Office
Devonshire MSS	Papers of 8th Duke, Chatsworth House
Dilke MSS	Papers of Sir Charles Dilke, British Library
Gladstone MSS	Papers of W. E. Gladstone, British Library
Goodwood MSS	Papers of 6th Duke of Richmond, West Sussex Record Office
Goschen MSS	Papers of 1st Viscount, Bodleian Library, Oxford
Halsbury MSS	Papers of 1st Earl, British Library
Hambledon MSS	Papers of W. H. Smith, archive of W. H. Smith and Son Ltd.
Iddesleigh MSS	Papers of 1st Earl, British Library
James MSS	Papers of Lord James of Hereford, Hereford and Worcester Record Office
Lothian MSS	Papers of the 9th Marquis, Scottish Record Office
Lytton MSS	Papers of the 1st Earl, Hertfordshire Record Office
Marlborough MSS	Papers of the 7th Duke, Cambridge University Library
Maxwell MSS	Papers of Sir Herbert Maxwell, National Library of Scotland
Ripon MSS	Papers of the 1st Marquis, British Library
Rosebery MSS	Papers of the 5th Earl, National Library of Scotland
St Aldwyn MSS	Papers of the 1st Earl, Gloucestershire Record Office
1st Earl of Selborne MSS	Papers of the 1st Earl, Lambeth Palace Library
2nd Earl of Selborne MSS	Papers of the 2nd Earl, Bodleian Library, Oxford

Zetland MSS   Papers of the 1st Marquis, North Yorkshire
                            Record Office

OTHER PRIMARY SOURCES

The most relevant and significant source for Conservative high politics in
the second half of the nineteenth century is the diary of the fifteenth Earl of
Derby, published in four volumes and edited by John Vincent. These
appeared out of chronological order as follows: *Disraeli, Derby and the
Conservative Party: Journals and Memoirs of Edward Henry, Lord Stanley
1848–1869* (Hassocks, 1978); *The Later Derby Diaries: Home Rule, Liberal
Unionism and Aristocratic Life in Late-Victorian England* (Bristol, 1981); *The
Diaries of Edward Henry Stanley, 15th Earl of Derby: Between September 1869 and
March 1878* (Royal Historical Society: Camden Series, 1994); and a further
volume covering the later years (forthcoming). They have the disadvantage,
from the point of view of thinking about Salisbury, that Derby and
Salisbury never got along personally because of their joint relationship
with Mary Sackville-West, Salisbury's stepmother and Derby's wife. But
Derby comments sharply on most of the issues that beset senior Conservative politicians and is good on everything except religion. He cannot match
the richness of Gladstone, whose vast diary is now complete in a superb
edition (M. R. D. Foot and Colin Matthew (eds.), *The Gladstone Diaries* (14
vols., Oxford, 1968–94)) and whose index-volume gives unrivalled access
to reflection on political events in general. But Gladstone had little to say
about the Conservative party, beyond predictable polemic, and is best used
for context. Of other Conservative diaries the most directly helpful is
Cranbrook's in a modern edition, Nancy E. Johnson (ed.), *The Diary of
Gathorne Hardy, later Lord Cranbrook, 1866–1892* (Oxford, 1981). Cranbrook
broadcast on Salisbury's wavelength for much of the period because of
their fellow-feeling about the church. Another sympathetic and important
perspective comes from Roundell Palmer, first Earl of Selborne whose
Memorials (4 vols., 1896–8) take one into a world of Anglican Liberalism
that turned to Liberal Unionism after 1886. He knew and greatly liked
Salisbury and his thoughtful, slightly prim remarks often present a starting-
point for reflection.

The most helpful collections of printed letters are the *Salisbury–Balfour
Correspondence*, edited by the Librarian of Hatfield House, Robin Harcourt
Williams (Ware, 1988) and the papers of the second Earl of Selborne, edited
by D. George Boyce under the title *The Crisis of British Power: The Imperial and
Naval Papers of the Second Earl of Selborne* (1990). There is some autobiography
– most of it of very limited value and some of it privately printed – of which
Frances Balfour's *Ne Obliviscaris: Dinna Forget* (2 vols., 1930) survives well with
unmatched vignettes of life at Hatfield House and Whittingehame, while
Lady Burghclere's compilation of *A Great Lady's Friendships: Letters to Mary,
Marchioness of Salisbury, Countess of Derby, 1862–90* (1933) also takes the reader

close to home. Collections of correspondence edited during the Victorian and Edwardian periods carry reticence to obsessive limits. A modern example of what, by contrast, can be done will be found in A. B. Cooke and A. P. W. Malcolmson (eds.), *The Ashbourne Papers 1869–1913* (Belfast, 1974), which contains a rich array of primary material, intelligently selected. At the parliamentary level, Lord George Hamilton's *Parliamentary Reminiscences and Reflections, 1886–1906* (2 vols., 1917–22), are helpful for the later years of the century and leave one wondering, as ever, how the author could be overlooked when he was patently so omniscient.

FURTHER READING

On Salisbury himself the best guides are his recent biographies, Andrew Roberts, *Salisbury: Victorian Titan* (1999) and David Steele, *Lord Salisbury: A Political Biography* (1999), though it should be noted that the present book was written independently of both and should not be seen as a commentary on them. An earlier collection of essays on *Lord Salisbury: The Man and his Policies* (ed. Lord Blake and Hugh Cecil, Basingstoke, 1987) is coherent and valuable, while the still-earlier accounts by Lord David Cecil of *The Cecils of Hatfield House* (1973) and by Kenneth Rose of *The Later Cecils* (1975) contain both insight and charm. On Salisbury's running of the Foreign Office the best guide is the formidable Agatha Ramm in her essay 'Lord Salisbury and the Foreign Office', albeit in a volume hard to acquire in Britain: Roger Bullen (ed.), *The Foreign Office 1782–1982* (Frederick, MD, 1984). The most helpful introduction to the place of politics in foreign policy in this period is Marvin Swartz (ed.), *The Politics of British Foreign Policy in the era of Disraeli and Gladstone* (Basingstoke, 1985). J. A. S Grenville's older monograph on *Lord Salisbury and Foreign Policy: The Close of the Nineteenth Century* (1964) retains its authority.

Disraeli has been well served over the past thirty years both by Robert Blake's majestic biography of 1966 and by vivacious introductions from John Vincent, *Disraeli* (Oxford, 1990) and Paul Smith, *Disraeli: A Brief Life* (Cambridge, 1996).

There is no decent life of Northcote. Catch 22: only a depressive could do it and no depressive can face it. 'I am not over-fond of cloudless skies,' he once told Disraeli. Hicks Beach shared his moments of gloom, and there is only a barely adequate memoir in Lady Victoria Hicks Beach, *Life of Sir Michael Hicks Beach, Earl St Aldwyn* (1932) to cover the contribution of this important politician. Cairns seems completely neglected, despite Lord Bryce's recollection in his *Studies in Contemporary Biography* (2 vols., 1903) that Salisbury himself had proved 'not superior to Cairns in political judgement or argumentative power'. An old biography of Cranbrook by A. E. Gathorne Hardy, *Gathorne Hardy, First Earl of Cranbrook: A Memoir* (2 vols., 1910) has been superseded largely by the Johnson edition of his diary. Sir Arthur Hardinge's *Life of Henry Howard Molyneux Herbert, fourth Earl of*

Carnarvon (3 vols., 1925) is all we have. There is a rather dull book about Cross who was rather a dull man: Dennis Mitchell, *Cross and Tory Democracy: A Political Biography of Richard Assheton Cross* (1891). Goschen has been updated – again without fireworks – in Thomas J. Spinner Jnr, *George Joachim Goschen: The Transformation of a Victorian Liberal* (Cambridge, 1973). Churchill did not know how to be dull; nor does his biographer, Roy Foster, whose *Randolph Churchill: A Political Life* (Oxford, 1981) is excellent on what it meant to be a Tory democrat.

For the party side of things, the best place to begin is with two volumes by Richard Shannon, who picks his way carefully and thoughtfully through the narrative in *The Age of Disraeli, 1868–1881: The Rise of Tory Democracy* (1992) and *The Age of Salisbury 1881–1902: Unionism and Empire* (1996). They are especially good on issues concerned with organization, fighting elections and discussions of intra-party tensions. On the party organization itself, Lord Chilston's account of Akers-Douglas, *Chief Whip: The Political Life and Times of Aretas Akers-Douglas, First Viscount Chilston* (1961) has stood the test of time but now has to be supplemented by recent work, in particular Jon Lawrence's *Speaking for the People: Party, Language and Popular Politics in England, 1867–1914* (Cambridge, 1998), which breathes fresh air into stale conceptions of how Victorian popular politics worked; and Martin Pugh, *The Tories and the People 1880–1935* (Oxford, 1985), which puts a major Tory initiative, the Primrose League, into perspective. For the early period after 1867, H. J. Hanham, *Elections and Party Management: Politics in the Time of Disraeli and Gladstone* (1969 (1st edn 1959)) remains essential.

On the themes chosen for review in the present volume, the nature of aristocratic society in the late nineteenth century is well depicted in Andrew Adonis, *Making Aristocracy Work: The Peerage and the Party System in Britain 1884–1914* (Oxford, 1993) and K. D. Reynolds, *Aristocratic Women and Political Society in Victorian Britain* (Oxford, 1998). The Tory idea of the state can be partially traced in E. H. H. Green, *The Crisis of Conservatism: The Politics, Economics and Ideology of the British Conservative Party 1880–1914* (1995) and Matthew Fforde, *Conservatism and Collectivism 1886–1914* (Edinburgh, 1990), though both of them go in different directions from the one followed here. On Conservative churchmen a mine of information has recently been made available by Nigel Yates in a study of *Anglican Ritualism in Victorian Britain 1830–1910* (Oxford, 1999). For the empire the best starting-point is now Robin W. Winks (ed.), *The Oxford History of the British Empire, Volume v: Historiography* (5 vols., Oxford, 1999). Conservative depictions of memory and the Tory construction of history, the subject of the last chapter of this study, permit little beyond tentative speculation at the moment; yet they deserve and demand so much more.

Index

Many names mentioned incidentally are not included here. I have included as many subject categories as possible to enable readers to follow a theme.